Put Away Your Sword

†

STUDIES IN WORLD CATHOLICISM

Michael L. Budde and William T. Cavanaugh, Series Editors
Karen M. Kraft, Managing Editor

Studies in World Catholicism offers scholarly, pastoral, and general readers alike the best of interdisciplinary research about and from the multifaceted worlds of Catholicism, which has seen its center of gravity shift from the so-called global North to Africa, Asia, and Latin America. In this series, authors from around the globe engage with both large-gauge theoretical questions and the particularities of specific communities and contexts, crossing disciplinary boundaries between theology, social ethics, history, cultural studies, political science and more.

This series is a project of the Center for World Catholicism and Intercultural Theology (CWCIT) at DePaul University in Chicago, one of the leading scholarly institutes focusing on Christianity as a transnational reality. More information on the Center and its work is available at http://cwcit.depaul.edu. Proposals for the series may be sent to series editors William T. Cavanaugh at wcavana1@depaul.edu or Michael L. Budde at mbudde@depaul.edu.

Recent Titles in This Series

Fratelli Tutti: *A Global Commentary*. Vol. 13, 2023.

Daughters of Wisdom: Women and Leadership in the Global Church. Vol. 12, 2023.

African Ecological Ethics and Spirituality for Cosmic Flourishing: An African Commentary on Laudato Sí. Vol. 11, 2022.

For God and My Country: Catholic Leadership in Modern Uganda. Vol. 10, 2020.

Gathered in My Name: Ecumenism in the World Church. Vol. 9, 2020.

Pentecostalism, Catholicism, and the Spirit in the World. Vol. 8, 2019.

For the complete list and ordering information, please visit www.wipfandstock.com/series and click on "Studies in World Catholicism."

Put Away Your Sword

Gospel Nonviolence in a Violent World

EDITED BY
Michael L. Budde

CONTRIBUTORS

Maria Clara Bingemer
Michael L. Budde
M. T. Dávila
Mauro Garofalo
Francis Gonsalves, SJ
Erico Hammes
Elizabeth Kanini Kimau

Robert Emmet Meagher
Jasmin Nario-Galace
Elias Opongo, SJ
Daniel Franklin E. Pilario, CM
O. Ernesto Valiente
Teresia Wamũyũ Wachira, IBVM

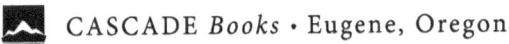

CASCADE *Books* · Eugene, Oregon

PUT AWAY YOUR SWORD
Gospel Nonviolence in a Violent World

Studies in World Catholicism 14

Copyright © 2024 Wipf and Stock Publishers. All rights reserved. Except for brief quotations in critical publications or reviews, no part of this book may be reproduced in any manner without prior written permission from the publisher. Write: Permissions, Wipf and Stock Publishers, 199 W. 8th Ave., Suite 3, Eugene, OR 97401.

Cascade Books
An Imprint of Wipf and Stock Publishers
199 W. 8th Ave., Suite 3
Eugene, OR 97401

www.wipfandstock.com

PAPERBACK ISBN: 978-1-6667-0595-9
HARDCOVER ISBN: 978-1-6667-0596-6
EBOOK ISBN: 978-1-6667-0597-3

Cataloguing-in-Publication data:

Names: Budde, Michael L., editor.

Title: Put away your sword : gospel nonviolence in a violent world / edited by Michael L. Budde.

Description: Eugene, OR: Cascade Books, 2024 | Studies in World Catholicism 14 | Includes bibliographical references and index.

Identifiers: ISBN 978-1-6667-0595-9 (paperback) | ISBN 978-1-6667-0596-6 (hardcover) | ISBN 978-1-6667-0597-3 (ebook)

Subjects: LCSH: Nonviolence—Religious aspects—Christianity. | Pacifism—Religious aspects—Christianity. | Just war doctrine.

Classification: BT736.6 .B80 2024 (print) | BT736.6 (ebook)

03/04/24

Scripture texts, prefaces, introductions, footnotes, and cross references marked (NABRE) are taken from the New American Bible, revised edition © 2010, 1991, 1986, 1970 Confraternity of Christian Doctrine, Inc., Washington, DC All Rights Reserved. No part of this work may be reproduced or transmitted in any form or by any means, electronic or mechanical, including photocopying, recording, or by any information storage and retrieval system, without permission in writing from the copyright owner.

Scripture quotations marked (NIV) are from the Holy Bible, New International Version®, NIV®. Copyright © 1973, 1978, 1984, 2011 by Biblica, Inc.™ Used by permission of Zondervan. All rights reserved worldwide. www.zondervan.com The "NIV" and "New International Version" are trademarks registered in the United States Patent and Trademark Office by Biblica, Inc.™

Scripture quotations marked (NJB) are taken from *The New Jerusalem Bible*, published and © 1985 by Darton, Longman & Todd Ltd and *Les Editions du Cerf*, and used by permission of the publishers.

Scripture quotations marked (NRSV) are from the New Revised Standard Version Bible, copyright © 1989 the Division of Christian Education of the National Council of the Churches of Christ in the United States of America. Used by permission. All rights reserved.

Contents

Contributors | ix

Introduction by Michael L. Budde | 1

Part One: Contributions to a Theology of Nonviolence

1: Christian Cross and Martyrdom: Jesus's Response to a Violent World | 35
O. Ernesto Valiente

2: A Spirit Christology of Peace and Active Nonviolence | 55
Erico Hammes

3: Christian Nonviolence for Secular Causes: The Case of Two Twentieth-Century Religious Communities | 73
Maria Clara Bingemer

Part Two: Practicing Gospel Nonviolence in a Violent World: Reports and Reflections

4: Peace Is an Open Workshop | 95
Mauro Garofalo

5: Martyrs at the Margins: Rethinking Martyrdom in the Time of Violent Populism | 105
Daniel Franklin E. Pilario, CM

6: The Catholic Church and Deeply Divided Societies: Utilizing the Potential of the Church to Build Sustainable Peace | 127
Elizabeth Kanini Kimau

7: Women and Nonviolent Indigenous Approaches to
Peacebuilding: The North Rift Region of Kenya | 142
TERESIA WAMŨYŨ WACHIRA, IBVM

8: Building Spaces of Nonviolence: Women's Work
to Challenge Armed Violence | 161
JASMIN NARIO-GALACE

9: "Be the Change You Want to See": Building
Interfaith Solidarity for Peace in India | 176
FRANCIS GONSALVES, SJ

**Part Three: Theopolitical Debates: Just War
and Responsibility to Protect**

10: Confessions of a Just War Theorist: My Challenges
Embracing a God of Absolute Nonviolence | 197
M. T. DÁVILA

11: Just War: A Convenient Untruth | 211
ROBERT EMMET MEAGHER

12: Responsibility to Protect and Nonviolence Discourse:
Implications on Conflict Militarization in South Sudan | 224
ELIAS OPONGO, SJ

13: Killing with Kindness: Can a Plague Cure a Plague? | 243
MICHAEL L. BUDDE

Index | 261

Contributors

Maria Clara Bingemer, professor of theology at the Pontifical Catholic University of Rio de Janeiro, Brazil. Her publications in English include *Latin American Theology: Roots and Branches*; *Mary: Mother of God, Mother of the Poor* (coauthor); and *Simone Weil: Mystic of Passion and Compassion*.

Michael L. Budde, professor of Catholic studies and political science and senior research professor at the Center for World Catholicism and Intercultural Theology at DePaul University, Chicago. His publications include *Foolishness to Gentiles: Essays on Empire, Nationalism, and Discipleship*; *Scattered and Gathered: Catholics in Diaspora* (editor); and *The Borders of Baptism: Identities, Allegiances, and the Church*.

M. T. Dávila, chair of religious and theological studies and associate professor of practice at Merrimack College, North Andover, Massachusetts. Her publications include "Making Spirits Whole: Homeless Ministries as a Tool for Integral Development," in *Land of Stark Contrasts* (Manuel Mejido Costoya, editor) and "A 'Preferential Option': A Challenge to Faith in a Culture of Privilege," in *The Word Became Culture* (Miguel Díaz, editor).

Mauro Garofalo, head of international relations for the Community of Sant'Egidio, Rome. He has also long been involved in the Community's secretariat for interreligious and ecumenical dialogue and has also served as one of its Conflict Resolutions Unit officers, supporting international rescue operations in Afghanistan and Senegal.

Francis Gonsalves, SJ, president of Jnana-Deepa Vidyapeeth, Pontifical Institute of Philosophy and Theology, Pune, India. His publications include *Corona of Thorns or Corona of Life? Changing Church in the COVID Context* (coeditor); *Romero and Pope Francis: Revolutionaries of Tender Love*; and *God of Our Soil: Towards Subaltern Trinitarian Theology*.

Erico Hammes, professor of systematic theology and coordinator of the postgraduate program in theology at the Pontifical Catholic University of Rio Grande do Sul, Porto Alegre, Brazil. Among his publications in Portuguese are *Filhas e filhos no filho: a divindade de Jesus na cristologia de J. Sobrino* [Daughters and Sons in the Son: The Divinity of Jesus in the Christology of J. Sobrino].

Elizabeth Kanini Kimau, founder of Horn of Africa Grassroots Peace Forum and a longtime grassroots peace builder in northern Kenya and South Sudan, fragmented by years of interethnic violence. She is currently pursuing her doctorate at the Centre for Nonviolence at Durban University of Technology, Durban, South Africa.

Robert Emmet Meagher, professor emeritus of humanities at Hampshire College, Amherst, Massachusetts. His publications include *Albert Camus and the Human Crisis*; *Killing from the Inside Out: Moral Injury and Just War*; and *Herakles Gone Mad: Rethinking Heroism in an Age of Endless War*.

Jasmin Nario-Galace, executive director of the Center for Peace Education and professor in the Department of International Studies at Miriam College, Quezon City, Philippines. She is also president of Pax Christi Pilipinas, and her publications include "Women Count for Peace: Women's Engagement in Track II Diplomacy of the Mindanao Peace Process" in *A Just Peace Primer Ethic* (Eli S. McCarthy, editor).

Elias Opongo, SJ, director of Hekima University College Institute of Peace Studies and International Relations, Nairobi. His publications include *Elections, Violence, and Transitional Justice in Africa* (coeditor); *Transitional Justice in Post-Conflict Societies in Africa* (coeditor); and *Catholic Leadership in Peacebuilding in Africa* (coeditor).

Daniel Franklin E. Pilario, CM, associate professor at St. Vincent School of Theology and director of research at Adamson University, Manila. His publications include *Back to the Rough Grounds of Praxis: Exploring Theological Method with Pierre Bourdieu*; *After the End: Reflections of the Happy Theologian in and on the Rough Grounds*; and *Signs of Hope in Christian-Muslim Relations* (coeditor).

O. Ernesto Valiente, associate professor of systematic theology in the School of Theology and Ministry at Boston College, Boston, Massachusetts. His publications include *The Grace of Medellín: History, Theology and Legacy* (coeditor); and *Liberation through Reconciliation: Jon Sobrino's Christological Spirituality*.

Teresia Wamũyũ Wachira, IBVM, copresident of Pax Christi International and senior lecturer and program leader of peace and conflict studies at St. Paul's University, Nairobi. She is also coordinator of Justice, Peace, Integrity of Creation—Eastern Africa Province; her publications include "Making Just Peace a Reality in Kenya: A New 'Flavor' to Peacebuilding" in *A Just Peace Ethic Primer* (Eli S. McCarthy, editor).

Introduction

Michael L. Budde

THE IDEA OF "NONVIOLENCE" in public life is sometimes treated like an eccentric, addled member of one's family: quaint, often well-intentioned, but not to be regarded as a role model for others. In political life, advocates for nonviolence are often dismissed as naïve, insulated from the realities of social struggle, and moralizers who privilege self-image over improving the world. Nonviolence has been described as an instrument of white supremacy that protects existing power structures from the threat of real or revolutionary change.[1]

In response, some advocates of nonviolence stress the effectiveness and radical bona fides of campaigns to confront oppression and injustice. A cornerstone of such defenses is the published work of Erica Chenowith, a Harvard scholar who has attempted to provide empirical support for the superior effectiveness of nonviolent social movements compared to those exercising violence.[2] These studies, in turn, are critiqued on methodological grounds by those seeking to expose the false promise of nonviolent social strategies.[3] These debates are not new and will continue well into the foreseeable future.

In contrast, consider the posture of a nonviolent leader of a most peculiar sort:

---

1. See, for example, Gelderloos, *Failure of Nonviolence*, and Churchill, *Pacifism*.

2. Chenoweth and Stephan, *Why Civil Resistance Works*.

3. Gelderloos, *Failure of Nonviolence*, chapters 3, 24–27; "Has XR the Successful Strategy."

> Love your enemies, do good to those who hate you, bless those who curse you, pray for those who abuse you. If anyone strikes you on the cheek, offer the other also; and from anyone who takes away your coat do not withhold even your shirt. (Luke 6:27–30 NRSV)

> You have heard that it was said, "You shall love your neighbor and hate your enemy." But I say to you, love your enemies and pray for those who persecute you, so that you may be children of your Father in heaven; for he makes his sun rise on the evil and on the good and sends rain on the righteous and on the unrighteous. For if you love those who love you, what reward do you have? Do not even the tax collectors do the same? And if you greet only your brothers and sisters, what more are you doing than others? Do not even the Gentiles do the same? (Matt 5:43–48 NRSV)

> Put your sword back into its place; for all who take the sword will perish by the sword. (Matt 26:52 NRSV)

Clearly, the nonviolence of political campaigners and tacticians is at some remove from the nonviolence of Jesus of Nazareth. "Love your enemies" is not a directive given with an eye toward superior political outcomes; "offer the other cheek," however subversive it may have been in terms of norms of social subordination and hierarchy, guarantees no greater likelihood of "victory" (whatever that may mean) than calls for the violent pursuit of one's rights, freedoms, or dignity.

This very particular sort of "nonviolence," which is a disposition and commitment to inhabit and extend the example of Jesus on matters of killing and coercion, makes sense only as an eschatological matter. Awareness of the eschatological nature of Christianity invites Christians and the church to begin living the newness of the kingdom of God today, just as Jesus's way of inhabiting the world inaugurated the kingdom of God. While the complete healing of creation awaits the culmination of the kingdom, Jesus's triumph over death means that we too are to live as though death does not have the final word. We do not have to kill to protect our lives; we can live here and now, however imperfectly, in a way that shows the world that God has inaugurated a new era in which love—even of enemies—is the means and the end of all life.

Some people call this way of inhabiting the world a matter of "gospel nonviolence," and it is the term we adopted in gathering people from around the world to reflect on the theories and practices of Christ-inspired love and action without recourse to lethal means. It is explicit in its theological grounding and teleology—it makes no sense without it—even as it hopes to contribute to movements for peace, justice, and resistance to exploitation. Results are not irrelevant, but neither are they determinative, in the world of gospel nonviolence.

More than a dozen scholars and practitioners committed to gospel nonviolence gathered in Chicago from May 3–5, 2019, and together explored the theme, "Put Away Your Sword: Gospel Nonviolence in a Violent World." This event, the annual World Catholicism Week gathering sponsored by the Center for World Catholicism and Intercultural Theology (CWCIT), dug deeply into crucial issues and challenges related to violence, nonviolence, and Christian discipleship: theologies of nonviolence, martyrdom, and the cross; practices of nonviolent peacemaking and the "responsibility to protect"; gender and violence; and grassroots formation of people in the practice of nonviolence. This book is the product of that gathering and is an attempt to broaden and deepen the conversation on being a transformed people in a world that remains addicted to the violent ways of the era before the "kingdom of God."

This exploration of the theologies, theories, and practices of gospel nonviolence does not hew to a single ideological or political position. Some of its participants are self-described pacifists; others are not. Some want to see Christian just war theory superseded by something else; others continue to see merit in it. Similarly, the contributions to the gathering (and to this volume) are diverse: some are formal scholarly papers, some are shorter reports on specific campaigns or experiences, and still others are synthetic reflections drawn from a number of experiences from around the world. What holds them together is a sense that the world and the church would benefit from a robust and gospel-based commitment to nonviolence as an alternative to lethal business as usual in addressing conflicts great and small.

The Role of Pope Francis

No account of contemporary Catholicism and questions of violence is complete without recognizing the profound influence of Pope Francis. Many modern popes have spoken eloquently and forcefully against war and violence in the world, but Francis has set in motion a reappraisal of long-standing Christian assumptions and frameworks. Unlike secular proponents of nonviolence, he rejects a purely instrumentalist view that stresses outcomes as the only relevant measure; at the same time, his understanding of nonviolence is not a passivity or bloodless pacifism that does not aim to make life better, especially for the vulnerable, in the world we inhabit between the old ways and the emerging kingdom of God.

It is no easy matter, trying to chart each of Pope Francis's calls for greater exploration of, and commitment to, nonviolence. It has suffused his papacy from the outset and has grown more frequent and emphatic. In 2016, the Pontifical Council for Justice and Peace cosponsored a conference with Pax Christi, the worldwide Catholic peace movement; he sent a strong message of support to the gathering, whose members later issued a statement that concluded:

> We believe that there is no "just war." Too often the "just war" theory" has been used to endorse rather than prevent or limit war. Suggesting that a "just war" is possible also undermines the moral imperative to develop tools and capacities for nonviolent transformation of conflict. We need a new framework that is consistent with gospel nonviolence.[4]

Pope Francis followed the call of this gathering with a powerful statement of his own, the World Day of Peace declaration of January 1, 2017. Here, he gave voice to his hopes for the church and the world:

> I ask God to help all of us to cultivate nonviolence in our most personal thoughts and values. May charity and nonviolence govern how we treat each other as individuals, within society, and in international life. When victims of violence are able to resist the temptation to retaliate, they become the most credible promoters of nonviolent peacemaking. In the most local and ordinary situations and in the international order, may nonviolence become the hallmark of our decisions, our relationships, and our actions, and indeed, of political life in all its forms. . . .
>
> Violence is not the cure for our broken world. Countering violence with violence leads at best to forced migrations and enormous suffering, because vast amounts of resources are diverted to military ends and away from the everyday needs of young people, families experiencing hardship, the elderly, the infirm, and the great majority of people in our world. At worst, it can lead to the death, physical and spiritual, of many people, if not of all.[5]

Jesus himself lived in violent times. Yet he taught that the true battlefield, where violence and peace meet, is the human heart: for "it is from within, from the human heart, that evil intentions come" (Mark 7:21 NRSV).

4. Pax Christi International, "Appeal to the Catholic Church."
5. Francis, "Nonviolence," para. 1–2.

But Christ's message in this regard offers a radically positive approach. He unfailingly preached God's unconditional love, which welcomes and forgives. He taught his disciples to love their enemies (cf. Matt 5:44) and turn the other cheek (cf. Matt 5:39). When he stopped her accusers from stoning the woman caught in adultery (cf. John 8:1–11), and when, on the night before he died, he told Peter to put away his sword (cf. Matt 26:52), Jesus marked out the path of nonviolence. He walked that path to the very end, to the cross, whereby he became our peace and put an end to hostility (cf. Eph 2:14–16). Whoever accepts the good news of Jesus is able to acknowledge the violence within and be healed by God's mercy, becoming in turn an instrument of reconciliation.[6]

To be true followers of Jesus today also includes embracing his teaching about nonviolence.[7] Peacebuilding through active nonviolence is the natural and necessary complement to the church's continuing efforts to limit the use of force by the application of moral norms. The church does so by her participation in the work of international institutions and through the competent contribution made by so many Christians to the drafting of legislation at all levels. Jesus himself offers a "manual" for this strategy of peacemaking in the Sermon on the Mount. The eight Beatitudes (cf. Matt 5:3–10) provide a portrait of the person we could describe as blessed, good, and authentic. Blessed are the meek, Jesus tells us, the merciful and the peacemakers, those who are pure in heart, and those who hunger and thirst for justice.[8]

Pope Francis's moves on nonviolence have gone beyond short annual pronouncements like those marking the World Day of Peace. He has also inserted his prioritization of nonviolence into major documents, most notably *Fratelli Tutti*, his 2020 encyclical on "fraternity and social friendship" (the document's subtitle). This document stands as Francis's major statement of diagnosis and prescription for a world facing crises on all sides, with political and social mechanisms of cooperation in need of serious repair, and with temptations to despair circulating throughout cultures and peoples.

He does not shy away from acknowledging the use and misuse of traditional Christian teaching on war and peace in ways that bless militarism and belligerence:

> War can easily be chosen by invoking all sorts of allegedly humanitarian, defensive, or precautionary excuses, and even resorting to the manipulation of information. In recent decades,

---

6. Francis, "Nonviolence," para. 3.
7. Francis, "Nonviolence," para. 3.
8. Francis, "Nonviolence," para. 6.

every single war has been ostensibly "justified." The *Catechism of the Catholic Church* speaks of the possibility of legitimate defence [*sic*] by means of military force, which involves demonstrating that certain "rigorous conditions of moral legitimacy" have been met. Yet it is easy to fall into an overly broad interpretation of this potential right. In this way, some would also wrongly justify even "preventive" attacks or acts of war that can hardly avoid entailing "evils and disorders graver than the evil to be eliminated." At issue is whether the development of nuclear, chemical, and biological weapons, and the enormous and growing possibilities offered by new technologies, have granted war an uncontrollable destructive power over great numbers of innocent civilians. The truth is that "never has humanity had such power over itself, yet nothing ensures that it will be used wisely." We can no longer think of war as a solution, because its risks will probably always be greater than its supposed benefits. In view of this, it is very difficult nowadays to invoke the rational criteria elaborated in earlier centuries to speak of the possibility of a "just war."[9]

About This Book

While Pope Francis's statements and initiatives on nonviolence are not the direct focus of this book, the topics and controversies explored aim to advance the dialogue across cultures and nations that he seeks. From a variety of contexts and with an array of tools—theological, historical, derived from direct experience, and more—contributors seek to enhance the role of nonviolence in contemporary Catholic thought and practice at all levels and in all parts of the world.

Part One: Contributions to a Theology of Nonviolence

The first section of the book aims to contribute to advancing a theology of gospel nonviolence. Three scholars explore fundamental areas of Christian theology and the reciprocal enrichments and extensions between classical theological concerns and the imperatives of enemy love and renunciation of violence.

Boston College theologian O. Ernesto Valiente suggests that a theologically worthwhile exploration of Christian nonviolence must engage

---

9. Francis, *Fratelli Tutti*, para. 258; internal citations omitted.

the meaning of the cross, and how best to understand martyrdom. For Christians, getting to the heart of such matters requires extended attention to the person and practices of Jesus. In "Christian Cross and Martyrdom: Jesus's Response to a Violent World," Valiente looks at the social and political structures of imperialism as they shaped life in first-century Palestine. He provides a welcome discussion of the kingdom of God and how best to understand it as promise and project, as both historical and the culmination of history.

Valiente offers five conclusions from his study of cross, martyrdom, and Jesus's response to oppression in occupied Palestine. Among them are the assertions that

> it is clear that Jesus rejects the possibility of a passive coexistence with the forces of oppression and, at a certain moment in his ministry, chooses to confront his enemies directly in Jerusalem, even when such confrontation seemed destined to seal his fate and martyrdom....[10]
>
> [T]hough Jesus seems to have foreseen his impending death, his ministry is never defined by the violence of his enemies. Jesus does not imitate them but remains faithful to the way of peace—to the way of the kingdom. Here it is important to stress that Jesus's followers must not only be attentive to the prophetic content of God's kingdom but also to the way of the kingdom—that is, the nonviolent manner in which it comes.
>
> Jesus's whole life reveals that eradicating sin and injustice cannot be accomplished indirectly—from a distance and without personal involvement. Rather, it calls for solidarity that is willing to take up and endure the consequences of sin—that is, a love willing to bear the weight of sin and to suffer on behalf of others.[11]

Moving into the area of Christology, Erico Hammes outlines what he calls a "Spirit Christology of peace and active nonviolence." A theologian at the Pontifical Catholic University of Rio Grande do Sul in Porto Alegre, Brazil, Hammes traces trends in recent Catholic theology, especially in the crucial area of Christology. His chapter aims to reconnect Christology to a robust pneumatology, the unity of which is essential to recognizing a theology of peace that is worthy of the name.

10. See p. 49.
11. See p. 50.

Hammes begins by offering a necessary deepening of basic categories that too often escape attention in discussions of nonviolence and violence. For example,

> Violence appears on personal, social or structural, national or international levels, and includes racism, sexism, terrorism, torture, dictatorship, human rights violations, and cultural, social, and religious discrimination, as well as economic and political practices. It is necessary to highlight the fact that violence is not the same in all countries and regions. There are countries where there is no war but where there are a great number of murders and assassinations; in other countries, social and economic inequality may prevail; and in still others, the exploitation of natural resources is the greatest form of violence.[12]

After noting the negative consequences of divorcing Christology from pneumatology for matters of gospel nonviolence ("Perhaps it was the identification of the church with Christ without pneumatological mediation that allowed the justification of war as an instrument of Christian political praxis"),[13] Hammes models what a christologically and spirit-filled theology of peace might include. He moves from a rereading of the synoptic accounts of Jesus's life and ministry to the early ecumenical councils of the church. He concludes his exploration by noting that

> [i]n a world of violence, injustice, and the destruction of creation, a Spirit Christology of peace explains the consequences of the confession that God has revealed himself in Jesus Christ. In Jesus, God appears as the God of peace pouring out his Spirit of life, reconciliation, peace, and nonviolence. Jesus not only reveals God, but also the merciful Father in the Spirit and the perfect image of man and woman. He appears not in strength and power but in weakness and slavery (cf. Phil 2:6–8), as the servant of God, the Prince of Peace . . . .[14]

Brazilian theologian Maria Clara Bingemer's contribution to the theology of nonviolence roots itself in the soil of ecclesiology. A particularly compelling idea of church, in service to the poor and the outsider, can sometimes lead to martyrdom as witness to the countercultural power of love and renunciation of the sword. To illustrate and deepen Christian thought and practice on nonviolence and martyrdom, she goes deeply into

---

12. See pp. 55–56.
13. See p. 58.
14. See pp. 69–70.

two contemporary experiences: the six Jesuits and two laypeople murdered by military forces (backed by the United States government) at the University of Central America in 1989 and the kidnapping and murder of Trappist monks by Islamic terrorists in 1997 in Tibhirine, Algeria.

Bingemer begins her study with a concise summary statement that highlights the close connections between ecclesiology, gospel nonviolence, and Christian martyrdom:

> Paul refers to the community of Christians as the "body of Christ." The church is the continuation of the bodily presence of Christ on earth. The boundaries of that body are rarely clear, for the Holy Spirit is not confined to the visible church. But the center of that body is clear: the weakest members, Paul says, are the indispensable ones (1 Cor 12:22), and when one member suffers, all suffer together (1 Cor 12:26). Christ identifies himself with the victims of this world (Matt 25:31–46). The church is that community that undoes the logic of violence by breaking the unanimity proclaiming the guilt of the victims. The church identifies God with the victims of this world and thereby unmasks the scapegoating mechanism. Nonviolence is not for a few heroic individuals; it is lived by the community's sensing the deep interconnection of all people because they share the same nervous system as the cosmic Christ. The Christian Church is called to be a community of witnesses who live the challenge of love and nonviolence every day.
>
> Siding with the victims of this world provokes opposition. Nonviolence is not a tactic that is always successful in the short run. Christians must be prepared for martyrdom, which is not just something that occurred in distant, ancient times but is a daily reality for Christians around the world today. Martyrdom is the ultimate witness to the truth of nonviolence. The martyr, in imitation of Christ, prefers to absorb the violence of the world rather than deal it out, in the secure knowledge that she or he is on the right side of history. The coming kingdom of God is nonviolent, and the martyr decides to live that reality now. But the martyr is not alone: the witness of the martyr depends on a church community that is ready to keep the memory of the martyrs alive as a proclamation of what God—and God's creation—is really like.[15]

Bingemer discusses the qualities of each community that placed them in continuity with church communities and ministries, and those that

---

15. See pp. 73–74; citations omitted.

marked them as distinctive—and how their qualities put them in the crosshairs of powerful and violent actors seeking domination and submission.

> [T]hey brought something new to the living out of a consecration to God and others. Both were dealing with new perspectives brought by the Second Vatican Council and incorporated by the whole church. Those new perspectives were only beginning to be assimilated and practiced. The monks of Tibhirine demonstrated the commitment to interreligious dialogue to the end, to the point of shedding their blood. They lived in a country where the religion of the other was the majority and practiced the monastic life that was theirs in close dialogue and in deep communion with this "other" tradition, assuming and integrating several of that tradition's elements. The Jesuits of the UCA did the same with the option for the poor. At the time of their death, this option had already been adopted by the Latin American church, but they found a way to live it in community and in academia. They redirected an entire university toward this option, responding to questions that came up everywhere about how to live this option when one is not poor. Therefore, both communities were pioneers of the options that the church was beginning to live and were like the light that illuminates the path of others that have followed them....
>
> [B]oth communities wanted to bring peace amidst conflict, injustice, and violence. And their testimony was evangelical and peaceful, even if violence seemed to have had the last word. The future has shown that their gestures, words, lives, and testimony remain and are victorious over violence.[16]

In the end, these communities testified to the nonviolence of Christ, becoming martyrs even though formal church recognition of their "martyrdom" has yet to be accorded them.

Part Two: Practicing Gospel Nonviolence in a Violent World: Reports and Reflections

Over the past half-century, few movements have engaged in nonviolent conflict resolution more than the Sant'Egidio Community. Formed in 1968 in Rome, Sant'Egidio now operates in more than seventy countries worldwide. It is a network of men and women committed to prayer, friendship with poor and marginalized people, and maintaining/restoring peace via

---

16. See pp. 80–81.

dialogue and negotiation. It helped negotiate an end to a civil war in Mozambique that had killed millions of people; its peacemaking work has since spread throughout Africa, the Balkans, and Latin America.[17] From a group of ten members in 1968, it now counts eighty thousand members spread across the globe.[18]

Mauro Garofalo, the head of International Relations for Sant'Egidio, has helped lead peace negotiations across Africa, East Asia, and the Middle East. His plenary lecture, "Peace Is an Open Workshop," has been transcribed and offered here as a set of reflections and lessons learned from the decades of experience gathered by Sant'Egidio members working to replace violent conflicts with negotiated peace settlements.

What Garofalo offers is not a standard scholarly paper, which allows for insights not always available through that often rigid genre. It moves from the history of Sant'Egidio and its diplomatic and peacemaking work to a nuanced reflection on the organic connections between prayer, life with the poor, and making peace.

Among its current projects are peacemaking efforts in Central African Republic—a country of four million people covering an area larger than France and where fourteen armed groups and dozens of political parties are vying for control, with divisions between and among religious groups.[19] Sant'Egidio is also engaged in Libya, working in small areas to address the colossal failures of the international community; it has also joined efforts to move toward peace in South Sudan, a conflict Garofalo says "casts shame on us as Christians. Because it is a country that became independent on the basis of Christians [being] free from the Muslim oppression."[20] On the second day of the country's formal independence, Christians began killing one another, with rival groups seeking to control the new government.

Garofalo said that this sort of work is not for the impatient or the naïve. He notes that his group was engaged for twenty-five years with people in southern Senegal before political conditions allowed for peace negotiations. As he reflects on his decades of peacemaking work as part of Sant'Egidio, he observes:

> We have to trust in the possibility of change for everyone. We can change. At the bottom of every man's [sic] heart, there is a desire for peace. We have witnessed change on multiple

---

17. For more information, see "The Community" page of the Sant'Egidio website.
18. See p. 97.
19. See pp. 100–1.
20. See p. 102.

occasions, change as the detoxification from the poison that is violence.

What can I say? These are the things that the UN should pay more attention to. So, in conclusion, everyone can change, and we need to heal men's [sic] souls and hearts from the wounds of violence. Peace is an open workshop. Peace is always possible. We know this from our thirty years of experience and hope, which guides the work of so many people. John Paul II was right. Peace is an open workshop, but we need lots of workers, so feel free to apply.[21]

Gospel nonviolence seems invariably to involve the risk of martyrdom—while several people have noted this connection, Daniel Pilario is uncommonly well-positioned to show the depth and breadth of this relation. Pilario is a noted scholar, the dean of a theology school, and a Catholic priest who ministers to people living in a garbage dump and slums in and near Manila. His essay, "Martyrs at the Margins: Rethinking Martyrdom in the Time of Violent Populism," situates the all-out war on the poor in the Philippines (led by President Rodrigo Duterte) within the worldwide surge in right-wing populist regimes; as the body counts rise, so does the need for Catholic theology to adjust its notions of martyrdom, witness, and fidelity to the gospel.

With more than thirty thousand people murdered by Duterte's police and paramilitaries, with untold numbers of people killed or consigned to preventable deaths under authoritarian regimes elsewhere, Pilario sketches the terrain upon which Christian love of neighbor and witness of Christ plays itself out. When love of neighbor and witness of Christ leads to death at the hands of ruling elites, it is proper that the language of martyrdom comes into play. For the church to discern its call to discipleship in areas where regimes rule through terror and profligate slaughter, its categories and commitments must be adjusted so that it might stay more true to its calling.

From the classical criterion of Christian martyrdom—being killed *in odium fidei* (out of hatred for the faith)—Pilario explores the evolution across the centuries of what else might constitute Christian martyrdom, including being killed *in odium conscientiae* (out of hatred for acts of conscience) and *in odium justitiae* (out of hatred for the pursuit of justice). The realities of political regimes that operate by killing large numbers of people, whose names are lost to all but their families—many of whom have disappeared and been made to vanish—merits a new category of Christian martyrdom, according to Pilario. He encourages the church to recognize

---

21. See pp. 103–4.

the martyrdom of those killed *in odium amoris* and *in odium misericordiae* (out of hatred for the love of neighbor, or for the practice of everyday love and mercy).

About such people, the victims of populist and authoritarian regimes of recent decades, Pilario notes:

> Their deaths were not as dramatic; their lives were so ordinary, commonplace, and unheroic. But they also met equally violent deaths as they expressed their commitment and fidelity to their families and friends. Many of them were ordinary sons or daughters, fathers or mothers, farmers or laborers—working on meager incomes for their families. Some of them were not even pious, nor were they staunch defenders of the faith. They were merely doing what an ordinary human person is expected to do: to love their neighbor, to take care of their families, to show compassion to someone in need, to be of help in any way whatsoever. Their violent deaths are signs of their Christian love for neighbor in living the way of compassion carved out by Jesus himself. Because of their great number—to the point of anonymity—the *Acta* of their martyrdom have not yet been collected, but the narratives of their deaths are even more chillingly gruesome.[22]
>
> I would like to consider that these simple people, who are among the socially excluded, did not die in vain. Beyond the narratives of "elite martyrs," theirs were not grand narratives, and they did not die in the name of fighting for justice and heroic causes of universal importance. I believe that there is a great Christian sense in ordinary expressions of love, in small narratives of day-to-day justice, in the daily lives of fidelity among the simple and the ordinary. These everyday people all met violent deaths, which they would have wanted to escape but did not in the name of charity and solidarity.[23]

Where Pilario focuses on the everyday martyrs in high-conflict areas of the Philippines, Elizabeth Kanini Kimau attends to the peacemaking potential of the church in what she calls the "deeply divided societies" of contemporary Africa. As she notes, the sheer numbers of people killed in recent African conflicts are staggering: 5.4 million in the Democratic Republic of Congo; two million each in Sudan and Sierra Leone; eight hundred thousand in Rwanda; and five hundred thousand in Angola, to name but a few.

---

22. See p. 116.
23. See p. 122.

In many places in Africa, where divisions seem intractable and sealed with years of bloodshed, the prospects of making authentic peace seem remote indeed. But in her experience, the Catholic Church is especially qualified to reconcile deeply divided societies and to heal those who have been broken by violence. This is because it is connected to people at all levels of society, including the few people at the top level, the larger group in the middle, and those at the grassroots, the largest group. Thus, the Catholic Church is found at every level of society and always accompanies the people.

Kimau speaks as someone with decades of experience in church-based peace work in Africa. She is the founder and coordinator of Seeds of Peace (Mbengu za Amani), a peace initiative in northern Kenya. She is also the coordinator of the Peace Building Cluster for the Alumnae Social Ministers in Tangaza College (part of the Catholic University of East Africa, based in Nairobi), as well as part of the Horn of Africa Grassroots Peace Forum. A teacher and peacemaker, she has facilitated reconciliation workshops among warring communities in the Rift Valley region of Kenya, having lived for a decade herself among warring factions in the area.

Kimau notes that many of the regions plagued with long-term violence are those in which people are most poor, neglected, or made worse off by state actors and forced to manage in areas of profound social instability. It is in such a context, she says, that "people at the grassroots feel justified taking up arms to protect themselves and their property. They see this as the only way to survive cycles of violence...."[24]

Many of the lessons Kimau shares in terms of church-based peace work derive from her decade of living among rival communities in northern Kenya and South Sudan. These were not areas in which the prospects would be seen as promising for reconciliation or gospel-based peaceableness. In one revealing section, she reports:

> From my ten years' experience of working with grassroots communities in northern Kenya and South Sudan, I have learned that revenge is embedded in the cultures of some ethnic groups. Children are socialized to believe that, when a relative is killed, one must avenge the death. For instance, when a father is killed in the Borana community, the father's clan has a responsibility to seek revenge. If it does not, it is mocked or disrespected by other clans. In addition, when the sons of the deceased father grow up, they are reminded of their responsibility to avenge their father's death. These quests for revenge trigger and also escalate the violence occurring in the community. Children in

---

24. See p. 130.

> this violent world learn that the only way to address violence is through violence. This was shown in responses I received from the Rendille[25] children I interacted with. I volunteered to teach in a school that had been closed several times for security reasons. The school was located at the fault line of the violence, so the children had seen many atrocities. Some children had even been killed as they cared for their cattle. When I asked the children, "What would you like to do when you grow up?" some replied, "When I grow up I will go kill Borana and bring back our livestock." Other times I asked, "When I bring Borana children to your school what will you do together?" and they responded, "We will kill them." I decided to help the children understand that we are all created by God and that even though some individual Boranas may be bad, not all are. I asked them, "Who created your parents?" and in unison they responded, "God." I went further and asked, "Who created the parents of Borana children?" All of the children responded with a loud voice, "Sheitani" (the devil).[26]

Despite such legacies, Kimau found that the church still possessed the capacity to build peace if it committed to the slow, mundane work such requires.

The church is endowed with many ways of serving as a channel for achieving sustainable peace at the grassroots. She is connected to people at all levels; she deeply values life and human dignity; her personnel have often sacrificed a lot in the service of God (e.g., religious people); she has channels that can form people in various ways; and she is guided by the values of Jesus: love, forgiveness, respect, and commitment. If the church conscientizes people at the grassroots to realize their potential for building peace and saying no to violence, they will be able to use their power not for violence but instead to contribute to a new generation that embraces peace, diversity, and participatory development.

This can happen if the church looks anew at what it already has and already does, with an eye toward peacemaking as a priority. Its everyday presence among rival groups . . . its ties to other religious communities . . . its commitment to education, formation, economic uplift, and more—the everyday life of the church, in other words—all are assets that can make peace something real at the local levels of conflict zones, even without large amounts of money. As Kimau notes:

---

25. The Rendille is an ethnic group in northern Kenya that has been in violent conflict with the neighboring Borana ethnic group.
26. See pp. 130–31.

> I have learned that building a culture of peace does not call for extraordinary actions but simply for being able to recognize opportunities for peace and utilize them to build a better environment. I also learned that it is possible to transform deeply rooted violence with little or no money. There is a need to demystify peacebuilding, which has been seen as a profession for a few educated people that involves a process that calls for a lot of money. Focusing on the church's potential for building a peaceful world gives peacebuilders a lot of hope and courage, something I experienced in collaborating with the church.[27]

At several points, Kimau notes that being a woman presented many of the local communities in which she lived with challenges: in these patriarchal societies, "[w]omen have historically not been permitted to attend gatherings of elders, nor to share ideas about how to build peace or make the community better."[28] Her experiences and insights complement those of Wachira Wamũyũ, another scholar focusing on Kenya's Northern Rift region; Wamũyũ echoes Kimau's remarks on women's role in society and provides an in-depth study of how women practice and narrate a range of indigenous nonviolence approaches to conflict and peacemaking.

A member of the Institute of the Blessed Virgin Mary (IBVM), better known as the Loreto Sisters, Wamũyũ is senior lecturer and program director of peace and conflict studies at the ecumenical St. Paul's University in Nairobi. In her chapter here, "Women and Nonviolent Indigenous Approaches to Peacebuilding: The North Rift Region of Kenya," she draws upon personal experiences and extended study of conflict in this important part of East Africa. Her chapter describes the scope and scale of violence in the region, explores some of the underlying causes, and describes several nonviolent indigenous approaches women have brought to bear on conflict in the region.

Whether it is violence associated with electoral cycles, cattle rustling, water conflicts, or grazing disputes, women disproportionately bear the brunt of regional violence. In addition, several but not all peoples in the region continue to practice gender-specific forms of violence, including female circumcision/genital mutilation, pressures toward early marriage, and various cultural exclusions affecting educational opportunities, decision-making, and more.

After offering some brief thoughts on the causes of regional violence, Wamũyũ offers an extensive list of nonviolent indigenous responses to

---

27. See pp. 133–34.
28. See p. 134.

violence. This list includes practices rooted deeply in the cultural firmament of the region's peoples, with traditional symbols and ideas deployed creatively in efforts to stop cycles of violence and oppression. Many of these nonviolent interventions build upon powerful symbols of female power and fertility, ranging from breastfeeding and the nude body to the traditional *legeteit* (birth belt). The latter is a symbol of female strength and potency, of communal life and protection, and is now used often to call for peace and protection by calling husbands and sons to refrain from warfare.

Wamūyū describes the development and spread of an alternative rite of passage for young women in the region, one that seeks to replace female circumcision/genital mutilation. This peaceful rite of passage seeks to affirm the intrinsic worth of all girls, joins them to an older female mentor, teaches them to experience God's love for them and their bodies as they are, affirms the value of female contributions to the community, and "teaches the girls about female sexuality, with an emphasis on the beauty of girlhood/womanhood and the uniqueness of each girl/woman."[29] The rite also includes outreach to boys that emphasizes the value of women's contributions to society rather than their continued exclusion; this is pursued through a Christian rite of passage for young men and boys.

Based on her observations and studies, Wamūyū offers numerous practical suggestions that promise to reduce or eliminate some of the violence experienced by women in the North Rift region. Some of these resemble the experiences and insights of Jasmin Nario-Galace, who draws attention to everyday practices of peace education and nonviolent action—with a special focus on women's experiences and capacities—in the Philippines and elsewhere. A professor of international studies at Miriam College in Quezon City, Nario-Galace is also the executive director of the college's Center for Peace Education. She also serves as president of Pax Christi Pilipinas and is a leader in the Philippine Council for Global and Peace Education. As a scholar-practitioner, she offers a blend of scholarly investigation and examples drawn from firsthand experience in "Building Spaces of Nonviolence: Women's Work to Challenge Armed Violence."

Part of what is needed, she says, is a reassessment of how attention to women and the gendered attitudes associated with war and violence should shape peacemaking and nonviolence efforts.

> Women are differently affected by armed violence, a situation that they do not normally perpetrate. They lose their source of livelihood due to displacement. They bear the responsibility of providing for children and household needs when men are

29. See p. 156.

killed or in the battlefield. They experience difficulty accessing services in evacuation centers . . . . In many armed conflicts, they have been raped, harassed, threatened, assaulted, and intimidated by those who wield the arms.[30]

Beyond the asymmetrical effects of violence on women, Nario-Galace notes that cultural constructions of masculinity are understudied and underappreciated in peace and conflict studies.

There are many known causes of armed violence—political, economic, cultural, situational—but not many have examined gendered causes. Cultural norms/constructions of masculinity expect men to exhibit power, dominate over others, take control, and exert physical strength. . . . Women have contributed to cultural conditioning that equates masculinity with violent behavior, encouraging their boys and men to fight or show force because they are boys or men. . . . Owning a weapon and aggressive behavior have, thus, become equivalent to being a man. Hence, the primary owners and users of weapons—and often the perpetrators and victims of armed violence—are men. Men and boys accounted for 84 percent of those who died violently in 2016.[31]

What gets overlooked in all of this, she says, is that the experiences of women in armed conflict is compounded by the exclusion of women from meaningful roles in conflict resolution, negotiation, mediation, and the like.

Women, in the face of armed violence, are normally viewed as vulnerable and victims. The role that they play in preventing violence and in conflict resolution is often overlooked. In many communities affected by armed violence, in times of both conflict and peace, women have played important roles: relief and rehabilitation coordinators, evacuation center managers, facilitators of dialogue, mediators between victims and government agencies, healers and counselors, etc. However, their diverse peace, conflict prevention, and security-related activities are referred to in passing and receive little or no support. Men, because they wage the war, often negotiate the peace. They dominate the public space and make the decisions in nearly all matters that relate to peace and security.

In a study done by UN women, women constituted only 6 percent of mediators, 13 percent of negotiators, and 6 percent

---

30. See p. 161.
31. See p. 162; citation omitted.

of signatories in all major peace processes between 1992 and 2019—and yet, women comprise 50 percent of the world's population. Their unique experiences and perspectives are hardly considered in matters of peace and security.

In developing solutions to the problem of armed violence, the views of women must also be considered. Hence, the adoption of UN Security Council 1325 . . . , which mandates member-states to include women and increase their participation in the different tracks of peace processes, conflict prevention, and peacebuilding, has been positively received.[32]

Complementing her attention to scholarly and theoretical considerations in the theory and practice of peacemaking, Nario-Galace offers a variety of examples from her and her colleagues' work on local, national, and international campaigns. In matters of education, she describes efforts that incorporate contextual awareness of violence and its victims, the importance of teaching mutual respect and equality as part of peace education, and awareness of the rights of women as well as the capacities of women in making peace.

She explores creative efforts that arise from the self-organization of women on matters of peacemaking, on various approaches to persuasion, and practical steps that have institutionalized nonviolent practices in the context of her own college. In addition to noting the difficulties attendant to working against armed conflict, she stresses the importance of noting and celebrating small victories and gradual progress as part of the long-term struggle to move beyond violence as a central feature of everyday life around the world.

Working for peace in Catholic-majority countries like the Philippines is very different than doing the same in places like India, where Christians of all types are a small minority of the population. In "Be the Change You Want to See: Building Interfaith Solidarity for Peace in India," Jesuit Francis Gonsalves relates the practical challenges and opportunities attendant to working for gospel nonviolence when only 2.3 percent of the population is Christian.[33] A professor at Jnana Deepa/Institute of Philosophy and Theology in Pune, India, Gonsalves also serves as an executive secretary for theology for the Conference of Catholic Bishops of India.

For persons unfamiliar with the complexities of modern India, Gonsalves offers a brief overview of religious and economic matters, and the inseparability of religion, economics, and politics:

32. See pp. 162–63; internal citations omitted.
33. See p. 177; internal citations omitted.

Indian religiosity has the following features: (a) porous boundaries, with a prolific exchange of religious practices and a strong eclecticism, leading to some level of integration; (b) the nonseparation between religion (*dharma*) and politics. Mahatma Gandhi's *sarva dharma samabhava* and Jawaharlal Nehru's *dharma nirpekshata* summarize what is implied by Indian secularism; (c) given the religious diversity in India, most believers acknowledge that their religion is but one among many others; (d) the renewal of religion is no longer the monopoly of the priestly class—Brahmins, priests/pastors, and imams—but rests in the hands of common people of all classes and castes, who practice *dharma* according to their concrete needs. Thus, we have seen a "democratization" of religion; and (e) while there are many positive elements in the Indian religious context, religion is often abused. Such abuse may appear, on the one hand, in hidden forms like the "Freedom of Religion" bill that actually robs people of their freedom to practice and propagate their religion, or, on the other, as open violence against religious minorities. One can cite the violence against Christians in Gujarat's Dangs District in 1998 and in Orissa's Kandhamal District in 2008, as well as the Gujarat genocide against Muslims in 2002. More recently, and in particular since the RSS-backed BJP government took power in May 2014, religious minorities have suffered much violence. The BJP won its second term in office in the national elections of May 2019 under the leadership of right-wing populist leader Narendra Modi—who has been accused of involvement in the 2002 Gujarat genocide.[34]

On the economic front, India's poverty amidst plenty is shocking. It is home to some of the wealthiest billionaires in the world, while millions of Indians eke out inhuman existences on its peripheries. In the 2022 Global Hunger Index, India stood at 107 out of 121 countries, and with a score of 29.1 (where 50 and above is "extremely alarming"), its level of hunger is classified as "serious." Such glaring inequalities in wealth are due not only to economic factors but also to religious beliefs that legitimize inequality on the basis of inherent factors like caste. Sadly, on the one hand, religions often legitimize poverty as a consequence of karma, predestination, or God-willed suffering, while, on the other, they widen the gap between the haves and the have-nots with a thriving "God Business" fueled by market mechanisms of globalization. In the recent past, the poor in India have also suffered severely due to a whimsical "demonetization" drive

---

34. See p. 178; internal citations omitted.

announced by India's Prime Minister, Narendra Modi, in 2016, while taxation and neoliberal policies, SEZs (special economic zones), illegal mining, and open market mechanisms, among other things, have crushed the rural poor and the daily wage urban laborers, many of whom have committed suicide.[35]

In such a challenging context, the church's commitment to peace might give rise to a different approach than might be pursued elsewhere. Might it be the case that, because Christians are so few in number, Catholics might need to think of gospel nonviolence in a more holistic, wide-ranging manner, perhaps including efforts at some remove from visible areas of conflict, violence, and peacemaking? Such seems to be the suggestion Gonsalves makes. For example, while he highlights a number church projects that might be seen as directly related to conflict, violence, and nonviolence, he also reports on several initiatives aimed at public health, youth development, and community well-being. The peace-related projects range from regional and national in scope, with one of them having marked its fiftieth anniversary in 2018. All of Gonsalves' cases deserve the sustained attention he provides them here.

Part Three: Theopolitical Debates: Just War and Responsibility to Protect

The final section of this book attends to some of the ongoing debates that attend to Catholic considerations of violence, security, peace, and theology. Two contributors offer challenging reflections on the notion of "just war" in the Christian tradition, while two others explore more recent questions and practices associated with what is known as the notion of Responsibility to Protect (R2P).

In "Confessions of a Just War Theorist: My Challenges Embracing a God of Absolute Nonviolence," M. T. Dávila, an associate professor of practice at Merrimack College, blends a discussion of theological positions on war and pacifism with honest and at times disarming personal reflections.

As a Christian ethicist who sees just war theory as a legitimate expression of Christian love of neighbor (while also aware of how the theory has been used and abused historically), Dávila notes that she has found herself challenged on several sides in recent years: from students who were not persuaded that just war theory was compatible with the Jesus of love and nonviolence they encountered in the Gospels, and from challenges to just

---

35. See p. 180; internal citations omitted.

war theory from various church circles, including the Vatican's 2016 conference on Gospel Nonviolence and Just Peace (which raised the question of setting aside just war theory as a legitimate Christian position).

As if that was not enough, she reports that she was asked to be part of a major initiative in 2017, which gathered Catholic theologians worldwide to engage in collaborative research in support of a proposed papal encyclical on gospel nonviolence. The task given to the group of which she was a member was to develop the theological rationale for understanding the God revealed in the Bible as a God of radical or absolute nonviolence. These experiences together, she says, inform her chapter as "a description of my journey," and have raised important methodological questions on "how we do and source theology and ethics grounded on gospel nonviolence."[36]

In the end, however, Dávila reports that the experiences, particularly in the 2017 collaborative project on nonviolence, reaffirmed the validity of the just war tradition and raised questions about problematic features of notions of "radical nonviolence."

> ... I was most challenged by my historical consciousness, which cautioned me to carefully consider the implications of proclaiming "gospel nonviolence" and a God of radical nonviolence. Questions that kept complicating my thoughts about this task included: Who gets to define these terms? Who benefits? What realities do they include and imply? What kinds of practices do they normalize? Do they overlook people's histories of colonial, economic, and other forms of violence? In short, I was suspicious that the drive to promote a God of nonviolence would result in a tool that could effectively erase peoples' particular experiences of unjust violence. As a Puerto Rican and a Latin American, I recognized that members of the roundtable from the global South also had similar concerns. More specifically, we wanted to make sure that any proposal for a foundational theology of nonviolence would not gloss over the Catholic Church's complicity with colonial and religious violence throughout the ages. Proposals that describe a God of radical nonviolence need to serve the purpose of putting a mirror to the church's lamentable links to European colonialism, conquest, and expansion.[37]

Even after reviewing the virtues and qualities of just war theory that serve Christian commitments to life and justice, and even as she notes that

---

36. See p. 199.
37. See p. 200.

many notions of radical nonviolence also rely on norms derived from just war theory, Dávila recognizes some changes in her views:

> I admit that these reasons I've just discussed grow weaker the more I engage with and learn from nonviolent practices and thinkers. They are, decidedly, heavily dependent on a structure of power that limits who the actors making policy and military decisions may be. As most often articulated and used, just war theory does not take into consideration the clamor of masses of people who, themselves having applied just war principles to particular situations (for example, the global mass demonstrations against the preemptive war against Iraq), have judged the use of force against particular populations and governments to be completely illegitimate. It often fails to incorporate the wisdom and on-the-ground work of civil actors who offer nonviolent resolutions to some or all parts of what was previously thought to be an intractable conflict, detailed examples of which are presented in this edited volume.[38]

She ends her reflections with a nod toward ideas about "Responsibility to Protect" (R2P), which may reflect an advance beyond some of the problems with just war theory, especially as it has been embedded in Western political history and contexts.[39] While Dávila continues to see theological and ethical value in the just war tradition, Robert Emmet Meagher does not. In "Just War: A Convenient Untruth," he places just war theory alongside other notions that he describes as "lies and promises drenched in blood."[40] A professor emeritus of humanities at Hampshire College, Meagher is a leading scholar working on the matter of "moral injury," defined as "the damage done to one's conscience or moral compass when that person perpetrates, witnesses, or fails to prevent acts that transgress one's own moral beliefs, values, or ethical codes of conduct."[41]

Meagher walks back through the various lies and untruths that have shaped his world over the past century—from those who made possible the mass slaughter of World War I to the commitment to murder on an unimaginable scale that undergirds the deployment of nuclear weapons. Ultimately, his review leads him back to the church and to its development of just war theory. Meagher the Catholic scholar is unsparing:

38. See pp. 202–3.
39. See p. 204.
40. See p. 211.
41. "What Is Moral Injury?"

> It is ironic and angering that the most lethal and effective public lie told to enable empires, kingdoms, and nations to martial armies and send them off to kill, destroy, and die is a lie invented by the church of the nonviolent Christ, more specifically by bishops Augustine of Hippo and Ambrose of Milan in the fourth century. I have little doubt that it was a lie first fabricated in good faith, a "white lie" as we say, but one that like a cancer eagerly metastasized and spread, becoming more deadly with the passage of time. The lie I have in mind is what we know as "just war theory." While its original aim may have been to limit as well as to allow the use of deadly force, it has had far more success in unleashing violence than in controlling it. Like a Wikitext, just war theory and its precepts have been freely expanded and updated across sixteen centuries to address and accommodate the open-ended evolution of warfare and the deepening of humanity's addiction to it. When we consider the Crusades, the conquest of the Americas, the religious persecutions and wars of Europe, the Great War, the Good War, the Cold War, the Forever War, the invention of gunpowder, the invention of nuclear fission, we may well wonder whether there is any war or weapon, any strategy or tactic, any exercise of force that just war theory won't eventually authorize or at least condone . . . provided we have the right intention (*recta intentio*).[42]

Like many contemporary scholars, Meagher traces the Christian compromise with violence to the changing social position (and its theological sequelae) symbolized by the rise of Constantine and Christianity's place in empire. He ascribes to Augustine the desire not only to make killing a defensible matter theologically but to provide assurances that Christians that kill in just wars commit no sin that would jeopardize their souls.

> To pray for the emperor and the legions, as the ardent pacifist Tertullian had done, was one thing, but to partner with the emperor and march in the legions was quite another. To do this in good conscience required the recalibration of that conscience, and it was Augustine and his mentor Ambrose who took on that task. Essentially, this meant arguing that there are two kinds of killing, one that offends God and alienates the killer from God, and the other, which does neither. With this simple distinction, Christian "just war" was born. War, after all, is all about killing. And so, with at least the theoretical possibility of sinless killing came the possibility of other forms of sinless physical violence, including torture, which Augustine explicitly defended, liberties

---

42. See pp. 214–15.

which not only Christian nations but also the church freely exercised in the centuries to come.[43]

And yet, just as Dávila the just war advocate recognizes how radical Christian nonviolence complicates her view, Meagher recognizes how an uncompromising refusal to kill sits uneasily with the need to protect vulnerable persons from threats when one has the ability to do so. A conversation with a military veteran who described himself as a "borderline pacifist," able to renounce all killing except if confronted with an immediate threat to children, left Meagher to conclude, "I was and remain conflicted, as even the nonviolent church has been and remains conflicted or, we might even say, confused."[44]

Meagher draws attention to Christian luminaries like Dietrich Bonhoeffer and Thomas Merton, neither of whom supported just war theory but nonetheless did not rule out lethal means in extremis. A onetime pacifist like Ernesto Cardenal similarly used the defense of children and the defenseless as the reason he came to accept violent resistance, a position criticized by fellow priest and pacifist Daniel Berrigan.[45] Meagher finds the tension between the two to be beyond resolution, which is not entirely a negative thing, in his view; at a minimum, it positions the peace movement to understand better the millions of military personnel for whom killing, moral injury, and self-sacrifice are critical questions. He believes "if we in the peace movement listen to them, we will discover uniquely credible and committed allies, brothers and sisters willing, even aching, to put away the swords they have wielded and beat them into ploughshares."[46]

The quandary of individual ethics—what should someone committed to gospel nonviolence do when vulnerable people are threatened with imminent harm?—becomes more complex when attention turns to large-scale versions of the question. The "international community" was said to stand by while eight hundred thousand people were killed in Rwanda in 1994; that and similar cases sparked renewed attention to whether military invasion and killing would be justified to stop large-scale atrocities as they occurred.

One person well positioned to explore the complexities of the issue is Elias Opongo, SJ. As a social scientist trained in peace and conflict studies, and director of the Hekima Institute of Peace Studies and International Relations in Nairobi, Opongo looks at the theory and practice of military intervention aimed at protecting vulnerable people in "Responsibility to

43. See pp. 216–17.
44. See p. 219.
45. See pp. 219–21.
46. See p. 222.

Protect and Nonviolent Discourse: Implications of Conflict Militarization in South Sudan."

Opongo begins his exploration of the South Sudan case by providing helpful background on R2P, which he notes is a successor concept to the idea of "humanitarian intervention," a vague term referring to sporadic use of military force in response to alleged large-scale violations of human rights. He notes that humanitarian intervention was often driven by the interests of major states rather than a consistent application of principle; sometimes the principle was invoked by individual states, other times by one or more states with or without the sanction of the "international community." The arbitrariness of the concept, and its association with what were sometimes judged as neocolonial invasions by powerful states at the expense of weaker ones, led to efforts to come up with a more adequate set of ideas and practices. Initiated by the United Nations and spearheaded by the Canadian government, these efforts generated the notion of R2P as an improvement on the logic of humanitarian intervention.[47]

As Opongo notes, the notion of R2P as ratified by the United Nations World Summit in 2005, qualifies the narrow Westphalian notion of state sovereignty by making it contingent on a state's ability and desire to protect the human rights of people inside its borders; when states are a threat to people inside their borders, or do nothing to protect them from severe threats, responsibility for people's well-being shifts to other states in the international community. The doctrine of R2P also added significant attention to initiatives and practices before, during, and after an armed intervention (the latter seen as a last resort), considerations that represent improvements on the "humanitarian intervention" framework.[48]

Opongo examines the application of R2P policies, including the insertion of armed force, to the civil war in South Sudan. The newest member of the state system, South Sudan split from Sudan in 2011 after a decades-long military and political campaign. The new state soon became the site of a protracted and bloody civil war, which has displaced more than a million people, killed several hundred thousand, and subjected untold number of women and girls to sexual violence. He discusses the efforts of many external actors—including neighboring states, the United Nations, the African Union, outside powerful states (including the United States)—and the invocation of R2P principles to justify military interventions into South Sudan. He traces these various campaigns, what they did and did not accomplish,

47. See pp. 227–28.
48. See p. 228.

and whether they seem to have made things better or worse for people at risk in South Sudan.

Opongo then examines initiatives that he sees as responding to the moral imperatives captured in R2P policy but in ways that might "bridge differences between belligerents and fighting communities." Principles and practices of nonviolence, drawn from both external sources (e.g., Gandhi, Martin Luther King) and local Sudanese culture, inspired a variety of attempts to resolve the conflict, in whole and in part, throughout the civil war.[49] While the war continues, Opongo nevertheless notes that in several of the campaigns he studied, nonviolent alternatives to militarized approach to conflict can work. Such processes are slow but have long-term impact on the change of attitudes and perceptions . . . in other words, encountering armed violence with nonviolent means takes time, but the long-term impacts are fulfilling.

He concludes by noting that despite the best intentions of several actors, R2P as practiced in South Sudan did not deliver as many had hoped:

> Militarized humanitarian interventions in the South Sudan conflict have cost the United Nations millions of dollars, without hope of ending the conflict in the near future. The UNMISS [UN military mission to South Sudan] may have also further fueled the conflict. Given the limited success of militarized conflict intervention by the UN, government forces, and militia groups, it is crucial—in order to save lives—to reconsider R2P initiatives that incorporate nonviolent strategies. Dialogue, tolerance, and reconciliation are important elements for successful conflict resolution, but for such interventions to succeed, they must be founded on the framework of South Sudan's cultural value system. Like many African countries, South Sudan integrates the cultural mechanisms of dialogue and reconciliation into conflict resolution structures. Largely communitarian, the approach involves active mediation by elders who work with community members to find common solutions to conflicts. . . . Other approaches like amnesty or pardon are built on the strong belief that, in certain situations, forgiveness of offenders is more expedient for the public welfare than prosecution and punishment, which can lead to vicious cycles of revenge and hate. Additionally, for conflict resolution strategies to be effective in Africa, there is a need to simultaneously link peacebuilding, democratization, governance, and economic development.[50]

---

49. See pp. 235–38.
50. See p. 240; internal citation omitted.

It is unclear whether Opongo sees R2P as an ethical framework that Christians can support, even though he finds it deficient thus far in the South Sudan case. There is no doubt where Michael L. Budde stands, in contrast, on whether Christians should embrace R2P. In "Killing with Kindness: Can a Plague Cure a Plague?" he argues that, even if R2P reflects good intentions and a desire to minimize casualties in the pursuit of the greater good, Christians committed to nonviolence should not embrace it. This is despite the serious work done by Christian ethicists working to advance frameworks like "just peacemaking," "just policing," or further developments of the just war tradition, all of which seek to embody Christian love and mercy while responding to violence in a fallen world.

> Persons like me, who insist Jesus meant what he said in the Sermon on the Mount and elsewhere that Christians shouldn't kill people, even with a good cause, are generally regarded as unrealistic, detached from the realities of suffering and oppression in the world, and putting abstract purity of principle over the flesh-and-blood needs of the most vulnerable in society—leaving them to the wolves, in other words. One needs a bracing dose of realism, grounded in the experiences of at-risk others, lest abstract principle lead to the death of others.[51]

With this demand for "realism" in mind, Budde proceeds to reframe the context in which Christian ethical discussion proceeds on R2P and similar applications of lethal force. These include both some of the unquestioned assumptions behind the Christian case for R2P, and the real-world means by which R2P is implemented in a world of states.

For example, he argues that state actors—the wielders of the violent means called upon in R2P—pay no regard to the limits imposed by Christian ethics in times of crisis; military adventures will occur whether or not Christian theologians approve of them; that whatever gains in the areas of nonviolence and peacemaking the churches have made in recent centuries may likely be overturned by embracing R2P; that arguments focusing on the number lives lost in the absence of military interventions depend on selective accounting that ignores potentially larger numbers of victims caused by such interventions or the inability of the church to speak against future invasions. He also draws attention to an unspoken assumption worthy of attention in discussions on Christians and the use of lethal force:

> There will always be actors and institutions that build some semblance of order using violence and coercion, but nowhere

---

51. See p. 246.

> in the New Testament does it say that Christians have to help build or enhance the formal institutions of violent order-keeping—neither Rom 13 nor 1 Pet 2:13–17 nor anywhere else. Lethality-created order is like the weather: it's going to be here whether you like it or not, and sometimes—like a rainstorm that generates a flood, which can renew the soil—some good can come from it by the grace of God. It doesn't follow from that, however, that Christians are under an obligation to make the flooding more powerful, or to wash away one's enemies, just because these things happen sometimes on their own.[52]

Given that most Christian defenses of R2P rely on some version of just war thinking as exemplified by Augustine, much of Budde's chapter looks at what happens to one of Augustine's primary criteria for assessing the morality of war in the real-world conditions under which humanitarian-based military interventions occur. This criterion—the need for warriors to operate with right intention, with internal dispositions toward love and not hate in their hearts—is not incidental to Augustine's framework, nor to the best Christian defenses of R2P. To see what happens to "right intention" in the conditions of modern warfare, including warfare waged for humanitarian purposes, is to respect the theological seriousness of those who see military force as an essential component of modern efforts to protect vulnerable persons.

What follows is an extended exploration of the socialization of soldiers, the dehumanization required to turn people into efficient killers. It is a grim and ugly process, designed to extinguish natural and Christian empathy for those designated as "enemy." From historical accounts to professional literature to first-person memoir, the story is the same: it involves

> more intensive psychological de- and re-construction of recruits (taking apart their sense of self and replacing it with loyalty to the military and especially to their small unit); systematic indoctrination in what many participants describe as dehumanization of others; a hyper-masculinity that generates sexual predation (among male and female recruits alike); and a profound disdain for civilian life and culture as weak, corrupted, and unworthy of the virtuous service of soldiers. These processes for formation begin in basic training, are sustained by military culture, and are deepened for those undergoing specialized training (e.g., elite forces of various types).

> The literature is extensive, and the personal testimonies from those who have experienced it are extensive (even as

---

52. See p. 248.

a powerful code of silence discourages sharing with outsiders the nature and depth of the dehumanization necessary to make modern soldiers). From physical brutalization and sleep-deprived exertions to countless repetitive drills—complete with racist and sexist cadences, invectives and insider-outsider language, and combat conducted while using powerful stimulants and psychotropic drugs—the modern soldier is different from the romanticized citizen-soldiers of Hollywood war films and July 4 parades.[53]

Given the significance of restraint and ethical conduct required of soldiers engaged in R2P actions, it seems that the training of modern military units works at cross-purposes with these concerns. Such is not to disparage individuals who become soldiers, but rather to recognize a structural incompatibility between the nature of war—even for good causes—and the restrictions and mindsets attendant to R2P and any ethical system that aspires to be anything other than window dressing. Budde ends with a proposal that might help reconcile the incompatibility of secularly formed soldiers with the exacting norms of R2P, just peacemaking, just policing, or other frameworks defended on Christian grounds. The proposal is undoubtedly an unpalatable one—Budde himself opposes it—but it is one that demands consideration if one takes seriously the call for moral realism undergirding the advocacy of Christian-approved lethal force in a good cause.

Postscript

Father Eliseo ("Jun") Mercado, a priest of the Oblates of Mary Immaculate, was a participant in the gathering that gave rise to this volume. He died on May 23, 2021, after contracting COVID-19; while his presentation is not included in this book, his ministry and lifelong dedication to peacemaking in his native Philippines and elsewhere will last in the hearts and memory of many people. His loss touches all of us who were lucky enough to have met him.

Bibliography

Chenoweth, Erica, and Maria J. Stephan. *Why Civil Resistance Works: The Strategic Logic of Nonviolent Conflict.* New York: Columbia University Press, 2011.

Churchill, Ward. *Pacifism as Pathology: Reflections on the Role of Armed Struggle in North America.* Chico, CA: AK, 2007.

---

53. See pp. 253–54.

"The Community." Sant'Egidio, n.d. https://www.santegidio.org/pageID/30008/langID/en/THE-COMMUNITY.html.
Francis, Pope. *Fratelli Tutti: On Fraternity and Social Friendship*. Vatican City: Libreria Editrice Vaticana, 2020. https://www.vatican.va/content/francesco/en/encyclicals/documents/papa-francesco_20201003_enciclica-fratelli-tutti.html.
———. "Nonviolence: A Style of Politics for Peace." Vatican, January 1, 2017. https://www.vatican.va/content/francesco/en/messages/peace/documents/papa-francesco_20161208_messaggio-l-giornata-mondiale-pace-2017.html.
Gelderloos, Peter. *The Failure of Nonviolence*. St. Louis: Left Bank, 2016.
———. "Has XR the Successful Strategy to Save the Planet?" Submitted August 16, 2019, to Libcom.org by Anna and Arthur (no last names given). https://libcom.org/library/has-xr-successful-strategy-save-planet.
Pax Christi International. "An Appeal to the Catholic Church to Recommit to the Centrality of Gospel Nonviolence." Concluding statement of the Nonviolence and Just Peace Conference, sponsored by Pax Christi International and the Pontifical Council for Justice and Peace and held in Rome, April 11–13, 2016. https://nonviolencejustpeace.net/wp-content/uploads/2016/05/appeal-to-catholic-church-on-gospel-nonviolence.pdf.
"What Is Moral Injury?" The Moral Injury Project at Syracuse University. https://moralinjuryproject.syr.edu/about-moral-injury/.

PART ONE

Contributions to a Theology of Nonviolence

I

Christian Cross and Martyrdom: Jesus's Response to a Violent World

O. Ernesto Valiente

THE TERMS "CROSS" AND "martyrdom" have always occupied a significant place in Christian tradition. Both words evoke the centrality of the Christ event and remind us that our faith is lived out in a violent world. "Cross" and "martyrdom" unveil the underside of historic reality, the frightful but real dimensions of Christian discipleship in a dangerous and conflicted world. From earliest Christianity, Jesus's crucifixion made him both our redeemer (1 Peter 1:18–19) and the exemplary Christian martyr[1] and has continuously generated polyvalent and, at times, conflictual interpretations.

Today, a vast number of Christians believe that God somehow willed Jesus's death on the cross and that his death was necessary for human salvation. Described as "substitutionary atonement," this theological explanation can be traced back to the medieval Benedictine monk, Anselm of Canterbury, who argued that Jesus's death on the cross served as a satisfaction or payment for human sin. While the Catholic Church has always acknowledged that there are different understandings of salvation and has never canonized one particular soteriological interpretation, this version of salvation largely became the main referent for understanding the

---

1. Eusebius of Caesarea noted that Christians "were also so zealous in their imitation of Christ . . . they cheerfully yielded the title of martyr to Christ, the true and faithful martyr (witness), the first begotten from the dead, the prince of divine life." Eusebius, *Ecclesiastical History,* 158.

meaning of the cross in Christian imagination and piety. Over the last fifty years, however, many theologians have challenged the widespread idea that God required Jesus's death for the salvation of sinful humanity. Although contemporary theologians acknowledge that certain aspects of atonement theories can be helpful pastorally, they warn against the implicit idea of a God who demands the sacrifice of his son or any other innocent victim to accomplish our salvation. They rightly insist that such an understanding of God is deeply problematic for Christians who are "called to be followers of Christ and imitators of God."[2] Theologians such as Rita Nakashima Brock, Delores Williams, and J. Denny Weaver have rejected this soteriological interpretation while others, like Edward Schillebeeckx, have even suggested that "we are not redeemed *thanks to* the death of Jesus but *despite* it."[3]

Closely related to the symbol of the cross is the understanding of Jesus as the authentic martyr. In Christian liturgy and devotion, we often hear that the blood of the martyrs was the seed for the church. Yet, as important as martyrdom has been for the church, this term has never possessed a univocal meaning within the Christian tradition. During the first three hundred years of Christianity, a martyr was described as one who witnessed to, and died like, Jesus.[4] As Candida Moss has shown, this link between martyrdom and *imitatio Christi* is widely found in martyriological accounts of the second and third centuries, including the *Letter of the Churches of Lyons and Vienne*; in Latin North African accounts such as the *Martyrdom of Montanus and Lucius*; and in some Syriac literature.[5] Unfortunately, this basic link between martyrdom and the imitation of Christ slowly eroded over time.[6] Today, the Catholic Church's criteria for martyrdom require that martyrs freely accept their death and that this death be both violent and caused by hatred for the faith.

In the last few decades, two main types of events have led us to reconsider our understanding of martyrdom. On the one hand, the persecution and assassination of many Latin American Christians actively struggling for greater social justice have led some theologians to argue that the Christian

---

2. Daly, "Images of God," 39.

3. Schillebeeckx, *Christ*, 729, italics original. See also Brock, "Little Child Shall Lead Us," 42–61; Williams, *Sisters in the Wilderness*; Weaver, *Nonviolent Atonement*; and Haight, *Future of Christology*, 87.

4. Candida Moss asserts that "from the proclamation of the churches to the footnotes of the academy, all agree: the martyr follows Christ both literally and literarily." Yet, her recent studies also show that early Christian views on martyrdom were not uniform. Moss, *Other Christs*, 3. See also Castelli, *Martyrdom and Memory*, 51.

5. Moss, *Other Christs*, 47.

6. See Valiente, "Renewing the Theology," 112–27.

understanding of martyrdom should be extended to include such victims.[7] Jon Sobrino, for instance, has noted that, while more Christians have suffered violent death in Latin America than any other place since Vatican II, most of "those who today are killed in a way that most resembles Jesus's death are not held to share in this supreme death, because they do not fulfill the canonical and dogmatic conditions for martyrdom."[8] On the other hand, the recent appropriation of the term "martyr" by perpetrators of violent actions by extremist groups has muddled the meaning of the word. Drawing on an ambiguous Christian tradition regarding the use of violence, some theologians are willing to consider the possibility of "bellicose" martyrs. In fact, Sobrino has noted that "St. Thomas [Aquinas] saw no problem in considering a soldier's death as a possible form of martyrdom, because 'the good of the republic is the highest of goods' and 'any human good may be a cause of martyrdom when it is related to God.'"[9] These developments have intensified the debate over whether Christians who take up arms against tyrants should ever be considered martyrs.

In response to the relative ambiguity attached to the significance of the cross and martyrdom, this paper proposes that Christians can better grasp the meaning of these two central terms when they are illuminated by Jesus's life and death. In other words, the significance of Jesus's cross and martyrdom is best understood against the conflicted background of his immediate situation and the manner in which he confronted it. The paper further argues that Jesus's nonviolent manner of engaging his conflicted world was essential to his understanding of God's reign and the only acceptable way to bring about God's kingdom. While Jesus's life and mission brings clarity to the meaning of the cross, this in turn sheds light on how we are to understand Christian martyrdom today. Hence, the paper takes the narratives of Jesus of Nazareth and the study of first-century Palestine as its points of departure and basis to offer a better understanding of the cross and Christian martyrdom. To this end, I will largely rely on the contribution of Scripture scholars belonging to the "Third Quest" who seek to locate Jesus within his historical context. While this study recognizes the theologized character of the New Testament accounts and the impossibility of gaining full access to the Jesus who walked in Palestine some two thousand years ago, it also accepts the fundamental structure of Jesus's life as portrayed by the Gospels and interpreted by the Christian tradition. Because the cross and martyrdom are the product of violent confrontations, my approach to the sources will privilege

---

7. See Rahner, "Dimensions of Martyrdom," 9–11.
8. Sobrino, *Jesus the Liberator*, 265.
9. Sobrino, "Jesuanic Martyrs," 131.

those narratives that reflect the situation of conflict in which Jesus found himself and the manner in which he confronted such conflict.

The essay is structured in three parts. First, it identifies the main sources of conflict in Jesus's context. Second, it turns to the narratives of Jesus's life and his response to this situation—that is, his reconciling mission in a conflicted world. Third, it examines the violent rejection to Jesus's mission and his nonviolent response to this rejection. To conclude, I offer some reflections on how Jesus's life sheds light on the meaning of the cross and Christian martyrdom today.

A Conflicted Context

The German historian Martin Hengel rightly argued that, to understand the uniqueness of Jesus's message and ministry, one must first consider them within the context of the conflicted Palestinian revolutionary situation of Jesus's day.[10] By the time Jesus was born, Palestine had already been under the control of the Roman Empire for sixty years. After the death of Herod the Great in 4 BCE, the Romans had placed his sons as the region's puppet rulers working in coordination with the Roman procurator in charge of Judea and Samaria. These proxies of Rome had complete control as long as they fulfilled three main conditions: collected taxes, maintained order and stability in the region, and protected the empire's borders. The ruling elites whose interests coincided with those of the Roman Empire included the puppet rulers' courts as well as the families of the chief priests who lived in the cities. The elites, who represented only one or two percent of the total population, were assisted in ruling Jewish Palestine by their bureaucracy: ordinary priests, temple officials, tax collectors, lawyers, clerks, toll collectors, and large merchants. The bureaucratic class accounted for 5 to 6 percent of Israelites in Palestine. The remaining 92 percent of the population consisted of a rural class of peasants, fishermen, and artisans who struggled to survive under unjust economic conditions. The relationship between these two main social classes—the urban elites and the rural workers—was dominated by economic exploitation.[11]

While recent studies have described Jesus's Galilean region as prosperous and relatively stable during Herod Antipas's reign, this general prosperity should not lead us to believe that there was an equitable distribution of goods.[12] On the contrary, this prosperity was a source of social tension and

---

10. Hengel, *Victory over Violence*, 45.
11. Borg, *Conflict Holiness*, 11.
12. Kloppenborg, "Jesus, Fishermen," 571–99.

conflict. Because land was the main source of revenue and employment, social stratification was largely a function of land ownership. Large landowners often rented their land and did not live on it but rather in the city. At the same time, small landowners and leaseholders lived under the threat of losing their holdings due to the triple tax structure: (1) tithes due to the priests and the temple tax; (2) levies (land tax and customs tolls) collected by Herod Antipas; and (3) the Roman tribute.[13] Richard Horsley notes, for instance, that oppressive taxation among agricultural producers amounted to "well over 40 percent of their production," thus worsening the division between the poor and the rich landowners and exacerbating social unrest in Galilee.[14] As Gerd Theissen and Annette Merz have noted, Jewish Palestine was "riven by deep structural tensions, tensions between Jew and Gentiles, town and country, rich and poor, rulers and ruled."[15] These tensions put a tremendous amount of pressure upon the Jewish population who resisted foreign occupation and oppression. Even if we agree with E. P. Sanders' argument that, at the time of Jesus, Jewish Palestine was not "tottering at the brink of revolt," it is important to remember that while Roman forces maintained a relative stability and order throughout Palestine, violent uprisings occurred right before and after Jesus's life, and that the possibility of violent insurrection was always latent.[16]

This is important because, to properly understand Jesus's ministry, one must remember that Jesus did not carry out his mission within some type of neutral or peaceful context but rather in direct response to the conflicted situation endured by the Jewish people at the time. This situation, in turn, hardened their hearts and filled them with hatred and resentment toward the Romans, whom they considered their enemy for political, economic, and religious reasons. As we will see in the following sections, Jesus rejects the options of (a) coexisting passively with this conflicted situation or (b) violently reacting against it. Rather, Jesus's reconciling ministry forges an alternative route by stressing what God has done in the past for the Jewish people and the promise, alive among the Jewish people, that God's reign of peace will soon become a reality.

---

13. Dunn, *Jesus Remembered*, 310–11.
14. Horsley, *Jesus and the Spiral of Violence*, 56.
15. Theissen and Merz, *Historical Jesus*, 175.
16. Sanders, *Historical Figure of Jesus*, 28. There were also different religious parties within Israel—Sadducees, Pharisees, Essenes—that distrusted one another and competed for the favor of the majority of the people.

Jesus's Reconciling Mission: God's Reign

Most scholars today agree that Jesus's life and ministry were centered in God and the promise of God's kingdom. As a dynamic symbol that communicated the hope that God would act in history, the kingdom of God was neither individualistic nor otherworldly. Rather, it had two basic connotations: "that God rules in [God's] acts" and that the kingdom "exists in order to transform a bad and unjust historical-social reality into a different good and just one."[17] As N. T. Wright has argued, within Second Temple Judaism, the idea of God's reign resonated among people, evoking a complete storyline. Such an idea embodied the promise of Israel's final return from exile, the return of Yahweh's Zion, and the final victory of Yahweh over evil and all of Israel's enemies.[18] If, in the present time, Israel were under Roman occupation while the wicked flourished and the Israelites disobeyed the Law, there would come a time when God would no longer hide God's face away from the people. In this new world order, God will assume God's kingship and overcome his enemies, the land will be cleansed of gentile pollution, and God will pour out his spirit in such a way that Israel will keep the Law from the heart. Jesus anticipated that this new reign would come fully in the near future as the consummation of God's purpose, but he also claimed that it was already breaking in through his own ministry.[19]

Jesus's ministry, Leonardo Boff tells us, introduces a new situation to the old world, now replete with God and reconciled with itself: "The kingdom of God means a total, global, structural revolution of the old order, brought about by God and only by God."[20] The kingdom that will take root in this world is also a social reality that consists of social-political arrangements among human beings and will not be established apart from them. While Jesus stressed that the kingdom is solely God's initiative and something God gives completely and freely, his ministry shows that the gratuitous character of the kingdom does not rule out human activity on its behalf. Rather, God's free, loving initiative places a claim on human cooperation with God's plan for humanity. As Gustavo Gutiérrez explains, "The kingdom is a gift but also a demand. It is a freely given gift of God, and it calls for conformity to God's will to life . . . it requires that we make others our brothers and sisters."[21] In this sense, it is important to stress the inclusive character of Jesus's mission.

---

17. Sobrino, *Jesus the Liberator*, 71.
18. Wright, *Jesus and the Victory*, 204–7.
19. Marshall, "Hope of a New Age," 212.
20. Boff, *Jesus Christ*, 63–64.
21. Gutiérrez, *God of Life*, 118.

As Gutiérrez writes, "the proclamation of the kingdom is directed to all; no one is excluded from either the gifts or its demands."[22]

At the same time, one cannot forget that the kingdom of God is primarily addressed to the victims of history. The essential relationship between the kingdom and the marginalized sheds light on those to whom the kingdom is bestowed. This is perhaps nowhere more evident than in Jesus's proclamation of the Beatitudes, which describe the "mindset of a person of the Reign": the pure of heart, the merciful, the peacemakers, those who are able to forgive, and the poor.[23] Indeed, Jesus's life and ministry were staked on the promise of a reconciled eschatological community rooted in God's merciful justice where the victims of history will be restored to life. That is, a community constituted, above all, by the poor and the victims and, by extension, the repentant and forgiven victimizers. As Latin American theologians have rightly argued, this kingdom "can be properly described as the ideal of reconciliation, especially because in [it] . . . will be present those who are always absent—the poor and the weak. And they will be there with their oppressors, now forgiven and converted."[24]

That Jesus's ministry is all-inclusive—but directed first to those who suffer and who have been excluded from the community—is also evident in Jesus's healing miracles, which are signs of the closeness of God's reign and of Jesus's utter compassion. As Scripture scholars have noted, these miracles not only bring physical healing to the recipients but also have a social component in that they enable the reincorporation, back into the worshiping community, of those who were maimed or sick and thus, considered ritually impure.[25] Particularly relevant to us are Jesus's exorcisms, which are a special type of healing miracle. Like the other healings, Jesus's exorcisms are directly related to the coming of the kingdom: "But if it is by the Spirit of God that I cast out demons, then the kingdom of God has come to you" (Matt 12:28 NRSV).[26] They reveal that Jesus's ministry was not exempt from conflict but rather brought him into direct contact with the spiritual forces occupying the people of Yahweh.

Another mark of Jesus's inclusive ministry was his welcoming of sinners, most clearly exemplified in his table fellowship. Indeed, more than just forgiving sinners, the Gospels often portray Jesus as talking, eating, and commingling with them. For those who had been traditionally ostracized

22. Gutiérrez, *God of Life*, 108.
23. Sobrino, *Spirituality of Liberation*, 127 and 36–37.
24. Sobrino, "Conflicto y Reconciliación," 1147.
25. Wright, *Jesus and the Victory*, 191–92.
26. All biblical citations are from the New Revised Standard Version (NRSV).

and marginalized from society by their religious leaders, Jesus's communion with them anticipates the coming of the kingdom and captures the experience of the sinner whose repentance is preceded and initiated by Jesus's acceptance.[27] This is not to say that Jesus was oblivious to human sinfulness or that he did not recognize the need for conversion. Rather, it is to stress that, in the Gospels, the sinners' acknowledgment of their shortcomings is accompanied and effected by his affectionate solidarity. In the Gospels, conversions are usually preceded by Jesus's welcoming and acceptance of the offender. It is only when illuminated by such compassion that sinners are able to recognize their failings. Only then, the call to engage their reality anew no longer represents a source of bleak impossibility but instead one of gratitude, hope, and ultimately, liberation.

Jesus's approach to sinners seems to depend largely upon the nature and the degree of their sinfulness. His interactions clearly differentiate between those who "sin 'from weaknesses' or those 'legally considered sinners' according to the dominant religious view of the time," and those who today we would call "oppressors."[28] From the first group, which includes prostitutes, the poor, and the sick, Jesus asks for a conversion in their understanding of God and of themselves—one that rejects the distorted images that their oppressors have imposed upon them, which they in turn have internalized. Above all, Jesus wants them to recognize that "the God who is coming is a loving God . . . one who seeks to welcome all those who think themselves unworthy to approach because of their sinfulness."[29]

In contrast, from the "oppressors" Jesus requires a radical conversion and an active cessation from oppressing. As exemplified in the story of the chief tax collector, Zacchaeus, Jesus's welcoming of sinners is offered freely and prior to the sinners' repentance. But this welcoming can also prompt the sinner to conversion and to establishing a new relationship with him, with God, and with those against whom they previously sinned. This gratuitous forgiveness generates a life of gratitude expressed in the pursuit of justice and reconciliation. As Jon Sobrino notes, "it is *the gratitude of knowing oneself to be accepted* that *moves a person to a de-centering from self*, to generous action, to a life of eager striving that the love of God that has been experienced may be a historical reality in this world."[30]

Through his actions and his preaching, Jesus communicated the good news of God's kingdom and challenged the worldview of his hearers. His

---

27. Meyer, *Aims of Jesus*, 155–56.
28. Sobrino, *Jesus the Liberator*, 96.
29. Sobrino, *Jesus the Liberator*, 97.
30. Sobrino, "Personal Sin," 96, italics original.

parables, for instance, not only convey the kingdom's imminence, dynamism, gratuitousness, and partiality toward the poor, but they also led their hearers into a moment of personal crisis, discernment, and ultimate decision so that they might realize that they must convert and put their talents to work on behalf of the kingdom. As we have seen, God's free, loving initiative both places a claim on human cooperation and enables our participation in God's plan for humanity. This participation, however, comes with a cost. Jesus warns his disciples that they will suffer violence as a consequence of their mission (Matt 10:22) and instructs them to flee when persecuted (Matt 10:23) but calls them to persevere in order to be saved.

Drawing on the prophecies of Jeremiah (31:31–34; 32:38–40) and Ezekiel (36:26–27) in which God promises Israel that their renewed heart and spirit will enable the renewal of the covenant, Jesus challenges his disciples to live as already-members of God's kingdom—that is, to become the salt of the earth and the light of the world. Indeed, they are to live "as the people of the new covenant, those who were truly returning from exile, those for whom and in whom the prophecies were coming true at last."[31] This invitation is also rooted in the command to love God and neighbor, which is "extended and intensified so that it explicitly applies to all human beings, especially foreigners, enemies . . . and sinners."[32] Jesus's challenge "to Israel to be Israel," as N. T. Wright puts it,[33] is nowhere clearer than in the Sermon on the Mount, which outlines a number of concrete practices and dispositions that reveal a new way of being in and relating to the world. In the Beatitudes, Jesus seems to be telling his disciples that the possibility of a renewed heart has become a reality with his coming. He is encouraging them to be poor in spirit and to meekly put their trust in God—to live today as if God's reign were fully present. New Testament scholar, Ulrich Luz, further explains that the main thrust of the Sermon on the Mount "supplies the contents of the mission to be proclaimed to the world by the [Christian] community, and the guiding principle by which that community is to measure its own works."[34] Hence, speaking from a situation riddled with conflict, Jesus invites his disciples to become peacemakers who mercifully thirst for justice, reject violence, and accept that persecution is part and parcel of the kingdom's way.

While the Sermon on the Mount in the Gospel of Matthew has traditionally been understood as structured by different sets of antitheses ("you

---

31. Wright, *Jesus and the Victory*, 277.
32. Theissen and Merz, *Historical Jesus*, 388.
33. Wright, *Jesus and the Victory*, 288.
34. Luz, *Theology of the Gospel of Matthew*, 44.

have heard that it was said . . . but I say to you. . . ."), scholars David Gushee and Glen Stassen suggest a more promising manner of understanding Jesus's teaching on the mount. They read the Sermon on the Mount as fitting the triadic pattern with which the Gospel of Matthew presents upwards of seventy-five of Jesus's teachings, which moves beyond the antitheses to a climactic *transformative initiative* that moves the hearer toward taking healing action. For instance, they argue that Matt 5:21–26 has the following threefold structure: (1) "You have heard . . . you shall not kill" (5:21); (2) "But I say to you that if you are angry with a brother or sister, you will be liable to judgment" (5:21); and (3) "first be reconciled to your brother or sister . . . (5:23–26)." In the third element of the triad, they argue, the *transformative initiative* expresses the practice that transforms the person into an active peacemaker "[that] transforms *the relationship* from one of anger into a peacemaking process; and . . . it hopes to *transform the enemy* into a friend."[35] Similarly, a threefold structure can be seen in Matt 5:43–48: (1) "You have heard . . . love your neighbor and hate your enemy" (5:43); (2) "do not even tax collectors do the same?" (5:46–47); and the transforming initiative in (3) to "love your enemies and pray for those who persecute you" (5:45–46).[36] For Gushee and Stassen, the "breakthrough of the kingdom"—or as the prophet Jeremiah would put it, the *grace of a renewed heart*—is revealed in the *transforming initiative* that offers us a new "way of deliverance" from our sinful patterns—that is, "the way of grace that Jesus is calling us to participate in."[37] In other words, these *transforming initiatives* emerge from a renewed and graced people who have God's law "written in their heart" and are now able to love their enemies and pray for those who persecute them. With his own life and transformational teaching, Jesus is inviting all of his followers—the renewed people of kingdom—to confront evil in a compassionate, creative, and nonviolent way.

The Way of Martyrdom and the Cross

That Jesus proclaimed a reconciling kingdom that welcomes sinners, blesses the meek, and rejects violent resistance does not mean that he passively shied away from conflict. Jesus not only proclaims God and God's kingdom, but this proclamation both unmasks lies and responds to a conflicted situation characterized by exclusion, abuse of power, and widespread oppression. He did not remain indifferent to this reality but rather took a side

---

35. Stassen and Gushee, *Kingdom Ethics*, 96, italics original.
36. Stassen and Gushee, *Kingdom Ethics*, 101.
37. Stassen and Gushee, *Kingdom Ethics*, 96.

consistent with the merciful God he knew and with the mission entrusted to him. Expressed in modern terms, Jon Sobrino explains, "Jesus [was] doing something like carrying on an ideological, de-ideologizing, and denunciatory struggle."[38]

It is within the context of his efforts to unmask the truth that one should understand the apparently contradictory passage in which Jesus affirms that he has come to bring the sword and division: "Do not think that I have come to bring peace to the earth; I have not come to bring peace, but a sword" (Matt 10:34–36). In exposing the truth, Jesus sheds light on the forces that oppressed and divided Palestinian society and revealed the inevitability of human conflict in a world permeated by sin. As Raymund Schwager explains, "The real cause of division is therefore not found in [Jesus]. But his coming uncovers the deep-seated tensions already present and thus provokes open enmity. He seems like a sword and a troublemaker because he unmasks as delusionary the familiar forms of human harmony."[39] For instance, Jesus denounces the use of wealth that dehumanizes the rich (Matt 6:21), leads them to tolerate the inhumane poverty of others (Luke 16:21), and places them in opposition to God's will (Luke 1:53). In a similar vein, he rejects a society structured around a purity system (Mark 7:15) that effectively excluded many, most particularly the vulnerable, from the community.[40]

In light of the theocratic nature of first-century Jewish Palestinian society, Jesus seems particularly concerned with confronting those groups who manipulate religion to defend their interests and oppress others. For instance, as both a religious movement and a political-religious party, the Pharisees felt threatened by the social, political, and cultural pollution brought about by the gentile Roman invaders. To protect their national and religious identity, the Pharisees consistently exhibited a great zeal in the study of and practice of the Mosaic law.[41] They also extended the purity and the dietary laws prescribed to priests to the people as a whole, and during the Hasmonean period had showed no qualms in enlisting "the power of the state to impose their legal practices on the general population."[42] While Jesus shared some theological convictions with the Pharisees, he rejected their practices related to ritual purity, which marginalized the most vulnerable from the community including those who were chronically ill, the lepers, the maimed, "children, women, and the poor who could not pay the

---

38. Sobrino, *Jesus the Liberator*, 161.
39. Schwager, *Must There Be Scapegoats?*, 155.
40. See Neyrey, "Idea of Purity," 91–128.
41. Wright, *Jesus and the Victory*, 378–79.
42. Meier, *Marginal Jew*, 331.

costly temple taxes and fees."[43] To be sure, Jesus often made enemies of the powerful because he chose to draw closer to the poor, the orphaned, the widowed, and sinners. Nonetheless, as we will see, Jesus's more immediate adversaries were the temple aristocracy in Jerusalem, particularly the high priests and the Sadducees.

Jesus performed two symbolic actions—similar to those performed centuries before by prophets such as Isaiah (Isa 20:3), Jeremiah (Jer 19:1–13), and Ezekiel (Ezek 12:1–16)—that may have led to his arrest during his last visit to Jerusalem. First, all the Gospels recount Jesus riding into Jerusalem on a donkey some days before the Passover, and a majority of scholars regard this event as mostly historical.[44] Jesus's entry into Jerusalem (Mark 11:1–11) hearkens back to Zechariah's prophecy (Zech 9:9–10) and serves to proclaim Jesus's messianic aspirations ("your king comes to you . . . humble and riding on a donkey"). Some scholars claim that the entrance was designed to spark some type of revolt.[45] In contrast, others more convincingly argue that Jesus was fulfilling Zech 9:9 in a humble but messianic way. Sanders, for instance, proposes that many Jews did not want a militaristic kind of king, and thus, that "Jesus's ride was a deliberate signal: 'king' yes, of a sort; military conqueror, no."[46] While Jesus presented himself as a humble and peaceful kind of Messiah, within Palestine's theocratic context his entrance into Jerusalem can be easily understood as a religious and political act of provocation. Such an entrance must have threatened the Sadducees and attracted the attention of the Romans, especially at the time of Passover—at times, an occasion of civil unrest when thousands of Jewish pilgrims were celebrating their liberation from Egypt.

Jesus's second symbolic action took place in the temple, which at the time was the heart of Judaism and the center of its religious life. The synoptic Gospels agree that Jesus entered the temple (Mark 11:15–17) and expelled both sellers and buyers from it, while accusing them of turning the temple from a "house of prayer" (Isa 56:7) into a "den of robbers" (Jer 7:11).[47] The accounts then attribute to Jesus a prediction that the temple would be destroyed (Mark 13:1–8). Most scholars agree that Jesus believed in and endorsed the imminent destruction of the temple, since the messiah was supposed to lead

---

43. Stassen and Gushee, *Kingdom Ethics*, 155.

44. See, for instance, Kinman, "Jesus's Royal Entry," 223–60; Meier, "From Elijah-like Prophet," 45–83; Tanm, *Zion Traditions*.

45. Brandon, *Jesus and the Zealots*, 332–40.

46. Sanders, *Historical Figure of Jesus*, 242.

47. The Gospel of John includes that Jesus made a whip to physically shoo sheep and cattle out of the temple (John 2:15).

Israel to liberation from the pagans and reform the temple.[48] There are, however, different interpretations of what this actually meant.

Some scholars, like E. P. Sanders, claim that Jesus wanted to replace the temple with one built anew by God.[49] Others reject the possibility that God would rebuild the temple and associate the temple with an implicit violent ideology condemned by Jesus. Building on the work of Ched Myers, William Herzog argues that Jesus's action was a protest against the economic violence generated by a corrupt temple system through which the religious elite exploited the poor peasantry.[50] By invoking the prophets, Herzog elsewhere adds, "Jesus identifies himself with the tradition of Israel's great prophets, but Jesus may be even more drastic than Isaiah, for Jesus does not envisage a reformed or even a transformed temple . . . for him . . . [t]he temple is beyond redemption."[51]

In a similar vein, N. T. Wright proposes that Jesus was not just attempting a reform. Stressing Jesus's eschatological perspective, Wright proposes that, with his action in the temple, Jesus was symbolizing a final judgment. For Wright, Jesus's prediction anticipates God's imminent destruction of the temple, because the Israelites had created an ideology of violent national resistance against Rome and had enlisted the temple as their talisman—their insurance—thinking that God would protect them, when in fact such an ideology, charged with violence, would lead to the destruction of the temple and of Jerusalem.[52] Thus, the arrival of God's reign was imminent and, with it, the expiration of the Jerusalem temple, which would now be replaced by Jesus and his eschatological community.

Whether one holds that the temple was going to be rebuilt or not, there is no doubt that Jesus's prediction of the temple's destruction must have been heard as a direct threat to the central religious institution and symbol of Judaism. It is no surprise, then, that the Gospel writers attribute to Jesus's accusers at his trial the testimony that he threatened to destroy the temple (Mark 14:58; Matt 26:61) and that the threat is again recalled during the crucifixion scene: "Aha! You who would destroy the Temple . . . save yourself, and come down from the cross!" (Mark 15:29ff; Matt 27:40).[53] In the final analysis, these two symbolic actions—the entry into Jerusalem and

---

48. See, for instance, Herzog, *Prophet and Teacher*, 165–66; Theissen and Merz, *Historical Jesus*, 432; Wright, *Jesus and the Victory*, 336–39; Sanders, *Jesus and Judaism*, 11.

49. Sanders, *Jesus and Judaism*, 256–62.

50. Herzog, *Jesus, Justice, and the Reign of God*, 136–45.

51. Herzog, *Prophet and Teacher*, 169.

52. Wright, *Jesus and the Victory*, 420–24; 494–95; 515.

53. Sanders, *Jesus and Judaism*, 278.

the judgment of the temple—combined with Jesus's solidarity with the poor may have played a central role in his capture and eventual death sentence.

From the perspective of the Sanhedrin, Jesus's condemnation could have been justified by appealing to the Jewish tradition. Wright, for instance, argues that, from this perspective, it is likely that "Jesus was killed because of crimes punishable by death in Jewish law—specifically, Deuteronomy 13 and similar passages, and the later rabbinic interpretations."[54] Unfortunately, the historical character of Jesus's trials is obscured due to the disagreement of the gospel accounts among themselves, our uncertainty regarding the Jewish and Roman law at the time, and the tendency of the early church to shift the responsibility of Jesus's death from the Roman authorities to the Jewish leaders. Nonetheless, it is very likely that Jesus's charges may have included his threat against the temple, his reinterpretation of the law and association with the ritually impure, and the accusation of leading the people astray as a false messiah, which constituted blasphemy in the eyes of the Jews.

There is no indication of any kind that Jesus was organizing a violent revolt or that he ever retaliated against his persecutors. Instead, he remained faithful to the values that the kingdom generates—peace, justice, and forgiving love. Yet, because Jesus understood himself as the Messiah, it appears that the Jewish leaders were afraid that he could actually become the focus of revolutionary activity and, thus, provoke the attack of Rome against Israel. In order to assure Roman cooperation, the Sanhedrin translated their religious charges into political ones, and Jesus was crucified by Pilate as a revolutionary. He was condemned as a false "King of the Jews," which was the charge placed on a placard on the cross.

It is important to insist, then, that Jesus's crucifixion was not part of some divine plan that required the Father's rejection of Jesus or the death of Jesus in order to expiate human sin and satisfy God's judgment. Powerful, fear-filled, but ordinary human beings put Jesus to death. As Gustavo Gutiérrez has noted, "what was rejected in [Jesus] and led to his death on the cross, was the same nucleus of his teaching: the kingdom of God."[55] In contrast, what was willed by God is the kingdom and the way to the kingdom, and thus, the manner in which Jesus responded to his rejection and condemnation on the cross.

---

54. Wright, *Jesus and the Victory*, 548.
55. Gutiérrez, *Spiritual Writings*, 64.

Conclusion

Jesus's Nonviolent Praxis of the Kingdom Illuminates the Meaning of the Cross

As we have seen, Jesus's crucifixion was the direct consequence and culmination of his faithfulness to God and to his mission on behalf of God's reign. It was the historical outcome of loving others and confronting evil in a situation of enmity, ill will, and sin. While Jesus's death must be categorically defined as an evil, the event of the cross reveals both the depths of human sinfulness and Jesus's unlimited solidarity and love for humanity. But how does the manner in which Jesus confronted enmity and human sinfulness shed additional light on the significance of the cross and the human struggle against evil?

First, it is clear that Jesus rejects the possibility of a passive coexistence with the forces of oppression and, at a certain moment in his ministry, chooses to confront his enemies directly in Jerusalem, even when such confrontation seemed destined to seal his fate and martyrdom. As the Gospel of Luke puts it, "When the days drew near for [Jesus] to be taken up, he set his face to go to Jerusalem" (9:51). Like other notable people in history who anticipated their deaths, Jesus set his face toward Jerusalem knowing the risks he was freely taking and the possible cost of his decision.

Secondly, one can assume that, like any other person in a similar situation, Jesus must have asked himself what his possible death might signify and what role it might play within the overall mission of the kingdom. Drawing from Jesus's words and actions at the Last Supper, theologians like Walter Kasper and Edward Schillebeeckx agree that Jesus likely thought that his death would be, in some way or other, beneficial to his mission and his friends.[56] In a similar way, N. T. Wright argues that Jesus uses this final confrontation both to model the *way of the kingdom* and to *bring about the kingdom*. Jesus, Wright tell us, "was dying as the rejected king, who had offered the way of peace which the city had rejected; as the representative king, taking Israel's suffering upon Himself, though not here even with any hint that Israel would thereby escape."[57] Through his passion, Jesus was going to confront evil and defeat it by letting "evil do its worst on him."[58] He was going to defeat it through his own suffering and death. Here, we are talking about Jesus's self-donation and loving sacrifice, as Wright explains, and not about some type of abstract atonement or transaction between human

---

56. Schillebeeckx, *Jesus*, 308. Kasper, *Jesus the Christ*, 120.

57. Wright, *Jesus and the Victory*, 570.

58. Wright, *Jesus and the Victory*, 565.

beings and God.[59] In the end, there is no indication that Jesus's death was willed or demanded by God.

Thirdly, though Jesus seems to have foreseen his impending death, his ministry is never defined by the violence of his enemies. Jesus does not imitate them but remains faithful to the way of peace—to the way of the kingdom. Here, it is important to stress that Jesus's followers must not only be attentive to the prophetic content of God's kingdom but also to *the way of the kingdom*—that is, the nonviolent manner in which it comes.

Fourthly, Jesus's whole life reveals that eradicating sin and injustice cannot be accomplished indirectly—from a distance and without personal involvement. Rather, it calls for solidarity that is willing to take up and endure the consequences of sin—that is, a love willing to bear the weight of sin and to suffer on behalf of others.

Finally, Jesus's cross confronts us with the reality that persecution, death, and martyrdom are a clear possibility for those who follow Jesus and work on behalf of God's reign. In a world corrupted by the historical accumulation of sinful choices that alienate us from God and one another, the question is not *whether* reconciling Christians will encounter conflict (they will!) but rather *how* they will respond to and humanize a conflicted world.

Jesus's Cross Illuminates Christian Martyrdom

Jesus's historical cross points to the millions of people in the world today who continue to be oppressed, impoverished, and marginalized, and who bear the consequences of sin—those who Monsignor Óscar Romero and Ignacio Ellacuría rightly called "the crucified people."[60] Because Christians are entrusted with the same mission that Jesus embraced—to pursue the fullest realization of God's reconciling kingdom in history—many of Jesus's followers will lose their lives as they seek to lower their brothers and sisters from the crosses that are generated by the many expressions of sin today: oppression, poverty, discrimination, etc. Like Jesus before them, these followers of Jesus lay down their lives for their friends (John 15:13).

Today, the Catholic Church celebrates as martyrs only those Christians 1) who freely accept their death; 2) whose deaths were violent or cruel; and 3) whose deaths were motivated by hatred for the faith—*odium fidei*.[61] But many martyrs today, especially in places like Latin America, do not die because of an *explicit* hatred of the faith, but rather die, *like* Jesus,

---

59. Wright, *Jesus and the Victory*, 561.
60. See Ellacuría, "Crucified People," 257–78.
61. Woestman, *Canonization*, 143.

for their pursuit of God's kingdom. As noted above, it is Jesus's own life and discipleship that best explains Christian martyrdom. They alone are indispensable for developing authentic criteria to identify Christian martyrs from whose blood the church may grow. Indeed, the fact that Jesus's death was the direct consequence of his faithful adherence to God's kingdom and to the nonviolent manner in which the kingdom unfolds sheds light on how the Christian community understands Jesus's cross and its understanding of Christian martyrdom.

First, the Jesus event tells us that a martyr's death cannot be separated from his or her life. A martyr's death is the direct consequence of the life they chose to live. As such, Christian martyrs *witness* to Christ's life and mission, even at the cost of their lives. Like Jesus, they choose to actively confront evil with the power and promise of God's reign, even when such confrontation put their lives at risk.

Secondly, what distinguishes Christian martyrs from other Christians is not only that they share in Jesus's mission and violent death but also that they follow him in embracing the *nonviolent* manner that characterizes the praxis of God's reconciling kingdom. As we saw above, Jesus's ministry was rooted in a compassionate and nonviolent love. To love nonviolently in a situation permeated by conflict is to be willing to suffer for others, to endure the consequences of the oppressor's sins. In a manner analogous to Jesus, the loving suffering of a martyr also has a redemptive dimension insofar as it stops, absorbs, and reverses the inherent tendency of evil and violence to generate even more violence.

Thirdly, while Christians may legitimately use physical violence in some extreme cases, "[Christian faith] regards violence as intrinsically related with evil and only explicable in a world of sin in which in the last resort death prevails over life."[62] It should be clear then that the excellence of the martyrs' lives and the superlative faithfulness with which they follow Jesus allows for the possibility of active and creative resistance but prevents them from embracing a violent path. As Ignacio Ellacuría notes,

> There are different gifts in the church, and different callings from the Spirit. While the personal vocation of each individual must be respected, provided it is genuine, it does not seem audacious or cowardly to claim that the Christian vocation calls for the use of peaceful means, which does not mean less effort, to solve the problems of injustice and violence in the world,

---

62. Ellacuría, "Violence and Nonviolence," 86–88, quoted in Sobrino, *Jesus the Liberator*, 218.

rather than violent means, however much these may sometimes be justified.⁶³

Finally, Christian martyrs are, in a manner of speaking, a "new compassionate creation" who exhibit a radical freedom and love that reflect the hope that God will overcome death and injustice. Indeed, their willingness to offer their lives as expressions of active resistance in solidarity with the victims of history and their bodies as loving vessels that absorb and neutralize their enemies' aggression demonstrate that they are bound to the indefensible logic of Christ's gratuitous love—a logic that excludes any type of harmful violence in its pursuit of communion.

Bibliography

Boff, Leonardo. *Jesus Christ, Liberator: A Critical Christology of Our Time*. Maryknoll, NY: Orbis, 1978.
Borg, Marcus. *Conflict Holiness and Politics in the Teachings of Jesus*. Harrisburg, PA: Trinity, 1984.
Brandon, S. G. F. *Jesus and the Zealots: A Study of the Political Factor in Primitive Christianity*. Manchester, UK: Manchester University Press, 1967.
Brock, Rita Nakashima. "And a Little Child Shall Lead Us: Christology and Child Abuse." In *Christianity, Patriarchy, and Abuse: A Feminist Critique*, edited by Joanne Carlson Brown and Carole Bohn, 42–61. New York: Pilgrim, 1989.
Brown, Joanne Carlson, and Carole Bohn. *Christianity, Patriarchy, and Abuse: A Feminist Critique*. New York: Pilgrim, 1989.
Castelli, Elizabeth A. *Martyrdom and Memory: Early Christian Culture Making*. Gender, Theory, and Religion. New York: Columbia University Press, 2004.
Daly, Robert. "Images of God and the Imitation of God: Problems with Atonement." *Theological Studies* 68:1 (2007) 36–51.
Dunn, James D. G. *Jesus Remembered*. Christianity in the Making. Grand Rapids, MI: Eerdmans, 2003.
Ellacuría, Ignacio. "The Crucified People." In *Systematic Theology: Perspectives from Liberation Theology*, edited by Jon Sobrino and Ignacio Ellacuría, 257–78. Maryknoll, NY: Orbis, 1996.
Eusebius. *Ecclesiastical History*. Translated by C. F. Cruse. Peabody, MA: Hendrickson, 1998.
Gutiérrez, Gustavo. *The God of Life*. Maryknoll, NY: Orbis, 1991.
———. *Spiritual Writings*. Maryknoll, NY: Orbis, 2011.
Haight, Roger. *The Future of Christology*. New York: Continuum, 2005.
Hengel, Martin. *Victory over Violence, and Was Jesus a Revolutionist?* Eugene, OR: Wipf and Stock, 2003.
Herzog, William R. *Jesus, Justice, and the Reign of God: A Ministry of Liberation*. Louisville, KY: Westminster John Knox, 2000.

---

63. Ellacuría, "Violence and Nonviolence," 86–88, quoted in Sobrino, *Jesus the Liberator*, 218.

———. *Prophet and Teacher: An Introduction to the Historical Jesus*. Louisville, KY: Westminster John Knox, 2005.

Horsley, Richard A. *Jesus and the Spiral of Violence: Popular Jewish Resistance in Roman Palestine*. San Francisco: Harper and Row, 1987.

Kasper, Walter. *Jesus the Christ*. New York: Paulist, 2018.

Kinman, Brent. "Jesus's Royal Entry into Jerusalem." *Bulletin for Biblical Research* 15:2 (2005) 223–60.

Kloppenborg, John S. "Jesus, Fishermen, and Tax Collectors: Papyrology and the Construction of the Ancient Economy of Roman Palestine." *Ephemerides Theologicae Lovanienses* 94:4 (2018) 571–99.

Luz, Ulrich. *The Theology of the Gospel of Matthew*. Cambridge: Cambridge University Press, 1995.

Marshall, Howard. "The Hope of a New Age: The Kingdom of God in the New Testament." In *Jesus the Saviour: Studies in New Testament Theology*, edited by Howard Marshall, 213–38. London: SPCK, 1990.

Meier, John P. "From Elijah-like Prophet to Royal Davidic Messiah." In *Jesus: A Colloquium in the Holy Land*, edited by Doris Donnelly and James D. G. Dunn, 45–83. New York: Continuum, 2001.

———. *A Marginal Jew: Rethinking the Historical Jesus*. Companions and Competitors. New York: Double Day, 2001.

Meyer, Ben F. *The Aims of Jesus*. London: SCM, 1979.

Moss, Candida. *The Other Christs: Imitating Jesus in Ancient Christian Ideologies of Martyrdom*. Oxford: Oxford University Press, 2010.

Neyrey, Jerome. "The Idea of Purity in Mark's Gospel." *Semeia* 35 (1986) 91–128.

Rahner, Karl. "Dimensions of Martyrdom: A Plea for the Broadening of a Classical Concept." *Concilium* 163 (March 1983) 9–11.

Sanders, E. P. *The Historical Figure of Jesus*. London: Penguin, 1993.

———. *Jesus and Judaism*. Minneapolis: Fortress, 1985.

Schillebeeckx, Edward. *Christ, the Experience of Jesus as Lord*. New York: Crossroad, 1981.

———. *Jesus, an Experiment in Christology*. London: Bloomsbury, 2014.

Schwager, Raymond. *Must There Be Scapegoats? Violence and Redemption in the Bible*. New York: Crossroad, 1987.

Sobrino, Jon. "Conflicto y Reconciliación: Camino Cristiano hacia una Utopía." *Estudios Centroamericanos* 661–62 (2003) 1139–48.

———. "Jesuanic Martyrs in the Third World." In *Witnesses of the Kingdom: The Martyrs of El Salvador and the Crucified People*, edited by Jon Sobrino, 119–33. Maryknoll, NY: Orbis, 2003.

———. *Jesus the Liberator: A Historical-Theological Reading of Jesus of Nazareth*. Maryknoll, NY: Orbis, 1994.

———. "Personal Sin, Forgiveness, and Liberation." In *The Principle of Mercy: Taking the Crucified People Down from the Cross*, edited by Jon Sobrino, 83–104. Maryknoll, NY: Orbis, 1994.

———. *The Principle of Mercy: Taking the Crucified People Down from the Cross*. Maryknoll, NY: Orbis, 1994.

———. *Spirituality of Liberation: Toward Political Holiness*. Maryknoll, NY: Orbis, 1988.

———. *Witnesses of the Kingdom: The Martyrs of El Salvador and the Crucified People.* Maryknoll, NY: Orbis, 2003.

Stassen, Glen, and David Gushee. *Kingdom Ethics: Following Jesus in Contemporary Context.* Downers Grove, IL: Intervarsity, 2003.

Tanm, Kim Huat. *The Zion Traditions and the Aims of Jesus.* Cambridge: Cambridge University Press, 1997.

Theissen, Gerd, and Annette Merz. *The Historical Jesus: A Comprehensive Guide.* Minneapolis: Fortress, 1996.

Valiente, O. Ernesto. "Renewing the Theology of Martyrdom." *Irish Theological Quarterly* 79:2 (2014) 112–27.

Weaver, J. Denny. *The Nonviolent Atonement.* Grand Rapids, MI: Eerdmans, 2001.

Williams, Delores S. *Sisters in the Wilderness: The Challenge of Womanist God-Talk.* Maryknoll, NY: Orbis, 1993.

Woestman, William H. *Canonization: Theology, History, Process.* Ottawa: St. Paul University, 2002.

Wright, N. T. *Jesus and the Victory of God.* Minneapolis: Fortress, 1996.

2

A Spirit Christology of Peace and Active Nonviolence

Erico Hammes

Introduction

THE FOLLOWING REFLECTIONS ATTEMPT an outline of a Spirit Christology of peace and active nonviolence that attempts to connect Christology, the Christology of peace, and Spirit Christology. One conceptual presupposition of these reflections is embracing an understanding of peace as creative conflict transformation. As such, according to the Earth Charter declaration, "Peace is the wholeness created by right relationships with oneself, other persons, other cultures, other life, Earth, and the larger whole of which all are a part."[1] The relationships that peace searches to establish must be right in order to build a just and sustainable peace that overcomes all kinds of violence and is in harmony with the whole environment. A second presupposition is the present reality of violence in all its forms. In the same way that peace is far more than the absence of war and has a positive definition, so too is violence far from a simple concept. Violence appears on personal, social, and structural levels, as well as national and international levels, and includes racism, sexism, terrorism, torture, dictatorship, human rights violations, and cultural, social, and religious discrimination, as well as harmful economic and political practices. It is necessary to highlight the fact that violence is not the same in all countries and regions. There are countries

---

1. The Earth Charter Commission, "Earth Charter," principle 16(f).

where there is no war but where there have been a great number of murders and assassinations; in other countries, social and economic inequality may prevail; and in still others the exploitation of natural resources is the greatest form of violence. Keeping in mind at least these two presuppositions, I would like to propose a pneumatological and peace hermeneutic of Christology.

As is well known, even if there are Christologies of peace,[2] there has been little reception of peace theology in common Christology. The challenge of peace and nonviolence often seems unrelated to Jesus Christ, salvation, liberation, justification, and other central issues. Similarly, pneumatology does not refer to peace, even if the hymn "Veni Creator Spiritus" asks the Holy Spirit "far from us drive our deadly foe; true peace unto us bring."[3] However, the Christian tradition of the Holy Spirit allows a true identification with essential subjects related to peace: internal peace, love, reconciliation, the new Earth, the Father of the poor, and the so-called seven gifts of the Spirit. Therefore, it seems that it is indeed possible to think of the Spirit as the Spirit of peace, for according to Rom 14:17,[4] "the kingdom of God is not a matter of food and drink, but of righteousness, peace, and joy in the Holy Spirit" (NABRE). In addition, in Eph 4:3, Paul explicitly urges the community "to preserve the unity of the spirit through the bond of peace." Finally, the Spirit Christologies, in explaining the Scriptures, describe the relationship between Jesus and the Spirit beginning at the moment of the incarnation and his relationship to the Father as the Son in his eternal existence. In and through Jesus, the Spirit is given as the Spirit of adoption and sonship "through which we cry, 'Abba' Father" (Rom 8:15; Gal 4:6), and by him all people are sisters and brothers. In this can be found the connection between Spirit Christology and peace.[5]

---

2. For example, those described in Biser, *Er ist unser Friede*; Jegen, *Jesus the Peacemaker*; Will, *Christology of Peace*; Coste, *Il est notre paix*; Rynne, *Jesus Christ*.

3. Silvahy, *Ritual Song*, 650.

4. All biblical citations herein are from the NABRE.

5. The best example is presented by Coste, *Il est notre paix*, 157–78. He develops the relationship between the "Spirit and the creativity of peace," identifying the manifestation of the Spirit as an "explosion" in the communities of the new covenant, "an incommensurable energy of communion and love, of dialogue and of peace." Coste, *Il est notre paix*, 158.

1. Spirit Christology

Since the 1960s, Spirit Christology has undergone significant development as a theological concept.[6] The first authors to discuss it came from Pentecostal or charismatic churches and movements highlighting the role of the Spirit in Jesus's existence and life.[7] From the point of view of Catholic theology, after the Second Vatican Council and the council's adoption of a pneumatological orientation toward the church and revelation, in the 1970s authors like Hans Urs von Balthasar, Walter Kasper, James Dupuis, and Yves Congar paved the way for Catholic pneumatological Christologies.[8] The encounter between trinitarian theology and Christology in the two decades from 1980 to 2000 produced a significant number of works showing how so-called "Christomonism" can be overcome. Jesus appears in these works in the light of the Spirit, in the "horizon of the Spirit," moved by the Spirit, or, in the expression of Rosato, as "the Spirit-filled Jesus."[9]

At this point, it is necessary to clearly distinguish this spiritual Christology from that which opposes Logos Christology.[10] The Spirit Christology proposed here reflects the triune and tripersonal God as the communion of Father, Son, and Spirit. The Son is the person who enters history in the incarnation in the Spirit as Jesus of Nazareth and reveals himself as the self-communication of the Father in the Spirit to humanity. Throughout his life, up to his crucifixion, death, and resurrection, in his deeds and preaching, he appears as the communion with the Father and the Spirit in love and mercy. Jesus's presentation in his relationship with the Father and the Spirit shows another dimension of his peaceful existence. In this, his deepest nature manifests itself as a relationship. In himself, he exists from and to

---

6. A general history of Spirit Christology from a Pentecostal point of view is presented by Herschel Odell Bryant in *Spirit Christology*. The book begins with a survey of the modern development of the concept until "the rise of Pentecostalism in the Twentieth Century."

7. See, for example, Berkhof, *Doctrine of the Holy Spirit*; Dunn, "Rediscovering."

8. Del Colle, *Christ and the Spirit*, 34–63, offers an overview from the neoscholastic tradition and presents the recent Catholic Spirit Christology of David Coffey; see also Schoonenberg, "Spirit Christology," 356–60; and Schoonenberg, *Der Geist*, 59–62; even if this author does not, from my point of view, do justice to the integral trinitarian faith. It seems that in *Der Geist* he denies the preexistent personality of the Son and the Spirit (cf. 177–95).

9. Rosato, "Spirit Christology," 427.

10. I disagree with the thesis presented by Jörg Weber in *Geist-Christologie* contesting Spirit Christology without distinguishing between the recent investigations, the historical discussions on the subject, and the attempts made during the transition from the almost exclusive Logos Christology to pneumatological- and trinitarian-oriented Christologies. Rosato, "Spirit Christology," 429–38, presents a stronger evaluation.

another—the Father, the Spirit, human persons, and the whole of creation. He is not in himself from himself and to himself, but from the Father and the Spirit and to them in creation and history.

2. Christology of Peace

Research in the theology of peace and nonviolence shows that the early Christian tradition presented Jesus as the peace of God and the victory over all kinds of violence.[11] Unfortunately, the later history of Christianity broke with this view. In order to live in the Roman Empire, Christians not only accepted the just war theory, but also formulated a Christian version of it.[12] Even if the theory had a restrictive intention—only wars that fulfilled the conditions were and are acceptable for Christians—historically it was used to justify many different kinds of war. Violence and war were used as a form of defense and evangelization both internally in Christianity as well as against other peoples. Perhaps it was the identification of the church with Christ without pneumatological mediation that allowed the justification of war as an instrument of Christian political praxis.

Nevertheless, throughout the centuries of Christianity, many people and movements lived and promoted peace and nonviolence, including Francis of Assisi, Nicholas of Cusa, Erasmus of Rotterdam, the Mennonites, and the Anabaptists—but christological reflections scarcely received and developed their practices. Identifications of Jesus Christ as emperor or king had more impact than his titles of the Suffering Servant or the Prince of Peace (Isaiah) or even the Crucified Lord. The "kingdom of God" was identified with the sovereignty of the church or with the Holy Roman Empire.

Since the tragic experiences of World War I and World War II, the challenge of peace has appeared more clearly in Christian and Catholic theology. To overcome the connection between Christianity and violence, Christian laypeople have involved themselves in peacebuilding actions. Leadership, including popes and bishops, have promoted peace, and theologians have set forth the outlines of a theology of peace and nonviolence. Even as early as World War I, Pope Benedict XV advocated peaceful means for the resolution of international conflicts. During and after World War

---

11. For what follows, see Cahill, "Traditional Catholic Thought"; Guimarães, *Correspondance*; Coste, *Theologie*, 129–37; Rynne, *Jesus Christ*, chap. 3.

12. There is a considerable amount of literature on this subject. A recent historical presentation covering the theory from Cicero to the present day can be found in Schockenhoff, *Kein Ende der Gewalt?*, 104–394. A shorter overview may be found in Coste, *Théologie*, 138–63.

II, especially Pope Pius XII delivered messages about peace. In the decades of the Cold War, other forms of violence were identified: social and economic injustice, ecological crises, structural violence, and many others that weaken peace. Here, it is worth mentioning Pope John XXIII's statements in his encyclicals *Pacem in Terris* and *Mater et Magistra*. From a theological perspective, Joseph Comblin published his two-volume *Théologie de la Paix* (1960–63). The Second Vatican Council's Pastoral Constitution *Gaudium et Spes*, as well as Pope Paul VI's visit to the UN conference in 1965, his encyclical *Populorum Progressio*, and his establishment of the World Day of Peace, were landmarks for a new Catholic perspective on peace and nonviolence.

After Vatican II, it became important to think about systematic theology and Christology. The early approaches to peace theology were mostly grounded in ethics. They looked for biblical foundations, developed some criteria for outlining peaceful behaviors and attitudes, and tried to understand how Christians might address questions about war, justice, structural sin, violence, and the just war theory. The Sermon on the Mount, the Beatitudes, and the kingdom of God were explained in terms of their ethical requirements. This work resulted in works on peace Christology, focusing especially on the historical Jesus, his peaceful and merciful life of forgiving sins, defending the weak, proclaiming blessed the peacemakers, and sending his disciples to announce peace and to proclaim the "gospel of peace" (Eph 6:15). But only in further reflection did the intrinsic relationship between peace and Jesus himself come to the fore, a relationship meaning that he is "our peace" (Eph 2:4).[13] A pacifist hermeneutics of Jesus as peace Christology thus became possible.

Relating the faith to Christ as "our peace," anointed by the Spirit, allows the possibility for a Christology of peace and nonviolence in the Spirit. It is worth remembering that in 1983 the United States Conference of Catholic Bishops published the pastoral letter *The Challenge of Peace*, and the World Council of Churches launched the World Council Process of Justice, Peace, and Creation in Vancouver. Both events referred explicitly or implicitly to the Holy Spirit, to Jesus Christ, and peace.

As Jegen points out, the bishops were, when they asked for a theology of peace, "even though Christology was not mentioned explicitly," but "Jesus and the Reign of God," and "Jesus and the community of Believers" *were* mentioned explicitly, also pointing to research on Christology.[14] As demonstrated by René Coste in *Il est notre paix*, and by James Will in *A Christology*

---

13. Cf. e.g., Dear, *Put Down Your Sword*, 1–19; Dear, *God of Peace*, 18–29, 52–58; Coste, *Théologie*, 81–128; Biser, *Er ist unser Friede*; Puig i Tàrrech, *Jesus*, 178–218; Rynne, *Jesus Christ*.

14. Cf. Jegen, *Jesus the Peacemaker*, 7–8.

of Peace, the Holy Spirit acting in Jesus is at the roots of his peacemaking. The God of peace, according to Coste, reveals himself through Jesus of Nazareth in a form that can be explained as "the mystery of communion in the love of the three divine persons."[15] Similarly, Will affirms that "the theology that emerges from being grounded in and participating in Christ's Holy Spirit is finally a Trinitarian Christology."[16] In this way, and taking into account Karl Barth's observation about the Holy Spirit as "the advocate of peace,"[17] it is possible to think about a Christology of peace in the discipleship of Jesus in the Spirit, or a Spirit Christology of peace in the discipleship of Jesus.

3. Spirit Christology of Peace and Nonviolence

3.1 The Beginnings of the Gospels

The incarnation of the Word or the Son of God is confessed as the incarnation of God's peace through the Spirit. If it is possible with John Dear to say that the "Christology of nonviolence . . . invites us to see Jesus as the incarnation of nonviolence,"[18] and if he "by the Holy Spirit was incarnate of the Virgin Mary" (Nicene-Constantinopolitan Creed), then it follows that he is God's peace in the Spirit. Now, the incarnation is a threefold revelation. First, the entrance of God into human history as a human being theologically expresses the transformation of the human condition from foreign or strange into the other of transcendence, of the mystery of God. The abyss between creator and creature is more than bridged because the "Word became a human being" (cf. John 1:14). From this basic reality derives the second part of the revelation—that the peace of God became flesh is peace itself, even if, as James Will points out, this christological peace is a "dialectical" one "whose coming includes struggle, rejection, and death."[19] And third, this change in the Son of God, in God, into dialectical, human peace on Earth can be understood as an action of the Spirit of God. Human expectations enter into the trinitarian offer of peace, transforming both the human in the divine and the divine in a "dialectical," conflictive human.

---

15. See Coste, *Théologie*, 86.

16. Will, *Christology of Peace*, 60.

17. Hofheinz, "Er ist unser Friede," 95, citing Karl Barth, *Kirchliche Digmatik*, vol. 4, part 2, 412.

18. Dear, *God of Peace*, 52; see also Dear, *God of Peace*, 19: "The gospel portrays Jesus as the incarnation of nonviolence."

19. Will, *Christology of Peace*, 48.

The beginning of Jesus's existence, as presented by the Gospels of Matthew and Luke, is associated with the presence of the Spirit in his mother: "But before they lived together, she was found with child through the Holy Spirit.... For it is through the Holy Spirit that this child has been conceived in her" (Matt 1:18–20), and, "The Holy Spirit will come upon you, and the power of the Most High will overshadow you. Therefore the child to be born will be called holy, the Son of God" (Luke 1:35). In the same way, the Spirit is described as being present to Elizabeth and to Zechariah and Simeon. The incarnation and birth of Jesus are presented by Matthew and Luke in the tradition of the expected Messiah who will bring peace to Israel and to all people. By the Spirit, the power of the Most High will come to Earth, and peace will come "to those on whom his favor rests" (Luke 2:14).

3.2 Jesus's Public Life of Peacemaking in the Spirit

The narratives of the baptism of Jesus in the four Gospels refer to the Spirit descending or coming down upon Jesus: "And the Holy Spirit descended upon him in bodily form like a dove" (Luke 3:22). For Jesus, the baptism of John represents a religious option. Among the different ways of living the faith, he adopts the way of John. This choice is not so much related to the temple, even if Zechariah, John's father, was a priest; on the contrary, the Baptist, as he is presented by the Gospels, preached an ethically oriented faith grounded in justice and repentance expressed to the Lord of Israel, open to all who search for righteousness. This accessible and embracing form of Jewish tradition, which is expansive enough to include soldiers and tax collectors, prepares the way on which Jesus will walk. The Spirit of God descending upon him sets him free for his mission. It is the manifestation that the existence of Jesus, his religious option, is at the same time as a disciple of John the Baptist in his universality and in the commitment of the Father to Jesus as his Son in the Spirit. Jesus does not share the Pharisees' narrow interpretations of Judaism or the calls to take up arms against the Roman Empire; nor does he hold with some of the forms of Essenianism. The baptism of Jesus represents his liberation and his empowerment to be free in the face of God as his Father and in front of all peoples searching for hope and life.

"Filled with the Holy Spirit, Jesus returned from the Jordan and was led by the Spirit into the desert" (Luke 4:1). The narratives of the temptations are also associated with the Spirit who leads or accompanies Jesus. They can be seen as temptations against living a peaceful life. The sense of life, the word of God, is as important as the bread; the worship of the only true God is necessary to overcome idolatry and all kinds of evil. At the same time, the temptations reveal self-training in prayer and fasting as a means for living peaceful lives. The desert represents for the Jewish tradition the environment of the Lord's care for his people and the occasion for the people's repentance and acceptance and fidelity to the covenant with God. At the same time, it represents grace, openness to the Spirit, and personal education so that violence can be faced. In recent history, great peacemakers, including Mahatma Gandhi, Martin Luther King, Dorothy Day, Thomas Merton, Dorothy Stang, and so many others, saw prayer and fasting in the Spirit of Jesus as a means for peacemaking and active nonviolence. At the same time, Jesus's temptation narratives show the reality of everyday difficulties and as risks for those attempting to live a peaceful life. According to Luke 4:16–19, referring to Isa 61:1–3, Jesus's public life begins with the proclamation of the anointing with the Spirit "to bring glad tidings to the poor . . . to proclaim liberty to captives and recovery of sight to the blind, to let the oppressed go free, and to proclaim a year acceptable to the Lord." This Spirit, through whom he became human, was upon him at his baptism and with him during the temptations. The Spirit would continue to be with him in his deeds, words, suffering, passion, and resurrection. The expression "to bring glad tidings to the poor" translates the Greek word *evangelísastai* associated with the prophetic mission of Jesus. But this mission, the text continues, is a conflictive one, especially in "his native place" (Luke 4:24). The prophetic mission is related to the poor, the captives, the blind, and the oppressed. All these peoples, as well as the sick, the widows, the orphans and the strangers, and the hungry and thirsty, were the recipients of the good news. When John the Baptist, from prison, sent his disciples to find out whether Jesus could be the Messiah, the answer they received connected Jesus to these suffering people (cf. Matt 11:5). His actions on behalf of these people were signs pointing to Jesus as the Messiah, the anointed one, who was expected to establish shalom, or peace (e.g., Isa 61:1–3; 32:1–5; cf. Isa 9:5–6; Jer 22:1–3), and the one whose Spirit guarantees an all-embracing peace: "Until the spirit from on high is poured out on us . . . the work of justice will be peace, the effect of justice calm and security forever. My people will live in a peaceful country, in secure dwellings and quiet resting places" (Isa 32:15–18). As Comblin stated at the beginning of the 1960s, "the Gospel breathes a climate of peace."[20]

While Luke inaugurates the public mission of Jesus with the narrative of his anointing by the Spirit of the Lord, in Mark instead, Jesus appears

---

20. Comblin, *Theologie des Friedens*, 252. This volume is a translation from the French of Comblin's *Théologie de la paix*, published in 1960.

after the imprisonment of John the Baptist, proclaiming: "This is the time of fulfillment. The kingdom of God is at hand. Repent, and believe in the Gospel" (Mark 1:15). This message of the kingdom of God, as generally accepted by biblical scholars, summarizes Jesus's teachings in the synoptic Gospels and corresponds to Jewish expectations of a time of peace and plenty. There will be no more war, and everyone will have the conditions to live a life in the covenant with the Lord in dignity and fraternity (cf. Isa 65:17–25). There is also a broad consensus that the kingdom of God is for the poor, including the orphans, the widows, the strangers (we could say the migrants and refugees), the sick and the prisoners, as well as the hungry and the thirsty (cf. Matt 25:31–46). The kingdom stands for God's governance in favor of those abandoned by kings of this world, by them who had forgotten their responsibility to the weak and had oppressed them: "But it shall not be so among you. Rather, whoever wishes to be great among you will be your servant; whoever wishes to be first among you will be the slave of all. For the Son of Man did not come to be served but to serve and to give his life as a ransom for many" (Mark 10:43–45).

This means that Jesus's whole life and preaching of the kingdom of God, his deeds and words, are in the Spirit of God. Thus, on the one hand, the exorcisms of Jesus are, according to the Gospel of Matthew, related to the power of the Spirit: "If it is by the Spirit of God that I drive out demons, then the kingdom of God has come upon you" (Matt 12:28; cf. Luke 11:20). On the other hand, Jesus prays in the Spirit: "At that very moment he rejoiced [in] the Holy Spirit and said, 'I give you praise, Father, Lord of heaven and earth, for although you have hidden these things from the wise and the learned you have revealed them to the childlike. Yes, Father, such has been your gracious will'" (Luke 10:21).

In this light, the Beatitudes and the Sermon on the Mount reveal their peaceful content. The kingdom of God belongs to the poor, to the hungry, to those who are weeping, to the persecuted. And one of the specific blessed, according to Matthew, "are the peacemakers, for they will be called children of God" (Matt 5:9). The sense of this beatitude includes the meaning of "making"—*eirenopoioi*—what has to do with shalom, the embracing peace that prevents war and violence, that overcomes both passivity and the violent reaction in order to resist, to establish new relations. Furthermore, peacemakers, as Schockenhoff remarks, "commit themselves passionately to the rebuilding and conservation of peace."[21] These peacemakers will be called "children of God," because God is peace and Jesus, the Son, is also peace. The Sermon on the Mount includes some other important teachings

---

21. Schockenhoff, *Die Bergpredigt*, 167.

that promote peace. These are about retaliation: "Offer no resistance to one who is evil" (Matt 5:39) and the love of enemies (Matt 5:43–45), which came with the promise "that you may be children of your heavenly Father." In the same perspective, the Lord's Prayer itself can be seen as a peacemaking prayer, especially with its injunction to forgive others' transgressions as the Father forgives ours (Matt 6:9–15).

Jesus not only announces and testifies to peace, but he also calls his disciples and followers to proclaim and spread peace. He sent them "to every town and place he intended to visit.... Go on your way; behold, I am sending you like lambs among wolves.... Into whatever house you enter, first say, 'Peace to this household.' If a peaceful person lives there, your peace will rest on him; but if not, it will return to you" (Luke 10:1–6; cf. Matt 10:13). To be sent like lambs points to the risks they may face on their mission. But in the light of a peace hermeneutic, it is possible to remember that "the wolf shall be a guest of the lamb" (cf. Isa 11:6) and that "the wolf and the lamb shall pasture together" (Isa 65:25). Therefore, the mission of the disciples includes the overcoming of enmity, or in any case to act and have the same attitude as the servant of God (cf. Isa 42:1–9), whom Matthew equates with Jesus (cf. Matt 12:15–21). It is noteworthy that in contrast to their announcement of peace, the Gospels also mention divisions and violence that may be associated with Jesus. Matt 10:34 (cf. Luke 12:51–53) has Jesus saying: "Do not think that I have come to bring peace upon the earth. I have come to bring not peace but the sword." But at the same time, it is said that "whoever does not take up his cross and follow after me is not worthy of me" (Matt 10:38). The meaning is not that he may use the sword but, rather, that he is invited to give his life: "Whoever finds his life will lose it, and whoever loses his life for my sake will find it" (Matt 10:39; cf. Mark 8:35; Luke 9:24; John 12:25).

One of the important practices of Jesus throughout his life, table fellowship, must also be highlighted for its relevance to peace.[22] In many Christologies, Jesus's table fellowship appears as one of his deeds actualizing the kingdom of God. It is a sign of forgiveness for sinners, a sign of friendship and celebration. One example of such Christologies is that of Jon Sobrino.[23] He concludes his reflections on the kingdom of God with a paragraph about the celebration of the coming of the kingdom: "Jesus's meals are signs of the coming of the kingdom and the realization of its ideals: liberation, peace, universal communion." At the table Jesus celebrates and rejoices with the

---

22. It seems that even a work as comprehensive as Hellholm and Sänger, *Eucharist*, does not recognize the connection between table fellowship and peace.

23. See especially Sobrino, *Jesucristo liberador*, 139–41.

sinners and marginalized so that "God reveals Himself to them."[24] Because it is such good news, the kingdom cannot but be celebrated, "for this would be a strange good news if it did not lead to it."[25] The celebration takes place especially at meals (Mark 2:15; Luke 7:6–47), in descriptions of the great human community in terms of a "feast" and a "wedding banquet," symbolizing the future of the kingdom (cf. Luke 14:15),[26] especially evidenced by the fact that it welcomes at its table "those who for centuries have been prevented from taking part."[27] This scandalous attitude of Jesus does not come unaccompanied by reaction: Jesus is accused of being "a glutton, drunkard, friend of publicans and sinners" (cf. Matt 11:19). Sitting at table with all sorts of people demonstrates his radical solidarity with the marginalized, "not only individually, but communally, re-creating them as a social group and certainly through the materiality of the table."[28]

At the very end of his life, Jesus celebrated the Last Supper, his last table fellowship, with his disciples, utilizing plenty of peace symbols and words. Following the eucharistic praxis as a praxis of identification with Jesus calls for peace. The first Christian communities and the general Christian tradition has held that in order to participate in the Eucharist, it is necessary to be baptized; that is, to be incorporated in Christ. The Eucharist includes prayers for peace and salutations and gestures toward and among the participants. As the remembrance of the loftiest, most important table fellowship of Jesus, the Last Supper is the eschatological sign of eternal peace and the foundation of the new covenant. Therefore, as highlighted by James Will, this anamnesis is received "as the very spirit of the eschatological prophetic-messiah who had been anointed with God's Spirit during his life, and even unto death."[29]

3.3 The Cross and Resurrection

The cross and resurrection, according to the Gospel of John, are framed by the promise of peace and the outpouring of the Spirit (cf. John 14:15–28; 20:19–29). The promise of peace is related to the overcoming of the political and religious violence of the Pax Romana, under which Jesus lived. The Roman Empire was of course ruled by the Caesars, whose political authority as

24. Sobrino, "¿Es Jesús una buena noticia?," 299.
25. Sobrino, *Jesucristo liberador*, 139.
26. Sobrino, *Cristología desde América Latina*, 36.
27. Sobrino, *Jesucristo liberador*, 140.
28. Sobrino, *Jesús en América Latina*, 147.
29. Will, *Christology of Peace*, 60.

pontifex maximus was also a religious authority. Both political and religious power supported each other to maintain a specifically Roman kind of peace. To ensure the stability of the empire, its rulers resorted to every possible means, including various kinds of violence: war against resistance movements, religious control, and co-option or defense of religious institutions, including the Jerusalem temple.[30] Any "suspicious" gathering or movement of people, or any questions about the temple or the religion of the empire, could lead to persecution and even to a sentence of death on the cross.

Besides the imperial power, there was also the Jewish political, social, and religious violence. The different Jewish religious parties conflicted with one another about the interpretation of faith and praxis in such a way that Jesus's life was a source of conflict from the very beginning of his public ministry. As the Gospels testify, political authorities such as the Herodians joined together with the Pharisees to attack and harass Jesus: "The Pharisees went out and immediately took counsel with the Herodians against him to put him to death" (Mark 3:6; cf. Luke 4:28–30; Matt 12:14). The same coalition is also mentioned in the episode of the tax to be paid to Caesar: "They sent some Pharisees and Herodians to him to ensnare him in his speech" (Mark 12:13; cf. Matt 22:15–16). What appears clearly in both cases is that in his public ministry Jesus suffered under the power of violence. Even if he was not directly involved with political parties, it was Pontius Pilate, in the name of the Roman Empire, who accepted the political distortion woven by some of Israel's religious and political authorities and condemned Jesus to death on the cross as a political rebel.

However, for Jesus the cross is not just suffering and death under the power of oppression. The cross was not just the destiny of someone who was condemned by the Roman Empire or by religious powers; rather, Jesus assumed his cross as part of his life of love and fidelity to his and our Father (cf. John 14:31), in solidarity with his people and the whole of oppressed human history, as a sacrifice and offering (cf. Heb 9:14)[31] for peace in the Spirit. Jesus dies in peace, without offering violent resistance, because for him peace is nonviolence. The peace he promises is "not as the world gives" it (cf. John 14:27), not the Pax Romana or something similar, but his peace.

30. For a classical work on the subject, see Wengst, *Pax romana*, especially "Erster Hauptteil," 19–72; see also Horsley, *Jesus and the Politics of Roman Palestine*, 26–79.

31. As François-Xavier Durrwell says: "It's Jesus who ascends, who dies to the Father; but the Eternal Spirit is the one who is this movement. He is the dying of Jesus 'who through the eternal spirit offered himself' (Heb 9:14). The death is the supreme act of filial love for the world to 'know that I love the Father' (Jn 14:31). It is Jesus who dies loving, but the dying of filial love is the Holy Spirit. Jesus gives himself as a sacrifice, he offers himself, he consecrates himself: 'I consecrate myself'" (Jn 17:19). Durrwell, *Jésus fils de Dieu*, 116.

Together with his peace, he promises "another Advocate" from the Father who will always be with the apostles: "The Spirit of truth, which the world cannot accept because it neither sees nor knows it" (John 14:16–17). The Spirit will teach us everything and remind us of everything Jesus told his disciples (cf. John 14:26). This surprising new peace will be part of the outpouring or sending of the Spirit of truth who will remain with the disciples. Thus, his peace is not as the world gives it, but is divine like the Spirit who comes from above, from the Father.

The peace Jesus promises appears in its strength at the cross. As he was being arrested, Jesus put a stop to all kinds of violent reaction. "Put your sword into its scabbard" (John 18:11), he orders Peter, who had used the sword against Malchus, a slave of the high priest. John Dear remarks that these "were the last words to the church before he [Jesus] was killed." The Gospels then describe Jesus as the suffering servant of God, the Lamb of God, the one who gives his life in obedience to the Father and for many. As Jürgen Moltmann says, he is the suffering God. And Ignacio Ellacuría, as well as Jon Sobrino, add the concept of the crucified people on the cross. This means that Jesus's cross stands for all people suffering violence in history. In other words, Jesus and the crucified people suffer violence, but do not, or may not, react violently. According to some traditions, Jesus forgives those who are taking part in his crucifixion: "Father, forgive them, they know not what they do" (cf. Luke 23:34). In any case, Jesus acts according to the new law: "Love your enemies, and pray for those who persecute you" (Matt 5:44; Luke 6:35–36; cf. 1 Cor 4:12; 1 Pet 3:9). Historically, the crucifixion represents the culmination of Jesus's persecution by the Pax Romana and of his conflicts with some oppressive interpretations of the Hebrew faith. Theologically, Jesus reveals his fidelity to the Father and to the kingdom of peace. He gives not only his life (cf. 1 Cor 11:24–25; Luke 22:17–19), but according to John 19:30, "he handed over the spirit." In him, human beings find the peace he reveals, the merciful forgiving God, the Father, "the God of peace" (Rom 16:20; Heb 13:20) who dwells in him (cf. John 14:10–11).

On the third day, Jesus is resurrected, through the Spirit, from death (cf. Rom 8:11).[32] Indeed, as the cross was in the Spirit (cf. Heb 9:14), so too the resurrection from the dead is the work of the Spirit (cf. Rom 8:10–11) and reveals Jesus as Christ and Lord—"Son of God in power according to the spirit of holiness" (Rom 1:4). He received the "promise of the Holy Spirit from the Father," and he "poured it forth" (Acts 2:33).

---

32. Both Will, *Christology of Peace*, 61–79, and Coste, *Il est notre paix*, 137–78, underline the connection between the resurrection, the gift of the Spirit, and peace.

The resurrection affirms the victory of nonviolence in the life-giving Spirit. The power of violence is overcome, which represents "the great explosion of peace and ... the definitive victory over the violence in the world."[33] Therefore, according to John, on the evening of that first day of the week, while the disciples were in fear, "Jesus came and stood in their midst and said to them, 'Peace be with you'" (John 20:19). Then he repeats the same message (cf. John 20:21, 26), and gives the disciples the Spirit so they can forgive sins (cf. John 20:22–23). The disciples become empowered to forgive one another, reflecting on earth what their Father does in heaven, for he forgives and is merciful. By forgiving as the Father does, the disciples pave the way toward peace and stop the spiral of violence. From now on, as Paul states, "Let the peace of Christ control your hearts, the peace into which you were also called in one body. And be thankful" (Col 3:11–15; cf. Eph 4:1–6).

This is the message of the resurrection, the new and peaceful life for all. The Spirit of the Father is the greatest gift Jesus left his disciples and followers in order to create a new earth, to change hearts, and to build a just and peaceful world.

3.4 "He Is Our Peace"—Christological Councils and Peace

Jesus, our peace, is the one who calls us to the discipleship of peace and active nonviolence. Being a Christian means to confess in the Spirit of God (cf. 1 Cor 12:3) through a praxis of peace and nonviolence that he is the Lord and the servant of God, the meaning of life and the way to the Father, to the other, and to nature.

The Christian tradition has developed the Christology of peace in the form of a confession of faith, beginning with the church fathers, and continuing with the christological councils of Nicaea and Chalcedon. For the moment, it may be enough to highlight that Constantine intended to restore peace among Christians by calling the Council of Nicaea. Even if in many other aspects the Roman emperor used Christians to further the purposes of his Pax Romana, it is necessary to accept that the Nicene faith expresses a fundamental perspective on christological peace. The Nicaean confession expresses the human-divine unity in Jesus: "Son of God" and "from the being (*ousia*) of the Father ..., one in the being (*homousios*) with the Father. . . . For us men and our salvation, He came down and became flesh, was made man, suffered, and rose again on the third day."[34] Theologically, this is an attempt to translate the original and biblical faith into a new

---

33. Coste, *Il est notre paix*, 138.
34. Translation in Neuner and Dupuis, *Christian Faith*, n7.

culture with new debates, to mediate religious as well as political conflicts. At the same time, in spite of all statements about the "divine," the confession explicitly refers to the human and historical conditions of Jesus's existence with both the ambiguity and the conflicts the incarnation implies. The Son not only became flesh and was made man, but he also suffered. Nevertheless, he is "God from God," which means that God entered human history and is the foundation of the possibility for peace.

With respect to the Council of Chalcedon, it is important to remark that in its introduction, the council fathers evoked the promise of peace described in the Gospel of John (14:27). After the preamble, the council begins the definition of faith with the words: "Our Lord and Savior Jesus Christ, confirming the knowledge of the Faith to His disciples, said, 'My peace I leave with you, My peace I give to you,' to the end that no one should differ from his neighbor in the doctrines of orthodoxy, but that the proclamation of the truth should be shown forth equally by all."[35]

As did Nicaea, Chalcedon aims to establish peace through a definition of faith. In the central part of the confession, Chalcedon affirms "the one and the same Christ, Son, Lord, only-begotten, made known in two natures without confusion, without change, without division, without separation."[36] From the point of view of a peace hermeneutic, the unity between the human and divine nature in one person—the Son of God—makes clear that he is the real, ontological, peace. He is the one in whom the friendship between God, humankind, and all human beings are "indivisibly" united in the same Christ, the only Son of the Father, from all eternity, and born as a human in time. He is the possibility of the "new man," the *Homo pacis*, as Hofheinz interprets it, following Karl Barth.[37] As the Second Vatican Council puts it, he is the fulfillment of the human mystery: "Through Christ and in Christ, the riddles of sorrow and death grow meaningful. Apart from His Gospel, they overwhelm us. Christ has risen, destroying death by His death; He has lavished life upon us so that, as sons in the Son, we can cry out in the Spirit: Abba, Father."[38]

Conclusion

In a world of violence, injustice, and the destruction of creation, a Spirit Christology of peace explains the consequences of the confession that God

---

35. Text translated from Alberigo et al., *Conciliorum Oecumenicorum Decreta*.
36. Alberigo et al., *Decrees*, 86.
37. Cf. Hofheinz, *"Er ist unser Friede,"* 165–237.
38. Vatican Council II, *Gaudium et Spes*, 22.

has revealed himself in Jesus Christ. In Jesus, God appears as the God of peace pouring out his Spirit of life, reconciliation, peace, and nonviolence. Jesus not only reveals God, but also the merciful Father in the Spirit and the perfect image of man and woman. He appears not in strength and power but in weakness and slavery (cf. Phil 2:6–8), as the servant of God, the Prince of Peace, in whom the strength of peace is greater than the strength of violence. As his revealer, Jesus shares the Father with his brothers and sisters in the Spirit. In the same Spirit, the disciples can cry "Abba," because there is no more fear and no more violence in the relationship between the triune God and humankind. The disciples are now empowered by the Spirit to proclaim the kingdom of God, the message of peace (Matt 10:1–42), even in the midst of persecution and conflicts.

A Spirit Christology of nonviolence reflects faith in Jesus, in his nonviolent incarnation, life, death, and resurrection. While the real starting point of Christology is faith in Jesus as Christ and Lord, as the Son of God made flesh, the depth of his existence appears only in the cross and resurrection. Only in the resurrection can the crucifixion and the entire history of his life be transcended. The confession of faith in Jesus as Christ and Lord includes the confession that he is the peace made flesh, the insurmountable union between God and human beings in his person, the one divine Son of the Father who became human through the Spirit. He is "the face of the Father's mercy."[39] And still more: he is Mercy. To be a disciple of Jesus consists of a life in the Spirit of the crucified and risen Jesus, who promises and gives his peace and forgives sins (John 20:19–23).

Bibliography

Alberigo, Giuseppe, et al. *Conciliorum Oecumenicorum Decreta*. Edizione Bilingue. Bologna, Italy: Dehoniane, 1991.
———, ed. *The Decrees of the Ecumenical Councils*. Vol. 1. Translated by Norman Tanner. Washington, DC: Georgetown University Press, 1990.
Balthasar, Hans Urs von. *Theologik III: Der Geist der Wahrheit*. Einsiedeln, Switzerland: Johannes, 1987.
Berkhof, Hendrikus. *The Doctrine of the Holy Spirit: The Annie Kinkead Warfield Lectures, 1963–64*. Richmond, VA: John Knox, 1964.
Biser, Eugen. *Er ist unser Friede*. Freiburg im Breisgau, Germany: Herder, 1984.
Bryant, Herschel Odell. *Spirit Christology in the Christian Tradition: From the Patristic Period to the Rise of Pentecostalism in the Twentieth Century*. Cleveland, TN: CPT, 2014.

---

39. Francis, *Misericordiae Vultus*, 1.

Cahill, Lisa Sowle. "Traditional Catholic Thought on Nonviolence." In *Choosing Peace: The Catholic Church Returns to Gospel Nonviolence*, edited by Marie Dennis, 105–18. Maryknoll, NY: Orbis, 2018.

Comblin, Joseph. *Théologie de la paix*. 2 vols. Paris: Editions Universitaires, 1960.

———. *Theologie des Friedens: Biblische Grundlagen*. Graz, Austria: Styria, 1963.

Congar, Yves M.-J. *El Espíritu Santo*. Barcelona, Spain: Herder, 1983.

Coste, René. *Il est notre paix*. Paris: Ouvrières, 1991.

———. *Théologie de la paix*. Paris: Cerf, 1997.

Dear, John. *The God of Peace*. Maryknoll, NY: Orbis, 1994.

———. *Put Down Your Sword: Answering the Gospel Call to Creative Nonviolence*. Grand Rapids, MI: Eerdmans, 2008.

Del Colle, Ralph. *Christ and the Spirit: Spirit-Christology in Trinitarian Perspective*. New York: Oxford University Press, 1994.

Dunn, James D. G. *Jesus and the Spirit: A Study of the Religious and Charismatic Experience of Jesus and the First Christians as Reflected in the New Testament*. London: SCM, 1975.

———. "Rediscovering the Spirit." *The Expository Times* 84:1 (1972) 7–12.

Dupuis, James. *Jesus Christ and His Spirit: Theological Approaches*. Bangalore, India: Theological, 1977.

Durrwell, François-Xavier. *Jésus fils de Dieu dans l'Esprit Saint*. Paris: Desclée, 1997.

The Earth Charter Commission. "The Earth Charter." 2000. https://earthcharter.org/library/the-earth-charter-text/.

Francis, Pope. *Misericordiae Vultus*. Vatican City: Libreria Editrice Vaticana, 2015. http://www.vatican.va/content/francesco/en/apost_letters/documents/papa-francesco_bolla_20150411_misericordiae-vultus.html.

Guimarães, Irénée Rezende. *Correspondance avec Irène: Méditations d'un chrétien sur la paix et la non-violence*. Tournay: les Ateliers de l'abbaye, 2015.

Hellholm, David, and Dieter Sänger. *The Eucharist—Its Origins and Contexts: Sacred Meal, Communal Meal, Table Fellowship in Late Antiquity, Early Judaism, and Early Christianity*. Wissenschaftliche Untersuchungen zum Neuen Testament 376. Tübingen, Germany: Mohr Siebeck, 2017.

Hofheinz, Marco. *"Er ist unser Friede": Karl Barths christologische grundlegung der friedensethik im gespräch mit John Howard Yoder*. Göttingen, Germany: Vandenhoeck & Ruprecht, 2014.

Horsley, Richard A. *Jesus and the Politics of Roman Palestine*. Columbia: University of South Carolina Press, 2013.

Jegen, Carol Frances. *Jesus the Peacemaker*. Kansas City: Rowman & Littlefield, 1986.

Kasper, Walter. *Jesus der Christus*. 2nd ed. Mainz, Germany: Grünewald, 1975.

Moltmann, Jürgen. *The Crucified God: The Cross of Christ as the Foundation and Criticism of Christian Theology*. Minneapolis: Fortress, 1993.

Neuner, Josef, SJ, and Jacques Dupuis, SJ. *The Christian Faith in the Doctrinal Documents of the Catholic Church*. Rev. ed. London: Collins, 1983.

Puig i Tàrrech, Armand. *Jesus: An Uncommon Journey: Studies on the Historical Jesus*. Wissenschaftliche Untersuchungen zum Neuen Testament 288. Tübingen, Germany: Mohr Siebeck, 2010.

Rosato, Philip J. "Spirit Christology: Ambiguity and Promise." *Theological Studies* 38 (1977) 423–49.

Rynne, Terrence J. *Jesus Christ, Peacemaker: A New Theology of Peace.* Maryknoll, NY: Orbis, 2014.

Schockenhoff, Eberhard. *Die Bergpredigt: Aufruf zum Christsein.* Frieburg, Germany: Herder, 2014.

———. *Kein Ende der Gewalt? Friedensethik für eine globalisierte Welt.* Freiburg, Germany: Herder, 2018.

Schoonenberg, Piet. *Der Geist, das Wort und der Sohn: Eine Geist-Christologie.* Regensburg, Germany: Friedrich Pustet, 1992.

———. "Spirit Christology and Logos Christology." *Bijdragen* 38:4 (1977) 350–75.

Silvahy, Michael, ed. *Ritual Song.* 2nd ed. Chicago: GIA, 2016.

Sobrino, Jon, SJ. *Cristología desde América Latina: Esbozo a partir del seguimiento del Jesús Histórico.* 2nd ed. Teología Latinoamericana 1. Mexico City: CRT, 1977.

———. "¿Es Jesús una buena noticia?" *Revista Latinoamericana de Teología* 10 (1993) 292–304.

———. *Jesucristo liberador: Lectura histórico-teológica de Jesús de Nazaret.* Madrid: Trotta, 1991.

———. *Jesús en América Latina: Su significado para la fe y la cristología.* 2nd ed. Santander, Spain: Sal Terrae, 1982.

United States Conference of Catholic Bishops. "The Challenge of Peace: God's Promise and Our Response." A Pastoral Letter on War and Peace. Washington DC, May 3, 1983. https://www.usccb.org/upload/challenge-peace-gods-promise-our-response-1983.pdf.

Vatican Council II. *Gaudium et Spes.* Vatican City: Libreria Editrice Vaticana, 1965. https://www.vatican.va/archive/hist_councils/ii_vatican_council/documents/vat-ii_const_19651207_gaudium-et-spes_en.html.

Weber, Jörg. *Geist-Christologie im Neuen Testament?: Erwägungen zu einer exegetischen These über das Verhältnis von Jesus Christus und dem Heiligen Geist.* Trier/Waldrach, Germany: Books on Demand, 2000.

Wengst, Klaus. *Pax romana: Anspruch und Wirklichkeit. Erfahrungen und Wahrnehmung des Friedens bei Jesus und im Urchristentum.* Munich, Germany: Kaiser, 1986.

Will, James E. *A Christology of Peace.* Louisville, KY: Westminster/John Knox, 1989.

3

Christian Nonviolence for Secular Causes: The Case of Two Twentieth-Century Religious Communities

MARIA CLARA BINGEMER

PAUL REFERS TO THE community of Christians as the "body of Christ." The church is the continuation of the bodily presence of Christ on earth. The boundaries of that body are rarely clear, for the Holy Spirit is not confined to the visible church. But the center of that body is clear: the weakest members, Paul says, are the indispensable ones (1 Cor 12:22), and when one member suffers, all suffer together (1 Cor 12:26). Christ identifies himself with the victims of this world (Matt 25:31–46).[1] The church is that community that undoes the logic of violence by breaking the unanimity proclaiming the guilt of the victims.[2] The church identifies God with the victims of this world and thereby unmasks the scapegoating mechanism.[3] Nonviolence is not for a few heroic individuals; it is lived by the community's sensing the deep interconnection of all people because they share the same nervous system as the cosmic Christ. The Christian church is called to be a community of witnesses who live the challenge of love and nonviolence every day.

Siding with the victims of this world provokes opposition. Nonviolence is not a tactic that is always successful in the short run. Christians

1. Cf. Cavanaugh, "Very Preliminary Sketch."
2. Cf. Girard, *Battling to the End*.
3. Cf. Sobrino, *La Fe en Jesucristo*.

must be prepared for martyrdom, which is not just something that occurred in distant, ancient times but is a daily reality for Christians around the world today. Martyrdom is the ultimate witness to the truth of nonviolence. The martyr, in imitation of Christ, prefers to absorb the violence of the world rather than deal it out, in the secure knowledge that she or he is on the right side of history. The coming kingdom of God is nonviolent, and the martyr decides to live that reality now. But the martyr is not alone: the witness of the martyr depends on a church community that is ready to keep the memory of the martyrs alive as a proclamation of what God—and God's creation—is really like.[4]

In this text we present the case of two religious communities of the twentieth century:[5] the Jesuits of the Catholic University of El Salvador, whose entire community was murdered in November 1989,[6] and the Trappist community of Tibhirine, all of whose members were kidnapped on March 27, 1996, and killed two months later, on May 21.[7]

Eccentric Communities?

On November 16, 1989, both the church and the world received with pain and surprise the news of the execution of an entire Jesuit community, the one that led the Universidad Centroamericana José Simeón Cañas (UCA) in San Salvador, the capital of the Central American country of El Salvador. The murder was carried out by the *batallón ATLACATL*, an elite unit within the Salvadoran army.[8] Those killed were the rector of the university, Fr. Ignacio Ellacuría, and five other Jesuits—Segundo Montes, Ignacio Martin-Baró, Ignacio Lopez y Lopez, Juan Ramon Moreno, and Amando Lopez—who were in the residence, and two women, a mother and her daughter—Julia Elba Ramos and Celina Ramos—who worked in the service of the university and Jesuit residence. One member of the community, the theologian Jon Sobrino, survived because he was in Thailand at the time giving a theology course.

---

4. See my book with Casarella, *Witnessing*.

5. This reflection is considered more in-depth in my recent book *Mística e Testemunho em Koinonia*.

6. Relevant works include Instituto De Estudios Centroamericanos Y El Rescate, *Jesuit Assassinations*, and Lassalle-Klein, *Blood and Ink*.

7. Relevant works include Kiser, *Monks of Tibhirine*, and Chenu, *Sept Vies pour Dieu*.

8. See Whitfield, *Paying the Price*.

On May 21, 1996, on the other side of the world, a communiqué sent by the radical Islamic group GIA announced the death of seven Trappist monks, the whole community of Notre Dame de l'Atlas, which lived in the mountains of Tibhirine in Algeria. They were the prior Christian de Chergé and novice master Christophe Lebreton, Br. Luc Dochier, Br. Michel Fleury, Fr. Bruno Lemarchand, Fr. Célestin Ringeard, and Br. Paul Favre-Miville. The monks, who had been kidnapped on March 27, two months before, were beheaded. The GIA blamed the French government for not being able to negotiate the liberation of some Muslim prisoners being held in France in exchange for the monks. Two of the monks, Fr. Jean Pierre and Fr. Amedée, survived because they slept apart from the others and were not found by the kidnappers. The bodies were not found; the monks were recognized only by their heads.[9]

These were religious communities, a model of Christian life found mostly in Catholicism, which has been present in the church since very early in its history. They were men who consecrated their lives to God through vows of chastity, poverty, and obedience. The Trappists took, in addition, a vow of stability, which attached them to the same monastery for the rest of their lives. The Jesuits make a special vow of obedience to the pope for everything related to their mission. But even though similar in some respects, the two cases were different in others. Trappists are contemplatives and live in the cloister. Jesuits, on the other hand, are active and not attached to anything but their mission, which can be diverse and global. Despite these differences, however, both communities experienced a similar kind of death, a violent one, because of their faith. The church considers them martyrs—which means witnesses—even if they have not been officially canonized. They are so considered because of their attitude, radically in line with the gospel, toward significant political and religious problems present in their historical context.

Ex-centric Communities?

In what sense did these two communities share traits in common? In the first place, they were both Christian communities and therefore church cells. Like every group of Christians who come together, they both believed that Jesus Christ is in their midst.[10] It is constitutive of Christianity to live faith in community. Far from being something individualistic and solitary

---

9. Olivera, *How Far to Follow?*
10. See Matt 18:20: "For where two or three gather in my name, there am I with them."

that alienates people from the fellowship of their fellow men, Christianity is gregarious, requiring and demanding community.

By the simple fact of claiming for themselves the name of Christian and by belonging to two religious orders of the Catholic Church, one of the most important and numerous denominations within historical Christianity, the Trappists and the Jesuits demonstrate that their community ties are part of their identity, which by itself means that they have more in common than differences between them. In addition, both the Tibhirine Trappists and the Jesuits of El Salvador lived a community style that is different from that of the other communities in their religious orders, and this difference made them even more similar: both lived a self-understanding of community as extended and eccentric ("ex-centric").

"Extended" because both communities housed and recognized as members, to at least some degree, people who did not belong to the religious order itself; in the case of the Trappists, the inhabitants of the village that surrounded the monastery, who were not even Christians but Muslims, and the participants in the group Ribat el Salam (Lien de Paix in French, Bond of Peace in English). The monastic community understood itself as inextricably linked to this larger community by faith, prayer, and the desire for communion. This desire was enhanced and explained in a clearer and stronger way with the arrival of Christian de Chergé and then with his election and service as prior, but it was present in the community before his arrival. Had not Brother Luc served the people of the village as well as anyone else who presented themselves in need of medical care as brothers? Is it not a fact that the monks participated in the life of the residents, in their family and even religious celebrations? Was it not affirmed and reaffirmed by all the works commenting on and describing the life of the monastery of Notre Dame de l'Atlas that other religious, linked together by the same dedication and love for the church of Algeria, formed a broader circle around the monastery?

I believe that one can say without fear of forcing the claim that the Tibhirine community was a community present in concentric circles, from the nuclear circle formed by professed monks with vows, including a vow of stability (among whom were the seven martyrs), passing into the larger circle of the village community, of the neighbors—mostly Muslim—and reaching the most scattered ecclesial communities not only in Tibhirine, but also in Fez, Algiers, and in so many other cities where love for the Algerian people and their church and people is the greatest motivation. It was a community in concentric circles and became so because it was an ex-centric community; that is, a community that does not find its beginning, middle, and end in itself and in the life of its nuclear members, but that understands its life and vocation as consisting in service to others, even if it is a quiet, prayerful service, without much stridency or visibility.

It was a community that exists outside of itself, living outside itself, finding within itself the gifts and grace that must not be jealously guarded but, rather, shared in generous solicitude for the building, expansion, and strengthening of communion. It was a community that pointed not to itself but to the communion of saints, a mystery to which the martyred prior had a special devotion.[11] It was a community, that is, a cell of communion that lived of the communion and for the communion and pointed toward the communion.

In the case of the Jesuits of the UCA of El Salvador, something similar happened. The UCA community had a common mission with very clear objectives: to employ knowledge to transform the suffering within the Salvadoran reality. Inspired by the theology of liberation, which at the time of the murders was having its heyday on the Latin American continent, the UCA community of the time in fact presented the profile described by one of liberation theology's most important exponents, the Peruvian priest Gustavo Gutiérrez.

Liberation theology suggests a conception of community that is defined and motivated by a common commitment to tradition and that results in action that is in line with the tradition but developed in a way that allows debate and disagreement with it. Through his expressive conception of action, Gutiérrez develops a concept that justifies the creation of a community of people sharing a common praxis, but that may mean very different traditions supporting the interpretation of this praxis. The Peruvian theologian provides an argument from within his tradition that some types of collaboration with members of other traditions, whether liberalism, Marxism, or other religious traditions, should be considered, reflecting a common fundamental choice and ultimately the basis for a community, not merely a matter of short-term convenience or strategy.[12]

It is also worth mentioning Gutiérrez's statements in Medellin that the current problem of the church is not so much people who do not believe in God, but rather, people who do not practice their faith.[13] From there the Peruvian theologian argues that the integration of differences—different

---

11. De Chergé and Chenu, *L'Invincible Esperance*; Salenson, *Christian de Cherge*; Salenson, *Prier 15 Jours*.

12. Lewis, "Actions as the Ties," 562. Lewis notes that Gutierrez's conception of community is deeply shaped by the Vatican II documents *Lumen Gentium* and *Gaudium et Spes*. Lewis also notes the relevance of the ecclesiological model developed by Avery Dulles in *Models of the Church*.

13. Gutiérrez, *Theology of Liberation*, cited by Lewis, "Actions as the Ties," 556n26.

people, different perspectives, different traditions—will lead to an enrichment of praxis. Because our actions are a more authentic expression of our fundamental choices than our words, this plural and multiform unity of gestures and attitudes is much more significant than a unity based only on common professions of faith.[14]

Thus, the community led by the brilliant philosopher and thinker Ignacio Ellacuría never ceased to open new doors to dialogue, not only with ecclesial, but also with academic, civil, and political sectors. This dialogue enriched the community's positions, reinforcing the community, expanding the role of the community responsible for the university beyond its campus to the city, the country, and the world. And it reinforced the idea that it was not only the Jesuit priests who wanted an end to injustice and violence in El Salvador. Many other people, communities, and religious, ecclesial, and nonreligious bodies supported the critical, utopian position of the rector and his community of Jesuit brothers and collaborators. Through this support, the community expanded its strength and historical and political significance.

This is what Gutiérrez is thinking when he states that despite the differences within such a group, his notion of common praxis provides the necessary basis for a meaningful and productive reflection on this praxis: "Only a sufficiently broad, rich and intense revolutionary praxis with the participation of people from different points of view, can create the conditions of a fruitful theory."[15] People who embody and live the same fundamental orientation, even if they belong to different intellectual and religious traditions, will produce a common experience that provides the foundation of a joint and meaningful theoretical reflection. One of Gutiérrez's fundamental concerns, especially at the beginning of his theological trajectory, is the dialogue between Marxists and Christians as they fight together in certain moments and revolutionary situations. Without ever suggesting that Marxists will eventually become Christians or that Christians will become Marxists, he sees Christian eschatology transformed as a result of the contact between Christians and Marxists, the latter of whom strive for a better world and live consistently with this striving.[16]

At bottom, liberation theology held dear the distinction between the church and the kingdom of God. No one remembers the document of John Paul II that discussed interreligious dialogue and criticized the kingdom-centeredness ("reinocentrismo") of some missionaries who did not explicitly

---

14. Gutiérrez, *Theology of Liberation*, cited by Lewis, "Actions as the Ties," 557.

15. Gutiérrez, *Theology of Liberation*, 56, 75, quoted by Lewis, "Actions as the Ties," 557.

16. Gutiérrez, *Theology of Liberation*, cited by Lewis, "Actions as the Ties" 557.

proclaim the gospel, believing more in dialogue and respecting the differences between people.[17] Long before this document, the Latin American theology of liberation, drinking from the new sap generated by the conciliar documents, distinguished kingdom, world, and church. Leonardo Boff thus emphasized the priority of the kingdom of God over the church, with the church being the community charged with carrying forward the kingdom project and making it grow.[18]

According to Boff, "The church is that part of the world which in the power of the Spirit has embraced the kingdom explicitly in the person of Jesus Christ, the Son of God incarnate in oppression, who keeps the permanent memory and conscience of the kingdom, celebrates its presence in the world and in itself and holds the grammar of its proclamation, in the service of the world."[19] The world is the place of the historical realization of the kingdom. And the kingdom, "which encompasses the world and the church, is the good end of the totality of creation in God at last liberated totally from all imperfection and penetrated by the Divine that realizes it absolutely."[20] Thus, the kingdom is realized in the world and the church is its mediator but not exclusively; being a mediator is one of its signs, but not the only sign.[21]

Tibhirine's monastic community experienced and understood that the best way to carry out their contemplative and incarnational vocation was to pray among the prayerful, and not only among Christian prayerful, but among the prayerful of other religious groups, mainly Islamic ones. They understood the necessity of doing this in order to realize the communion of the saints that so much inspired and attracted the mystic prior Christian de Chergé.

Because of that, they paid a price. Some have not looked favorably on mystical and prophetic movement across the boundaries of religious differences. And although the poor, humble Muslim people who knew and loved the monks welcomed and participated with them with open arms and hearts in this evangelical and pioneering experience, it was not so for others—the radical terrorist groups and even the Algerian army and government. Martyrdom and violent death were the price to be paid.

The Jesuit community at UCA had a similar experience. Instead of self-understanding and self-building only a theoretical academy that sees

---

17. John Paul II, *Redemptoris Missio*.
18. Boff, *Igreja*.
19. Boff, *Igreja*, 16.
20. Boff, *Igreja*, 16.
21. Boff, *Igreja*, 84, 139.

knowledge as an end in itself, they opened up the academy and their mission from faith and religious consecration to other segments of society, even if they did not share their reading of reality. The UCA at that time was in the forefront of not only knowledge and state-of-the-art education in the country and in Central America, but it was leading a political process as a liberator and a contributor to a serious breakthrough. As with the Trappists of Tibhirine, the price of their visibility and choices was martyrdom and violent death.

Martyrdom as a Communitarian Liturgy

After these reflections, we ask ourselves: What message do these two communities have for us today? *First*, they were both revolutionary, each in its own style. But their way of transforming the world was rooted in the particular charism and style of their respective communities; they both lived in a way that was different from the usual model of religious community.

Second, they brought something new to the living out of a consecration to God and others. Both were dealing with new perspectives brought by the Second Vatican Council and incorporated by the whole church. Those new perspectives were only beginning to be assimilated and practiced. The monks of Tibhirine demonstrated a commitment to interreligious dialogue to the end, to the point of shedding their blood. They lived in a country where the religion of the other was the majority and practiced the monastic life that was theirs in close dialogue and deep communion with this "other" tradition,[22] assuming and integrating several of that tradition's elements. The Jesuits of the UCA did the same with the option for the poor. At the time

---

22. Cf. Vatican Council II, *Nostra Aetate*, para. 2: "The church, therefore, exhorts her sons, that through dialogue and collaboration with the followers of other religions, carried out with prudence and love and in witness to the Christian faith and life, they recognize, preserve, and promote the good things, spiritual and moral, as well as the socio-cultural values found among these men"; and para. 3: "Since in the course of centuries not a few quarrels and hostilities have arisen between Christians and Moslems, this sacred synod urges all to forget the past and to work sincerely for mutual understanding and to preserve as well as to promote together for the benefit of all mankind social justice and moral welfare, as well as peace and freedom." Also cf. Vatican Council II, *Gaudium et Spes*, para. 26: "The social order and its development must invariably work to the benefit of the human person if the disposition of affairs is to be subordinate to the personal realm and not contrariwise, as the Lord indicated when He said that the Sabbath was made for man, and not man for the Sabbath. This social order requires constant improvement. It must be founded on truth, built on justice and animated by love; in freedom it should grow every day toward a more humane balance. An improvement in attitudes and abundant changes in society will have to take place if these objectives are to be gained."

of their death, this option had already been adopted by the Latin American church, but they found a way to live it in community and in academia. They redirected an entire university toward this option, responding to questions that came up everywhere about how to live this option when one is not poor. Therefore, both communities were pioneers of the options that the church was beginning to live and were lights that illuminated the path of others that have followed them.

Third, both communities were embedded in a particular and concrete reality but maintained an openness to the universal. The Trappists' context was Algeria and by extension the Middle East; the Jesuits' was El Salvador, then a strategic and explosive location in Central America. But both were also windows to the world. In both Algeria and El Salvador, these communities lived the Christian faith as proposed by the Gospel of Jesus for every man and woman living in this world.

Fourth, both communities accepted the challenge of staying where they were in spite of danger and threat. They did not withdraw or escape or adopt any change in their attitude or position driven by the fear of taking upon themselves and bearing the consequences of their choices. And they were guided by the desire and hope that their actions would have universal repercussions.

Fifth, both communities were sustained by a deep spirituality. The whole process they lived to the point of death was prayed over, discerned, and worked on in community, both *ad intra* and *ad extra*, from within and dealing with diversity.

Sixth, both communities had a remarkable leader. Neither Christian de Chergé nor Ignacio Ellacuría were charismatic or delirious dreamers unaware of the facts and the dangers they faced. They were spiritual and brilliant intellectuals with a broad and prophetic vision who followed the inspirations that were granted them by God and engaged in the projects that their historical time demanded of them. Their gifts were fundamental for enabling the communities to engage deeply in projects that responded to the historical and geographical context in which they were located.

Seventh, both communities wanted to bring peace amidst conflict, injustice, and violence. And their testimony was evangelical and peaceful, even if violence seemed to have had the last word. The future has shown that their gestures, words, lives, and testimony remain and are victorious over violence.

Eighth, both communities have left us some lessons from their testimony that can be lived by every person, every Christian, in any context, without needing to be a religious or a monk or something similar. These lessons are as follows:

- To be prayerful among the prayerful who are not only Christians, but also come from other faiths and religions. To find spiritual nourishment in the religion of the other, contributing from your own tradition and learning equally from the other.

- To serve the poor and to live simply among them. To receive from the poor friendship, forgiveness, and priorities that guide work, even academic research work.

- Not to respond to violence with violence. To practice the evangelical principle of not returning evil with evil to the extreme; instead, reacting to evil with good, love, and peace. This principle was patent in the community of Tibhirine and was even stated explicitly several times in the writings of Christian de Chergé and Christophe Lebreton.[23] In the Salvadoran community, this principle did not appear so clearly, but was practiced to the extent that the Jesuits tried in every way to enter into dialogue with anyone who might oppose them.[24] They were in dialogue with their enemies until the end, and even the apparent scouting mission, under the guise of a visit from some of the soldiers the day before the murders, was no reason for them to close off dialogue or take any more explicit defensive action.

- To face death with a certain style, the style of Jesus Christ, remaining resilient under threat, praying and discerning the possibility of martyrdom, making decisions to stay and remain faithful to their commitment to death even when it is very close on the horizon. The martyr receives martyrdom as a gift. Violent death because of fidelity to Jesus Christ and his gospel can be accepted, but not sought. This is the difference between a martyr and others who both kill and die. It is not the death of the kamikaze, nor of the suicide bomber, nor of Socrates, who quietly drank his poison in the presence of his disciples, uttering wise words. All of them, somehow, actively bring death to themselves. The martyr, in contrast, receives it passively, even while remaining clear about the story of his or her faith, just as Jesus of Nazareth did.

Both communities respond, inspired by the Spirit of God, to the challenges that their time puts to them. They are, as the Second Vatican Council envisions, readers attentive to the "signs of the times," which reveal where the will of God is present in this time and space. And at the same time, they have as the background of their lives and their witness of martyrdom the

23. See, for instance, "Testament of Christian de Chergé," certainly one of the most inspiring spiritual texts of the twentieth century. See also Christophe Lebreton's poetic and spiritual writings in *Born from the Gaze of God*.

24. See Lassalle-Klein, *Blood and Ink*.

presence and revelation of God, which paradoxically allows their mission to be verified according to the impotence and failure of the cross, a historical event that configured nascent Christianity, which was forced to find its identity in a man who was born, lived, suffered, and died violently in a certain period of human history.

Reading and meditating on the testimony of these two Christian religious communities, we see further that suffering and death are not barriers for God. The early Christian community understood this because when they experienced the resurrection of Jesus, they heard what God said through his death. From then on, they reread the story and realized that they were faced with an event that was not merely linear and chronological, but rather about something that represented a radical turning point. A new era was beginning, when it was necessary to announce the good news and to build the kingdom so that Jesus's proposal could spread throughout the world and not be stifled by institutions that were not suitable to it. Christianity is therefore based on Jesus Christ's proclamation of the kingdom of God, a fact that happened in history, and by the proclamation of Jesus personally acknowledged as the living word of God pronounced in history.

The fruits of his testimony will spread like seeds to the wind fallen on good soil, or they will be distributed to feed the hungry with truth, love, and meaning. The time of Easter will inevitably come. The prisons, hammers, nails, knives, and bullets apparently seem to always destroy everything, but in reality, they always arrive late, because the Word is already sown in many generous and fruitful wombs. These wombs are those of the men and women who receive the testimony and cause it to bear fruit. The earth opens its fruitful womb to receive the seed that will later become a leafy tree, turgid with fruit. The extirpated prophet had no apparent success, but he was fruitful in the womb of history, in which the novelty of God's plan is found without break or rest.

So too the community, the ecclesial cell, shows what the whole church is called to be. The martyrdom of those in the two communities is:

1. a call to attention to what is essential, not so much the rules, the irreproachable and radical following of the principles and what is written in the books and records of the religious order or congregation. The essential thing is to live the gospel, to be a group of people who closely follow the radical way of life of Jesus. These people are open and ready to develop loving and dialogical relationships with all people, cultures, and traditions. They call attention to love, the only thing that is unique and worthy of faith and that will define the identity and belonging of

the communities.²⁵ In the midst of the secularism and pluralism of the world today, Christianity is called to enter into this diversity and from there give its testimony. So it is with the testimony of the two communities.

2. a testimony that surprises the world. Why did the two communities give a testimony that shook public opinion and surprised the world? Partly because, for the Jesuits, the testimony resonated in a sociopolitical and socioeconomic context and not so much in an ecclesial context. In the case of the Tibhirine monks, it resonated in a multireligious or even theocratic context. The issues that brought about the radical engagement of both communities were secular, not theological or religious, at least not directly. In the case of the Jesuits this was clearly apparent. The community, in its charism and mystical aspect, wanted to be an instance of prophetic denunciation against an oppressive and unjust government, following in the footsteps of Monsignor Romero, a martyr himself nine years before the Jesuits. And this mystical aspect, with its expected consequences of liberation of the poor and oppressed of El Salvador, occurred within an academic, secular space, although Christian in inspiration. From the areopagus of the university, the Jesuits placed their study, their research, their teaching, and their activities in the service of transforming the unjust context in which they lived.²⁶ But they also added to this their insertion into poor communities in the periphery. Almost all of them worked alongside these communities, which were spread out on the outskirts of San Salvador, and from there preached the gospel and helped transform reality. The work of the monks had somewhat different characteristics. The space they had was not a university, but a monastery. However, they made this explicitly religious space a place of openness to the poor communities in the neighborhood. They provided services of all kinds to these communities, not just religious services. Among them is worth mentioning the medical services that the indefatigable and admirable Frère Luc provided, attending at times to more than 150 patients per day.²⁷ For his part, the prior Christian de Chergé created a movement, the Ribat al Salam, that involved religious and laity, Christians and Muslims, in prayer and in work toward the construction of peace. By acting in a religious way—prayer—but also universally in

---

25. Cf. Balthasar, *L'amour Seul est Digne de Foi*.

26. See John Paul II, *Redemptoris Missio*, which identifies the university, among other places, as a modern areopagus.

27. Cf. Kiser, *Passion pour l'Algérie*.

the construction of peace, de Chergé's movement witnessed that it was possible to transform the society in which it was present. De Chergé's work was done with absolute respect for the other religion that was working with him in this peacebuilding. The group was formed by Christians and Muslims who prayed together and thought about a way to advance peace in the country.[28]

3. a community liturgy of surrender of life for the glory of God and his kingdom.[29] In fact, the martyrdom of the two communities, expected and prepared for in a certain way, has the status of a liturgy. Such was martyrdom generally in the early days of Christianity: a public event with characteristics of celebration. The martyrs were displayed in spaces open to the whole population, such as the Roman circus, the streets of the city, or the roads in the outskirts of the cities. They were oblations of the liturgy of the Roman Empire, which preached the cult of the emperor. On the side of the martyrs, they accepted this death out of conviction and, above all, by the felt need to bear witness.[30] In fact, the martyrs were committed to making visible in the world, to the eyes of all, Jesus and what he represented; that is, the kingdom of God already present here and now, already happened. Their lives were lived for that purpose and their deaths were a consequence of it.[31] This liturgy was indeed eucharistic, for the martyrs and their testimony were food for all who could witness their deaths, including the executioners. One can recall here Ignatius, the bishop of Antioch, a second-century martyr who called the guards who led him to the execution "ferocious beasts," similar to the animals of the arena in which he would be killed, while declaring his desire to be food, understanding himself in eucharistic terms. "I am God's wheat, and I shall be ground by the teeth of beasts, that I may become the pure bread of Christ."[32] The effect, the consequence of this, would be "the distribution of Christ in person by the population."[33] In our two cases, it is the communities themselves that live this eucharistic vocation, made visible liturgically and actually realized. It is worth remembering that the monk Christophe Lebreton, in describing his community, used the Greek word that describes the

---

28. Cf. Ray, *Christian de Cherge*.

29. About martyrdom as liturgy, see the excellent reflections contained in Young, *In Procession*.

30. Young, *In Procession*.

31. Young, *In Procession*, 6.

32. Quoted in Young, *In Procession*, 8.

33. Young, *In Procession*, 8.

liturgical moment of consecration when the Spirit transforms the species into the body and blood of Christ to become the food of all the people: *epiclesis*.[34]

These two communities teach us today, first, a *way to be truly human*. There is a deep anthropological significance in the testimony of these two religious communities, which seal their lives and actions by the surrender of martyrdom. In a historical and cultural moment in which the purpose of human beings seems to have become synonymous with possessing, consuming, and seeking happiness in acquiring more and more material objects, they teach that being human involves, on the contrary, giving, offering, opening up and committing to the other, being faithful to the end, to the point of surrender. In this sense, rather than consuming, being human consists in "being consumed."[35]

In this understanding, human life is a given, surrendered life. This is what came to the mind of Christian de Chergé whenever he thought about his community. Their lives had already been given. What could happen in that moment when the threat of death was no more than a direct consequence of coherence with the surrender they had already made? And made not so they would be admired or venerated, but to serve others, to help others, even those belonging to another religion, another tradition, another culture? So it was for the Jesuit community, which understood itself as existing to bring the poor down from the cross. Their story was the story of a university's efforts to help the crucified people of El Salvador "to come down from the cross, supporting their efforts to build a society in which everyone had the opportunity to share a future where dignity, love, compassion, and sanity could prevail."[36]

Second, the communities teach us *a christological path*. In fact, what the testimony of the two communities says with their martyrdom is that being human is to be governed by the existence of otherness, by the presence of the other who, by the epiphany provided by his or her face, he or she interrogates and calls. Christian de Chergé, a profound connoisseur of Levinas, applied and taught this to his confreres.[37] Ellacuría, the brilliant philosopher, introduced this centrality of otherness by employing the concept of "reality" taught by his master Zubiri.[38] It is a reality that one

---

34. See Minassian, "Itinéraire et Spiritualité du Frère Christophe."
35. Cavanaugh, *Being Consumed*.
36. Lassalle-Klein, introduction to *Blood and Ink*, xxiii.
37. For instance, in de Chergé, *L'Autre que Nous Attendons*.
38. Comisión Teológica Internacional, *Bajar de la Cruz a los Pobres*.

must take charge of and carry, putting it on one's shoulders, announcing the kingdom of God.

In fact, it is the path of Jesus Christ himself that is reborn through those who follow him. Both communities are Christian and even Catholic but open to all the diversity and difference that they encountered on their path. The UCA served the poor of El Salvador who were, at least at the time the community lived and worked there, mostly Catholic. However, this was not recognized by their fellow Catholics who did not hesitate to write on the walls that to be patriotic they must kill the priests who wanted the revolution that would change the life of Salvadorans. Surely if any non-Catholic had written this, the UCA would have welcomed, listened, and entered into dialogue with them. There were certainly many nonbelievers who spoke at UCA, as is often the case in academic circles, where freedom of belonging and expression must always be undisputed. In any case, the murdered Jesuits were intellectuals who did not close themselves inside the known environment of their identity. They were not researchers who restricted themselves to their laboratories or teachers who only acted in the classroom. They went out to meet the different and the poor in their communities and they learned a new way of thinking, of celebrating life. They entered into communion with otherness, as did Jesus of Nazareth, who included at the table of his kingdom those who were considered godless as a result of their health status, their birth, or their political or religious belonging.

Tibhirine's Trappist community followed this path even more explicitly. As a contemplative Catholic community, they did not hesitate to walk to meet Muslims and their religion. And they did this in the style of Jesus, which is open to and allows the transformation of the predominant view that foreigners, like the Syro-Phoenician or the Samaritan, were idolatrous;[39] which allows touching by impure and sinful women without fear of contamination;[40] and which exalts the behavior of publicans, who, because of their difference, can teach those who consider themselves elect and can correct those who would presume to overrule the Lord's priorities.[41] Jesus opens the doors of his kingdom to all those who seek God with a sincere heart. Opening the space of their monastery so that Muslims could pray there, going out to meet these brethren of another faith to pray with them, welcoming them into their personal and communal space, and giving their lives to the end for them, the Tibhirine monks testified to their radical following of Jesus. By opening themselves to the difference of the other who

39. Cf. Matt 15:21–28; Mark 7:24–30; Luke 10:25–37.
40. Luke 7:36–50.
41. Cf. Luke 18:9–14 and John 19.

had a faith different from their own, they showed themselves to be followers of this Jesus to whom they had given their lives and whose teachings they wished to live and to encourage others to live. Both communities lived, transmitted, and proclaimed an open and inclusive gospel, the same good news that was announced by Jesus of Nazareth.

Finally, the communities teach us *a way to be church*. Both show an ecclesiological path through their witness. That is, they teach and seal with their blood a way, a style, of being church that can teach something to the whole church. In the case of the UCA, the Jesuit community's model of being church was firmly connected to the majority of the Latin American church as it existed throughout the 1970s and 1980s. This was a church that conceived itself as more horizontal and less vertical, more centered on the people, a model of church proposed by the Second Vatican Council in the Dogmatic Constitution *Lumen Gentium*, which sees the church as "the People of God," rather than seeing it as pyramid focused on the clergy and the episcopate. In addition, it was a church whose pastoral and missionary priority was focused on the poor, a church that wished to incarnate among the poorest and from there help them become craftsmen of their liberation and to fight against their poverty. This church continues to exist in Latin America, fueled by a popular reading of the Bible, by pilgrimages and walks that draw attention to the situation of the excluded, and by denunciations against the injustices committed by various autocratic and elitist governments. Some of its prophets were murdered, including the members of the UCA community, and a number of them were punished, curtailed in their right to write and teach. But the seeds they have sown continue to sprout and are slowly bringing about the dawn of a new day, which may take time but will come. The hope of the people is also sustained by the memory of these martyrs, who gave evidence of a committed church that is incarnated with the people.

The model of church witnessed to by the Tibhirine community is also characterized by solidarity with the poor and the excluded. It was clearly out of solidarity with the disinherited that the monks did not leave where they were, hoping by the example of their stability to help and protect those who were threatened by the violence that reigned in that place. But above all, they evidenced a model of the church that is humbly aware of not holding a monopoly on truth but, rather, shares it with other traditions that name God using other names. What was happening in the monastery of Tibhirine was a transreligious ecclesial community, which, while living its Christian and Catholic identity deeply, could be permeated by all the richness of dialogue with another tradition. It allowed itself to be shaped by its relationship with other traditions and religions. This relationship was a constitutive part of its identity and gave to its ecclesial profile the striking features of diversity. Today we see other communities that follow Tibhirine's model, while at the same time renewing and reconfiguring it. We can remember here the case of Taizé, an ecumenical monastery founded by Br. Roger de Taizé, which attracts thousands of young people from all over the world and has expanded its presence to many parts of the world. There is also the Bose monastery in Italy, whose prior, Enzo Bianchi, is an exponent of ecumenical dialogue,[42] and the monastery founded by the Italian Jesuit Paolo Dall'Oglio in Syria, which gathered people from the three monotheistic traditions for prayer-sharing.[43] Its mysterious disappearance several years ago has not stopped the seed it planted and the inspiration it gave to others to establish a place of transreligious prayer from bearing fruit in various parts of the Middle East and radiating a spirit of interreligious dialogue. The church that lived, suffered, and died in Tibhirine is still alive there. It's not over. And the spirit that inspired it continues to be present in the church of Christ, which has opened up more and more in the recent pontificates, and especially in the pontificate of Pope Francis, to a universal communion without frontiers.

Bibliography

Balthasar, Hans Urs von. *L'Amour Seul est Digne de Foi*. Saint Maur: Parole et Silence, 1999.

Bingemer, Maria Clara Lucchetti. *Mística e Testemunho em Koinonia: A Inspiração que vem do Martírio de Duas Comunidades do Século XX*. São Paolo: Paulus, 2018.

Bingemer, Maria Clara Lucchetti, and Peter J. Casarella. *Witnessing: Prophecy, Politics, and Wisdom*. Maryknoll, NY: Orbis, 2014.

Boff, Leonardo. *Igreja: Carisma e Poder: Ensaios de Eclesiología Militante*. Petrópolis: Vozes, 1981.

Cavanaugh, William T. *Being Consumed: Economics and Christian Desire*. Grand Rapids, MI: Eerdmans, 2008.

———. "A Very Preliminary Sketch for a Foundational Theology of Nonviolence." Paper presented as a contribution to the virtual working group on active nonviolence convened by Pax Christi, 2019.

Chenu, Bruno. *Sept Vies pour Dieu et l'Algerie*. Paris: Bayard, 2006.

42. Bose monastery is totally ecumenical, comprised of monks of both sexes and of various Christian denominations, but is also open to laypeople, nonbelievers, and people coming from other religious traditions.

43. In the 1980s, Dall'Oglio refounded in Syria the monastic Catholic-Syriac community Mar Musa (the Monastery of San Mosè L'Abissino), heir of an important cenobitical and eremitical tradition from the fourth century. The monastery also welcomes people from the Orthodox religion. Paolo Dall'Oglio is a Jesuit who is strongly committed to interreligious dialogue with the Islamic world. For this reason, he was strongly pursued by the Syrian government and was kidnapped in 2013. It is unknown whether he is still alive.

Comisión Teológica Internacional de la Asociación Ecuménica de Teólogos/as del Tercer Mundo. *Bajar de la Cruz a los Pobres: Cristologia de la Liberación.* Edited by José Maria Vigil. México, DF DABAR, 2007.

De Chergé, Christian. *L'Autre que Nous Attendons: Homélies de Père Christian de Chergé (1970–1996).* Montjoyer, France: Abbaye Notre Dame d'Aiguebelle, 2006.

De Chergé, Christian, and Bruno Chenu. *L'Invincible Esperance.* Paris: Bayard, 2007.

Girard, René. *Battling to the End.* Translated by Mary Baker. East Lansing: Michigan State University Press, 2010.

Gutiérrez, Gustavo. *A Theology of Liberation: History, Politics, and Salvation.* Translated and edited by Sr. Caridad Inda and John Eagleson. Rev. ed. Maryknoll, NY: Orbis, 1988.

Instituto de Estudios Centroamericanos y el Rescate. *The Jesuit Assassinations: The Writings of Ellacuría, Martin Baro, and Segundo Montes with a Chronology of the Investigation.* Kansas City: Sheed and Ward, 1990.

John Paul II, Pope. *Redemptoris Missio.* Vatican City: Libreria Editrice Vaticana, December 7, 1990.

Kiser, John. *The Monks of Tibhirine: Faith, Love, and Terror in Algeria.* New York: St. Martin's Griffin, 2002.

———. *Passion pour l'Algérie: les Moines de Thibirine.* Montrouge, France: Nouvelle Cité, 2006.

Lassalle-Klein, Robert. *Blood and Ink: Ignacio Ellacuría, Jon Sobrino, and the Jesuit Martyrs of the University of Central America.* Maryknoll, NY: Orbis, 2014.

Lebreton, Christophe. *Born from the Gaze of God: The Tibhirine Journal of a Martyr Monk (1993–1996).* Translated by Mette Louise Nygard. Monastic Wisdom Series 37. Collegeville, MN: Cistercian/Liturgical, 2014.

Lewis, Thomas A. "Actions as the Ties That Bind: Love, Praxis, and Community in the Thought of Gustavo Gutiérrez." *The Journal of Religious Ethics* 33:3 (September 2005) 539–67.

Minassian, Marie Dominique. "Itinéraire et Spiritualité du Frère Christophe, Moine de Tibhirine." *Liens Cisterciens* 11 (October 2006) 35–48. https://www.arccis.org/downloads/itinerairefrerechristophe.pdf.

Olivera, Bernardo. *How Far to Follow? The Martyrs of Atlas.* Petersham, MA: St. Bede's, 1997.

Ray, Marie-Christine. *Christian de Cherge, Prieur de Tibhirine.* Paris: Bayard-Centurion, 1998.

Salenson, Christian. *Christian de Cherge: Une Theologie de l'Esperance.* Montrouge, Francis: Bayard, 2009.

———. *Prier 15 Jours avec Christian de Chergé: Prieur des Moines de Tibhirine.* Collection Prier 15 Jours 102. Montrouge, Francie: Nouvelle Cité, 2006.

Sobrino, Jon. *La Fe en Jesucristo: Ensayo desde las Víctimas.* Madrid: Trotta, 1999.

"Testament of Christian de Chergé." Order of Cistercians of Strict Observance, n.d. https://ocso.org/history/saints-blesseds-martyrs/testament-of-christian-de-cherge/.

Vatican Council II. *Gaudium et Spes.* Vatican City: Libreria Editrice Vaticana, 1965. https://www.vatican.va/archive/hist_councils/ii_vatican_council/documents/vat-ii_const_19651207_gaudium-et-spes_en.html.

———. *Nostra Aetate: Declaration of the Relation of the Church to Non-Christian Religions.* Vatican City: Libreria Editrice Vaticana, 1965. http://www.vatican.va/archive/hist_councils/ii_vatican_council/documents/vat-ii_decl_19651028_nostra-aetate_en.html.

Whitfield, Teresa. *Paying the Price: Ignacio Ellacuría and the Murdered Jesuits of El Salvador.* Philadelphia: Temple University Press, 1995.

Young, Robin D. *In Procession Before the World: Martyrdom as Public Liturgy in Early Christianity.* Milwaukee: Marquette University Press, 2001.

PART TWO

Practicing Gospel Nonviolence in a Violent World: Reports and Reflections

4

Peace Is an Open Workshop

Mauro Garofalo

It's my honor to be here and I thank you for inviting me. This is my first time in Chicago, and it's a good chance for me to visit this beautiful city.

"Put away your sword"—what a great subject for a conference. It puts us exactly at the center of the Gospel of St. Matthew during the passion of our Lord.

The first question that comes to my mind is: Why did the disciples not understand? We know they were tired, they were sad, they could barely stand or stay awake in this moment. . . . And all of a sudden, violence enters in the form of a mob with swords and clubs, led by someone they knew very well, Judas, who had always been with them. And sadness and tiredness gave way to rage and violence. And violence came, and it was Peter, a leader for the Twelve, who struck the servant of the high priest.

It was not the first time in their three years of following and listening to Jesus that he had clearly rejected violence. Just a few hours earlier, during the Last Supper, Jesus was clear to his friends as they presented him with two swords, to which he said, "Enough."

And this "enough" is one of the keywords in the Gospel—"enough." Before that he said, "But I say unto you that you should not resist evil" (Matt 5:39). All throughout three years of public life, Jesus was always very clear about violence, but the disciples gave way to violence and eventually fled from Jesus in his moment of need. But again, I did not come all the way from Rome to preach on the gospel. I'm not a priest, and I'm not a theologian!

Maybe I'm the only one during these three days of conference who is not a professor or a theologian. I came all this way to tell you about the story of the Community of Sant'Egidio. Our moderator already said something about us: "They pray every day; they put the gospel at the center of their life," and other beautiful things!

So, in the first part of my [talk], I will try to explain very briefly what the Community of Sant'Egidio is. Very briefly, because I cannot squeeze fifty years of our story into forty minutes. It's impossible! In the second part, I will talk about why a Christian community like ours got involved in mediation and conflict resolution starting from zero. This is why we have chosen the title for this talk of "Peace Is an Open Workshop." And in the third and last part, I will try to underline some aspects of our work to [show] more concretely what we do, together with some notion of our methodology of conflict resolution. Some situations and some scenarios that we mentioned are still ongoing, so you will forgive me if I'm not too specific.

Let's get straight to the point . . . the Community of Sant'Egidio. Some of you have been to our central headquarters in Trastevere, a lovely neighborhood in Rome. It is in a small former monastery, a convent for Carmelite nuns that used to be a very strict cloister. The nuns could never go out. They were called by the people of the neighborhood the "buried-alive nuns." It became the central place of Sant'Egidio in 1973. To be very honest with you, we actually squatted in the place, because it was abandoned, so we gave new life to a Christian building. There, a small group of high school students, younger than the students of this university, began to gather every day to pray together and to serve the poor. This first group had already been formed by 1968, a year of movements, protests, and riots, but these young students understood that, truly, the world had to change. But first of all, they had to change their hearts and put the gospel at the center of their lives.

Today, in order to better explain what Sant'Egidio is, I will refer to the words of Pope Francis during his speech on the occasion of his first visit to Sant'Egidio in 2014, a few months after his election. He said, "In some countries suffering from war, you seek to keep hope for peace alive. Working for peace doesn't bring quick results, but it is the work of patient artisans who seek what unites and set aside that which divides, as Saint John XXIII said," and then he told us to "go forward on this path of prayer, the poor, and peace."[1]

These are the three main vocations of Sant'Egidio: prayer, the poor, and peace. These three elements stand together. You cannot imagine a member of Sant'Egidio such as I am who works for peace but does not serve the poor.

---

1. Francis, "To the Sant'Egidio Community," para. 8.

You cannot imagine a member of Sant'Egidio who serves the poor but does not attend to prayer—it is impossible. The three of them stand together.

Prayer. Prayer is the heart of the life of the community of Sant'Egidio and an absolute priority. At the end of the day, every community of Sant'Egidio, large or small, gathers around the word of God. A common, simple, and family prayer open to everybody is, in fact, the very basis of the whole life of the community. The disciples cannot do other than remain at the feet of Jesus.

The Poor. The poor are not, for us, a social target. Serving them is not only a way to restore social justice, but the poor are brothers and sisters, friends of the community, members of the community. The elderly, homeless, migrants, disabled, street children, minors, prisoners . . . these are our companions. The first students back in 1968 met around the word of God, and they felt the gospel was calling them to be close to the poor. Our dream was (and still is) to change the lives of the least in society by offering them our presence, a profound affection, and a second chance in life. Since then, this friendship has stretched out to other poor people: children in institutes, the lonely and sick elderly, the physically and mentally disabled, people living in the streets, the terminally ill, prisoners, gypsies, migrants, lepers, and people with HIV. Through the years, the community has developed a way to be sensitive to all forms of poverty, whether old, new, or emerging. On Christmas Day, immediately after Mass, we go into the lunchroom for a Christmas lunch with the poor. This is a true icon for Sant'Egidio. I am proud that, last year—just to give you some numbers—250,000 people had Christmas lunch in the church with us. Yes, the church is wherever we are. During Christmastime, those who are usually alone are even more so, so we need to spend time with our friends.

The Community of Sant'Egidio identifies itself with all of these people who are, without exception, part of the community. Service to the poor is rooted in gratuity and voluntary work, because we are all volunteers. No one is paid at Sant'Egidio. About this interpretation of friendship, let me quote Pope Francis again, who said to us, "It becomes unclear who helps and who is being helped. Who leads the action? Both of them, or, to say it better, the embrace leads."[2]

The first group of Sant'Egidio consisted of ten people. Now, we are around eighty thousand members in seventy countries.

I would love to switch now to the second part of my [talk], which is "peace is an open workshop."[3] Who said that? It was Pope Saint John Paul

2. Francis, "To the Sant'Egidio Community," para. 4.
3. This is my [the author's] translation from the original Italian, but the quote as

II. He told us at Sant'Egidio that "peace is something so important that it cannot be left only in the hands of professional mediators, politicians, and diplomats." It's something so important—I daresay, so essential—that it requires contributions from everyone. Common people, men and women of goodwill, believers, entrepreneurs, academics, students—I really mean everyone. The words "peace is an open workshop" were a great inspiration for us, because they were addressed to a community that was expanding its presence in various parts the world.

But becoming an international presence also meant that, for us, war and violence were suddenly not just a strategic thing or something that we could read about in a book . . . [these were] a real haunting presence in our lives. They were no longer something we heard about from our grandpa who was a soldier in the Second World War but instead a threat to brothers and sisters of the Community of Sant'Egidio in war-torn regions. They even became a tragic reality when members of Sant'Egidio were killed [in the] war in Mozambique, the nation of our first community in Africa.

We realized two things. First, it was impossible to help poor people through our communities, particularly in our community in Mozambique, because everything is lost in war. Second, war is very real. It's a wound on the skin of the Community of Sant'Egidio, so doing something about it was compulsory. Mozambique was a strange adventure, because it was the location of a civil war that had been going on for more than a decade with a stunning death toll. It was a war between an Afro-Marxist government and an almost unknown rebel group, the *barbudos armados* . . . the bearded bandits.

So, we decided to do something about that war, because it was necessary to do something. For various reasons, no one was paying attention to a conflict that had seen more than a million deaths. We first got involved to protect the church, which was seen by the Marxist FRELIMO government as a legacy of Portuguese colonization. We managed to secure some space of freedom for the church, and we got in contact with the guerillas. To make a long story short, I would simply say that a peace process started at our headquarters. It involved twenty-seven months of confidential negotiations with, of course, the help of some governments, including the US, the former colonial power, Portugal, and Italy, which secured visas for delegates, for example. . . . Not an easy thing to do even today. We "locked" the rebels and the government in that small convent while the war was still going on, and in the end, on the fourth of October, the day of Saint Francis, a peace

---

published on the Vatican's website is, "Peace is a workshop, open to all." John Paul II, "Address to the Representatives," 7.

agreement was signed. And all of a sudden, the world realized that there was this thing called Sant'Egidio.

Journalists and the international media became aware of Sant'Egidio and had a lot of questions for us: How did you do that? Why did a little humanitarian Catholic organization get involved in this process? Did you change your vocation? When? We told them that we never changed our vocation. It's the same vocation—helping the poor—and the truth is that, as stated by our founder, Andrea Riccardi, "war is the mother of poverty," and there is a link between conflict resolution and love for the poor. So, this is how it all began in Mozambique at the end of the 1980s.

Let me now go back to the words of Pope Francis about "patient artisans." Making peace involves the craftsmanship of patient artisans, not only mediators, experts, and diplomats. Peace, I want to stress, is a vocation for all the members of our community, at all levels. It is not by chance that many of the activities of Sant'Egidio fall into the category of peacemaking.

There is, for example, the School of Peace. The School of Peace is a free after-school program for children. In many countries in the developing world, this is the only school the children attend. It is a foundational activity of Sant'Egidio to gather the children and teach them. This was Sant'Egidio's and my personal first service to the poor—children and adolescents from all over the world and from every faith and ethnicity studied together and learned the beauty of living together and growing together in harmony. This involves peacebuilding, as does *the People of Peace,* which is a movement of former migrants, former refugees who were welcomed by Sant'Egidio not only in Italy but also in Belgium and most of the countries where we are present; its members also became members of Sant'Egidio in some way. They come from various ethnic groups and religions and carry with them difficult stories of suffering, but in contact with the community, they find the strength to become themselves as promoters of friendship and hospitality. I should also mention the March for Peace, which takes place wherever there is a community on New Year's Day to mark the Catholic Church's international day of peace.

These are a few examples of the life of the Community of Sant'Egidio. The community represents a prophecy of how we can live together; it is precisely the crises engendered by living together that is at the origin of many conflicts. Those who say they are from Sant'Egidio tell the world, "Yes, we can live together" and "Yes, the complexity of the world in which we live does not scare us." This is true of many communities around the world, and I especially think about members of Sant'Egidio in Burundi, in the Great Lakes region, but also about the communities in Russia and Ukraine where members are brothers despite the difficulties. And I will always proudly say that our evening prayer in Moscow, as well as our evening prayer elsewhere in Russia, is not a prayer for victory but a prayer for peace. We do not pray to defeat someone, because we have no enemies.

So, by learning the art of living together, peace can be built. And let's say that after Mozambique, many other countries came knocking on our door in search of peace. Algeria was more difficult and had different results, but there was also Guinea, Burkina Faso, Niger, Guatemala, etc. We work in North Korea as well—I've been there three times with a delegation from Sant'Egidio to help orphanages and elderly homes, because the situation there is quite terrible, as you can imagine.

Slowly, Sant'Egidio became an independent international subject recognized by many state and international organizations and was nicknamed by a journalist, "the small UN of Trastevere." He was exaggerating, of course, but we built credibility by doing something that is generally reserved for politicians and diplomats. And even though we never became diplomatic professionals, we are able to engage in dialogue with people at all levels.

So, where are we active right now? This is the third part of [this talk]. We are working on three or four different scenarios. The first is the Central African Republic [CAR], a country that, you may know, has been experiencing a lot of difficulties since 2013, and you could say since their independence in the sixties. There have been sixteen coup d'états in the history of the country. The normal way of becoming president is to kill or to exile the previous one. There is now a democratically elected president, which is a sign of hope. Sant'Egidio got involved in 2013. The CAR is bigger than France in area but has only four million inhabitants. It is situated in a difficult neighborhood, near Chad, South Sudan, Sudan, Cameroon, and DR Congo. The country was in big trouble in 2013 when President Bozizé was ousted by a coup d'état again by the so-called Seleka, which is an alliance of many Muslim groups, but there are many components of that. As usual, as often happens, the international community underestimated the impact of what happened. They said "OK. It is the sixteenth coup d'état. They will play around with power and share the money of the people and things will go as usual."

Unfortunately, that time was far more difficult, far more dangerous, because Seleka was characterized as Muslim. The Christians reacted by forming other armed groups called the anti-balaka. Thus, a conflict that began over the sharing of power became an interfaith conflict, and the situation spiraled out of control, resulting in three years of violence. Sant'Egidio intervened, and the result was meetings with representatives of the fourteen armed groups in the country, one for each group, which tells you a lot about the fragmentation of the scenario. Mozambique was different: there was one rebel group and one government. The CAR is more complicated. We started talking with the armed groups and working with the religious communities. Sant'Egidio has had a multilevel engagement with the country since 2013. An agreement was eventually signed among the numerous armed groups in June 2017.

We also worked with the political parties. There are dozens of political parties in the Central African Republic. Simply organizing free and fair elections and campaigns that use nonviolent language is an extremely difficult task but is extremely important, especially in African countries, in which the electoral process often leads to immediate violence. I'm not talking about civil war. I'm talking about riots, protests, and manifestations, but injuries and death always occur.

Then, there are the religious communities. You might think that at least the priests and nuns would agree. Well, not exactly. Even today, as we speak, there are some responsible religious communities that are against the peace agreement. They are against this process. . . . And now, as we speak, and I cannot go into detail, an agreement was signed in Khartoum.

And, of course, Sant'Egidio is also engaged at a humanitarian level in the disarmament process. This is something new for us. But imagine . . . fourteen armed groups—small, medium, and large—in possession of Kalashnikov rifles and nothing else. Their lives depend on their Kalashnikovs. This is a new thing for us—we have never participated in disarmament before, even in Mozambique. We are always taking on new challenges.

We are also engaged in Libya, which presents an almost impossible situation; it is a clear example of the failure of the international community. Because there is a UN mission, there is a mediation panel. There is a club of countries, seemingly friends of Libya, but everyone has a hidden agenda. Everyone has a different idea about what should happen, and the armed groups are profiting from that.

What we are doing now is working with the southern tribes. We are also working on local cease-fire agreements and treaties, whether among tribes, between one city and another, or within the same city. These are important, but it is often said that you also have to address the overall picture . . . you have to solve the main problem. Yes, but in a country as fragmented as Libya, even a small cease-fire in the town of Sabha—the capital of the Fezzan region in the south of the country with eight thousand inhabitants—is something that could improve the life of the people and ensure access to humanitarian aid. These small steps can lower the level of violence in the country and are very important. Pope Francis has said that we are living in the midst of a third world war in a time of peace. This is true, as we all know, and means that we need to work for peace in a time of peace as well. We should not give up on smaller problems, because there is a larger problem to solve. Who knows when the warring rivals Serraj and Haftar will arrive at an agreement? We don't know. But the general population has asked for our mediation, and we are doing that. I think that it is important to follow every single path for peace that is presented to us without giving up on anything.

I would love to tell you about our third engagement, also in the same region. . . . The vast majority of world conflicts are going on in Africa, unfortunately. I am talking about South Sudan. You may still have in your eyes the image of Pope Francis kneeling before the country's political rivals, Kiir and Machar. It was a shocking image. Even I thought, "This is too much. The pope should not kneel in front of them." But this tells us how far he is willing to go to achieve peace. It was really an example for everyone.

The first thing that must be said is that South Sudan casts shame on us as Christians. It is a country that became independent on the basis that Christians would be free from Muslim oppression. And on day two of their independence, finally free from this oppression, they commenced killing themselves. It's a defeat not only for the country—it's a defeat for us all. Whether they are Catholic, Presbyterian, or Anglican, they were killing each other with great enthusiasm.

An agreement was signed in December 2018, less than one year ago, which has resulted in a lowering of the violence. Some of the rebels did not sign it, and the reaction of the international community was "You did not sign; you're a spoiler. We'll sanction you." This has resulted in the violence ratcheting back up, especially in the south of the country. We are now working confidentially with some of these factions to bring them back into the framework of the agreement.

I also want to talk to you about the Casamance region of Senegal. All of you have heard about Senegal, but not all of you have heard about Casamance, which is in the southern part of Senegal. It is the richest and most fertile part of the country, and it has been the location of an independence movement that has been active since the 1980s. This movement (founded by a priest) has paralyzed the region; some areas contain so many land mines that they cannot be accessed by anyone. So, when Macky Sall was elected president of Senegal, we became the official mediator between the guerrilla movement and the country's government. There have been off-and-on negotiations for seven years. Once every two months, representatives come and discuss but thus far have not achieved an agreement. I am sometimes asked whether we are being a bit naïve, and the answer is that perhaps we are, but at the same time, no one has been killed in those seven years. There has been no fighting at all. There have been small agreements that have resulted in the freeing of hostages—I was present when they released the last seven soldiers captured by the guerrillas. To me, that's enough, but not the enough of Jesus. By enough, I mean it's something.

This has been characterized as a low-intensity conflict. Many people love to categorize conflicts and violence, but I don't [like] this. A conflict is a conflict. If a farmer cannot go to the field because there are mines, if truck drivers have to pay taxes at every checkpoint, this is not a society in which I would like to live. It can be a low-intensity conflict, but it's still a conflict if children cannot go to school.

If I had more time, I could also mention other conflicts we are engaged in, in Mindanao and other places.

Let me underline some aspects of our methodology. First of all, fidelity to a situation—the ability to maintain patience waiting for new roads to peace to be opened. I just mentioned Casamance, where we had to wait twenty-four years to do something. It was not possible, because previous presidents did not want to open negotiations, saying publicly that "we will defeat them." When Macky Sall was elected, however, we finally saw a space, and we moved.

Second is a certain disinterestedness, which means that we are not perceived to be an instrument of this power or that nation or international organization. As we said about Libya, the lack of an honest broker is a big problem for the negotiations. Sant'Egidio does not deal with natural resources, and we do not have a stake in any economic issues, so if you want to come to Sant'Egidio to discuss, you are very welcome.

Third is complementarity with other mediators. This is important because sometimes mediators compete with each other. Sometimes, meetings with the mediators are necessary to decide who will do what. It is becoming more and more complicated. We have to work with governments, international organizations, and other NGOs. An example is the negotiations related to Guatemala: there was a UN panel of mediation plus negotiations going on in Mexico City, and the entire process became paralyzed. A few meetings in Rome at Sant'Egidio helped to unblock, to jump-start, the process. We were able to make a small contribution to peace.

I should also mention interfaith dialogue, which was important in South Sudan and elsewhere.

Who are we then in this complicated world? We are the people who treat HIV for free. We are the ones who teach in the School of Peace. It's a good name—it identifies us. We have to trust in the possibility of change for everyone. We can change. At the bottom of every man's heart, there is a desire for peace. We have witnessed change on multiple occasions, change as the detoxification from the poison that is violence. What can I say? These are things that the UN should pay more attention to.

So, in conclusion, everyone can change, and we need to heal men's souls and hearts from the wounds of violence. Peace is an open workshop. Peace is always possible. We know this from our thirty years of experience and hope, which guides the work of so many people. John Paul II was right. Peace is an open workshop, but we need lots of workers, so feel free to apply.

Thank you so much.

Bibliography

Francis, Pope. "Address of Pope Francis to the Sant'Egidio Community." Speech given at the Basilica of Santa Maria in Trastevere, Rome, June 15, 2014. https://www.vatican.va/content/francesco/en/speeches/2014/june/documents/papa-francesco_20140615_comunita-sant-egidio.html.

John Paul II, Pope. "Address of John Paul II to the Representatives of the Christian Churches and Ecclesial Communities and of the World Religions." Speech given at the Basilica of St. Francis in Assisi, Italy, October 27, 1986. https://www.vatican.va/content/john-paul-ii/en/speeches/1986/october/documents/hf_jp-ii_spe_19861027_prayer-peace-assisi-final.html.

5

Martyrs at the Margins: Rethinking Martyrdom in the Time of Violent Populism

Daniel Franklin E. Pilario, CM

Martyrs are considered martyrs because they were killed out of their persecutors' hatred of the Christian faith (*odium fidei*). Beyond this classical criterion, however, there has been a direction toward its theological rethinking. Óscar Romero, ignored by Vatican authorities for a long time despite universal clamor after his murder by government forces in El Salvador, has been recently raised to the altars. His murderers did not kill him because they hated the Christian faith. They, too, could have been Catholics themselves. No, he was killed because he stood up for the rights of the poor and the downtrodden in his diocese, a position that clashed with the interests of political and military powers. For this, he is named a martyr—the "martyr of the Church of the Second Vatican Council," as Archbishop Vincenzo Paglia, the postulator of the cause of his beatification, called him.[1]

As the church opens its notion of martyrdom beyond *odium fidei*, this paper attempts to respond to a new challenge. In the context of violent populist regimes as presently experienced in the Philippines, more than 33,000 fathers, young men and, in some cases women and children, have been viciously killed because they were listed on the government list of drug users. To have a "drug-free country" is the government's banner political project. The victims were fathers killed while in the act of feeding their children; poor garbage workers resting with friends after a hard day's labor;

1. O'Connell, "Archbishop Romero."

young men who were merely doing errands at night; students going home from school—all fulfilling their everyday Christian duty of love, compassion, and service. I am not only talking of the thousands of victims in the Philippines. There are millions worldwide who are innocent and unwilling victims of rising populist regimes. Can the church raise them to the altars and consider them martyrs in the present times? I intend to answer this question in four parts: (1) I will narrate some details of the so-called "war on drugs" in the Philippines; (2) I will contextualize these events in the emerging populist regimes worldwide and their accompanying violence wrecked on poor and helpless victims; (3) to contextualize my argument, I will offer a cursory survey of the notions of martyrdom throughout the centuries, and lastly; (4) I will offer a theological reflection on the heroic lives of what I call "martyrs at the margins."

1. Extrajudicial Killings in the Philippines

The Philippine National Police reported that there were 5,526 persons—mostly men—who were killed in 134,583 anti-drug police operations from July 1, 2016 (the day after President Rodrigo Duterte assumed office) to June 30, 2019.[2] At the time of this writing (March 2020), the number has risen since the president announced this government's flagship program in a "more chilling manner." Beyond the official police report, human rights organizations and media outlets record 27,000 to 33,000 "deaths under investigation" (DUI) which are drug-related, although there is really no official count on this to date. There was only one case that led to conviction—that of a seventeen-year-old boy, Kian de los Santos, whose murder was caught on CCTV camera. Three police officers now suffer twenty to forty years of imprisonment without parole,[3] while the other hundreds go scot-free. As of this writing, the UN Human Rights Council has officially received the report of the high commissioner for human rights, Michele Bachelet, which talks of 8,663 documented drug-related killings and 248 deaths of human rights defenders, human right professionals, journalists, and other government critics.[4] The majority of cases in police records indicate that the victim "fought back" in a firefight with police personnel, though some deaths were strangely labeled in the police reports as stroke or heart attack.

---

2. Cabico, "Revised Drug War," paras. 2–3.
3. Buan, "Policemen Guilty," para. 2.
4. UN Human Rights Office of the High Commissioner, "Philippines," para. 4.

These gruesome killing sprees are documented by journalists and filmmakers, sometimes with the consent of the police authorities themselves.[5]

Together with those killed are 193,086 arrested drug suspects who are in unhealthy prisons overflowing with inmates all throughout the country. "Arrests of suspected drug offenders have also contributed to a 534 percent prison congestion rate—among the highest in the world," the Office of the High Commissioner for Human Rights (OHCHR) report points out.[6] These arrests were made without warrants, and crime evidence was often tampered with or falsified. To date, no investigations or trials have been initiated by police authorities, government agencies, or local courts. When the United Nations, international media, and human rights groups became interested in the situation, Duterte and his minions prohibited the release of police records even when demanded by the Supreme Court.

In later developments, the targets went beyond drug users and sellers; they were extended to include human rights lawyers, activists, critics of the government, church workers, local politicians, and poor farmers suspected of being communists. On September 25, 2019, three years after his inauguration, Duterte was relentless in his resolve: "If you go into drugs, I will kill you. Even with the United Nations listening, I will kill you, period."[7]

To give a face to this violent situation, let me narrate the story of Constantino de Juan, or just "Juan," as his friends call him. I was present at his wake and later at his funeral. And I have journeyed with his family ever since.[8] Juan was a father to six children, and his wife was pregnant with their seventh child; he worked as a waste-picker at the Payatas garbage dump in Quezon City. He was told that his name was on the drug hit list. One night, a group of policemen came into his house, breaking down his walls to force themselves in, but he was not there. They captured his pregnant wife instead. When she was interrogated at the police station, they asked for the whereabouts of her husband. If she could point out where he was, she would be freed. She did not. For this, she was incarcerated for a year and eight months without charges. And she delivered her seventh child in prison.

In the meantime, Juan was working in another city to escape the police but could not take it anymore, knowing that his children were left to the care of his eighty-five-year-old mother. He knew he was placing his own life in danger, but he decided to go home, even if to see his children for just

---

5. For example, see in general, Frontline PBS, "On the President's Orders"; CBC News: The National, "Horror of the Philippines' Drug War"; Human Rights Watch, "Police Fake Evidence"; and CBS News, "In-Depth Look."

6. UN Human Rights Office of the High Commissioner, "Philippines," para. 9.

7. Human Rights Watch, *World Report 2020*, 462.

8. See, in general, St. Vincent School of Theology, "Street Theater."

a few moments. He went home at night to avoid the surveillance cameras stationed all over the place. He was with his children that night and cooked spaghetti for breakfast. It was the birthday of one of his daughters. They were happy that morning. He missed his children, and they missed him. He first fed them and prepared them for school. But when it was his turn to eat, five armed men barged into the house and let him raise his hands in surrender. They dragged the children out the door and shot him. He was still able to beg for his life and knelt, pleading, "Please don't kill me. Imprison me if you want but please do not kill me. I have seven children, and my wife is still in prison. No one is going to take care of them." The armed men did not listen; instead, they landed four more bullets in different parts of his body. One of his daughters saw what happened. Before the shooting, she had hugged her father, and he told her, "Do not leave your younger sisters and brothers." When he was lying there dead, the armed men put a small gun to his right and illegal drugs on his left. They took a photo of the crime scene and sent it to news outlets. The next day, the headlines said, "He fought back."[9] Juan is just one among the many thousands with parallel narratives.[10] In Payatas alone, we estimated more than a hundred deaths. After their funerals, the families left the place in fear; others continued to grieve in silence, not wanting to see anyone or talk about it, while others decided to fight in order to survive. These widows, mothers, and orphans organized themselves into a group called "Solidarity with Orphans and Widows" (SOW) to take care of themselves, to look for livelihood that will bring food to their tables, which was done before by their dead breadwinners, and to seek justice for the deaths of their loved ones.[11]

On the one hand, the government storyline is that Juan was both a drug user and small-time drug dealer, and for this, he deserved his death. Since he fought back, he had to be "neutralized" (police jargon for "killing") in the name of self-defense. Beyond that, in the government's view, Juan was a pest to society. Drugs had destroyed his human capacities beyond

9. This is my own narration of what happened, based on my numerous discussions with Juan's family. For the original news article that reported on Juan's death, see Enano, "QC Cops Kill 7." It says, "One operation ended in the killing of a man known only as 'Buhay' and his unidentified companion. Another drug-bust cornered their neighbor, 30-year-old scavenger Constantino de Juan. The QCPD said two .38-caliber revolvers, a .45-caliber pistol, and five sachets of suspected 'shabu' were recovered from the three slain suspects."

10. For examples of such parallel narratives, see Buan, "Gruesome Tale of Tokhang"; Buan, "TokHang Victim"; Smith, "Families Ripped Apart"; Malig and Taguines, "Left-Behind Children."

11. For more about SOW, see Pilario, "Of Mothers, Widows and Orphans"; Watford, "Finding Hope in the Dark"; and Agence France-Presse, "Grieving Children's Choir."

repair, and all addicts like him are hopeless to rehabilitate—or so the official narrative goes. Juan's neighbors, mostly supporters of Duterte, believe this dominant storyline, because it is popularized on the airwaves and social media. They did not come to the wake. They did not condole with the family. They were afraid the police might come back, or they might also have thought that the government was right.

On the other hand, in the eyes of his family, Juan was a caring and responsible father. They were only happy that he came back. "They were happy that morning," grandmother Remy recalled. "He was always a loving father to them." Knowing that his name was on the list and he was being hunted, returning to the area was a huge risk to his life. But he did not mind it. He was worried about the children. And then, the inevitable came.

2. Populism and Violence

During the 2016 presidential campaign, Duterte proclaimed that, once elected, "The funeral parlors will be packed. . . . I'll supply the bodies."[12] Critics refer to his war on drugs as a "Kill, Kill, Kill" program, mimicking his government's hyper-infrastructure venture called "Build, Build, Build." The police were transformed into a killing machine aimed at sowing fear among the populace, putting off dissent, and demanding subservience. Paul Chevigny, who studied police killings in Latin America in the 1980s, found parallel characteristics: the victims are mostly poor, and the killings happen in urban districts, all done in deterrence to crime. "Police violence can serve as an instrument of coercive social control as long as it can be characterized as a justifiable response to violent crime."[13] He argues that these everyday killings should be distinguished from political deaths under dictatorial rule. The intention in Latin America was not to punish political opponents but to make ordinary people toe the line. This seems to be the same objective in the Philippines. The chilling effect on the population wards off uproar against the violence and widespread dissent among the populace. Thanks to the propaganda machine of social media and trolls, Duterte consistently enjoys an 80 percent approval rating in opinion polls. However, the distinction between populist and dictatorial violence was blurred as the war on drug addicts later metamorphosed into a battle against political rivals, government critics, and human rights workers.

Regarding the violence of populist regimes, one can discern two directions. On the one hand, there is performative violence, which is directed

12. Agence France-Presse, "Kill the Criminals," para. 6.
13. Chevigny, "Police Deadly Force," 407.

against local dissent and used to project a strong domestic government for the international community to see. With Singapore as a model, the Filipino government wants to assert that our local situation has unique needs and circumstance, thus, we owe it to our people to interpret the universal human rights discourse in context. In this view, the insistence on noninterference becomes the government's rallying cry against what is sometimes rightly perceived as foreign imposition. On the other hand, strong rhetoric against foreign bodies—e.g., the United Nations, United States, European Union, and human rights organizations—aims to tell the people that the president has full control of the defense of our national sovereignty.[14]

But Duterte is not alone in this. Populist politics have been in existence for quite some time.[15] The populist governments growing worldwide are characterized by similar rhetorical violence against local populations, ethnic minorities, and secessionist groups. Leaders of such governments include Recep Erdogan of Turkey; Vladimir Putin of Russia; Jair Bolsonaro of Brazil; Narendra Modi of India; Norbert Hofer of Austria; Marine Le Pen of France; Viktor Orban of Hungary; Geert Wilders of the Netherlands; and Donald Trump of the United States.[16] Having surprisingly gained massive support among their peoples, all of these populist leaders display the necessary violence needed both to keep people "in place" and to project a particular international image. Because of this, their nameless victims—dead, disappeared, or effectively banished—also abound.

The headlines give us a hint about who and where these victims are. How many victims among immigrant families died while being held at the US-Mexican border, and how many boatloads of people capsized in the sea that borders Europe and North Africa or Europe and the Middle East? How many indigenous peoples were slaughtered or pushed to deadly hunger and poverty by Bolsonaro's pro-capitalist policies in the Amazon? How many indigenous suffer in the refugee camps of Asia and Africa? How many deaths are caused by the aerial bombings and chemical weapons in Assad's Syria with support coming from Putin's Russia? How many Rohingya Muslims died on the rough seas after being refused entry by Myanmar and neighboring countries? There are no existing statistics, but these brutal situations exist all over the world, and the victims are impossible to name and count.[17]

14. McCoy, "Philippine Populism," 514–22.

15. For some current literature on populism, in general, the following: Gidron and Bonikowski, "Varieties of Populism"; Allcock, "Populism"; Moffitt, *Global Rise of Populism*; Kaltwasser et al., *Oxford Handbook of Populism*; Taggart, *Populism*.

16. See generally, "Global Rise of Populism."

17. For a helpful overview of populism around the world, see Roth, "Dangerous Rise of Populism."

Our focus is on the victims of violence in populist regimes. Beyond that, in the context of our globalized world, there are many others who died violent deaths, most of them nameless and unrecognized. Ours is a world of victims and victimizers. Writing in 2003, the Latin American liberation theologian, Jon Sobrino, observes:

> Auschwitz, Hiroshima, and the Gulags are behind us, but millions of human beings continue to suffer massively, unjustly, and innocently in repressions, wars, and massacres. Many millions more suffer a slow death from poverty, particularly women and children, besides the death of their dignity and their cultures. So-called globalization has not changed things; it has rather increased the number of the "excluded." Two figures from the present: 1,300 million people live on less than a dollar a day; in the Democratic Republic of Congo, around three million have died over the past four years in a war provoked by powerful nations' control of its mineral wealth. Most of these deaths have definite causes: either active, when they are inflicted by institutions and authorities, or passive, when many of these tragedies are not prevented, even though they could have been.[18]

There are identifiable individuals but there are unknown masses too—all victims of the world's cruelty. Some stood up in faithful defiance; others were mere unwilling victims, and others, more unwitting casualties. They all suffered violent deaths in their struggle to survive and live decent lives. How do we name them? We are at a loss for words. They are given many names: "crucified peoples"; "the pierced Christs" (Óscar Romero); "Jesus martyrs" (Jon Sobrino).[19] Can they be called martyrs?

Perspectives on Martyrdom: A Cursory Survey

My concern with the above analysis of the worldwide sociopolitical context is its victims and martyrs: those who are killed by the empire. If "martyrs" are, traditionally, believers who died "out of hatred for the faith," can these new victims also be called martyrs? There are always two perspectives to the martyrdom narratives in the different epochs of Christian history: the dominant perspective, "from above," of those who hold power—that is, from the official storyline of the empire—and the minority view, "from below," of the persecuted Christian communities themselves. From above, the victims were killed because they were criminals, threats to the existing social order

18. Sobrino, "Our World," 15–16.
19. Sobrino, "Our World," 15–23.

and disobedient to the laws of the regime. From below, these martyrs were killed because they were faithful—to the point of dying—to their human and Christian calling in the face of hostile powers. These two views are understandable because of their interested sociopolitical locations. But even within the Christian narrative itself, the historiography of martyrdom keeps shifting according to different times and contexts.

First, the Christian martyr is one who died in *odium fidei* (hatred of the faith). When the Roman Empire was threatened by the new Christian movement, the believers were sought out as criminals. Before they were led to the stake or the lions, they were asked whether they believed in Christ and were members of the Christian sect. The main sign of martyrdom was their personal confession of the faith as the *Acta*, or accounts of death of early martyrs, show.[20] What is the main motive of the Roman persecution of early Christians? Lawrence Cunningham locates it in the threat Christians pose to the state.[21] Though they were an "obscure and secretive alien religious sect"[22] emerging from the margins of the empire, their refusal to externally express their homage to the gods of Rome made them appear blasphemous and disloyal and, thus, a danger to the state's common good. In their refusal to honor the values that the empire represented, they have violated the Roman *pietas* expected of every citizen. Thus, faith in Christ was crucial to confess. It represents an outright defiance to the ideals of the state, and the Christians' subsequent deaths were a consequence of the empire's *odium fidei*. Though there were localized and sporadic persecutions from Nero (64 AD) to Trajan (112 AD), the empire-wide and systematic persecution came in the time of Decius (250 AD) and Diocletian (303–12 AD). Martyrdom was not the only response to persecution. Many complied with the edict and performed the sacrificial ritual in honor of the Roman gods; many others escaped through bribes and forged certificates. Only a tiny minority—those we call martyrs—resisted to the point of death. "It has been estimated that in the entire Roman Empire," Cunningham writes, "less than a thousand died, but it was the constancy and bravery of that singular minority which has been remembered for centuries by the Christian church. The compliance and evasion of the many has been all but forgotten except by historians of the period."[23]

The second step in martyrology's journey can be tagged as deaths *in odium conscientiae*. In the medieval period, when the Catholic Church's

---

20. As an example, see Owen, *Some Authentic Acts*.
21. Cunningham, *Catholic Heritage*, 8–27; this is Cunningham's chapter, "Martyrs."
22. Cunningham, *Catholic Heritage*, 11.
23. Cunningham, *Catholic Heritage*, 13.

hegemonic rule was exercised in collusion with worldly powers—or better still, when Christianity became a political power itself—martyrdom was seen as suppression of individual consciences for the individuals' nonacquiescence and nonsubservience to dominant powers of which the church institution was a crucial player. "They were assailed with dogma, Bible, obedience, judgment, and another salvation. Worse, they were regarded as negative figures to the degree that they were critical, and people did not hesitate to attribute the conflicts which broke out in the mother church to their impiety."[24] They were victims of the system's hatred of conscience (*odium conscientiae*). The accounts of the martyrdom of Joan of Arc, Jan Hus, Girolamo Savonarola, Thomas Beckett, and Thomas More are quite popular, but there were many others who were relegated in the shadows. They stood up for their consciences and were condemned to death by the powerful Christian Church to which they professed allegiance.

Let me give two famous examples. Joan of Arc was an illiterate farm girl who was appointed to head the French army in its battle with the English military sometime in 1429. Only an ailing and desperate regime can agree to a girl who claimed that she was led by the voice of God to bring the French army to victory. And victory she did indeed bring. But the tide turned against her and the French. She was captured and brought before the Inquisition for charges of heresy and cross-dressing with all pro-English clerics as judges. Her trial was rigged from the start, financed as it was by the English Crown. She was executed by being burned in a square in Rouen on May 30, 1431. Her name was rehabilitated at a later trial years after her death, and in 1920, she was canonized and given the liturgical title, "St. Joan of Arc, virgin." The French historian Daniel-Rops comments: "[T]hough its validity is, theologically speaking, somewhat dubious, does not the title 'martyr' spring spontaneously to mind whenever we think of her?"[25] Even in the time of her rehabilitation five hundred years later, "martyrdom" as a description of her death was not taken-for-granted fact.

John Hus, a Czech-Bohemian Catholic theologian, was also burned at the stake, about which Luther later wrote: "I was overwhelmed with astonishment. I could not understand for what cause they had burnt so great a man, who explained the Scriptures with so much gravity and skill."[26] Considered the forerunner of the Reformation, he preached against the abuse of indulgences which were used to collect money to fund war. He also advanced the idea that Jesus was the head of the church, not the popes and

---

24. Chenu et al., *Book of Christian Martyrs*, 10.
25. Daniel-Rops, *Protestant Reformation*, 78.
26. Forrest et al., *Legacy of Preaching*, 247.

bishops. He went to the Council of Constance to avail of the opportunity to defend himself but was, instead, imprisoned. He was later tried and condemned to be burned. The bones of his master Wycliffe were exhumed and burned with him. He refused to retract, despite being given the chance to do so. Instead, he mounted the stake, bravely reciting the *Miserere*. Showing the effect of the hegemonic power of the church, a story is told that "an old woman . . . had brought a log for the stake because she had heard someone say that such an act would win her indulgences. On seeing her, Hus murmured, '*Sancta simplicitas*.'"[27]

However, there were still many missionaries in foreign lands who were killed in the name of *odium fidei*, as they met new cultures and powerful rulers. While Western colonizers exercised high-handedness in proclaiming the faith in the New World, and thus, murdered many natives and destroyed their cultures, the missionaries who went to Asia encountered great opposition from ancient autocratic regimes that led to the martyrdom of the missionaries themselves and their new converts. In China, Japan, Korea, and the Middle East, Christians died for the faith at the hands of kings and emperors.[28]

The third development is a rethinking of martyrdom beyond the previous perspectives to include deaths caused by people's hatred of justice (*odium justitiae*). In the 1983 *Concilium* issue, Karl Rahner argues for broadening the traditional concept to include "a death suffered in active struggle for the Christian faith and its moral demands (including those affecting society as a whole)."[29] Twenty years later, *Concilium* published one whole volume on this very issue. Jon Sobrino argues that martyrs are those who followed the demands of Jesus up to his violent death as the culmination of a life of praxis of justice and defense of the poor and the oppressed. "In the way deaths come about in the Third World today," Sobrino writes, "martyrs are above all those who die like Jesus because their lives, words, and praxis have been essentially—allowing, of course, for matters of degree—like those of Jesus. They suffer a violent death for being like Jesus. This is why I call them 'Jesus martyrs.' In this case, Jesus martyrs are not, strictly speaking, those who die *for* Christ or *because of* Christ, but those who die *like* Jesus and *for the cause of* Jesus."[30] In this reading, Jesus is the first martyr, the first witness. And those who followed his life, those who testified to his truth, those who took up his cause, those who took up his mission to the point of dying—in *sequila Christi*—are martyrs, too. Maximilian Kolbe, Dietrich

27. Daniel-Rops, *Protestant Reformation*, 163 n1.
28. See, for instance, Meroni, *Martyrs in Asia*.
29. Rahner, "Dimensions of Martyrdom," 9–11.
30. Sobrino, "Our World," 19.

Bonhoeffer, Martin Luther King Jr., and, more recently, Óscar Romero, are prominent examples of these "Jesus martyrs" coming from different Christian denominations.

The most controversial path to martyrdom, in my view, is that of Óscar Romero. One hundred thousand people attended his funeral, but the hierarchy—except for a few—were nowhere in sight. He was a saint by popular acclaim, but it took more than two decades for him to be canonized. There are many possible reasons. First is the theological criterion of martyrdom as *odium fidei*. The enemies of Romero always return to this classical definition: Romero died not because his assassins hated the Catholic faith but rather, he was politically assassinated and, thus, not eligible to be raised to the altars as a martyr. A second factor is the opposition against liberation theology, brought about by the growing conservatism in Latin American churches and backed up by some influential personalities at the Vatican and their local ecclesiastical cohorts. Despite his initial conservatism, Romero grew to be a vocal defender of the oppressed in El Salvador and became the face of liberationist ecclesiology in the years following his death. A third factor, which I think is most significant, is political. One author recently commented: "To celebrate Romero, the church has to address unholy episodes in its past—episodes as troubling, in their own way, as the current sexual-abuse scandal."[31] It forces the present church—both in Latin America and Rome—to confront its complicity with past dictatorial regimes, its silence on the killing of thousands during this rule, the disappearances of activists and *campesinos*, the collusion with political and economic policies of the United States and local rulers, etc. When these agents within the church still hold power, raising Romero to the altars can also be seen as an act of self-indictment.

The fourth step in rethinking martyrdom are the deaths out of hatred for love of neighbor (*odium amoris, odium misericordiae*). Jon Sobrino differentiates three kinds of martyrs: the classical martyrs; the "Jesus martyrs" like Romero or Bonhoeffer; and the "crucified peoples" of the Third World who die *en masse,* without recognition or dignity, as victims of political repression, ethnic cleansing, or poverty. "This martyrdom is produced not out of *odium fidei* but out of *odium justitiae*, or—more deeply and extensively—*odium misericordiae*, hatred for a mercy that defines the deepest nature of Jesus and his God, described by Luke as being 'moved to compassion.' This is martyrdom in the line of John's 'greater love.'"[32]

---

31. Elie, "What Óscar Romero's Canonization," para. 4.
32. Sobrino, "Our World," 19.

These contemporary martyrs have lives far different from the prominent trajectories of Bonhoeffer or Romero. Their deaths were not as dramatic; their lives were so ordinary, commonplace, and unheroic. But they also met equally violent deaths as they expressed their commitment and fidelity to their families and friends. Many of them were ordinary sons or daughters, fathers or mothers, farmers or laborers—working on meager incomes for their families. Some of them were not even pious, nor were they staunch defenders of the faith. They were merely doing what an ordinary human person is expected to do: to love their neighbor, to take care of their families, to show compassion to someone in need, to be of help in any way whatsoever. Their violent deaths are signs of their Christian love for neighbor in living the way of compassion carved out by Jesus himself. Because of their great number—to the point of anonymity—the *Acta* of their martyrdom have not yet been collected, but the narratives of their deaths are even more chillingly gruesome.

3. Martyrs at the Margins: Theological Reflection

What I would like to argue for is the recognition of nonheroic martyrs, persons who were not, at first, actually resolved to offer their lives joyfully for the faith like the martyrs of old who were said to be singing while being led to the lions. These individuals could not even be said to have been full dedicated and lifelong witnesses to the mission of Jesus. Their lives were very ordinary, and their violent deaths were not as resolute—we might even say, hesitant. If they had been given a chance to escape, they probably would have taken it. But their dedication and fidelity to their loved ones and neighbors were ultimately uncompromising. And for this, they met violent deaths. The Spanish theologian, José Ignacio González Faus, describes these martyrs as "witnesses to love," "killed by the hatred of love."[33] Ignacio Ellacuría calls them "crucified peoples." I call them "martyrs at the margins." In the following section, I offer some reflections by situating their narratives in the context of contemporary martyrological conversations.

Witnesses to Love

Recovering Thomas Aquinas' fundamental insight in *Summa Theologiae* IIa-IIae, Question 124, José Ignacio González Faus argues that martyrs are

---

33. González Faus, "Witnesses to Love," 59–66.

persons who are "witnesses to the perfection of love."[34] In Article 5,[35] the Angelic Doctor asked whether faith alone is the cause of martyrdom. He answered in the affirmative. However, for Aquinas, faith is not only about inward belief but is also an external profession, not only articulated in words but also in deeds (in reference to James 2:8). He gives, as an example, the martyrdom of John the Baptist that was caused not by his denial of faith but by his denouncing of the evils of Herod's rule. St. Thomas, in a previous article (Art. 4), writes that a martyr is one who "does not abandon faith *and justice* even when faced with imminent death."[36] Faus suggests three points. First, martyrdom in the church must be seen as an assimilation into the death of Jesus—that is, dying not so much *for* Jesus as *like* Jesus, "who did not die exactly from *odium fidei.*" Second, quoting Vatican II, Faus says, "The church therefore considers martyrdom as *an exceptional gift and as the highest proof of love.*"[37] Third, martyrdom should be seen not so much from the motives of those who kill but from the motives of the victim.[38] Focusing on the victim brings to the fore an early church tradition of looking at the martyr as *witness* to God's love and fidelity and concrete love to the neighbor. Witnessing to the life and dangerous memory of Jesus becomes a grave threat to the dominant power of the empire. The victims turned themselves into witnesses of love and justice, and for that reason, they have been killed. The intention of Faus is clear:

> *If there are martyrs, it is because there are victims.* Reclaiming the phrases "hatred of love" allows us to state this and, so, to incorporate the victims of Latin America into the subject of martyrdom. There are an impressive number of these: anonymous *desaparecidos* ("disappeareds"); indigenous people of Brazil and Guatemala; many of the mothers and grandmothers of the Plaza de Mayo, still trying to establish the paternity of a son or a granddaughter. Many of them are not merely victims but true anonymous martyrs, like those the martyrology of my own country calls "the innumerable martyrs of Zaragoza."[39]

By extension, I argue that the victims of populist regimes can also be considered martyrs—for example, the anonymous martyrs of the Duterte regime, some 33,000 victims whose bodies were slaughtered like animals.

34. González Faus, "Witnesses to Love," 61.
35. Aquinas, *Summa Theologiae*, II-IIae.124.5.
36. González Faus, "Witnesses to Love," 61, italics original.
37. Paul VI, *Lumen Gentium* 42–3, italics mine.
38. Paul VI, *Lumen Gentium*, 62.
39. Paul VI, *Lumen Gentium*, 64, italics original.

Many of them could not be claimed by their families for lack of funds or because they were unidentifiable beyond recognition and, thus, were only buried in common graves or thrown into the sea.[40] Their horrible deaths were even more cruel and inhuman than those of the early martyrs. They were not considered human threats to the empire; they were used and disposed of as animals without significance and value. From the perspective of the regime, they are "hopeless cases," less than human, pests of society who need to be eliminated. This was how the regime saw Juan, for example. But from the view of his children, Juan was a loving father who risked his life, because he wanted to see his children. He wanted to be there, despite the danger, on his daughter's birthday. Like many others, he died as a "witness to love."

Voluntary Martyrdom Revisited

This brings us to the ongoing debate on "voluntary martyrdom" in contemporary research.[41] G. E. M. de Ste. Croix argues that early Christian martyrs voluntarily sought out arrest, willfully and enthusiastically offered their lives, singing as it were while being fed to the lions. According to Tertullian, early Christians actually longed for martyrdom: "Now we are in the midst of an intense heat, the very dog star of persecution . . . the fire and the sword have tried some Christians, and the beasts have tried others; others are in prison, longing for martyrdom which they have tasted already, having been beaten by clubs and tortured."[42] The foremost example of this is Ignatius of Antioch who, on the way to his trial and execution in Rome, wrote the churches there: "I plead with you not to be an 'unreasonable kindness' to me. Allow me to be eaten by the beasts, through which I can attain God. I am God's wheat, and I am ground by the teeth of wild beasts, so that I may become pure bread of Christ. . . . Do me this favor."[43] According to Ste. Croix, these voluntary martyrs stampeding to the arena were "surprisingly large" in number, and the phenomenon actually aggravated, or even caused, more outbreaks of persecution. Authors following Ste. Croix argue that

---

40. See, in general, among others, Berehulak, "They are Slaughtering Us"; Ramos, "Unclaimed Corpses"; "Philippine Police."

41. See, among others, de Ste. Croix, "Aspects of the 'Great' Persecution," 75–109; Buck, "Voluntary Martyrdom Revisited," 125–35; Middleton, "Early Christian Voluntary Martyrdom," 556–73.

42. Tertullian, *Scorpiace* 1, 5, 7, cited in Middleton, "Early Christian Voluntary Martyrdom," 557.

43. Ignatius of Antioch, "Epistle to the Romans," 4.1–5.3, cited in Middleton, "Early Christian Voluntary Martyrdom," 557.

some Christians provoked authorities to arrest them or even killed themselves without having been provoked by the authorities.[44]

P. Lorraine Buck, on the contrary, argues that many of these martyrs did not provoke their own deaths or hardly attracted the attention of the Roman authorities. It might be true that the Romans were thrilled by the blood in the gladiatorial arenas. Some intellectuals also idealized the Socratic "suicide" tradition. But there is little proof that early Christians sought death by presenting themselves *en masse* to the authorities to be fed to the lions. According to Buck, "the number of martyrdoms in the first three centuries was, in relative terms, very small . . . there were approximately five million Christians in the Empire in 300 CE. Of that five million, only one tenth of one percent, or 5,000 Christians, spread over an empire of 5.7 million square kilometers, were martyred, and only a fraction of these martyrdoms was voluntary."[45]

Many of these martyrs were just doing the "ordinary" tasks Christians were expected to do: take care of the sick, feed the hungry, show compassion for the persecuted, etc. Buck points to some data from the narratives of Eusebius, the historian of the early church:

> Theodosia, for instance, was arrested when she saluted some confessors and asked them to remember her in their prayers. Dionysius was beheaded after he attended to six voluntary martyrs prior to their deaths. Agapius was denounced to the governor when he made frequent trips from Gaza to Caesarea to visit his brother in prison. Ares was condemned to the flames, and Probus and Elijah to the sword, when, upon being questioned at the gate of Ashkelon, they admitted they were taking food to the confessors in Cilicia. Indeed, all of these martyrs, and many others, attracted attention to themselves by doing nothing more than was expected of them as Christians. . . . Indeed, it was these very acts of charity, compassion, and cohesion that set Christianity apart from paganism, especially during times of adversity, and made it an attractive option.[46]

There are many other names all throughout the Christian history beyond Buck's list. A little-known martyr is Emerentiana, a catechumen and the foster sister of St. Agnes. She went to pray and shed tears at the tomb of her friend, Agnes, who was just martyred. She was mocked by Agnes's mur-

---

44. See, generally, Droge and Tabor, *Noble Death*.
45. Buck, "Voluntary Martyrdom Revisited," 135.
46. Buck, "Voluntary Martyrdom Revisited," 128.

derers and was also stoned to death over her friend's tomb.[47] Fast-forward in history: a five-volume book entitled *Guatemala, Nunca Más* (1988),[48] compiled by an interdiocesan group called "Recovery of Historical Memory" (REMHI), contains narratives of massacres and abuses that occurred in Guatemala from 1977 to 1996. For sure, these victims did not sing their way to their common graves. They were forced, coerced, raped, abused, buried on their own farms, or thrown into rivers. Most of them anonymous until their names were recently recovered. They committed their lives to defend their families, friends, and neighbors. Imagine the same things happening in violent regimes in the African or the Asian continents of our times. These victims—including those ordinary fathers and young men in the Philippines like Juan—are what I call "martyrs at the margins." They were merely practicing their Christian responsibility, within their ordinary lives, to care and be compassionate, to love and be faithful—to the point of death. They did not volunteer their own deaths. When his friends told Juan that he was on the "drug list," he moved to Manila to escape the police. He was careful not to provoke them. It is the same predicament of thousands of others. But they could not renege on their duty to service and compassion. Like Juan, they were killed while "on duty." One lawyer was going to court to defend a poor farmer; another man was ferrying his children to school; another was driving a jeepney to earn a few pesos for food that night; and one young boy was begging the police to stop their torture of him because he had classes the next day. In all these instances, the police did not listen. They shot and killed them anyway.

Crucified People

This brings us to Ignacio Ellacuría's concept of crucified people, later appropriated by Jon Sobrino to proclaim the new martyrs of our times.[49] Ellacuría argues that there is a "vast portion of humankind, which is literally and actually crucified by natural oppressions and especially by historical and personal oppressions."[50] Beyond religiously and politically motivated martyrdoms are the deaths of millions caused by the present world's socioeconomic arrangement, what Pope Francis describes as an economy that "kills."[51] "Auschwitz, Hiroshima, and the Gulags are behind us," Sobrino

47. Kirsch, "St. Emerentiana."
48. REMHI, *Guatemala, Never Again!*
49. Ellacuría, "Crucified People," 580–603.
50. Ellacuría, "Crucified People," 580.
51. Francis, *Evangelii Gaudium*, 53.

writes, "but millions of human beings continue to suffer massively, unjustly, and innocently in repressions, wars, and massacres. Many millions more suffer a slow death of poverty, particularly women and children, besides the death of their dignity and their cultures."[52] United Nations research shows that twenty-five thousand die each day due to hunger;[53] many others are refugees and migrants, victims of ecological degradation and climate change, terrorism, discrimination, and violence. These are crucified peoples, victims of globalization, anonymous martyrs of our times.

Crucified people is not a mere metaphor or abstract description of all human suffering in the world. This crucifixion and martyrdom are material, historical, concrete, and real. These deaths are caused by the sum total of collective sociopolitical, economic, cultural, and religious forces that exercise dominion over peoples' everyday lives. The category of *crucified people* can be understood in a dialectical manner. The first movement is spatial: the social permeates the personal, and the personal impinges on the social. In other words, as crucifixion happens in the people's personal, everyday lives, it also impacts the structural and global realities—and vice versa. The second dialectical movement is hermeneutical. On the one hand, "the crucified peoples of the Third World," writes Sobrino, "are today the great theological setting, the locus, in which to understand the cross of Jesus."[54] Since we are not there at the foot of the cross, present-day Christians understand what that crucifixion meant by standing at the foot of crucified peoples. On the other hand, the cross of Jesus and the history of our understanding of it bring into deeper perspective our experiences of the crucifixion of peoples in our time. While the death and suffering of peoples in today's world becomes the privileged hermeneutical guide to understanding the historical event of Jesus's own death on the cross, this same death and suffering give meaning and hope in the midst of the martyrdom of innocent and unwilling victims in our world.

The Christian reflection on Jesus goes all the way back to the Suffering Servant of Second Isaiah: "But he was wounded for our transgressions, crushed for our iniquities; upon him was the punishment that made us whole, and by his bruises we are healed" (Isa 53:5 NRSV). The "Servant of Yahweh" finds himself in a paradoxical situation. On the one hand, he is totally deformed by the torments done to him. Considered a sinner by all, God has abandoned him in the eyes of his tormentors. On the other hand, by his wounds we are healed. Jesus was seen as Isaiah's Suffering Servant.

---

52. Sobrino, "Our World," 15.
53. Holmes, "Losing 25,000 to Hunger," para. 7.
54. Sobrino, *Jesus the Liberator*, 196.

But what is true for Jesus is also true for the crucified peoples: "The crucified people has a twofold thrust: it is the victim of the sin of the world, and it is also the bearer of the world's salvation."[55] Besides being the main object of the effort of salvation, this same crucified people might also *"in its very crucified situation* be the principle of salvation for the whole world."[56]

If martyrdom is understood as following the cross of Jesus, then those who die as victims of the present socioeconomic and political arrangements—the crucified people—are martyrs themselves—"Jesus martyrs"—to borrow Sobrino's term. The scandal of the death of crucified peoples goes back to the scandal of Jesus on the cross and further back to the Suffering Servant. "It is precisely the reign of sin that continues to crucify most of humankind," Ellacuría writes, "that obliges us to make real in history the death of Jesus as the actualized Passover of the Reign of God."[57]

4. Conclusion

This attempt to rethink the notion of martyrdom is intended to make sense of what many people call "senseless killings" taking place in some of the populist regimes of our times. I would like to consider that these simple people, who are among the socially excluded, did not die in vain. Beyond the narratives of "elite martyrs," theirs were not grand narratives, and they did not die in the name of fighting for justice and heroic causes of universal importance. I believe that there is a great Christian sense in ordinary expressions of love, in small narratives of day-to-day justice, in the daily lives of fidelity among the simple and the ordinary. These everyday people all met violent deaths, which they would have wanted to escape but did not in the name of charity and solidarity.

In July 2017, Pope Francis issued *motu proprio*, a document suggesting a new way toward beatification, "*Maiorem Hac Dilectionem*," on the offering of one's life.[58] Traditionally, the Catholic Church has had three paths toward beatification: martyrdom, a life of heroic virtues, and exceptional cases called "equipollent" canonization based on a long tradition of the people's veneration of an individual's holiness. The causes of beatification of Óscar Romero and Teresa of Calcutta have alluded to all of these criteria. But in this 2017 document, Pope Francis has introduced a fourth way. His opening

---

55. Ellacuría, "Crucified People," 603.
56. Ellacuría, "Crucified People," 591.
57. Ellacuría, "Crucified People," 584.
58. Francis, "*Maiorem Hac Dilectionem*."

sentence comes from the Gospel of John: "Greater love has no man than this, that a man lay down his life for his friends" (John 15:13).

"These Christians, who following more closely the steps and teachings of the Lord Jesus, offered voluntarily and freely their life for others and persevered in this intention up to death, are worthy of particular consideration and honor. It is certain that the heroic offering of their life, suggested and sustained by charity, expresses a veritable, full, and exemplary imitation of Christ, and it is why they merit the admiration that the community of the faithful usually reserves to those who voluntarily accepted the martyrdom of blood or exercised the Christian virtues to a heroic level."[59]

The document gives some criteria for this fourth way of beatification—for instance, the free and voluntary offering of life and heroic acceptance, out of charity (*propter caritatem*), of a certain death and, in the short term, a link between the offering of life and premature death. There are also other criteria to be fulfilled, but for certain, these everyday people I have described—these "martyrs at the margins"—had "offered voluntarily and freely their life for others and persevered in this intention up to death."[60] For this, their lives and deaths are a "veritable, full, and exemplary imitation of Christ."[61] Thus, we also owe them the "admiration that the community of the faithful usually reserves to those who voluntarily accepted the martyrdom of blood or exercised the Christian virtues to a heroic level."[62] Moreover, recovering the lives of these "martyrs at the margins" goes beyond honoring the martyrs themselves. It also leads us to live the ordinary Christian life in the martyrial key—that is, to borrow the words of Rowan Williams, to appreciate the "quotidian character of martyrdom" and to live our baptismal challenge in a nondramatic manner of everyday existence.[63]

Bibliography

Agence France-Presse. "Grieving Children's Choir Breaking Philippine Drug War Cycle." *World Asia*, March 9, 2020. https://gulfnews.com/world/asia/philippines/grieving-childrens-choir-breaking-philippine-drug-war-cycle-1.1583732906320.

———. "Kill the Criminals! Duterte's Vote-Winning Vow." *Philippine Daily Inquirer*, March 16, 2016. https://newsinfo.inquirer.net/774225/kill-the-criminals-dutertes-vote-winning-vow.

Allcock, John. "Populism: A Brief Biography." *Sociology* 5:3 (1971) 371–87.

59. "Motu Proprio," paras. 4–5.
60. "Motu Proprio," para. 4.
61. "Motu Proprio," para. 5.
62. "Motu Proprio," para. 5.
63. Williams, *Why Study the Past*; Medley, "Always Carrying," 475–93.

Aquinas, St. Thomas. *The Summa Theologiae of St. Thomas Aquinas*. 2nd and rev. ed. Translated by Fathers of the English Dominican Province. London: Burns, Oats, and Washbourne, 1920. https://www.newadvent.org/summa/3124.htm#article5.

Berehulak, Daniel. "They Are Slaughtering Us Like Animals." *The New York Times*, December 7, 2016. https://www.nytimes.com/interactive/2016/12/07/world/asia/rodrigo-duterte-philippines-drugs-killings.html.

Buan, Lian. "A Gruesome Tale of TokHang: 'Sir, May Humihinga Pa'." *Rappler*, January 30, 2017. https://rappler.com/nation/gruesome-tokhang-payatas-quezon-city-petition.

———. "Policemen Guilty of Kian delos Santos Killing." *Rappler*, November 28, 2018. https://www.rappler.com/nation/217770-caloocan-policemen-convicted-murder-kian-delos-santos-killing.

———. "TokHang Victim Files Murder Charges vs Cops." *Rappler*, March 1, 2017. https://rappler.com/nation/tokhang-victim-murder-cops-efren-morillo-ombudsman.

Buck, P. Lorraine. "Voluntary Martyrdom Revisited." *The Journal of Theological Studies* 63 (April 2012) 125–35.

Cabico, Gaea Katreena. "Revised Drug War Death Toll Is Thousand Less than Previous Figure." *Philstar*, July 19, 2019. https://www.philstar.com/headlines/2019/07/19/1936097/revised-drug-war-death-toll-thousand-less-previous-figure.

CBC News: The National. "Horror of the Philippines' Drug War." YouTube Video, 17:44. April 12, 2017. https://www.youtube.com/watch?v=q0v9IcZRfhY.

CBS News. "In-Depth Look at the War on Drugs in the Philippines." YouTube Video, 11:05. March 6, 2017. https://www.youtube.com/watch?v=wyAHmMMORCs&list=PLoJyM3hC2NZFSPNtS8sSRLaag5egemH4X&index=57&t=0s.

Chenu, Bruno, et al. *The Book of Christian Martyrs*. New York: Crossroad, 1990.

Chevigny, Paul. "Police Deadly Force as Social Control: Jamaica, Argentina, and Brazil." *Criminal Law Forum* 1:3 (1990) 389–425.

Cunningham, Lawrence S. *The Catholic Heritage*. New York: Crossroad, 1988.

Daniel-Rops, Henri. *The Protestant Reformation*. His History of the Church of Christ 4. Translated by Audrey Butler. London: J. M. Dent and Sons, 1961.

Droge, A. J., and J. D. Tabor. *A Noble Death: Suicide and Martyrdom among Christians and Jews in Antiquity*. New York: Harper San Francisco, 1992.

Elie, Paul. "What Óscar Romero's Canonization Says about Pope Francis: Reassessing the Catholic Church's Dubious History in Latin America." *The Atlantic*, November 2018. https://www.theatlantic.com/magazine/archive/2018/11/the-martyr-and-the-pope/570835/.

Ellacuría, Ignacio. "The Crucified People." In *Mysterium Liberationis: Fundamental Concepts of Liberation Theology*, edited by Ignacio Ellacuría and Jon Sobrino, 580–603. Maryknoll, NY: Orbis, 2004.

Enano, Jhesset O. "QC Cops Kill 7, including Trash Collectors 'Wielding Guns'." *Philippine Daily Inquirer*, December 8, 2016. https://newsinfo.inquirer.net/851675/qc-cops-kill-7-including-trash-collectors-wielding-guns.

Forrest, Benjamin K., et al. *A Legacy of Preaching: The Life, Theology, and Methods of History's Greatest Preachers*. Vol. 1. Grand Rapids, MI: Zondervan, 2018.

Francis, Pope. "*Maiorem Hac Dilectionem*: On the Offer of Life." Apostolic letter issued at St. Peter's, Rome, July 11, 2017. http://www.vatican.va/content/francesco/en/

motu_proprio/documents/papa-francesco-motu-proprio_20170711_maiorem-hac-dilectionem.html.

———. *Evangelii Gaudium: The Joy of the Gospel*. Vatican.va, 2013. http://www.vatican.va/content/francesco/en/apost_exhortations/documents/papa-francesco_esortazione-ap_20131124_evangelii-gaudium.html.

Frontline PBS. "On the President's Orders." YouTube Video, 54:47. October 16, 2019. https://www.youtube.com/watch?v=qugduxazBBg.

Gidron, Noam, and Bart Bonikowski. "Varieties of Populism: Literature Review and Research Agenda." Weatherhead Center for International Affairs Working Paper No. 13–004. Harvard University, 2013.

"The Global Rise of Populism." *World Politics Review*, September 23, 2019. https://www.worldpoliticsreview.com/the-global-rise-of-populism/.

González Faus, Jose Ignacio. "Witnesses to Love, Killed by Love." In *Rethinking Martyrdom*, edited by Teresa Okure, et al., 59–66. London: SCM, 2003.

Holmes, John. "Losing 25,000 to Hunger Every Day." *UN Chronicle*, June 27, 2013. https://www.un.org/en/chronicle/article/losing-25000-hunger-every-day.

Human Rights Watch. "Police Fake Evidence in Philippines' Drug War Killings." HRW Video, 3:22. March 2, 2017. https://www.hrw.org/video-photos/video/2017/03/02/300523.

———. *World Report 2020: Events of 2019*. New York: Seven Stories, 2020. https://www.hrw.org/sites/default/files/world_report_download/hrw_world_report_2020_0.pdf.

Kaltwasser, Cristóbal Rovira, et al. *The Oxford Handbook of Populism*. Oxford: Oxford University Press, 2017.

Kirsch, Johann Peter. "St. Emerentiana." In vol. 5 of *The Catholic Encyclopedia*. New York: Robert Appleton, 1909. http://www.newadvent.org/cathen/05401b.htm.

Malig, Kaela, and Andrea L. Taguines. "Left-Behind Children Cry 'Papa!' What Happens to the Children Left Fatherless by the Philippine Drug War?" *The Guidon*, January 3 2018. https://www.theguidon.com/1112/main/2018/01/left-behind-children-cry-papa/.

McCoy, Alfred. "Philippine Populism: Local Violence and Global Context in the Rise of a Filipino Strongman." *Surveillance and Society* 15:3–4 (2017) 514–22.

Medley, Mark. "Always Carrying in the Body of Jesus: Baptism, Martyrdom and Quotidian Existence." *Anglican Theological Review* 94 (2012) 475–93.

Meroni, Fabrizio, ed. *Martyrs in Asia*. Rome: Urbaniana University Press, 2019.

Middleton, Paul. "Early Christian Voluntary Martyrdom: A Statement of Defense." *The Journal of Theological Studies* 64 (October 2016) 556–73.

Moffitt, Benjamin. *The Global Rise of Populism: Performance, Political Style, and Representation*. Palo Alto: Stanford University Press, 2016.

"Motu Proprio on the Offering of Life (Complete Translation): A New Way Towards Beatification." Zenit.org, July 11, 2017. https://zenit.org/2017/07/11/motu-proprio-on-the-offering-of-life-complete-translation/.

O'Connell, Gerard. "Archbishop Romero Is a Martyr of the Church of Vatican II." *America*, February 4, 2015. https://www.americamagazine.org/content/dispatches/archbishop-romero-martyr-church-vatican-ii.

Owen, Edward Charles Everard, ed. *Some Authentic Acts of the Early Martyrs*. Oxford: Clarendon, 1927.

Paul VI, Pope. *Lumen Gentium: Dogmatic Constitution on the Church*. Boston: Pauline, 1965.

Philippine Human Rights Information Center. *The Killing State: 2019 Philippine Human Rights Situationer.* Quezon City, Philippines: PhilRights, January 2020. https://www.philrights.org/wp-content/uploads/2020/02/WP-Copy-2019-HR-Sit.pdf.

"Philippine Police 'Dumping Bodies' of Drug War Victims." *Al Jazeera*, July 28, 2017. https://www.aljazeera.com/news/2017/7/28/philippine-police-dumping-bodies-of-drug-war-victims.

Pilario, Daniel Franklin E. "Of Mothers, Widows and Orphans: Stories of Resistance on the Philippine War on Drugs." KULeuvenTheologie Video, 1:38:18. March 17, 2017. https://www.youtube.com/watch?v=9-EtAoWhVp4&t=10s.

Rahner, Karl. "Dimensions of Martyrdom: A Plea for the Broadening of a Classical Concept." In *Martyrdom Today*, edited by Johannes Baptist Metz and Edward Schillebeeckx, 9–11. London: SCM, 1983.

Ramos, Mariejo S. "Unclaimed Corpses: Drug War's Forgotten Fatalities." *Philippine Daily Inquirer*, November 2, 2018. https://newsinfo.inquirer.net/1049590/unclaimed-corpses-drug-wars-forgotten-fatalities.

REMHI (Recovery of Historical Memory Project), Human Rights Office, Archdiocese of Guatemala. *Guatemala, Never Again!* Maryknoll, NY: Orbis, 1999.

Roth, Kenneth. "The Dangerous Rise of Populism: Global Attack on Human Rights Values." Human Rights Watch. https://www.hrw.org/world-report/2017/country-chapters/dangerous-rise-of-populism.

Smith, Nicola. "The Families Ripped Apart by the Philippines' Brutal, Bloody War on Drugs." *The Telegraph*, August 18, 2019. https://www.telegraph.co.uk/global-health/terror-and-security/saw-grandfather-lying-pool-blood-unseen-impact-philippines-brutal/.

Sobrino, Jon. *Jesus the Liberator: A Historical-Theological Reading of Jesus of Nazareth.* Maryknoll, NY: Orbis, 1993.

———. "Our World: Cruelty and Compassion." In *Rethinking Martyrdom*, edited by Teresa Okure, et al., 15–16. London: SCM, 2003.

de Ste. Croix, G. E. M. "Aspects of the 'Great' Persecution." *Harvard Theological Review* 47 (1954) 75–109.

St. Vincent School of Theology. "Street Theater on the Drug War: Huwag Kang Papatay (Thou Shall Not Kill)." YouTube Video, 12:47. September 23, 2017. https://www.youtube.com/watch?v=ML1wOiQApVg.

Taggart, Paul. *Populism.* Birmingham, UK: Open University Press, 2000.

UN Human Rights Office of the High Commissioner (OHCHR). "Philippines: UN Report Details Widespread Human Rights Violations and Persistent Impunity." June 4, 2020. https://www.ohchr.org/en/press-releases/2020/06/philippines-un-report-details-widespread-human-rights-violations-and.

Watford, Joy. "Finding Hope in the Dark." Positively Filipino: Your Window on the Filipino Diaspora, May 28, 2018. http://www.positivelyfilipino.com/magazine/finding-hope-in-the-dark.

Williams, Rowan. *Why Study the Past: The Quest for a Historical Church.* Grand Rapids, MI: Eerdmans, 2005.

6

The Catholic Church and Deeply Divided Societies: Utilizing the Potential of the Church to Build Sustainable Peace

Elizabeth Kanini Kimau

The words of Jesus to Peter, "Put back your sword"(Matt 26:25, NIV)[1] seem to fall on deaf ears in today's world, which is characterized by unending conflict, as exemplified by the large number of violent situations in Africa. The region has continually been torn by violence, ranging from terrorism to civil wars to genocides to interethnic and political violence to religious and economic- and resource-based violence. This violence has affected the lives of millions of innocent people. In 1994, 800,000 people were killed in Rwanda in just three months,[2] the war in the Democratic Republic of the Congo between 1998 and 2003 claimed the lives of 5.4 million people, and 2 million died in Sudan between 2003 and 2009.[3] In Darfur, fighting resulted in 400,000 deaths and in northern Uganda, civil war claimed an estimated 100,000 lives; civil war in Angola killed 500,000, in Sierra Leone 2 million, and in Liberia 200,000.[4] Scenes of deadly violence have been witnessed as well in Somalia, Mali, South Sudan, the Central African Republic, and in northern parts of Kenya. These wars are mostly fought at

1. All biblical citations herein are from the NIV.
2. Stedman, Rothchild, and Cousens, *Ending Civil Wars*, 1.
3. Rupesinghe and Anderlini, *Civil Wars*, 2.
4. Habeeb, *Civil Wars in Africa*.

the margins of communities that are experiencing poverty, inequality, and underdevelopment,[5] and these populations at the grassroots are typically the worst affected.

The violence that characterizes many regions of Africa clearly evidences that a voice urging people to "take up your instruments of violence" has rung louder than Jesus's words, "Put back your sword." In such a violent environment, who is able make the words of Jesus louder in order to stop the bloodshed, to enable people to live in full dignity, and to restore respect for human dignity and life? What does the call of Jesus to his disciples, "Go out to the whole world and proclaim the good news" (Mark 16:15) mean to Christians who can see their brothers and sisters living miserable lives in a violent environment? In his message on World Peace Day in 2019, Pope Francis said, "Bringing peace is central to the mission of Christ's disciples,"[6] echoing the words of St. Paul to the Corinthians that we are called to join Jesus in his mission of reconciliation.[7] In reflecting on Paul's letter, Lederach says that "this mission as articulated by St. Paul is about facing divisions and restoring people in their relationship with others and with God. It is about joining God in the mission of reconciliation by building bridges and bringing down the dividing walls of hostility between individuals and groups."[8] Each person is called to build peace in this broken world. The church should take a leading role to prevent and transform violent conflict and to protect the lives and dignity of people at the grassroots whose environment is immersed in violence. If properly utilized, the gifts that the church possesses are able to create a peaceful world where life flourishes and people are left free to collaborate on developmental activities.

The Catholic Church is especially qualified to reconcile deeply divided societies and to heal those who have been broken by violence. This is because it is connected to people at all levels of society, including the few people at the top level, the larger group in the middle, and those at the grassroots, the largest group. Thus, the Catholic Church is found at every level of society and always accompanies the people.[9]

Journeying toward a culture of peace with people who are at present rooted in a culture of violence is a difficult task full of challenges. This mission calls for actors seeking peace who are always with the people and who are committed and have the right motivation. The church has most of these

---

5. Lederach, *Building Peace*, 16.
6. Francis, *Message for the Celebration of the 52nd World Day of Peace*, 1.
7. See 1 Cor 5:18–20.
8. Lederach, *Reconcile*, 130–31.
9. Lederach, *Building Peace*, 37–43.

qualities and is capable of attaining even more. The first step in accompanying people at the grassroots who are entangled in violence is to understand the people, their cultures, how violence has affected them, and how they have responded to it.

The Grassroots Population and Violence

In the African context, the majority of the population lives at the grassroots level, mostly in areas that are marginalized in terms of security and development. Many of these people are chained to poverty, making them more vulnerable to violence. Poverty in sub-Saharan Africa continues to escalate, as indicated by its growth from 278 million people in poverty in 1990 to 413 million in 2015.[10] Many families in the region are not able to fly their families to safe places; instead, some walk for long distances to refugee camps or remain in violent zones. They often have direct experience of the violence and struggle to find food, shelter, water, and safety. Paradoxically, the groups who are fighting each other live as neighbors and yet are locked into long-standing cycles of hostile interaction.[11] As the violence deepens, the divisions into hostile groups deepen. The hatred, enmity, mistrust, intolerance, and revenge escalate and are passed on from generation to generation in a vicious cycle. The people at the grassroots are entangled in violence, the history and causes of which the majority do not even understand. Many were simply born into the violence. The enmity and hatred they inherited drives them to continue fighting the perceived "enemy." In some cases, children are forced to become soldiers, which destroys their childhood and humanity. Integrating them back into the same society in which they have committed atrocities is an enormous challenge. People who are surrounded by such severe violence are easily manipulated into continuing to fight the "enemy."[12] Those who incite the people ironically often suffer less from the violence, because they live in safe areas far from the war. Their own children are secure, attending good schools in a peaceful environment conducive to learning and holistic growth.

---

10. World Bank Group, *Poverty*, 2.
11. Lederach, *Building Peace*, 23.
12. Lederach, *Building Peace*, 23.

The Violent Voices at the Grassroots

In the gospel, Peter took his sword to protect his master whom he loved so much. He felt he was justified in taking up the sword because the life of his friend was in danger. However, Jesus told him to "put back your sword," and despite the danger, Peter heard and obeyed. In a similar way, the masses at the grassroots level are deeply pained by the violence occurring around them. Lederach describes how the contemporary violence usually occurs in marginalized areas where people are struggling with inequality and a lack of development and security.[13] For these reasons, the people at the grassroots feel justified taking up arms to protect themselves and their property. They see this as the only way to survive cycles of violence in which there is a limited government presence. How can these people hear the words of Jesus to lay down their arms? The insecurity, the image of the other as the "enemy," and the quest to simply survive are big obstacles to hearing any message of peace. This situation calls for innovative ways to break the chains of violence.

From my ten years' experience of working with grassroots communities in northern Kenya and South Sudan, I have learned that revenge is embedded in the cultures of some ethnic groups. Children are socialized to believe that when a relative is killed, one must avenge the death. For instance, when a father is killed in the Borana community, the father's clan has a responsibility to seek revenge. If it does not, it is mocked or disrespected by other clans. In addition, when the sons of the deceased father grow up, they are reminded of their responsibility to avenge their father's death. These quests for revenge trigger and also escalate the violence occurring in the community. Children in this violent world learn that the only way to address violence is through violence. This was shown in responses I received from the Rendille[14] children I interacted with. I volunteered to teach in a school that had been closed several times for security reasons. The school was located at the fault line of the violence, so the children had seen many atrocities. Some children had even been killed as they cared for their cattle. When I asked the children, "What would you like to do when you grow up?" some replied, "When I grow up, I will go kill Borana and bring back our livestock." Other times I asked, "When I bring Borana children to your school, what will you do together?" and they responded, "We will kill them." I decided to help the children understand that we are all created by God and that even though some individual Boranas may be bad, not all are. I asked

---

13. Lederach, *Building Peace*, 11–18.

14. The Rendille is an ethnic group in northern Kenya that has been in violent conflict with the neighboring Borana ethnic group.

them, "Who created your parents?" and in unison they responded, "God." I went further and asked, "Who created the parents of Borana children?" All of the children responded with a loud voice, "*Sheitani*" (the devil). Whenever I gave these children paper for drawing, they drew people killing each other or cows being stolen in raids. These children are already unconsciously arming themselves. Some who had witnessed lots of violence shared with me how they saw the police run away at the peak of the violence. It is clear that they do not trust that the police can protect them.

In these insecure environments in which people are so strongly attached to their instruments of violence, how can they hear the words of Jesus to "put down your swords"? Through whom does Jesus utter these words today? Why are Jesus's other "voices" (e.g., love your enemy, do not kill, forgive) seemingly forgotten? What will make the church's voice louder than the voices emitted by political leaders, criminals, rebel group leaders, elites, businesspeople (especially those trading in arms and natural resources), and the media? The transition from a culture of violence to a culture of peace involves a long journey. It calls for motivated agents of social change who are committed to spending time with the people, seek to protect life, are able to recognize the potential of every person, and are skilled in exploring the potential for peace and development.

The church is endowed with many ways of serving as a channel for achieving sustainable peace at the grassroots. She is connected to people at all levels, she deeply values life and human dignity, her personnel have often sacrificed a lot in the service of God (e.g., religious people), she has channels that can form people in various ways, and she is guided by the values of Jesus: love, forgiveness, respect, and commitment. If the church conscientizes people at the grassroots to realize their potential for building peace and saying no to violence, they will be able to use their power not for violence but instead to contribute to a new generation that embraces peace, diversity, and participatory development.

The Potential within the Structure of the Church

Reconciling people who have a long experience of violent trauma that they associate with perceived enemies and that has accumulated over generations involves a long and slow process. The journey calls for a faithful servant who is not in a hurry, has the right motivation, is committed, and is ready to sacrifice to be with people in their own settings. Many people live in marginalized areas with poor infrastructure, making it difficult for agents of social change—or even in some instances the government—to penetrate these regions. The challenges of reaching people most affected by violence are often beyond the institutions of civil society, which tend to focus primarily on short-term projects. Processes involving a few individuals seeking to make peace by meeting in hotels, leaving many affected people out of the process, are ineffectual. Attempts to jump-start the peace process through the distribution of monetary allowances incentivizes people to attend meetings not out of a desire for peace, but simply to get money.

In contrast, the Catholic Church has a long-term presence in and connection to many people in these marginalized areas. As one example, the northern parts of Kenya have been marginalized for a long time. A report published by the Kenya Human Rights Commission in 2000 referred to the people of this region as "the forgotten people."[15] Since 1963 the Catholic Church has accompanied the people of Marsabit (a town in this region) and provided almost all of the necessary social services to the people without discriminating. Some people call the church their "government" because she has provided them with health care, education, humanitarian assistance, and social services. In contrast, the national government was not very visible to them, and this was one reason they felt they had to take up arms to protect themselves and their property. I did my master's program with a lady who was educated by the Catholic Church. She was from the AIC Church, but the Catholic Church provided an opportunity for education to everyone. She shared with us that the Catholic Church was always with the people and they knew her as a government would. She stated that it was with them during war and drought, as well as in the schools.

The connection the Catholic Church has with people at every level of society places her in a good position to influence social change. Many warring groups are neighbors, and the church frequently has connections to both hostile groups. These connections can be utilized to rebuild relationships, tolerance, and trust. In addition, because of its structure, the church is able to mobilize other religions and form interreligious groups that wield considerable influence.

Building peace is often perceived to depend heavily on financial resources, leading many to think that absent these resources peace is not possible. Moreover, the majority of people at the grassroots level have a low level of education, whereas many who are chosen to participate in gatherings aimed at peace have at least a bit of education. This means that many people who are skillful in resolving local disputes yet lack a formal education are left out of the peace process. Critical local resources—*the people*

---

15. Kenya Human Rights Commission, *Forgotten People Revisited*.

themselves, and their cultures—which are powerful in building a culture of peace are not mobilized.

The church is connected to the grassroots through catechists, the leaders of small Christian communities, youth, women, and Sunday school teachers. This makes it easy for the church to demystify peacebuilding and mobilize the local resources that can build peace. The church's grassroots leaders can be empowered with the necessary skills and knowledge to become peace ambassadors and with the will to educate others to take responsibility for building their own peace. In my peace mission in northern Kenya in 2016, I collaborated with grassroots church leaders to begin the process of reconciling the Rendille and Borana ethnic groups. These grassroots religious leaders have started bringing people from the two ethnic groups together each year for worship, which strengthens their relationships.

The Catholic Church also operates schools ranging from kindergarten to primary to secondary to institutes of higher learning. This is a very powerful channel for peace and can be used to form a new generation equipped with alternative and constructive ways of resolving conflicts. The church can form agents of social change who are committed to building a culture of peace for current and future generations.

The Catholic Church's system of formation, which produces catechists who in turn form catechumens, can also be used for peace. Peace studies and methods of nonviolent action can be integrated into this formation, which places a heavy emphasis on respect for life and human dignity. The Catholic Church is guided by the Holy Bible, the *Catechism of the Catholic Church,* and its social teaching. All of these teach about respect for the human person, who is created in the image of God. They also contain values that guide Christians in their interactions with each other. Revisiting approaches to teaching these values in settings of protracted conflict could be a powerful tool for re-evangelizing people, enabling them to embrace peace and sacrifice their lives to sow seeds of peace.

Rays of Hope in the Midst of Violence

Christians may have a strong desire to contribute to building a culture of peace in settings of protracted violence, but they might not know how to do it or where to begin. How to start the journey from unpeaceful relations to peaceful relations poses a number of challenges. Despite the potential of the church, Christians can lose hope and fail to take action. From my ten-year experience in South Sudan and of reconciling the Rendille and Borana ethnic groups, I have learned that building a culture of peace does not call for extraordinary actions, but simply for being able to recognize opportunities for peace and utilize them to build a better environment. I also learned that it is possible to transform deeply rooted violence with little or no money. There is a need to demystify peacebuilding, which has been seen as a profession for a few educated people that involves a process that calls for a lot of money. Focusing on the church's potential for building a peaceful world gives peacebuilders a lot of hope and courage, something I experienced in collaborating with the church.

When I went to northern Kenya in 2009, the Rendille-Borana violence was deeply rooted and had left the communities divided and very hostile to one another. People had lost any hope of living in a peaceful environment. I found that I possessed the skills, knowledge, and motivation to bring a message of hope and peace to these broken people, but I was a stranger and also a woman entering into a patriarchal society in which women have no voice. In that society, women have historically not been permitted to attend gatherings of elders, nor to share ideas about how to build peace or make the community better. In addition, I had no money or automobile, both of which were associated with people working for peace.

I observed that people in this region, including Muslims, other Christian denominations, and traditional religions, had a lot of respect for the Catholic Church, since she has always accompanied people and served them all without discrimination for years. I also noticed that the Catholic Church was present among both the Boranas and the Rendilles and that there was only one Catholic priest serving the village churches. I started accompanying the priest (Fr. Joao) to these grassroots churches. The priest always gave me a chance to greet people after mass. Sometimes he requested that I prepare the homily. On weekdays, we went to primary school to teach a pastoral program. I started to interact with the people, and after some time people got to know me. I noticed that the Leyai primary school had been closed several times due to the violence. I told the people if they wanted me to teach their children to give me a place to live and food—nothing special, but only where they sleep and what they eat. They identified a family who welcomed me to live with them. On the first day, Fr. Joao took me to the community because I had no other means of transportation. When the elders saw me, they called the priest aside and asked, "Will this small girl manage to teach our children?" The priest assured them that I have a lot of experience in teaching, even in colleges, and they trusted him. The elders said it was their first time seeing a woman teacher.

Living at the grassroots gave me an opportunity to create close relationships with people and to deeply understand the violence and the attempts at intervention by the government and the civil society. I walked from village to village with the people, and I ate their food and lived with them. Initially most people perceived me to be a person who was very different from them. They observed carefully the way I interacted with them, and they saw that I ate their food and even slept on skins without complaining. They began to accept me and to see some similarities between us that they had not noticed when I was a stranger to them. During this period, I never talked about peace with them.

The government sent teachers to the school and after some time I stopped teaching and began focusing on shepherd education and bonding with the people. I was eventually accepted by the elders, who invited me to join in their meetings and even contribute my ideas. Even the Morans/Warriors[16]—who are the key perpetrators of the violence and do not ordinarily interact with women or eat food cooked by women—welcomed me. I created relationships with them that enabled me to interact freely with them and influence them toward peace.

In collaboration with other actors of positive change, I began to help reconcile these people through the promotion of activities that regenerated relationships and built trust, tolerance, and understanding. They were also trained in nonviolent communication skills by Irmtraude Kaushat, an international trainer in nonviolence communication from Germany, who helped them perceive each other as fellow human beings, as opposed to simply the "enemy." My ten-year journey with these people enabled many to become agents of their own change. Elders started returning raided livestock, a practice that was previously unheard of. Both Borana and Rendille elders started tracing their livestock together and ensuring that it went back to the rightful owners. Interactions between the two communities became more frequent. Initially, the Borana and the Rendille used separate means of transportation but eventually began sharing these. New relationships were created when young people and older people from the two groups began visiting one another. Intermarriages began to happen, and the two groups began engaging in trade relations. The youth continued to sustain these relationships through sports. The children who told me that they wanted to kill Borana children are now organizing sports that they play with the Boranas. People who lived in Leyai IDP (Internally Displaced Persons camp) went back to their farms and resumed farming. Initially, I brought together an

---

16. Morans are unmarried Maasai (or Samburu) warriors in the Rendille community. The majority of Morans do not go to school and instead take care of livestock in the bush. Morans cannot marry unless they pay a dowry, so they raid cows from neighboring communities (typically the Borana). However, due to the commercialization of cattle raiding, some are now connected to business people who steal and sell cattle, triggering violence.

interreligious group, which then began organizing people to pray together. Each year they organize a big worship celebration that brings people together to celebrate and pray. The Catholic bishop of the Diocese of Marsabit is always with the people at this event.

The transformed Morans worked to prevent raids by their peers. They also became peace ambassadors to other Morans. Morans who come from remote villages have continued to pose a big challenge, but there have not been any immediate counterattacks because people are waiting for the livestock to be tracked. Cattle raiding used to be accompanied by a lot of killing, but now the killings have stopped; the Morans take the cattle and leave the people unharmed. Despite the continuing challenge from the Morans, the two ethnic groups are more connected and have not engaged in the level of violent conflict that had prevailed before.

The peace between the Borana and the Rendille was achieved only because of the excellent entry point I had through the church. Because they had a positive image of the church, the elders trusted even when they had doubts that a young woman could teach their children. The entry point is very important in any process of social transformation, which can be seen in God's mission to save the world—in order to redeem humankind, God sent his son. For the son to succeed in his mission, he had to humble himself and become human. In this form, it was easier for people to understand Jesus. In a similar way, the method of insertion is very important as one starts a journey to break cycles of violence. The church, because of its connection with people and the trust the majority at the grassroots have in her, offers a rich opportunity to people who feel called to sow seeds of hope and peace but do not know how to enter into settings of violence.

Another example is that of Msgr. Bishop Peter Kihara, who led other religious leaders who had formed an interfaith team to calm violence between the Borana and the Gabbra, which started to escalate after the 2017 general elections in Kenya. While the violence between these groups has continued to claim lives, religious leaders are collaborating to prevent a massive loss of lives such as the one that occurred in the Turbi massacre of 2005.[17]

In areas where the potential of the church has been tapped for peace, losses of lives and atrocities have been prevented. Other examples of how the power of the church has been used include the participation of Archbishop Baptist Odama in transforming violent conflict in northern Uganda, and Paride Taban, the bishop emeritus of Torit, now living in Kuron peace village, who was involved in building peace during the civil war in South

---

17. Baregu, *Understanding Obstacles*, 159.

Sudan and has continued this work after the creation of an independent South Sudan.[18]

My experience and the examples of church leaders who have taken leading roles in missions of peace has helped me to understand that the church has an excellent opportunity to contribute to the building of a peaceful world if she is able to fulfill her potential. These experiences are also signs that if Christians recommit themselves to gospel teachings and take responsibility for responding to the call for them to serve as reconcilers, the world—and especially Africa—will become a safer place in which people can live in their full dignity.

Recommitting the Church to the Mission of Peace

While building peace in settings of protracted conflict has been frequently associated with civil society, or with the work of a few individuals, building a culture of peace is in fact a responsibility of each Christian. Living a Christian way of life is the first step in building peace. Jesus's message to each Christian is love of God and neighbor, forgiveness, and respect for life, and Jesus also calls Christians to love their enemies.[19] If Christians truly live these values, conflicts will be resolved constructively and nonviolently before they escalate to violence. Jesus also calls and sends each Christian out into the whole world to proclaim the good news. The best news that people living in a violent environment could hear is one of hope and peace. St. Paul stresses that Christians are called to be reconcilers, and by doing so they join God in his mission of reconciliation.

Peace is also referred to in the Scriptures, the social teaching of the Catholic Church, and the *Catechism of the Catholic Church*. All of these sources provide guidance to Christians as they follow Christ. The first chapter of the book of Genesis speaks of the human person as being created in the image of God. The social teaching of the Catholic Church explains more deeply what it means for a human to be created in God's image: "The church sees in men and women, in every person, the living image of God himself. This image finds, and must always find anew, an ever deeper and fuller unfolding of itself in the mystery of Christ, the Perfect Image of God, the One who reveals God to man and man to himself."[20]

Part III, chapter 1 of the *Catechism of the Catholic Church* repeats this message on the dignity of the human person, which is rooted in the

18. Byassee, *Discerning the Body*, 116.
19. Luke 6:27.
20. Pontifical Council for Justice and Peace, *Compendium*, 105.

individual's being created in the image and likeness of God.[21] Chapter 2, article 3 of the same part adds the aspect of social justice. It states:

> Social justice can be obtained only in respecting the transcendent dignity of man. The person represents the ultimate end of society, which is ordered to him: What is at stake is the dignity of the human person, whose defense and promotion have been entrusted to us by the Creator, and to whom the men and women at every moment of history are strictly and responsibly in debt.[22]

In his address on the 2017 World Day of Peace, Pope Francis stated that "to be true followers of Jesus today also includes embracing his teaching about nonviolence."[23] The pope explains that nonviolence is a way of life in which one is able to forgive and love the enemy. He quotes Mother Teresa from 1979 when she received the Nobel Peace Prize: "We in our family don't need bombs and guns, to destroy to bring peace—just get together, love one another.... And we will be able to overcome all the evil that is in the world."[24] As we noted above, in 2019 the pope wrote another message on the World Day of Peace: "Bringing peace is central to the mission of Christ's disciples."

Thus, the Scriptures, the message of Jesus, the social teaching of the Catholic Church, the *Catechism of the Catholic Church,* and Pope Francis's messages for peace all emphasize respect for human dignity and the preciousness of life and call for each Christian to take responsibility for building peace within him or herself by living Jesus's message of love and forgiveness and spreading the message of defending human life and dignity. What are these messages saying to Christians in Africa, where we continue to witness massive loss of lives?

First there is a need for conscientization, or creating deep awareness among Catholics—and especially among the leaders of the church—of the potential of the church's structure to help build a peaceful world. The church needs to revisit modes of evangelization and the message of Christ in a world affected by endless violence. The conscientization needs to reach the clergy, religious orders, and every Christian so that they embrace the gospel of nonviolence and take responsibility to sow seeds of peace in families, villages, churches, communities, and countries. While many people hate to see violence, in general people are not aware of how they contribute to the ongoing violence with their words and actions. Others are not aware of the

---

21. *Catechism of the Catholic Church,* 1707–9.
22. *Catechism of the Catholic Church,* 1929.
23. Francis, *Message for the Celebration of the Fiftieth World Day of Peace,* 3.
24. Francis, *Message for the Celebration of the Fiftieth World Day of Peace,* 4.

preconditions of violence, such as stereotyping, hatred, discrimination, and prejudice. So as to avoid creating new situations of violence, Christians are called to deeply reflect on the actions they model for their children and the words and thoughts they transmit to their children.

Second, it is important to recall that the Catholic Church already has a structure (the Dicastery for Promoting Integral Human Development) for peace and justice, which flows from the top of the church hierarchy (the Vatican) to the grassroots. There is an urgent need for this entity to collaborate with other actors promoting peace, such as the Catholic Nonviolence Initiative of Pax Christi International, and formulate materials that will help create awareness among Christians regarding the messages of Jesus aimed at promoting peace and the call for each person to live by gospel values and be ambassadors for peace.

Third, it is important to integrate peace and the gospel of nonviolence into Sunday school programs and the formation for catechists, priests, and religious sisters and brothers. Peace programs also need to be taught in church-owned institutions, including schools, universities, colleges, and technical schools.

Fourth, in order to transform present-day violent conflicts, it is very important to understand the nature of the conflicts. This will inform the approaches needed to build sustainable peace. The primary parties to these conflicts are frequently neighboring ethnic groups, with the conflict being fought out in marginalized areas. These wars leave people at the grassroots deeply divided, traumatized, and filled with enmity, revenge, hatred, and fear. Where there is deep fear, long-standing animosity, and a direct experience of violence that sustains the image of the enemy, people are easily manipulated.[25] And unfortunately, the people directly caught up in the violence tend to be left out of the peace processes.

Sustainable peace will be achieved only if there is a recognition of the potential for each person at the grassroots to contribute to peace. The resources available at the grassroots for galvanizing support for peace must be mobilized. The people must be empowered to be agents of their own peace. The church needs to acquire the necessary skills and knowledge that will enable her to understand the roots and manifestations of contemporary violence and the appropriate approaches that can be applied, including exploring and facilitating wisdom at the grassroots level, giving people space to work for their own peace.

Finally, Pope Francis has written several messages of peace asking Christians to not only live peace, but also take responsibility for building

---

25. Lederach, *Building Peace*, 37–43.

a culture of peace. These messages, however, rarely reach people at the grassroots. I myself was able to learn of the pope's messages only because of my own interest and reading—I have never heard these messages being discussed in church. Channels for disseminating these messages should be revisited and strengthened. My own personal experience may be instructive. I grew up in a very rural area of the Diocese of Machakos in eastern Kenya. There were no mobile phones or computers. In my area there were only two priests and forty-three outstations, so we had Mass only once per month. On the other Sundays, the catechist presided over services. Since the diocese was so large, the bishop paid a visit only once a year, but he wrote messages to all the churches. The priest would print a copy for each village church, and the catechist would read the message to Christians for three weeks to ensure that they understood it. The same channel could be revived so that the messages of Pope Francis could be widely disseminated and translated into local languages, making it possible for each Christian to hear and understand them.

Conclusion

Violent conflicts in Africa have continued to claim the lives of innocent people and have forced many to live in dehumanizing situations. The majority of people who suffer as a result of these wars are found at the grassroots level of the societies where most of the violence takes place. The Catholic Church has enormous potential, which can be utilized to create a peaceful environment in which people coexist and collaborate in developmental activities. Christians follow their master Jesus, who teaches them to love even the enemy, to forgive, and to sacrifice in order to reach others who are in need. Christians are also guided by other values, such as a respect for life and human dignity. If Christians truly lived this message, there would be peace. Those who embrace the mission for peace will engage in it not because of the lure of money, but because they are called by Jesus to do so. The church is already with the people, and remains with them, which makes the church's peace mission believable. The church also has institutions through which messages of peace can be transmitted. Using these institutions, a new generation skillful in transforming conflicts constructively before they escalate into violence can be formed. In societies experiencing so much violence and the conditions that lead to violence, the church needs to take urgent action to utilize her potential to transform violence and prevent future wars.

Bibliography

Baregu, Mwesige, ed. *Understanding Obstacles to Peace: Actors, Interests, and Strategies in Africa's Great Lakes Region*. Kampala: Fountain, 2011.

Byassee, Jason. *Discerning the Body: Searching for Jesus in the World*. Eugene, OR: Cascade, 2013.

The Catechism of the Catholic Church. 2nd ed. Washington, DC: United States Catholic Conference, 2000.

Francis, Pope. *Message for the Celebration of the Fiftieth World Day of Peace*. Vatican City: Libreria Editrice Vaticana, January 1, 2017. http://www.vatican.va/content/francesco/en/messages/peace/documents/papa-francesco_20161208_messaggio-l-giornata-mondiale-pace-2017.html.

———. *Message for the Celebration of the 52nd World Day of Peace*. Vatican City: Libreria Editrice Vaticana, January 1, 2019. http://www.vatican.va/content/francesco/en/messages/peace/documents/papa-francesco_20181208_messaggio-52giornatamondiale-pace2019.html.

Habeeb, William Mark. *Civil Wars in Africa*. Africa Progress and Problems 6. Broomall, PA: Mason Crest, 2014.

Kenya Human Rights Commission. *The Forgotten People Revisited: Human Rights Abuses in Marsabit and Moyale Districts*. Nairobi: Kenya Human Rights Commission, 2000.

Lederach, John Paul. *Building Peace: Sustainable Reconciliation in Divided Societies*. Washington, DC: United States Institute of Peace, 1997.

———. *Reconcile: Conflict Transformation for Ordinary Christians*. Harrisonburg, VA: Herald, 2014.

Pontifical Council for Justice and Peace. *Compendium of the Social Doctrine of the Church*. Vatican City: Libreria Editrice Vaticana, 2004.

Rupesinghe, Kumar, and N. Sanam Anderlini. *Civil Wars, Civil Peace: An Introduction to Conflict Resolution*. London: Pluto, 1998.

Stedman, Stephen John, Donald Rothchild, and Elizabeth M. Cousens, eds. *Ending Civil Wars: Implementation of Peace Agreements*. Boulder, CO: Lynne Rienner, 2002.

World Bank Group. *Poverty and Shared Prosperity 2018: Piecing Together the Poverty Puzzle*. Washington, DC: The World Bank, 2018.

7

Women and Nonviolent Indigenous Approaches to Peacebuilding: The North Rift Region of Kenya

Teresia Wamũyũ Wachira, IBVM

IN THIS CHAPTER, THROUGH the personal narratives of women, I explore the nonviolent indigenous approaches they utilize to address the violence they experience and/or observe in the North Rift Region, Kenya—in particular, the four counties of Samburu, Elgeyo Marakwet, West Pokot, and Turkana.[1] My specific objectives are threefold: first, to highlight the different types of violence experienced and/or observed by women in this region; second, to examine the underlying causes of violence here; and third, to evaluate the nonviolent indigenous approaches that women engage in to address this violence.

Violent conflicts, in all forms (direct, structural, and cultural),[2] are a common phenomenon both globally and locally. In the context of Kenya, episodes of violent conflict occur on both the local and national levels. Nationally, for example, violence has broken out in the periods prior to, during, and after elections.[3] At the local level, there are different forms of violence. In the North Rift Region, it takes the form of cattle rustling

---

1. There are several counties in the North Rift Region, but due to the scope of this work, I cover only four counties, which are mainly arid or semi-arid. The people are mainly nomadic and pastoralists, with some such as the Marakwet engaging in mixed farming and cattle rearing. In all four counties, the people equally engage in cattle raiding as a cultural practice. Wachira, "Making Just Peace a Reality," 209–26.

2. See, in general, Galtung, *Peace by Peaceful Means*.

3. See, in general, Wambua, "Ethnification of Electoral Conflicts in Kenya."

(traditionally referred to as cattle raids), an activity that also exacerbates another problem—the proliferation of small arms and light weapons. Other forms of violent conflict in this region are resource-based, occurring mainly over water points and grazing fields for the people's cattle and goats.[4] And it is the women that tend to bear the brunt of this type of violence. Additionally, as in other parts of Kenya, the North Rift Region experiences various types of cultural violence that primarily target the female gender—for instance, female circumcision, an initiation rite of passage also known as female genital mutilation (or FGM) and female genital cutting (or FGC). Of the four counties I have studied, only the Turkana community does not practice FGM. This initiation rite of passage has numerous adverse effects including fistulas, HIV/AIDS, depression, and other illnesses, as well as early marriages that deprive the girl child of her right not only to experience childhood but also of her right to education, which curtails her potential to realize her goals.[5] In addition to FGM, the Samburu community also practices "beading," a cultural tradition that encourages early marriages and, to some extent, further entrenches the practice of FGM. In this tradition, the warriors (Morans) who are family relatives bring red beads to an uncircumcised girl and approach her parents, who give him permission to engage in sexual relations with their daughter. Because the young man and the girl are blood relatives, they are only allowed to have a temporary sexual relationship; marriage and pregnancy are forbidden, and should pregnancy occur, it must be terminated through the use of poisonous herbs. The main objective of beading in the Samburu culture is to prepare the young girl for marriage in the future.[6]

Other expressions of cultural violence include the exclusion and abuse of women and girls in patriarchal systems where they are treated as "second-class" citizens and often deprived of their freedom to associate and be involved in decision-making at all levels. Similar to other parts of the world, decision-making in the North Rift Region is highly gendered to the disadvantage of women. In addition, violent conflicts have led to livelihood impoverishment, because they prevent the women from accessing food and water. When their husbands are killed or wounded, the women are left to provide for their families. They also often face human security threats like forced displacement, which shatters their social lives and that of their

4. See, in general, Muigua, "Natural Resource Conflicts."

5. For more information on FGM's adverse effects, see "Termination of Female Genital Mutilation (TFGM) Project" and the World Health Organization's fact sheet, "Female Genital Mutilation."

6. For a more extensive exploration of the beading tradition, see Young, "Silent Sacrifice."

families. Susceptible to further exclusion and socioeconomic suffering, they can become specific targets for further violent attacks.

Some Underlying Causes of Different Types of Violence in the North Rift Region

The causes of violence in this part of Africa are multifaceted. For example, in some of the communities in Kenya, oral literature—such as myths, legends, songs, poetry, and dance that are passed on from one generation to the next—can be used to endorse stereotypical systems like exclusion and masochism. An apt example is a proverb from the Agikũyũ (also known as the Gikũyũ or Kikuyu—one of the ethnic communities in Kenya, a few of whom live in the counties I researched), which generally states that one should not believe a woman's word until it is actualized. In essence, this cautions people against trusting a woman's word and encourages them to disregard the female voice in general, but it can also play out in gatherings where key decisions are made. The same holds true in other North Rift communities. Women in these communities are perceived as, and sometimes treated as, children. It is not uncommon for a man to report, after visiting a home and finding a woman and her children, that there was no one in the house except the children. Such statements, as insignificant as they may seem, can hide violence against women and be passed on wholesale from one generation to the next and become the norm.

While there are governmental structures in place that stress equality and equity and should support women, little is actually done to reinforce these laws and policies. This is true even at the highest level—for instance, the Constitution of Kenya promulgated in 2010 gives equal rights to all[7] in spirit, but this is not the case in reality. Furthermore, the approaches currently taken to address violent conflict serve only to marginalize women more by excluding them from the various tables of fellowship and negotiation. How, then, do women find spaces where their voices can be heard in their own right, where they can comfortably sit at the table and contribute to decision-making?

---

7. See Constitution of Kenya, 2010, chap. 4, part 2, §27(3): "Women and men have the right to equal treatment, including the right to equal opportunities in political, economic, cultural and social spheres." See also Constitution of Kenya, 2010, chap. 4, part 2, §27(4): "The State shall not discriminate directly or indirectly against any person on any ground, including race, sex, pregnancy, marital status, health status, ethnic or social origin, colour, age, disability, religion, conscience, belief, culture, dress, language or birth."

Nonviolent Indigenous Approaches: Women's Responses to Violence in the North Rift Region

Although their contributions often remain on the periphery, women engage in peacebuilding activities at all levels—globally, regionally, and locally. For example, in Liberia, women used nonviolent means to help bring about an end to the nation's fourteen years' war. In Sierra Leone, Sudan, and Kenya, indigenous women used their nakedness as a nonviolent way to force their sons to stop the violent conflicts.[8] Distinct from that of men, the women's role is key to the success of any peacebuilding process and instrumental in reestablishing the social fabric following conflict.

Bridge Builders of Peace in Warring Communities

In almost all communities across Africa, women earn great respect and are considered the "bonding factor of families." Traditionally, it is believed that a married woman has no clan, and therefore, she is expected to transcend her own ethnic community in every way. Marrying into a different ethnic community, the woman is considered the new link between the two groups. Consequently, those within one ethnic group who are keen to go to war with the other can be dissuaded from doing so by being reminded that, because of their interethnic marriages, they are now kinsmen with their enemies. As one woman from the Turkana community explains in Kiswahili:

> *Unajua mama akiolewa kwa adui, kama vile mimi ni mturukana lakini bwana wangu nimpokot, sasa watu wakitaka kupigana wanakumbuka ya kwamba mtoto wao ameoleka huko kwa hivyo hi ni familia sasa—hawa wamekua in-laws. Sasa ya muhimu ni kuongea na kusikilizana.* [You see, when a woman is married to the enemy, just as I have done—I am a Turkana, and my husband is a Pokot—now, if the people want to fight, they will remember that their child is married there, and so they are family now—now they are in-laws. Now of importance is to dialogue and agree.][9]

This is also supported by a narrative from a woman of the Samburu ethnic community:

---

8. Schirch, *Ritual*. For additional information, see note 22 of this chapter.

9. Female respondent (coded F1T) from Turkana, interviewed in 2018; this and all subsequent translations from Kiswahili are my own.

> *Unajua sisi kina mama hatuna ukoo. Ukiolewa unaenda kwa bwana yako naunatulia ukifwatilia vile wanaishi. Ukiwa na kiburi utajipata na shida nyingi sana.* [You see, we women do not have a clan. When you get married, you go to your husband and you live there and adjust to the way of life. If you are proud, you will find yourself in many problems.]¹⁰

It is important to note that, while it is noble to recognize women as the symbolic bearers of cultural and ethnic identity and as the producers of a community's future generations, the flip side of this is this recognition can make them more vulnerable; it creates a tendency in society to blame them for the ills that befall individual family members, entire communities, or the country in general. Thus, a key component of the peacebuilding process is recognizing the woman's important and unique role as a bridge builder in the family setting, their local communities, and globally. One of the male respondents in my study highlights this bridge builder role in his own experience:

> You see, even if you see us Kalenjin men so strong and that we are the ones who are in charge, at home we listen to the good counsel of our wives. Sometimes, there can be a discussion among us men. If, for instance, I find that I am uncomfortable with it, I will ask my friends to give me time and that I will get back to them the following day. Actually, what I am planning is to check with my wife and see what she feels. If, after discussing with her, she is against the idea, I will go back and tell my friends that, after reflection, I am not supporting the idea.¹¹

This view is supported by one respondent, a woman from the Pokot community who shared in Kiswahili: *Unajua mama ndiye kila kitu. Ukitaka nyumba yako iwe na amani wewe ndiye mpatinishe. Usingonjee bwana kuleta amani nyumbani.* [You know, the woman is everything. If you desire your home to be peaceful, you are the bridge builder. Do not wait for your husband to bring peace into the home.]¹² An elderly woman from the Turkana community expresses a similar view, on the key role women play in their society to ensure stability and peace. She spoke in Turkana, which my research assistant, a young man familiar with the language, translated into English:

> You know, women have a lot of wisdom and, in fact, I think a very strong sense of good judgement and do not rush to making

---

10. Female respondent (coded F2S) from Samburu, interviewed in 2018.
11. Male respondent (coded M1K) Kalenjin living in Samburu, interviewed in 2018.
12. Female respondent (coded F5WPF from West Pokot), interviewed in 2019.

decisions; they consider an issue in totality and not just speaking carelessly. Women have seen a lot in life as they face a lot of problems from their husband and children as well. They have to deal with all that comes with patience and wisdom. Women play a key role as reconcilers in cases of divisions and differences. They have a caring and listening heart. This they do mainly to ensure they protect their livelihoods, maintain reconciliation because when war breaks, they are the ones who will suffer and have to bear the burden of taking care of the children and the elderly.[13]

The Power of the *Legetiet* (Birth Belt), the Spoken Word, and Symbolic Actions and Peacebuilding

In all of the communities in the North Rift Region, the women use a birth belt known as *legetiet* (also known as *leketyo* or *leketio*). The main function of this belt is to strengthen and shape the "womb" (belly) once the woman has given birth; it also serves as a means of birth control and brokering peace, which will be explained below. It is made of leather and decorated with cowrie shells that are strategically arranged. The women that participated in my research shared that, normally, the cowrie shells are arranged in odd, rather than even, numbers. They also reported that, in some communities such as the Samburu, there are two types of belts, one worn by older women and another by young women. Furthermore, they shared that, in order to differentiate the different belts, one has to check the arrangement of the cowrie shells, especially the number of rows of shells. One of the respondents, a church leader, explained:

> The significance of the *legetiet* is to restore, replace, relieve, and subsequently use [it] to deal with issues that require prayers for children, sons, warriors on special expeditions/missions. It is also used to relieve pain and to restore. This was also used by women to resolve conflicts as they grew older; having been elevated to wear *seemweett* (a necklace), they would use it instead.[14]

---

13. Female elderly woman and mentor to the young Turkana women (coded EWT1), interviewed in 2018.

14. Male church leader from the Kalenjin community (coded MCL), interviewed in 2021.

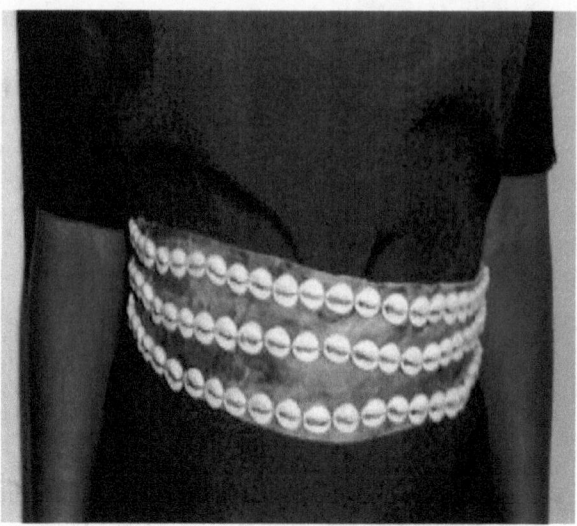

A *legetiet (leketyo, leketio)*, or birth belt. Source: Tulel, "Women and Peacebuilding in Pastoral Conflicts," 60.

Traditionally, the *legetiet* was also used for birth control, because once a woman is wearing it, her husband is not allowed to enter into a sexual relationship with her. It also acts as a shield for the woman—when she has it on, the man cannot attack her as he will be afraid of attracting a curse. Equally, in the situation of war, the women place the *legetiet* strategically on the ground, and as they are doing this, they utter these words, "*Leketio! Murenju!*" ("The belt is before you, warriors!"). Since crossing over the birth belt means attracting a curse, which usually leads to death, the warriors will not dare cross it to go and fight "the enemy," and their thoughts and desires of war will cease immediately. Hence, women use the birth belt to bless or to curse. One of the women respondents in my survey confirmed the power of the *legetiet* as a blessing, a symbol of life, or a curse:

> *Mimi nimeona vijana huko kwetu ambao aliruka hiyo legetiet akijifanya ati hizi ni mila za zamani na alipofanya hivyo aliangu-ka chini akakufa. Si hii inamaanisha uhai. Kwanini mtu achague kifo akikiona kikundolea macho?* [In fact, I witnessed a young person die after crossing over a *legetiet*. In our community, the *legetiet* is a symbol of life for us, so why does one want to choose death when seeing it right in front of them?][15]

---

15. Female respondent (coded F7WP) from West Pokot, interviewed in 2019.

The following is an excerpt of a song sung by a Pokot warrior to prompt the women to wear the *leketyo* to protect him as he goes to war:

> *Chepomoi amadawa ahaya* [Lady Chepomoi, wear the safety belt]
> *Amadawa haya* [Assure me that I can go]
> *Amadawa haya* [Assure me that I can go][16]

Women are using the *legetiet* more today to call for peace and to discourage their husbands and sons from going to war, due to the losses it has brought them, their children, and society as a whole.

Besides the *legetiet*, the other powerful symbol is a mother's, or woman's, nakedness. In African culture, showing a woman's—more so, a mother's—nakedness is a taboo and therefore can attract a curse on the individual who forces a mother to do this.[17] In the communities residing in the location of my research study, when mothers do not want their children to go to war, they will expose their breasts and press the milk out onto the ground as a symbol of dissatisfaction. A mother's milk is considered sacred, as it feeds the child and gives it life. Pressing it directly onto the ground symbolizes killing the future generation,[18] and this is culturally unacceptable, as expanding a clan and upholding its values are symbols of wealth and continuity. As one woman from the Elgeyo Marakwet community explains,

> *Mama akimkatasa mtoto kwenda vitani naye hasikilizi, mama anaweza kutoa maziwa kwa titi nikama anataka kunyonyesha mtoto. Akifanya hivi anajaribu kukumbusha mtoto wake vile alimunyonyesha lakini sasa anajiona ati ni mtu mzima hawezi kuambiwa chochote hasa na mwanamke. Kitendo hiki hata ikiwa ni cha aibu kwa mzazi na hata mtoto, chaweza kuleta balaa kwa mtoto huyu. Basi, mtoto akiona hivi na akikumbuka ile inaweza kumpata anaacha.* [When a mother wants to dissuade her male child from going to war and he is adamant, the mother might spill the milk from her breast to show him how hurt she is that her child is disobedient. When she is engaging in this act, she is trying to remind her son that she provided him the same milk from her breast and now he thinks that he is a grown-up man so he cannot be advised by a woman. Though such an action from his mother is shameful, to both her and him, it can bring a curse to the son. As a result, he might be afraid and decide to listen to his mother in case he calls a curse upon himself.][19]

16. Ong'eta and Salome, "Culture, Peace, and Development," 139–40.
17. Among the Agĩkũyũ, for instance, the curse of a mother is the most feared. Wachege, "Curses and Cursing among the Agĩkũyũ," 3.
18. Gichohi, "Women's Experiences," 52.
19. Female respondent (coded F9EM) from Elgeyo Marakwet, interviewed in 2020.

Similarly, lactating mothers extend the gesture of reconciliation by swapping babies with their "opponent" and breastfeeding them.[20] This is to show their willingness to create harmony, communion, and sisterhood. More importantly, as one woman from the Kalenjin community told me, this gesture is aimed at passing on new life and the reconciliatory spirit to generations to come: "What greater thing can a mother give someone than to nurture them through the milk that has and continues to nurture life?"[21] The spoken word and a mother's displaying of her nakedness carry power in African communities. For instance, it is a curse to see parents' private parts as these are associated with the creation of life, which is sacred and is always to be treated with the utmost decorum and respect. For example, beginning on February 28, 1992, in Kenya, during the one-party system under the late second president, Daniel arap Moi, mothers whose children had been held without trial as "political detainees" staged strikes that lasted for eleven months; at one point in early March, police came with batons and tear gas to break up their protest, and in response to such violence, the women stripped before the officers. This violence also triggered local demonstrations and headlines worldwide, as well as some international criticism of Kenya's government, all of which ultimately aided the mothers as they continued working for their sons' release.[22]

Early Warning Signs: Interpretation of Daily Events and Peace

Within these communities, there are some diviners who are women; they give early warning signs, predicting an attack or the chances of an attack, and are viewed as the best "medicine persons (*chesakttian*) and seers (*kapoloktin*)."[23] The important role of women diviners is to assist in preventing an impeding war. Since it is the women who go out in search of water, food, and herbs for treatment when their children and family are ailing, it is the women who will hear of impending attacks and may also sometimes observe footprints that are foreign to their land. In addition, their children may report seeing

---

20. Akinyi, "Participation of Women," 74.

21. Elderly woman (coded F7EM) from Elgeyo Marakwet, interviewed in 2020.

22. See "Bare-Breasted Crusade": "In retaliation, the *cūcūs* [the Gikūyū word for grandmothers] stripped naked and shook their breasts at the cops. The policeman ran away. It is deemed a curse when a mother or old woman strips in anger, but the violence against them made world headlines, sparking stone-throwing riots in Nairobi. *Matatus* [public sixteen-seater vans] staged strikes in solidarity. The US and German embassies condemned the Kanu [Kenya African National Union] regime."

For additional information on the women's protests, see Tedia, "Kenyan Mothers."

23. Loyatum, "Role of Women," 4.

footprints or unusual sights, as they tend the animals in the field. A male peacebuilder working in Samburu affirms the important role of women in identifying signs of impending danger: "When women are going out to fetch firewood, water, and are looking for food, they might notice a number of monkeys lining up on the road, a sign that the forest is not safe. These women will come home and share with their husbands that all is not well."[24]

In addition, some of the respondents in my research said that some elderly women can tell when there is a war brewing by looking at the color of the milk or the feeding habits of the animals. For example, these women know when a cow has eaten in a hurry, indicating that there must be some destruction in the grazing fields, which is often because the enemy has occupied the land. They communicate all this to their husbands who then will meet with other men and strategize how to protect themselves and their families. As one of the women from West Pokot describes,

> *Wakati mwingine unakamua ngombe halafu onaone ndume wengine wakiwa na mori ya kupigana. Hii ni ishara ya kwamba adui amekaribia kwetu. Nahata unaeza ona yakwamba ngombe haijashiba vizuri, inatoa maziwa kidogo ndio unajiuliza, ni kwanini hasijashiba na kuna nyasi kiasi? Si hii ni ishara ya kuonyesha sinakula kwa haraka siondoke au kuna mtu huko ambao hazimjui anasizuia zikule na kushiba?* [Another time, you are milking and then you see nearby some bulls with the spirit of aggression. This is a sign that the enemy is near home. Even you can see that the cows are not satisfied and are not producing much milk. Then, you ask yourself why these animals are not well-fed and yet there is plenty of grass? Is this not a sign . . . that they were eating in a hurry so that they can go home, or that there is someone they do not know who is preventing them from eating their fill?][25]

This testimony concurs with the narratives recorded in a research study carried out by Angela Wangui Gichohi on the role of women in averting violent conflicts by relaying information of an impending threat or raid—for example, identifying unfamiliar footprints that could be interpreted as belonging to the enemy.[26] In today's context, these are treated as early warning signs that need to be incorporated into the peacebuilding process.

---

24. Male peacebuilder (coded M5S) from Samburu, interviewed in 2018.
25. Female respondent (coded FWP6) from West Pokot, interviewed in 2019.
26. Gichohi, "Women's Experiences," 41.

The Power of the Spoken Word and Modeling Just Peace Virtue Ethics through Oral Literature

In these communities, a woman is held in high esteem because she nurtures life inside her womb, brings forth life, and ensures the perpetuation of the clan. Therefore, showing disrespect to a woman—and more so, a mother—is seen as disrespecting the whole community. Anyone who does not take heed of a mother's words or advice is making a choice to reject the opportunity for life. As highlighted by this male peacebuilder working in Samburu, the spoken words are, therefore, a source of life or death: "The women are the mothers of the warriors and the advice they give them is taken seriously—she [the mother] is considered the 'gate to a Moran's heart,' [and] thus, holds the key to a Moran's heart. Thus, her words carry so much power, blessings, or a curse."[27]

One male community leader from Elgeyo Marakwet emphasized the fact that one cannot replace the position a mother holds in the family and community: "After the young men have undergone through [sic] the rite of passage, the mother is the last person to open the gate to allow the initiate (her son) back to the community. She speaks some words of wisdom to him, crowns, and anoints him with words of blessings. Thus, mothers have a very central role to play in the transition of their sons from boyhood to manhood."[28] As a result, when the mother dissuades her male children, for example, from engaging in wars or violent conflicts, they heed her advice and will not engage in warfare. This shows the power of the mother in ensuring a peaceful society. Finding ways to build on this powerful peacebuilding role of the mother can help to address the violent conflicts in the North Rift Region and, indeed, in all of Kenya and beyond.

Culturally, the North Rift Region communities do not allow women or children to engage in warfare and/or to shed blood. Thus, warriors cannot kill a woman or child, and if this happens, a cleansing ritual must be performed. However, it is the women that sometimes hide and shelter the cattle and/or goats that have been brought home after cattle rustling. Therefore, the women can easily identify the cattle rustlers, their point of entry, as well as the specific markets where they sell the looted cattle, and thus, expose them and stop the violence. It is the women who are in the best position to be the custodians and gateways to peace in their communities. Furthermore, as explained by the community leader from Elgeyo Marakwet who was quoted earlier,

27. Male peacebuilder (coded M5S) from Samburu, interviewed in 2018.
28. Male community leader (coded M8CL) from Elgeyo Marakwet, interviewed in 2020.

> Every man that engages in warfare must undergo cleansing before going back to normal life. Therefore, they should not enter their house before engaging in this cleansing ritual. This is because it is assumed that those who go to war must have killed or observed someone being killed and, therefore, have blood on their hands. Furthermore, these communities believe that if the man does not go for cleansing after war, the blood could affect his children, and this can continue for generations to come. However, some men are adamant and are not willing to go through the cleansing rituals. In such cases, the wife is expected to report to the elders so that they can summon the man to be cleansed.[29]

Women actively contribute to peacebuilding in their own unique ways. Some of the approaches they utilize are song, dance, peace missions, and marriage. Oral literature (including song) is another strategy used to honor the giftedness of humanity and also to promote harmony and development.[30] Most importantly, in the traditional communities of Africa, oral literature plays an important role in the early formation of children and also throughout the adult life as a means to dialogue, correct, and show language prowess. For instance, long ago, children (especially in the rural areas) would sit around a fire listening to their mothers or grandmothers tell stories, offer riddles, or share tongue twisters as they prepared a meal. The stories would involve primarily animal characters that would symbolize different community virtues such as honesty, love, generosity, sharing, kindness, compassion, justice, peace, and harmony. Stories would also be used to discourage children as well as adults from behavior that would show disrespect, greed, or selfishness—for instance, the stories of the tricky hare who later was caught and punished; of the cunning ogre who waylays a pregnant woman but later is killed by the sons she gives birth to; of the animals that unite during the drought season to dig a common well, each using its different gifts. Children also learn these virtues through legends, myths, songs, dances, and poetry. Young girls and women would also use song, poetry, and dance to motivate the young men/warriors to go to war as well as to praise them when they returned home victorious. On the other hand, songs could also be used to criticize and ridicule those who showed cowardice. Thus, just as women in the past were at the forefront of inciting and ridiculing the warriors, today they are at the forefront of dissuading the warriors and the men from engaging in violent conflicts which, as noted

---

29. Male community leader (coded M8CL) from Elgeyo Marakwet, interviewed in 2020.

30. Ong'eta and Salome, "Culture, Peace, and Development," 134–46.

earlier, have led to the loss of lives and property, leaving some of them widowed and also having to provide security for themselves and their families. Take, for a contemporary example, the women crusaders who are acting as agents of change by discouraging young men from participating in cattle raiding. They ensure that they attend meetings of the community elders to apply pressure in order to make peaceful resolutions whenever they are addressing issues of conflicts in their families and communities.

Traditionally, older women also created occasions and opportunities for bonding, especially in the evenings after work when they would use themed songs and dances to educate, for example, the young married women on how to take care of their families and to cement their relationships with their husbands. These forums created an environment for older women to share both their wisdom and their grievances and also for the younger women to learn from the wisdom and experience of the older women. The older women also mentored the new mothers in caring for and protecting their children while also teaching the young mothers how to ensure peace in their homes and what to do if their husbands turned violent. This mentorship both taught and planted the culture of peace in families and communities. It gave the young mothers confidence as they mentored their own children. This journey continued as formation in the community's values of sharing, community living, caring for the environment, being honest, working hard, and showing justice; giving thanks to the Creator of all human beings and the environment—through prayers and libations and also through efforts to live harmoniously—was a community affair. As a result, this contributed to harmony and unity in families and communities. Some of these practices have continued to be embraced in the rural settings and have helped bring communities together in both happy and challenging times.[31]

As a young married Turkana woman in Samburu describes:

> *Unajua sisi kina mama ambao wameolewa jusi huwa tunastress sana. Kwa mfano, bwana zetu hata ikiwa wamesoma zaidi, hata wawe na madegree bado wanashikilia ile mila zao za zamani. Hawataki useme chochote. Sasa sisi hufurahia wakati tuko na nafasi na kina mama wale wazee ambao wanatupa mawaidha, tunafuraha sana tukiwa nao hii inatoa stress yote tunayo hata ikiwa ni ya muda mfupi tu.* [You see, we young married women have a lot of stress. For instance, our husbands, even those that have attended higher education, keep holding to their traditions.

---

31. Seven women respondents in a focus group (coded 7W) from Turkana, Samburu, and West Pokot, interviewed in 2020; though living in Nairobi, they are in touch with their home counties and supporting grassroots initiatives.

They do not want you to contribute in any conversation. We are happier when we go to listen to the elderly woman that gives us counsel; we are so happy when we are with them, because this helps us deal with all our stress, even if this is for a little while.][32]

Bonding and Bridging through Preparing and Sharing Meals and Barter Trade

As in other communities, both locally and globally, food is a uniting factor in the African culture, as it brings everyone to the table regardless of their color, gender, status, and orientation. As a result, in the African culture (without generalizing), food is the symbol of peace. During the different celebrations such as births, naming ceremonies, rites of passage from childhood to adulthood, marriage, and death, the women come together to prepare meals to celebrate life. When the food is ready, all are welcome to partake of it. As one of the women of the Kalenjin community shared, "Only a witch likes to eat alone."[33] Food brings women together as they plant, weed, harvest, and build granaries for the future storage of extra food; they engage in hearty conversation, song, and dance, thanking the Creator for the gift of food. Food also creates an opportunity for barter trade; for instance, one woman from West Pokot explained that she sells her honey to the women from Turkana, and in return, she buys vegetables from them.[34]

Alternative Rite of Passage: A Nonviolent Approach to Female Circumcision (Female Genital Mutilation)

Except for the Turkana, the communities in the North Rift Region practice female circumcision, or FGM. As noted early in this chapter, this rite of passage has adverse side effects, especially on women's health and their socioeconomic contributions, with far-reaching negative consequences, including women's contributions to sustainable development. As a result, today there are various initiatives aiming to end this violence against women. One of the best examples of such initiatives is the alternative rite of passage, based on Christian principles,[35] at the Loreto Abundant Life Centre oper-

---

32. Female youth respondent (coded FY6T) from Turkana, interviewed in 2018.
33. Female respondent (coded F6K) from Turkana, interviewed in 2018.
34. Female respondent (coded F6EM) from Elgeyo Marakwet, interviewed in 2020.
35. Ephigenia W. Gachiri, IBVM, details this alternative rite of passage in her book, *Christian Initiation for Girls*.

ated by the Institute of the Blessed Virgin Mary (also known as the Loreto Sisters) in Isinya, Kajiado, Kenya. Advocating the "termination of female genital mutilation," this redefined rite of passage teaches its young female participants that Jesus came so that all—including girls and women—"may have life and have it to the full" (John 10:10, NJB), and they are no exception. The program helps young girls to learn and experience God's love for all people, emphasizing love and acceptance of themselves as being unique and "as beautiful as God made them."[36]

The program teaches the girls about female sexuality, with an emphasis on the beauty of girlhood/womanhood and the uniqueness of each girl/woman. The girls are educated in virtues such as human dignity and self-love (care and respect for themselves and their developmental uniqueness), which promotes the rejection of violence as well as a healthy self-image and respect for one's body. The program offers its participants the opportunity to learn about—and value—the unique and important role that girls and women play in their local communities as well as all over the world, in general.

In addition, the program teaches the history of the traditional rite of female circumcision, explaining the facts and analyzing the possible emotional, physical, and psychosocial consequences. It also readapts the traditional role of the "sponsor." In the traditional FGM rite of passage, the sponsor accompanies the initiate from the time of circumcision throughout the rest of her life. In the Loreto Abundant Life Centre's alternative nonviolent rite of passage, the sponsor has an enhanced role, acting as a role model for the young girl/woman as she progresses through life. Additionally, the program offers outreach to the boys of the community through a Christian rite of passage, educating the young men to respect women through capacity-building as opposed to excluding them.[37]

---

36. "Termination of Female Genital Mutilation (TFGM) Project." The Loreto Abundant Life Centre has developed out of the TFGM Project, started by Sr. Ephigenia Gachiri in 1998 in the Murang'a Catholic Diocese of Kenya "to promote the well-being and rights of the girls" and ensure "that they attain their highest potentials." For more information about the TFGM Project, visit its website, https://stopfgm.or.ke.

37. These values and others—such as hard work, obedience, perseverance, peaceful coexistence, and desisting from violent practices like cattle raiding—are taught during this Christian rite of passage. The details of the rigorous training that the young men undergo through this rite are captured in Sr. Gachiri's book, *Rite of Passage for Christian Boys*. Through this book, Sr. Gachiri addresses and aims to counter the harmful traditional values inculcated in the young men during the traditional rite of passage to manhood. These harmful values include killing, machismo, negative stereotyping of ethnic communities other than their own, and disrespect for the female gender (especially those who have not undergone FGM), inclusive of their female teachers. The boys also take secret oaths and are inducted through intense, painful, and violent experiences, which are intended to make them tough and ready to face the wider world, but which are, in actuality, detrimental to them.

Practical Suggestions

The following are initiatives that, if enhanced, can address some of the violence that women experience and/or observe and that they themselves are making efforts to address in the North Rift Region of Kenya:

- Women's voices are unique and key for sustainable peacebuilding/development. At both the local and national levels, special efforts should be made to include women at the different tables of fellowship and decision-making. Additionally, the inclusivity of women should not be tokenism but rather based on equality and equity and respected as a human right.
- Communities should be encouraged to learn and adopt some of the nonviolent indigenous approaches utilized by different indigenous groups in addressing violent conflicts they encounter. The approaches in this text can act as a point of departure.
- The FGM rite of passage for girls—and the corresponding rite for boys—usually happens between the ages of thirteen and fifteen (though in some communities, it is earlier than this), and in the Catholic Church, this age group corresponds to the age of Christian initiation, through the sacrament of confirmation. Therefore, the Catholic Church can use the time and preparation for this sacrament as an opportunity to teach young men and women about the gift of life, which is precious, sacred, and should be protected; about God's unconditional love for each person irrespective of gender, religion, and age; and about such virtues as forgiveness, harmony, peace, mercy, justice, and compassion. The church can incorporate some of the virtues that the girls were taught before, during, and after the traditional rite as well as the idea of having a mentor to guide them. And it should discard, on the other hand, the harmful and violent aspects of the traditional rites. For the girls, these include the "cut" and other lessons that deny them a voice; for the boys, they include the physical challenges they are put through that aim to make them tough as well as some of the oaths they take that serve only to numb their humanity.
- Harmful myths and misinformation concerning sexuality should be examined and dispelled.
- Leaders at all levels of governance should model inclusivity and respect, especially for women and children who often experience different forms of exclusion and vulnerability.

- Women, as the first custodians of culture and educators for peace, should utilize their moral authority, modeling for their children the virtues of community: sharing, harmony, justice, peace, and compassion, among others. They should advocate against "gun culture" by refusing to sing and dance for warriors heading out for cattle rustling. Parents should discourage the purchase of toy guns for children and avoid taking them to entertainment centers where they can watch and/or play violent games. Indeed, they should shun all purchases of arms and any programs or entertainment centers that foster violence in families, communities, and institutions.

- The Kenyan government should reinforce the Bill of Rights sections in the 2010 Constitution's chapter 4 that promote the equal rights and freedom of all people, including women, children, the elderly, refugees, and minorities.[38]

- Having ratified UN Resolution 1325—a "landmark resolution on women, peace, and security"[39]—the Kenyan government must also ensure that it is implemented and evaluated to establish its successes and challenges.[40]

- The church should also encourage and support women's associations such as the Catholic Women's Association and the Women's Guild. Working closely with the women at the grassroots level, these groups can thereby harness the different nonviolent peacebuilding approaches the women are engaged in. The church should also encourage the different Catholic men's organizations to work collaboratively and peacefully with these women's organizations.

---

38. See note 7 for the specific language in these sections.

39. "Landmark Resolution." Adopted by the UN Security Council on October 31, 2000, Resolution 1325 "urges all actors to increase the participation of women and incorporate gender perspectives in all United Nations peace and security efforts. It also calls on all parties to conflict to take special measures to protect women and girls from gender-based violence, particularly rape and other forms of sexual abuse, in situations of armed conflict."

40. Since Kenya has ratified this resolution, it should implement it in full to support women's efforts in security and peacebuilding. For instance, women's voices need to be brought to the fore by ensuring that the two-thirds gender rule is passed by Parliament and also that there is gender mainstreaming, from the grassroots to the top level.

Conclusion

In this chapter, I have argued for nonviolent indigenous approaches in addressing violent conflicts, and from the personal testimonies I have shared, it is evident that the peacebuilding role of women is valued within the communities. This is rarely appreciated, however, at the top level of peacebuilding processes, whether in traditional or modernized settings, and for a long time, women's peacebuilding roles have been relegated to the grassroots level. Whether within the church or other spheres of life, not involving women as equal collaborators at the high-level negotiation tables creates a lacuna in the peacebuilding process that has adverse effects on sustainable peacebuilding and development. Therefore, I argue that we must bring women's voices and contributions to the fore, engaging them beyond simply the grassroots level. Lederach's pyramid framework of actors can be the starting point for this engagement. In his arguments, Lederach highlights the importance of involving actors at each and every level of the peacebuilding process (top, middle, and grassroots); as he points out, each level has its own unique expertise to contribute to ensure sustainable peace.[41]

Bibliography

Akinyi, Eunice Ochieng'. "Participation of Women in Peacebuilding in the Cross Border Conflict between the Luo of Upper Nyakach and Kipsigis of Sigowet Sub-Counties: 1963–1992." Master's thesis, Kenyatta University, 2017. https://ir-library.ku.ac.ke/bitstream/handle/123456789/18637/Participation%20of%20women%20in%20peacebuilding%20in%20the%20cross%20border%20conflict.pdf?isAllowed=y&sequence=1.

"Bare-Breasted Crusade: When Mothers of Political Prisoners Stripped at Uhuru Park." *The Standard*, August 31, 2018. https://www.standardmedia.co.ke/entertainment/nainotepad/2001261426/bare-breasted-crusade-when-mothers-of-political-prisoners-stripped-at-uhuru-park.

Constitution of Kenya, 2010. Kenya Law, Laws of Kenya, n.d. http://kenyalaw.org:8181/exist/kenyalex/actview.xql?actid=Const2010#KE/CON/Const2010/chap_4/hc_chap_4/sec_27.

"Female Genital Mutilation." World Health Organization, January 31, 2023. https://www.who.int/news-room/fact-sheets/detail/female-genital-mutilation.

Gachiri, Ephigenia W. *Christian Initiation for Girls*. Nairobi: Paulines Africa, 2006.

———. *Rite of Passage for Christian Boys*. Nairobi: Paulines Africa, 2006.

Galtung, Johan. *Peace by Peaceful Means: Peace and Conflict, Development and Civilization*. London: Sage, 1996.

Gichohi, Angela Wangui. "Women's Experiences in Peace Building Processes: The Case of Turkana County, Kenya." Master's thesis, University of Nairobi, 2016. http://

---

41. Lederach, *Building Peace*, 39.

erepository.uonbi.ac.ke/bitstream/handle/11295/100405/Gichohi-Women's%20 Experiences%20In%20Peace%20Building%20Processes%20The%20Case%20 Of%20Turkana%20County%2c%20Kenya.pdf?sequence=1&isAllowed=y.

"Landmark Resolution on Women, Peace, and Security." Website of the United Nations OSAGI (Office of the Special Adviser on Gender Issues and Advancement of Women), n.d. https://www.un.org/womenwatch/osagi/wps/.

Lederach, John Paul. *Building Peace: Sustainable Reconciliation in Divided Societies.* Washington, DC: United States Institute of Peace Press, 1997.

Loyatum, Irene Cherotich. "The Role of Women in Peace Building in Conflicting Society: The Case of West Pokot County, Kenya, 2000–2018." Master's thesis, United States International University–Africa, 2019. https://erepo.usiu.ac.ke/bitstream/handle/11732/5003/LOYATUM%20IRENE%20CHEROTICH%20 MAIR%202019.pdf?sequence=1&isAllowed=y.

Muigua, Kariuki. "Natural Resource Conflicts: Addressing Inter-Ethnic Strife through Environmental Justice in Kenya." Kariuki Muigua and Co. Advocates, September 2019. http://kmco.co.ke/wp-content/uploads/2019/09/Natural-Resource-Conflicts-Addressing-Inter-Ethnic-Strife-Through-Environmental-Justice-in-kenya-Kariuki-Muigua-7th-September-2019.pdf.

Ong'eta, Mose Wyclife, and Nyambura Salome. "Culture, Peace, and Development: A Case Study of West Pokot County, Kenya." *Machakos University Journal of Science and Technology* 1:1 (November 2018) 134–46. https://dvc-ril.mksu.ac.ke/wp-content/uploads/2019/06/MksU-JOURNAL-Final-2abcd.pdf.

Schirch, Lisa. *Ritual and Symbol in Peacebuilding.* Bloomfield, CT: Kumarian, 2005.

Tedia, Aden. "Kenyan Mothers Win Release of Political Prisoners and Press for Democratic Reform, 1992–1993." Swarthmore College Global Nonviolent Action Database, March 11, 2010. https://nvdatabase.swarthmore.edu/content/kenyan-mothers-win-release-political-prisoners-and-press-democratic-reform-1992-1993.

"Termination of Female Genital Mutilation (FGM) Project." Mary Ward JPIC Office, July 5, 2020. http://www.marywardjpic.org/2020/07/05/termination-of-female-genital-mutilation-tfgm-project.

Tulel, Irene Chepoisho. "Women and Peacebuilding in Pastoral Conflicts: A Case Study of Pokot Women in Sigor Region of West Pokot County, 1984–2000." Department of History and Archeology, University of Nairobi, 2013.

Wachege, Patrick N. "Curses and Cursing among the Agĩkũyũ: Socio-cultural and Religious Benefits." Faculty website, Philosophy and Religious Studies Department, University of Nairobi, 2012. http://erepository.uonbi.ac.ke/handle/11295/39934.

Wachira, Teresia Wamũyũ. "Making Just Peace a Reality: A New 'Flavour' to Peacebuilding." In *Just Peace Ethic Primer: Building Sustainable Peace and Breaking Cycles of Violence*, edited by Eli S. McCarthy, 209–26. Washington, DC: Georgetown University Press, 2020.

Wambua, Muema. "The Ethnification of Electoral Conflicts in Kenya: Options for Positive Peace." *African Journal on Conflict Resolution* 17:2 (2017) 9–40. https://www.ajol.info/index.php/ajcr/article/view/167168.

Young, Laura A., ed. "Silent Sacrifice: Girl-Child Beading in the Samburu Community of Kenya. Samburu Women Trust, 2012. https://www.iwgia.org/images/publications/0607_SEEDO_research_report.pdf.

8

Building Spaces of Nonviolence: Women's Work to Challenge Armed Violence

Jasmin Nario-Galace

Introduction

WOMEN ARE DIFFERENTLY AFFECTED by armed violence, a situation that they do not normally perpetrate. They lose their source of livelihood due to displacement. They bear the responsibility of providing for children and household needs when men are killed or in the battlefield. They experience difficulty accessing services in evacuation centers, which pose concern particularly for the pregnant and lactating. In many armed conflicts, they have been raped, harassed, threatened, assaulted, and intimidated by those who wield the arms.

Armed violence is the intentional use of physical force, threatened or actual, against oneself, another person, or against a group or community that either results in or has a high likelihood of resulting in injury, death, psychological harm, or deprivation.[1] In 2016, over half a million people were violently killed, both in conflict and non-conflict settings.[2]

---

1. Krug et al., *World Report*, 4.
2. McEvoy and Hideg, *Global Violent Deaths*, 10.

Gender and Violence

There are many known causes of armed violence—political, economic, cultural, situational—but not many have examined gendered causes. Cultural norms/constructions of masculinity expect men to exhibit power, dominate others, take control, and exert physical strength. This is why they dominate public spaces like government and business. They are the heads of states and the chief executive officers of business organizations. They dominate the military and police institutions, media, and religious organizations. They call the shots in every institution there is from family to international organizations. Women have contributed to cultural conditioning that equates masculinity with violent behavior, encouraging their boys and men to fight or show force because they are boys or men. They reprimand their boy children when they cry. They buy them war toys and encourage them to play games and sports that are tough and rough. Owning a weapon and exhibiting aggressive behavior have, thus, become equivalent to being a man. Hence, the primary owners and users of weapons—and often the perpetrators and victims of armed violence—are men. Men and boys accounted for 84 percent of those who died violently in 2016.[3]

Women, in the face of armed violence, are normally viewed as vulnerable and victims. The role that they play in preventing violence, keeping the peace, and in resolving conflict is often overlooked. In many communities affected by armed violence, in times of both conflict and peace, women have played important roles: relief and rehabilitation coordinators, evacuation center managers, facilitators of dialogue, mediators between victims and government agencies, healers and counselors, etc. However, their diverse peace, conflict prevention, and security-related activities are often referred to in passing and receive little or no support. Men, because they wage the war, often negotiate the peace. They dominate the public space and make the decisions in nearly all matters that relate to peace and security.

In a study done by UN Women, women constituted only 6 percent of mediators, 13 percent of negotiators, and 6 percent of signatories in all major peace processes between 1992 and 2019[4]—and yet, women comprise nearly 50 percent of the world's population.[5] Their unique experiences and perspectives are hardly taken into account in matters of peace and security.

In developing solutions to the problem of armed violence, the views of women must also be considered. Hence, the adoption of UN Security

---

3. McEvoy and Hideg, *Global Violent Deaths*, 12.
4. UN Women, "Facts and Figures," para. 8.
5. World Bank Group, "Population, Female."

Council Resolution 1325 on October 31, 2000, which mandates member-states to include women and increase their participation in the different tracks of peace processes, conflict prevention, and peacebuilding, has been positively received. The landmark resolution underscores the importance of women's equal participation and full involvement in both the maintenance and promotion of peace and security. In essence, the resolution has two important aims: to get to peace and to give women the equal right to participate in building it.

Why Peace?

Why develop solutions to armed violence? First, it is a practical alternative. The 1.7 trillion US dollars spent globally for military purposes in 2017[6] could have been used to deliver the essential basic services for the world's poor. Approximately half of the world's population of nearly seven billion live in poverty.[7] Second, it's our legal obligation to the community of nations. We are signatories to important human rights and disarmament conventions and treaties. But the quest for peace should not be simply rooted to practical and legal reasons. We work for peace, because it is an ethical imperative, a strong teaching of our faith. The rejection of violence, of killing, and of harming are strong teachings in the Catholic tradition. We are taught to respond to evil with good (Rom 12:17–21). When Peter drew out his sword and *cut off* the right *ear* of the high priest's servant, Jesus instructed him to put his sword back. In Isa 2:4, we are warned against war and taught peaceful settlement of disputes and converting our weapons into food-gathering implements. Love and reconciliation, rather than retaliation, are at the heart of Christian teachings. Jesus instructed us to love one another (John 13:34), not to repay injury with injury (Rom 12:17), and instead to turn the other cheek when a person strikes us on one cheek (Matt 5:39). Jesus also refused to stone a woman accused of adultery (John 8:1–11).

In his message for the celebration of the Fiftieth World Day of Peace on January 1, 2017, Pope Francis has also called on all—not just the Catholic flock—to respect each other's dignity and make active nonviolence our way of life. He enjoined people to cultivate nonviolence in their thoughts and values and in their treatment of others. He underscored that countering violence with violence will lead to greater suffering, positing that war takes

---

6. Stockholm International Peace Research Institute, "Global Military Spending," para. 1.

7. Lardieri, "World Bank," para. 1.

away resources that otherwise would have benefited those who experience hardship.[8] Indeed, we are called to be people of peace and nonviolence.

Women and Nonviolence

Women have a rich history of challenging armed violence and of building spaces of nonviolence. The oldest record in world literature of civil disobedience can be found in the Second Book of Moses, where midwives spurned a government decree to kill all male newborns and, instead, saved them all. In olden times, women were almost invisible in discourses of war and peace, but in a more contemporary example from the nineteenth century, the civil rights activist Lucretia Mott used methods of "moral suasion" to end slavery, call out racial discrimination, and fight for women's rights. She maintained that struggle should be pursued with moral force alone.[9] Many of these women abolitionists believed that Christian principles and the struggle for justice and peace are one and the same. In Argentina, the mothers at Plaza de Mayo who wore their missing children's cloth diapers on their heads persistently called on the government to account for their missing children and eventually caused political change.[10] From 1976 to 1983, the government of Argentina abducted, tortured, and killed political opponents of the regime. Mothers gathered in the plaza weekly, demanding that the government tell them where their children were. Their nonviolent protest earned international attention and became an inspiration for women in Chile, Brazil, Bolivia, Paraguay, and Uruguay who were in similar situations. In 1988, Women in Black in Israel called for an end to the occupation in Gaza. Since then, Women in Black groups have sprouted in various parts of the world protesting war, nuclear proliferation, and the arms race, among other atrocities.[11] In September 1980, Molly Rush, a Catholic antiwar activist, entered a General Electric nuclear weapons plant with eight others and pounded parts of nuclear warheads, rendering them less dangerous. She was accompanied by seven others, including one other woman, who are collectively called the Plowshares Eight and will always be remembered in history for this brave act of nonviolent protest against nuclear weapons.[12] The following year in England, women challenged the decision to store nuclear weapons at the Greenham Common military base in Berkshire. Chaining

8. Francis, "For the Celebration," para. 6.
9. Vetter, "Most Belligerent Non-Resistant," 600–30.
10. See, generally, "History of Abuelas."
11. See, generally, "Israel."
12. Muller and Brown, "Plowshares Eight," para. 7.

themselves to the fence there, they became instrumental in the removal of cruise missiles from this base.[13]

Building Spaces of Nonviolence: Experience in the Philippines

Prior to the signing of the Comprehensive Agreement on the Bangsamoro (CAB), there were two major armed conflicts in the Philippines. One was between the government (GRP, or Government of the Republic of the Philippines) and the Moro Islamic Liberation Front (MILF), and the other was between the government and the Communist Party of the Philippines, the New Peoples' Army (CPP-NPA). Both armed conflicts began in the 1960s. Over the decades, these armed conflicts have killed and displaced thousands of people. Civilians, particularly indigenous peoples who live in the highlands, are the ones always caught in the crossfire. The Moros were fighting for independence not only because of their difference in religion and ethnicity but also because of their experiences, over time, of marginalization, historical injustice, land grabbing, and political alienation. The armed struggle of the CPP-NPA is rooted in the goal of replacing what it calls an oppressive system.

There are many women's initiatives in the Philippines to challenge this armed violence. The initiatives I will share here are those of women from the Center for Peace Education in Miriam College, a twenty-one-year-old advocacy center housed in and supported by a Catholic educational institution, Miriam College.[14] Our story is that of nonviolent resistance to armed violence, of building spaces of peace and nonviolence in peoples' minds and hearts, in practices and institutions aided by research, and through education, organizing, nonviolent persuasion, and nonviolent action. They are modest initiatives but done with the intention of saving and building lives as taught in the Gospel.

Education

Pope Paul VI once said that, to reach peace, we must teach it.[15] Jesus Christ did so. To help build spaces of nonviolence, we at the Center for Peace

---

13. Imperial War Museums, "Women Who Took."

14. For more information on the Center for Peace Education, see its website, https://www.mc.edu.ph/cpe.

15. John Paul II, "To Reach Peace." Before he died, Paul VI decided that the upcoming 1979 World Day of Peace should be titled, "To reach peace, teach peace." John Paul II, his successor, honored his wishes.

Education at Miriam College utilize the power of peace education. Before we teach peace and nonviolence, we first work to understand the context of the people we engage. Our peace initiatives are normally preceded by conversations or focus group discussions that center on peoples' experiences of violence, their perspectives, their hopes and aspirations. Then, we dialogue with them about important concepts such as respect for life, all life: Muslim, Christian, indigenous peoples, man, woman, gay, rich, poor, black, white. We talk about nonviolence and nonharming. We teach peaceful conflict resolution skills, emphasizing that an eye for an eye will leave everyone blind. We teach that all humans are "brothers and sisters" and that human rights are to be respected and promoted and that basic needs should be fulfilled. We teach the respect, acceptance, and appreciation of diversity. We educate around gender norms to deconstruct toxic masculinities and teach our boys and girls that partnership, rather than domination, is the way to go. If our participants are Catholic, we teach about the Catholic Nonviolence Initiative (CNI),[16] to remind many that nonviolence was how Jesus lived his life and, hence, how we should live ours. If they are not, we teach about the ethical teachings on peace and nonviolence shared by major religious and philosophical traditions: Islam, Buddhism, Hinduism, Taoism, and indigenous traditions. We teach peace to as many sectors as possible: students, youth, community women, religious leaders, teachers, parents, even the military, paramilitary, and police.

We teach about gender equality and the right of women to participate in processes and decision-making that relate to peace and security, that women are an important agency that can challenge armed violence. But this will remain merely empty rhetoric if the encouragement is not accompanied by skills-sharing. And so, we share skills with community women, so that they can meaningfully participate in the mission of peacebuilding. We share skills on conflict resolution, peacekeeping, and mediation. We build skills on the documentation, monitoring, and reporting of human rights violations through a gender lens. We share skills on leadership and political participation.

---

16. See, generally, Catholic Nonviolence Initiative, "Who We Are." As this page of its website says, CNI "is a project of Pax Christi International, the Catholic peace movement, affirms that active nonviolence is at the heart of the vision and message of Jesus, the life of the Catholic Church, and the long-term vocation of healing and reconciling both people and the planet."

Organizing

Aware that there is power in numbers, we encourage women to organize themselves. With armed conflict so entrenched, people often think that nothing can be done in relation to violence. In the Philippines, violence is not confined to armed conflict; it can also be political in nature. Provinces are ruled by political clans, many of whom are considered warlords. Many of them have been in power since the time of the ousted dictator, Ferdinand Marcos. Challenging political violence is a tall order. But after a training on women and gun control, a group of women in Abra, a province known for intense political violence, sought a dialogue with the province's politicians and asked them to commit to taping over the nozzles of their guns during the election period. Politicians in this province are known to kill each other during elections. This initiative bore fruit—no killings were reported during that election period. Organizing efforts in other parts of the country has also resulted to the birth of women's organizations on the ground doing work such as human rights incidence monitoring, peacekeeping, and peacemaking. Our mantra is that we can help make communities safer if we ourselves give our share in keeping the peace.

Nonviolent Protest and Persuasion

We have also protested and continue to protest the violent approach taken by our government to resolve the menace of drugs. Thousands of lives have already been lost from the drug war. We have gone to Congress, concerned government offices, and the streets to make known that we oppose the killings, as well as the government's plan to revive the death penalty, the lowering of the age of criminality from fifteen to nine years old, and the compulsory military training of students.

For decades, Moros or Muslims in the Philippines have suffered from historical injustice and marginalization. The war in Mindanao killed roughly one hundred and twenty thousand and has displaced over a million over time.[17] We accompanied our Muslim sisters and brothers in their lobby for greater political autonomy and right to self-determination, and we accompanied our Muslim sisters in lobbying for women's meaningful participation. We were regular guests in Parliament, talking to as many legislators as possible, practically knocking on each legislator's door, asking them to sign a statement of support, handing out collaterals such as chocolates and postcards, persuading them to support our cause. After all,

---

17. Adriano and Parks, *Contested Corners of Asia*, 12.

the passage of the Bangsamoro Organic Law and the eventual establishment of the Bangsamoro Government would mean an end to war. The hard work of all stakeholders to ensure success of the peace process paid off. The Bangsamoro Organic Law was passed, and women are assured that they will no longer remain invisible in public space. The law is peppered with provisions to ensure that women have a role in peacebuilding—for example, "the Bangsamoro Government shall recognize the role of women in governance and ensure their fundamental equality before the law. It shall guarantee full and direct participation of women in governance and development process, ensuring that women shall benefit equally in the implementation of development programs and projects."[18]

We take our campaign of arms control seriously. The Philippines is home to 3.9 million guns, many of them loose, and approximately twenty-one people die each day in the Philippines from gun violence.[19] Consequently, we campaigned hard for the Arms Trade Treaty (ATT) in both our country and at the UN. Disappointed that, while there were global rules regulating the trade in bananas, there was no treaty to regulate the trade in weapons, and so we delivered bananas to our Department of Foreign Affairs and gave out "banana" postcards to key decision-makers. We organized several forums, consulted many communities, went to malls, markets, and churches to gather signatures of everyday people to support the adoption of an arms trade treaty. We got priests to discuss gun violence in their Sunday homilies, went cheerleading in front of our Department of Foreign Affairs to get its attention, and followed Asian parliamentarians on their beach excursions to remind them to support the treaty. There was nothing we were not ready to do to win an ATT.

At the UN, we used the same nonviolent strategies: we handed out letters to UN delegates, delivered speeches at UN conferences, circulated petitions, put up exhibits, and gave out collaterals like buttons and flowers to delegates who mentioned gender in their speeches. In a desperate move to get gender language into the ATT text, we mustered all of our courage to approach the president of the conference to lobby our cause. We were yelled at but were approached later and asked what specific language we wanted in the treaty. The Arms Trade Treaty is now known for its gender-specific provision that obligates exporting states to undertake a risk assessment prior to authorizing the transfer of any conventional weapons.[20] We were persistent.

---

18. Congress of the Philippines, "Republic Act No. 11054," Art. 8, Sect. 5.

19. Nario-Galace, "Women's Agency Against Guns," para. 1.

20. See, generally, UN Regional Centre for Peace and Disarmament in Africa, "Gender Dimensions."

We were courageous. We were nonviolent in our approach, language, and strategies. And we were heard.

It was not easy to explain the difference between women and gender. It was also not easy to explain that we wanted to transform the image people have of women, from that of victims to that of agents of change. It was even more difficult to explain that the socialization process has led to the association of weapons and violence with power, domination, and control. This mindset has led to the normalization of weapons, which has enabled and sustained armed conflicts and various forms of armed violence throughout the world. This is why, in our campaign against gun proliferation and gun violence, we attempt to show the link between gender constructions of masculinity and gun proliferation and violence. We bring the issue to light on Wear Orange Day (observed since high school student Hayida Pendleton was shot in Chicago in 2013).[21] Her classmates wore orange as a tribute to her during the Global Week of Action against Gun Violence and during the "Global 16 Days Campaign," which strives to eliminate gender-based violence.[22]

Even Pope Francis saw the gendered aspect of nuclearization, stating that we "cannot be held captive to military force . . . and the parading of stockpiles of arms." In a statement on nuclear arms, he condemned not only "the threat of their use" but also "their very possession."[23] We are doing our share to raise awareness of the urgent need to ban the bomb: exhibits, seminars, forums, visits to legislator's offices. We have marched against the bomb and have haunted a bank that is investing in these horrible weapons of mass destruction.

Yes, women back home pull every trick out of "Gene Sharp's Methods of Nonviolent Action[24] hat" to prevent and challenge armed violence. We are huge supporters of the peace processes in Mindanao and between the government and the Communist Party of the Philippines and the New Peoples' Army (CPP-NPA). In *Gaudium et Spes*, we are told that "it is our clear duty to strain every muscle in working for the time when all war can be completely outlawed."[25] Successful peace talks translate to an end of armed conflict and, consequently, violence on the ground. We lobby, we march, we speak. When the Bangsamoro Law was up for deliberation in Congress,

21. See, generally, "About Wear Orange,"
22. See, generally, "About the Global 16 Days Campaign."
23. Francis, "To Participants," para. 3.
24. For the list of Gene Sharp's nonviolent actions, see, generally, Albert Einstein Institution, "198 Methods." As stated there, "A description and historical example of each [method] can be found in volume two of *The Politics of Nonviolent Action* by Gene Sharp," published in 1973 in Boston by Porter Sargent.
25. Vatican Council II, *Gaudium et Spes*, 81.

we went around the country speaking to Catholic students about why the Muslims, the Bangsamoro, deserve greater autonomy. It is not only winning the law that was important but also winning the hearts of people who did not belong to the Islamic faith tradition, the Catholic faithful in this case.

The armed conflict between the government and the CPP-NPA is one of the longest running armed conflicts in the world. It has killed more than forty thousand over the years, many of them indigenous peoples.[26] We have consistently been asking both parties to go back to the table through various means: dialogues, consultations with those affected by the crossfire (especially indigenous peoples), public actions, statements, letters of appeal—all because we believe that, in war, everybody loses. "Justice can never be wrought by killing," Pope Francis said.[27] We traveled to many areas of armed conflict and held focus group discussions with community women who were directly affected by the conflict, and their response was similar throughout: "we are tired of war . . . please tell both armed parties to leave us in peace."

There are groups, however, that do not want to speak to the military because of its record of human rights violations during the time of Marcos. We broke that traditional adversarial paradigm by organizing a tea with the military to let them know that we want them to stay loyal to the Constitution in the face of populism. Together with community women, we have dialogued with the lawyers of the National Democratic Front to inform them of cases of human rights violations apparently committed by their troops. We find dialogues to be very important; there are times when we are met with indifference, but we persist.

We have issued many statements to protest armed violence and appeal for a stop to it. We have issued public statements on the extrajudicial killings related to the war on drugs, the proposed death penalty, the plan to lower the age of criminality to twelve years old, the plan to revive a form of conscription, the resumption of peace talks, condemnation of terror attacks—all because we stand with victims of armed violence and their families. Violence only begets more violence.

Jesus led his life nonviolently. As the Catholic Nonviolence Initiative says, we need a "renewed moral framework [that] would enable . . . the institutional church as a moral authority to be more consistent with the nonviolent creativity of the Gospel. . . . In turn, a moral framework built on

---

26. Minority Rights Group International, "Philippines," para. 8.
27. "Pope Francis," para. 6.

nonviolence and just peace would better illuminate the sacred dignity of all persons and creation."[28]

Understanding the importance of mainstream media and the number of people they can reach, we ask radio and television shows to invite us to speak about the importance of the nuclear ban, the need to control arms proliferation, or the importance of supporting greater autonomy for the Muslim population so that the war will end. Thanks to connections we have, we get invited; we send op-eds to newspapers, and they get published.

We understand the power of social media as well—with just one click, you reach so many. Consequently, our Facebook and Twitter pages are replete with messages challenging armed violence or asking people to support a cause that will bring more peace. We post infographics about gun violence and nuclear proliferation. We sponsor Twitter Parties, inviting people to join us on Twitter for one hour on a designated day, and we flood Twitter for one hour with tweets about a certain issue—calls to end gun violence, for example. We use a hashtag like #ThisIsNonviolence, so that we can monitor how many have attended our Twitter Party.

Social Action

We also open up spaces for people to give directly to a cause. Tweets that we want to see more peace in Mindanao are not enough to make a difference. Students at Miriam College, for example, organize annual fundraisers to support causes that challenge armed violence and build peace. They sell old clothes, muffins, ice cream, food. And the proceeds all go to a scholarship fund for students living in an area that is affected by armed conflict or to people displaced by war or affected by extrajudicial killings, etc.

Institutionalizing Nonviolent Practices

We also institutionalize practices that can help promote peace. We have, for example, declared our college a "Zone of Peace." As you enter, you will see a manifestation of our Zone of Peace declaration. We have visited and successfully encouraged Catholic schools to establish anti-bullying programs. We have also changed our discipline philosophy to one of restorative discipline, believing that punishment does not really help reform the offender. We also work with kindred spirits; there are many groups with similar

---

28. Catholic Nonviolence Initiative, "Nonviolence," 4.

causes, aspirations, and visions. We have joined or established coalitions, networks, and associations so that we can do more.

We also recognize the importance of building peace and challenging violence in our hearts and in our relationships. And so, we offer trainings on mediation and peacekeeping. We train our students and faculty in peaceful conflict resolution and anti-bullying. We have established a twinning project with a Muslim school in Mindanao. Biases abound between Christians and Muslims, and so, in order to build bridges of friendship and understanding between the youth from both faith traditions, we partnered with a school in Mindanao attended by Muslims. Their students and ours have been writing to each other as pen pals. At the end of every school year, we bring the pen pals together for a face-to-face interaction. We call this a people-to-people peace process. The students write their reflections in a shared newsletter, and this is where you will see how beliefs and attitudes toward each other have changed over time.

Engaging the Men

Gender is not just about women, and so, we have been educating about gender norms, challenging constructions of masculinity, but not without the men. It is important to acknowledge that many men and boys choose not to engage in violence. We actively engage men in our work in challenging armed violence and building spaces for peace. We share peacebuilding skills with young men, and we talk peace, even with the police and the military.

Gains

Considering all these efforts, what gains have been made? At Miriam College, research results have indicated changes in beliefs and attitudes amongst our students—for example, in relation to war or those who are different from them. We have students actually stopping fights on campus and see an increasing number of students participating in peace clubs, public actions, campaign work, and lobby work. We have alumnae doing peacebuilding, humanitarian, and human rights work. We have inspired other schools to declare their schools Zones of Peace, establish peace education centers, and develop anti-bullying programs. We have inspired community women to believe that they are not secondary citizens, consequently motivating them to run for public office. And indeed, some of them have thrown their hats into the election ring and won! We have inspired the creation of grassroots peace organizations working for conflict prevention and resolution.

Our engagement with local communities and other sectors has also helped women to become part of the Councils of Elders, which for centuries did not have women members. We have helped develop a National Acton Plan on Women, Peace, and Security that would ensure women's meaningful participation in leadership and peace processes. Local governments are now legislating women's participation in governance; one example is the Bangsamoro Organic Law discussed earlier. And on the global front, women and men together helped bring about the passage of two treaties at the UN: the Arms Trade Treaty, which regulates the sales of arms to ensure that they don't end up in the hands of those who will use them for atrocities, and the Nuclear Ban Treaty, which now prohibits State Parties from manufacturing, selling, deploying, and acquiring nuclear weapons.

These are modest gains but loud in their message that nonviolence works to prevent and stop armed violence. And so we call on the church, governments, academic institutions, and other organizations and sectors to allocate resources to nonviolent approaches in order to build a culture of peace. Let us all remember what Pope John Paul II told us: "Violence destroys what it claims to defend: the dignity, the life, the freedom of human beings."[29]

Let us, therefore, choose life. Let us choose nonviolence as a pathway to just peace.

Bibliography

"About the Global 16 Days Campaign." 16 Days Campaign, n.d. www.16dayscampaign.org.

"About Wear Orange." Wear Orange, n.d. https://wearorange.org/about/.

Adriano, Fermin, and Thomas Parks. *The Contested Corners of Asia: Subnational Conflict and International Development Assistance—The Case of Mindanao, Philippines*. San Francisco: The Asia Foundation, 2013. https://asiafoundation.org/wp-content/uploads/2013/10/The-Contested-Corners-of-Asia_The-Case-of-Mindanao.pdf.

Albert Einstein Institute. "198 Methods of Nonviolent Action." https://www.aeinstein.org/198-methods-of-nonviolent-action.

Catholic Nonviolence Initiative. "Nonviolence and Just Peace: A Moral Framework for Catholic Theology in the Context of a Violent World—Catholic Nonviolence Initiative Roundtable #3." N.d. https://nonviolencejustpeace.net/wp-content/uploads/2020/08/Nonviolence-just-peace-new-moral-framework.pdf.

———. "Who We Are." https://nonviolencejustpeace.net/who-we-are/.

Congress of the Philippines. "Republic Act No. 11054." The LawPhil Project: Arellano Law Foundation, Philippine Laws and Jurisprudence Databank, July 24, 2017. https://www.lawphil.net/statutes/repacts/ra2018/ra_11054_2018.html.

29. John Paul II, "Do Not Be Overcome," 4.

Francis, Pope. "For the Celebration of the Fiftieth World Day of Peace—Nonviolence: A Style of Politics for Peace." Message delivered from the Vatican, Rome, December 8, 2016. https://www.vatican.va/content/francesco/en/messages/peace/documents/papa-francesco_20161208_messaggio-l-giornata-mondiale-pace-2017.html.

———. "To Participants in the International Symposium 'Prospects for a World Free of Nuclear Weapons and for Disarmament.'" Address given at the Vatican, Rome, November 10, 2017. https://www.vatican.va/content/francesco/en/speeches/2017/november/documents/papa-francesco_20171110_convegno-disarmointegrale.html.

"History of Abuelas de Plaza de Mayo." Abuelas, n.d. https://abuelas.org.ar/idiomas/english/history.htm.

Imperial War Museums. "The Women Who Took On the British Government's Nuclear Programme." IWM, n.d. https://www.iwm.org.uk/history/the-women-who-took-on-the-british-governments-nuclear-programme.

"Israel." Women in Black, Vigils Around the World, n.d. https://womeninblack.org/vigils-arround-the-world/middle-east/israel/.

John Paul II, Pope. "Do Not Be Overcome by Evil but Overcome Evil with Good." Message delivered from the Vatican, Rome, December 8, 2004. https://www.vatican.va/content/john-paul-ii/en/messages/peace/documents/hf_jp-ii_mes_20041216_xxxviii-world-day-for-peace.html#fn4.

———. "For the Celebration of the Day of Peace: 'To Reach Peace, Teach Peace.'" Message delivered from the Vatican, Rome, December 8, 1978. https://www.vatican.va/content/john-paul-ii/en/messages/peace/documents/hf_jp-ii_mes_19781221_xii-world-day-for-peace.html.

Krug, Etienne G., et al. *World Report on Violence and Health*. Geneva: World Health Organization, 2002. https://apps.who.int/iris/handle/10665/42495.

Lardieri, Alexa. "World Bank: Half the World Lives on Less than $5.50 a Day." *U.S. News and World Report*, October 17, 2018. https://www.usnews.com/news/economy/articles/2018-10-17/world-bank-half-the-world-lives-on-less-than-550-a-day.

McEvoy, Claire, and Gergely Hideg. *Global Violent Deaths 2017: Time to Decide*. Geneva: Small Arms Survey, 2017. http://www.smallarmssurvey.org/fileadmin/docs/U-Reports/SAS-Report-GVD2017.pdf.

Michals, Debra, ed. "Lucretia Mott (1793–1880)." National Women's History Museum, 2017. https://www.womenshistory.org/education-resources/biographies/lucretia-mott.

Minority Rights Group International. "Philippines: Current Issues." https://minorityrights.org/country/philippines/.

Muller, Mary Anne, and Anna Brown. "The Plowshares Eight: Thirty Years On." Waging Nonviolence, September 9, 2010. https://wagingnonviolence.org/2010/09/the-plowshares-8-thirty-years-on/.

Nario-Galace, Jasmin. "Women's Agency Against Guns." *Isis International*, July 27, 2014. http://www.isiswomen.org/index.php?option=com_content&view=article&id=1707:women-s-agency-against-guns&catid=22&Itemid=229.

"Pope Francis: No Matter What the Crime, 'the Death Penalty is Inadmissible.'" *Catholic News Agency*, March 20, 2015. https://www.catholicnewsagency.com/news/31715/pope-francis-no-matter-what-the-crime-the-death-penalty-is-inadmissible.

Sharp, Gene. *The Politics of Nonviolent Action*. Boston: Porter Sargent, 1973.

Stockholm International Peace Research Institute (SIPRI). "Global Military Spending Remains High at 1.7 Trillion." May 2, 2018. https://www.sipri.org/media/press-release/2018/global-military-spending-remains-high-17-trillion.

UN Regional Centre for Peace and Disarmament in Africa (UNREC). "Gender Dimensions of the Arms Trade Treaty." https://front.un-arm.org/wp-content/uploads/2016/12/Gender-Dimensions-of-the-ATT_English.pdf.

———. Recommendations published by UNREC's "Workshop on the Implementation of ATT Obligations relating to Human Rights and Gender-Based Violence," December 7–8, 2015, Addis Ababa, Ethiopia. https://www.un.org/disarmament/unscar/unrec2014/.

UN Women. "Facts and Figures: Peace and Security." https://www.unwomen.org/en/what-we-do/peace-and-security/facts-and-figures.

Vatican Council II. *Gaudium et Spes*. Vatican.va, 1965. https://www.vatican.va/archive/hist_councils/ii_vatican_council/documents/vat-ii_const_19651207_gaudium-et-spes_en.html.

Vetter, Lisa Pace. "'The Most Belligerent Non-Resistant': Lucretia Mott on Women's Rights." *Political Theory* 43 (October 2015) 600–30. https://www.jstor.org/stable/pdf/24571648.pdf.

The World Bank Group. "Population, Female (% of Total Population)." https://data.worldbank.org/indicator/SP.POP.TOTL.FE.ZS?end=2015&start=2015&view=bar.

9

"Be the Change You Want to See": Building Interfaith Solidarity for Peace in India

Francis Gonsalves, SJ

Introduction: Be the Change You Want to See

"BE THE CHANGE YOU wish to see in the world"[1] are words attributed to Mahatma Gandhi, the renowned Indian prophet of nonviolence (*ahimsa*), truth (*satyagraha*), and peace. His "walk the talk" approach taught the world how to resist violence and build peace and inspired many world leaders to tread in pathways of peace. Indeed, unless you and I are ready for inner conversion and change, we will never be agents of peace and reconciliation in our own neighborhoods, countries, or in the wider world. Aware of the urgent need to build a nation and world on firm foundations of peace—beginning with transforming themselves—some individuals and groups have been involved in interfaith ministries for peace in India. These ministries seek to pool resources not only of Christians, but also of firm believers in other religions and of those who practice no religion whatsoever. I shall focus on the aims and activities of some of these peace initiatives in India, but first a brief word about the Indian context will help us to understand them.

---

1. See Quote Investigator, "Be the Change." It has not been conclusively proven that this quotation is verbatim from Mahatma Gandhi. However, because he expressed similar views in his writings, it has been attributed to him.

The Indian Context: Plagued by Paradoxes and Polarities

The Religious Context

India is undoubtedly a deeply religious country, with millions of believers representing almost all religious traditions. Mother India has birthed the world's so-called "Cosmic/Mystic/Indic" religions (Hinduism, Buddhism, Jainism, and Sikhism) and been a gracious hostess to the so-called "Abrahamic/Prophetic/Word" religions (Judaism, Christianity, Islam, and Baha'i). According to the 2011 Indian national census, 79.8 percent of the population of India practices Hinduism, 14.2 percent adheres to Islam, 2.3 percent practices Christianity, and 1.7 percent adheres to Sikhism. Zoroastrianism and Judaism also have an ancient history in India, and each has several thousand Indian adherents. Although there are approximately twenty-eight million practicing Christians in India,[2] and though Indian Christianity traces its origins to the apostle Thomas, it comprises only 2.3 percent of the total population and therefore its contribution to the larger national life is minimal and focused on the fields of education, public health, and social work. Furthermore, Catholics comprise less than 2 percent of the Indian population, and they are subdivided in terms of ritual practice.[3] Indian Christians are mostly lower class, both economically and socially.[4]

Indian religiosity has the following features: (a) porous boundaries, with a prolific exchange of religious practices and a strong eclecticism, leading to some level of integration;[5] (b) the nonseparation between religion (*dharma*) and politics. Mahatma Gandhi's *sarva dharma samabhava* and Jawaharlal Nehru's *dharma nirpekshata* summarize what is implied by Indian secularism;[6] (c) given the religious diversity in India, most believers

---

2. "India's Population," para. 6.

3. The Catholic Church in India is made up of three *sui iuris* churches—the Latin, Syro-Malankara, and Syro-Malabar—each with its own liturgical rites and administrative apparatus, all under the governance of the Roman pontiff.

4. According to the 2016 Catholic Bishops' Conference of India, "Policy of Dalit Empowerment," n. 24, Dalits (formerly the "untouchables") make up about twelve million of the nineteen million members of the Catholic Church in India. In addition, the Adivasis (indigenous or tribal peoples) also form a sizable percentage of Indian Christians.

5. See, generally, Desai, "National Integration and Religion," 54–67.

6. Nehru desired to divorce religion from politics and to keep the state neutral toward all forms of religion (*dharma nirpekshata*), while Gandhi intended that all religions would be treated with equal respect (*sarva dharma samabhava*). For further readings on secularism in India, see Bhargava, *Secularism and Its Critics*.

acknowledge that their religion is but one among many others;[7] (d) the renewal of religion is no longer the monopoly of the priestly class—Brahmins, priests/pastors, and imams—but rests in the hands of common people of all classes and castes, who practice *dharma* according to their concrete needs. Thus, we have seen a "democratization" of religion; and (e) while there are many positive elements in the Indian religious context, religion is often abused. Such abuse may appear, on the one hand, in hidden forms like the "Freedom of Religion" bill that actually robs people of their freedom to practice and propagate their religion, or, on the other, as open violence against religious minorities. One can cite the violence against Christians in Gujarat's Dangs District in 1998[8] and in Orissa's Kandhamal District in 2008,[9] as well as the Gujarat genocide against Muslims in 2002.[10] More recently, and in particular since the RSS-backed BJP government took power in May 2014,[11] religious minorities have suffered much violence. The BJP won its second term in office in the national elections of May 2019 under the leadership of right-wing populist leader Narendra Modi—who has been accused of involvement in the 2002 Gujarat genocide.[12]

The Political Context

India is the largest functioning democracy in the world. Despite its many pitfalls in practice,[13] democracy has proved to be a good form of governance since it protects against both *majoritarianism* and *minoritarianism* (the appeasement of a minority).[14] Premised on the principle of egalitarianism, the Indian Constitution guarantees rights[15] and establishes reservation quotas

---

7. See, generally, Klyuev, *Religion in Indian Society*, which highlights the diversity of religions in India.

8. See Chenoy, *Violence in Gujarat*.

9. Apoorvanand, "On the Anniversary," para. 5.

10. Mander, "Soul-Wounds of Massacre," para. 1.

11. RSS stands for Rashtriya Swayamsevak Sangh (meaning the Nationalist Volunteer Association in Hindi), which has been promoting militant Hindu nationalism, called *Hindutva*. Its political wing—which is currently the ruling party in India—is a populist right-wing party known as the BJP, the Bhartiya Janata Party. See, generally, Dayal and Hashmi, *365 Days*.

12. Gonsalves, "Populism," 35.

13. See, generally, Kohli, *Democracy and Discontent*, for views on the crises affecting democratic governance.

14. See, generally, Bhargava, "What Is Democracy?" for the strengths of democracy.

15. See the Constitution of India, Part III, articles 25–30.

(i.e., affirmative action) to certain sectors of society.[16] Today, some of these rights and reservations are being contested, if not blatantly denied, in the public realm. Moreover, there is a growing tendency to categorize citizens into two groups: "nationals" versus "antinationals" or patriotic versus unpatriotic, with the latter terms always referring to those who do not subscribe to the pseudonationalism of the *Hindutva* brand[17] or who do not endorse the divisive policies of the government. When political power is used to further an obscurantist agenda or marginalize minorities, the very nature of secular democracy is jeopardized.

The Social Context

Indian society is changing rapidly to keep pace with both internal and external influences. However, the caste structure and its inherent violence never change. The virus of caste (Varna and Jati) has infected almost all Indians in one way or the other. Moreover, we have Adivasis (tribals)—sometimes referred to as Adijati and Vanyajati—who do not fall within the ambit of the caste structure.[18] Recent events show that atrocities against Dalits are on the rise. It is estimated that some 70 percent of Indian Christians are either of Dalit origin (BCs ["backward classes"] or OBCs ["other backward classes"])[19] or are tribals (STs ["scheduled tribes"]). While STs are given benefits on account of their tribal status, the Christians of Dalit origin are not considered underprivileged as such. Hence, they are not accorded the educational and employment benefits provided to underprivileged people by the Indian state. Consequently, they suffer from double discrimination—in both the society and the church.[20]

---

16. There is sound logic behind the Indian Constitution granting reservation quotas and minority rights. See Heredia, "Justifying Reservation Quotas."

17. For the basic tenets of *Hindutva*, see in general the works of its founders: Golwalkar (*We, or Our Nationhood Defined*) and Savarkar, *Hindutva*. The twenty-third annual meeting of the Indian Theological Association (ITA) discussed the theme of *Hindutva*, and the resulting papers were published in Mattam and Arockiadoss, *Hindutva*.

18. See Atal, *Changing Indian Society*, 145–66.

19. Banerjee, *Struggle for Justice*, 42.

20. See Catholic Bishops' Conference of India, "Policy of Dalit Empowerment," nn. 9–40.

The Economic Context

On the economic front, India's poverty amidst plenty is shocking. It is home to some of the wealthiest billionaires in the world,[21] while millions of Indians eke out inhuman existences on its peripheries.[22] In the 2022 Global Hunger Index, India stood at 107 out of 121 countries, and with a score of 29.1 (where fifty and above is "extremely alarming"), its level of hunger is classified as "serious."[23] Such glaring inequalities in wealth are due not only to economic factors but also to religious beliefs that legitimize inequality on the basis of inherent factors like caste. Sadly, on the one hand, religions often legitimize poverty as a consequence of karma, predestination, or God-willed suffering, while, on the other, they widen the gap between the haves and the have-nots with a thriving "God Business" fueled by market mechanisms of globalization.[24] In the recent past, the poor in India have also suffered severely due to a whimsical "demonetization" drive announced by India's Prime Minister, Narendra Modi, in 2016,[25] while taxation and neoliberal policies, SEZs (special economic zones), illegal mining, and open market mechanisms, among other things, have crushed the rural poor and the daily wage urban laborers, many of whom have committed suicide.

The Crux of the Clashes and Crises

In view of the above-mentioned polarities and paradoxes, while India is depicted on the world stage as a well-developed, peaceful country, it is only partly so. What is most distressing is that *dharma*—loosely translated as "religion"—is turning out to be *adharma*, or "irreligion," and the root of conflict. Some further points must be noted in any discussion pertaining to religion.

---

21. For example, India's Mukesh Ambani and Lakshmi Mittal are usually ranked in the *Forbes* list of top billionaires. In 2022, Ambani ranked number 10 and Mittal number 89; Dolan and Peterson-Withorn, "Forbes World's Billionaires List." Ambani owns Antilia, the costliest private home in the world, worth two billion US dollars, with twenty-seven floors and a staff of six hundred; Gorgan, "Antilia," para. 3.

22. See, generally, Dhage, "Poverty Alleviation Programmes in India," which argues that poverty alleviation programs do not address the root causes of poverty and hunger and cannot ensure that the poor get enough food throughout the year because of flaws in the public distribution system (PDS).

23. von Grebmer et al., *2022 Global Hunger Index*, 13.

24. See, generally, Radhakrishnan, "Globalization, Faith, and Development Politics," for an analysis of how gurus and godmen thrive in these times.

25. See, generally, Basu, "Life after Demonetisation."

First, "secularism" is not univocally understood in all parts of the world. In the West, it means a clear separation between politics and religion, the public sphere and the private, while in India it mostly refers to respect for all religions.

Second, in India there is not only a conflation of politics and religion, but daily life is seen as an integral whole embracing the social, economic, and cultural realms. Hence, what may appear to be a "religious issue" (e.g., *Hindutva* or religious nationalism) will certainly have roots, ramifications, and repercussions in these realms as well.

Third, in most of our interfaith exchanges, we normally think in terms of polarities: "we" versus "they"; superior versus inferior; morally right verses morally wrong; ritually pure versus ritually impure; the "saved" as opposed to the "damned"; and so on, with the former label describing one's own religion and its adherents and the latter characteristic of the "other."

And fourth, we normally tend to compare the best of our own religion with the worst of the other's religion. For instance, in the post-9/11 world, we often blanket-brand Muslims as "terrorists" since the radicalized Islamists from ISIS or Al-Qaeda were involved in terrorist strikes in New York, Madrid, France, London, Brussels, and Mumbai. But when a white-skinned New Zealander—presumably Christian—murdered and injured some one hundred Muslims on March 15, 2019,[26] we seemed to think that he was an "exception" to the ranks of normal, peaceful Christians.

With all of this in mind, let us now reflect upon some interfaith initiatives undertaken by individual Christians and Christian groups that seem to be doing much good in India, especially among the youth. Interestingly, by 2020 India will be the youngest country in the world, with 64 percent of its population being of working age.[27] Hence, addressing the needs of the young is of utmost importance. This is the target group of all the interfaith ministries whose work we shall examine.

The Universal Solidarity Movement of Value Education for Peace

The Universal Solidarity Movement of Value Education for Peace (USM) was begun by a Catholic priest, Varghese Alengaden, on July 16, 1993. Inspired by the axiom, "Better to light a candle than to curse the darkness," Fr. Alengaden left the comfortable confines of his church and moved into a small apartment in Indore city, Madhya Pradesh, central India. He describes USM's founding as follows: "A passionate vision for a world of peace and

26. See, generally, Gelineau and Gambrell, "New Zealand Mosque Shooter."
27. "With an Average Age," para. 1.

universal solidarity, confidence in the power and goodness of the youth and unfailing trust in the providence of God were my assets for launching this mission."[28] The expansion of USM throughout India and abroad was the result of an uncompromising commitment to its two fundamental principles: personal transformation and pluralistic spirituality. Adherence to the values of total transparency, pluralism, emphasis on self-transformation, not owning property, submission to evaluation at all levels, teamwork, and inclusive community living makes the USM different from other organizations. Membership in the USM is open to all people who are interested in building interfaith relationships.

Each USM member must fulfill the "Five Conditions" and walk the "Five Paths," failing which s/he loses her/his membership. These are:

1. Praying daily for peace and forgiveness so that the member can be an agent of reconciliation. Everyone is expected to pray the following prayer daily, silently in one's heart: "Give peace in my heart, in our family, in our country, and in the whole world." This prayer can be offered anytime, anywhere by people of all faiths.

2. Skipping a meal once a week to express solidarity with the poor and marginalized and donating the money saved to the poor. This is not a religious fast, as such, but more an act of solidarity.

3. Doing a good deed daily, consciously, without a selfish motive. The fruit of doing a good deed daily is that one good deed leads to a snowballing of good deeds, and persons develop a habit of doing good deeds.

4. Honoring your parents, teachers, and all human beings. Honor is given to people regardless of their economic status, age, religious affiliations, or positions they hold.

5. Respecting Mother Earth and conserving its resources. Developing ecological consciousness and preserving the environment are essential for the peace and prosperity of the world. A lack of respect toward the earth and violence inflicted on nature will bring disaster.

With respect to its spiritual vision, the USM believes in building community, society, nation, and world into a "civilization of love," harmonizing the best offered by every religion as its heritage to humankind. Therefore, it seeks inspiration from the religious values of the following religions:

- The universal family spirit of Hinduism and the Baha'i faith
- The discipline and fellowship of Islam

---

28. Personal correspondence with the author, September 8, 2019.

- The courage of Sikhism
- The compassion of Buddhism
- The nonviolence of Jainism
- The creativity of Zoroastrianism (the religion of the Parsees)
- The indomitability of Judaism
- The cosmic solidarity of the tribal religions
- The self-sacrifice and forgiveness of Christianity

In terms of its *modus operandi* over and above fulfilling the five conditions for self-transformation, the USM has a ten-point action program for social transformation as follows:

1. *Enlightened Leadership*: To promote leadership qualities of self-discipline, fellowship, universal vision, courage, compassion, selfless service, love, and respect for all religions. These are developed by practicing the five paths, studying the lives of great persons, and developing organizational skills.

2. *Empowering Women*: To undertake activities that will promote the dignity of women and empower them by giving them more opportunities and creating a healthy attitude of respect toward them.

3. *Caring and Sharing*: To promote a compassionate and caring attitude toward needy fellow beings. This is realized by giving financial support and extending personal help to the needy, sharing meals with the poor, building houses for the homeless, etc.

4. *Art and Culture*: To develop latent talents in individuals for the purpose of promoting personal growth and the common good. This is achieved through creating opportunities for individuals to exercise their talents in music, dance, drama, art, painting, and writing, with a focus on each person's own cultural tradition.

5. *Light and Life*: To promote respect for life and uphold human dignity. Eye donations, blood donations, the promotion of human rights, and antiabortion campaigns are some of the means for realizing this objective. (The eye is the light of the body and blood is life.)

6. *Literate India*: To create awareness among students and use their talents and the available infrastructure to eradicate illiteracy at all levels.

7. *Green India*: To create awareness regarding the protection of nature and the maintenance of ecological balance. Tree planting, gardening, organic farming, antipollution campaigns, campaigns against consumerism, and the formation of ecoclubs are some suggested activities.

8. *Clean India*: To promote a sense of cleanliness in personal and public life. Keeping one's home and surroundings clean and undertaking cleanliness drives in school/college and public areas are some of the activities recommended.
9. *Knit India*: To promote national integration and communal harmony. Joint celebration of religious and national festivals, interreligious prayer meetings and dialogue, and organizing regional and national youth camps are proposed.
10. *Heal India*: To promote better health care for all. Visiting the sick, organizing health camps, sponsoring rural dispensaries, promoting the use of herbal medicines, and antinarcotic campaigns may be adopted.

USM has already celebrated its silver jubilee, which was in 2018. Since then, 7,403 student leaders in 370 batches have come to Indore from twenty-two states of India for this unique training. Apart from the training sessions conducted at the center, several sessions are conducted in outreach programs in schools across the country for teachers, students, and their parents. One might ask: What is the future outlook for USM? Fr. Alengaden, the founder and national coordinator, answers this question with great confidence and optimism:

> A Movement should exist only if it is relevant to the times. If it is relevant and needed, people will support it. When it ceases to be relevant it should die. The role of USM is to infuse values into individuals and institutions and bring transformation in their structure and style of functioning. The attitudinal change in individuals would enable them to create alternative systems and structures to rebuild the nation. Through these individuals and institutions, the Movement will be alive. Then a national structure and organization will not be required. In the death of the structure the spirit of the Movement will be alive.[29]

Three Indian Campaigns Specifically Involving Children

Because India is a young country, it is important that Christian ministers and ministries target and train young minds; there are many evil forces eager to influence young minds, pulling them in the wrong directions. Let us look at three initiatives focusing on children not only as passive recipients of education, but as agents and creators of their own destinies.

29. "What's Unique," para. 2.

The "Nine Is Mine" Campaign and the Children's Circus

The "Nine is Mine" campaign is a participatory children's advocacy initiative calling for 9 percent of India's GDP to be committed to health and education (3 percent to health and 6 percent to education), as promised by the Indian government in 2004. Under the aegis of the Christian Brothers in New Delhi, the movement was inaugurated on the annual International Day for the Eradication of Poverty on October 17, 2006. It is now coordinated by PRATYeK—a registered society that came into existence on October 9, 2013, recognizing children as primary stakeholders of society and therefore seeking to provide them with local, national, and international forums aimed at effectively engaging with policies and policymakers, while ensuring the effective implementation of the same. PRATYeK, which in Hindi means "everyone," captures the essence of protecting and promoting rights and opportunities for every child in India by creating a vibrant array of child rights and NGOs spanning across every state of India.

Nine is Mine "grew out of Nelson Mandela's call to ordinary citizens to keep governments accountable to fulfilling the MDGs [Millennium Development Goals]. Children in India took upon themselves the task to ensure the fulfillment of Goals 2 and 3 and 4—all of which refer to children. Later the campaign grew to realize the exclusion issue of children, particularly in the context on India. They, therefore, incorporated a strong focus on the 'last child' . . . [ensuring that all sectors] of India (the children of privileged middle-class [parents] and [members of] excluded communities interact together to find common solutions. The Nine is Mine campaign believes that child rights abuses anywhere are a concern for children everywhere."[30]

Many children—especially poor, orphaned, and specially abled children—have achieved great honors, like scaling Mount Everest and representing children at the UN and in other global forums, or as part of a "children's circus" that performs in order to conscientize people of their roles and rights in society.[31] At present, Br. Steve Rocha is the driving force behind all the activities and programs.

---

30. "Who Are We," para. 2. Respectively, goals 2, 3, 4 of the MDGs are to "achieve universal primary education," "promote gender equality and empower women," and "reduce child mortality"; United Nations, *Millennium Development Goals*, 4–5.

31. For an example of the children's circus, see Ceska, "Art for Change"; for examples of other Nine is Mine activities, see the numerous videos on their YouTube channel, https://www.youtube.com/user/9isM9/videos. Br. Steve Rocha provided these links to the author in personal email correspondence.

Small Christian Communities Working with Neighborhood Children's Councils (NCCs)

Small Christian Communities (SCCs) first began in Latin America in the 1960s and then spread to North America, Europe, Africa, and Asia. The first initiatives in India came from the dioceses of Kottar and Trivandrum in the state of Tamil Nadu in southern India. Later, SCCs took root in Kerala and in the Archdiocese of Bombay (now Mumbai) in 1984. There are SCCs in almost all the parishes in Mumbai, and each organizes a host of activities depending on the needs of the particular place and time. The main purpose behind establishing the SCCs was and is to create a participatory church enabling the lay faithful to meet in their own localities to pray, discuss their lives, and respond to common concerns.

An SCC animated by Sr. Manisha Gonsalves, RSCJ, and Sr. Daphne Furtado, RSCJ, works with children residing in the Malad West neighborhood in Mumbai. The children they minister to are members of what is called a Neighborhood Children's Council (NCC); it is comprised of students of all religions of the age of roughly nine to sixteen years.[32] All of the children are requested to choose an area of interest and belong to a "ministry"—not in the Christian sense of the word but in an eco-socio-political sense. The children are "ministers" who are asked to reflect on their areas of interest and to devise measures that first serve their immediate neighborhood but also their country. The nine ministries relate to:

a) care for Mother Earth;
b) health care;
c) sports;
d) spiritual connections;
e) arts, crafts, and culture;
f) talent search;
g) food and diet;
h) media and communications; and
i) outreach.

Each ministry chooses a leader to coordinate the activities of the group, which meets at least once a month. The emphasis for each ministry is teamwork. Each month, the members of three of the ministries are asked to make a brief, creative presentation to highlight a message pertaining to their ministry that promotes holistic growth and life, individually and

---

32. Gonsalves, "SCCs Inspiring NCCs," 18.

collectively. At the end of each presentation, all of the children are asked to give some positive feedback to the presenters, state what they have learned from the presentation, and conclude with a word of thanks to the presenters.

What follows are some examples of the activities organized by the NCC ministries with the support of the SCC:

1. The Care for Mother Earth Ministry presented a project about the hazards of noise pollution and made a plea to all to avoid using microphones and amplifiers and spread the message wherever they can. The group also takes the lead in creating awareness to avoid wasting electricity, to conserve water, to dispose of garbage in an eco-friendly way, and other such issues.

2. The Sports Ministry presented a chart with the final results of football's World Cup tournament. In addition, a young woman of the neighborhood who has emerged as a football champion was invited to share her success story. She shared personally what this journey has entailed in terms of discipline, hard work, perseverance, good health, etc., thereby inviting the young to do likewise. She served as a role model for the other children.

3. The Spiritual Connections Ministry highlights important religious events every month. For example, in September 2018, a Catholic girl shared her understanding and experience of Mother Mary, whose birth is celebrated on the eighth of the month, explaining the devotions, rosaries, novenas, etc., that are conducted. A Hindu boy spoke about the significance of the festival of Ganpati, a popular celebration in the Indian state of Maharashtra commemorating Lord Ganesh.

4. The Talent Search Ministry interviewed each member of the group prior to the meeting and then at the meeting shared with everyone what they discovered about each one's talents. As "homework," all were asked to go home to their parents and conduct a similar interview to highlight their parents' talents with a word of appreciation from the children, in order to encourage their parents to contribute their part to the larger society. The main target group is women—there is a need to encourage them in a special way since many women are unaware of and diffident about their own capabilities.

5. The Food and Diet Ministry presented different possible ingredients in a salad (e.g., carrots, tomatoes, cucumbers, and beetroot), pointing out the nutritive value of each. The idea is to persuade the children to eat all kinds of nourishing foods in this day and age when many prefer fast food, which may not be conducive to their good health, to home-cooked food.

Says Sr. Manisha, "In all our plans, we hope to form our children to be 'multipliers' of good wholesome values by sowing in them the seeds of a more promising, peaceful, and humane future for all. We have succeeded in creating a lot of goodwill among people of different religions."[33]

Peace Education Courses from the Indian Salesians of Don Bosco

The Salesians of Don Bosco (SDB) offer a peace education course for schools in India based on the teachers' manual, *Exercises in Peace Education*.[34] The training is given to teachers or animators in charge of students, who then use their training to train the students. The main architect and animator of the courses is Fr. Peter Gonsalves, SDB, who says in the course proposal that "[o]ur vision is to promote a positive, non-violent environment through participatory training of committed teachers, leaders, parents, and activists eager to educate young people to mutual respect, collaboration, and peace in a pluralistic society through a concrete training program based on a ready-to-use manual of lesson plans in schools and youth centers of South Asia."[35] Breaking this sentence down into easy-to-understand bits with a corresponding summary for each, Fr. Peter has created the following chart:[36]

Our vision is to promote a positive, non-violent environment	*Aim*
through participatory training	*Method*
of committed teachers/leaders/parents/activists	*Agents*
eager to educate young people	*Target*
to mutual respect, collaboration, and peace in a pluralistic society	*Content*
through a concrete training program based on a ready-to-use manual of lesson plans	*Strategy*
in schools and youth centers of South Asia.	*Context*

33. Email correspondence with the author, May 24, 2019.
34. See, generally, Gonsalves, *Exercises in Peace Education*.
35. Gonsalves, "Proposal," 1.
36. Gonsalves, "Proposal," 1.

The objectives of the Peace Education courses are to:

- "make schools places of peace;
- ensure they are free of violence, conflict, discrimination, and bullying;
- teach mutual respect, empathy, appreciation of diversity, inclusion of differences, conflict resolution, clean environments, peace theory, and peaceful practices and strategies; and
- enable selected teachers to put the manual *Exercises in Peace Education* to good use in their schools."[37]

The beneficiaries of the peace exercises are usually students from the ages of five to seventeen years; "[t]hey are encouraged to develop their knowledge, attitudes, and skills in order to become peace-filled persons and proactive peacebuilders through experiential and participatory learning. The lessons raise awareness, provoke thinking, challenge stereotypes, point to solutions, and incite to action. To be relevant to all South Asians without distinction, an attempt has been made to sustain a multiethnic, pluricultural, and interreligious viewpoint."[38]

South Asian Jesuit Initiative: Loyola Institute of Peace and International Relations

While the initiatives described above focus more on the school context in collaboration with teachers and the parents of students, the Jesuits of South Asia have established an institute specifically set up to teach peace and reconciliation to youth in universities and to other secular groups working for peace. Aware of the violence—direct, structural, and cultural—that threatens to fragment human societies and destroy Mother Earth, the Kerala Jesuits founded the Loyola Institute of Peace and International Relations (LIPI) on November 1, 2015, in Kochi.[39]

The founding and fostering of this venture must be seen in the light of GC 36—that is, the 36th General Congregation of the Jesuits worldwide, which was very deeply influenced by the ecclesial, social, ecological, pastoral, and missiological thrusts of Pope Francis. The aims of LIPI are as follows:

- To explore various conceptual resources: scientific, religious, academic, and cultural;

37. Gonsalves, "Proposal," 1.
38. Gonsalves, "Proposal," 2.
39. "Lipi Jesuits," para. 1.

- To envisage new strategies and concrete steps for conflict resolution at various levels;
- To achieve its goals through strategic plans for research facilities, publications, conferring academic degrees, spiritual programs, and campaigns to popularize the theme of peace;
- To network with similar institutes and organizations sharing a common vision of peace.

All of the above, it is believed, will contribute to bringing about peace to all groups of people in the multicultural context of India. Most importantly, the vision and mission of LIPI is strongly rooted in the Jesuit tradition.

LIPI has been engaged in the following activities for the past two years:

1. *Ezhuthu magazine*—new in the last few years, this publication is creating waves of impact on secular society irrespective of its readers' caste, creed, or class. It draws inspiration from Pope Francis's call to embark upon a new mode of evangelization.
2. *Peace clubs*—Indian schools and universities have numerous forums aimed at enhancing student life, but few specifically promote peace and harmony. LIPI sets up peace clubs in schools and peace forums in colleges to help students engage in activities that promote peace.
3. *Cultural immersion programs*—in an attempt to broaden the horizons of understanding across cultures and nations, LIPI organizes cultural immersion programs for foreign students. One was organized for the students of Santa Clara University, Berkeley, CA, USA, in January 2017.
4. *Seminars and conferences*—this relates to the organization of various national and international seminars, conferences, and workshops on peace-related topics. Through these, individuals and groups engage in critical and constructive interactions leading to peacebuilding activities.
5. *Centre for Art and Peace (CAP)*—art is a very effective means of alleviating suffering, curtailing violence, and promoting peace. With the Jesuit artist Roy Mathew as director, the center conducts art workshops and exhibitions for children and youth as a means of tapping into their creativity and talents.
6. *Centre for Science and Religion for Peace (CSR)*—"Science can purify religion from error and superstition. Religion can purify science from idolatry and false absolutes," wrote Pope Saint John Paul II.[40] Drawing inspiration from the complementarity of science and religion, this center, under the leadership of the Jesuit scientist Binoy Jacob,

---

40. John Paul II, "Letter of His Holiness," para. 29.

makes use of advancements in both science and religion for promoting peace. Cosmic retreats, seminars, and publications are the main tools for this venture.

Conclusion: Being Interreligiously Religious in India

In a multireligious context like India, it is said that to be religious is to be interreligious. Along these lines, Hans Küng said, "No peace among the nations without peace among the religions. No peace among the religions without dialogue between the religions. No dialogue between the religions without investigation of the foundation of the religions."[41] No one can disagree with this, for even a cursory glance at the many hot spots of so-called religious violence worldwide will convince anyone that there is a dire need for a deeper understanding of the many religions through interfaith dialogue that leads to the promotion of interfaith initiatives and lasting peace for all. In this regard, India is richly blessed because it is the mother of or hostess to all of the world's major religions. India must be a trailblazer in providing inspiration for interfaith dialogue.

John Paul II prayed for peace at Assisi in 1984 with the leaders of all religions. Pope Francis has moved this initiative for peace forward by his status as a third millennium Francis of Assisi, showing a three-part love for God, humankind, and the cosmos. Pope Francis has taken active steps to foster dialogue among religions. On the eve of his visit to Morocco as an ambassador of peace, he said: "I come as pilgrim of peace and fraternity, in a world which has great need of both," and added, "as Christians and Muslims, we believe in the Creator and Merciful One, who has created men and women and placed them on the earth so that they might live together as brothers and sisters, respecting each other's diversity and helping each other in their need. He has entrusted the earth—our common home—to them, to care for it responsibly and to preserve it for future generations." In the same address, the pontiff also encouraged the Christian community to meet with "migrants, who represent an appeal to build together a more just and solidary world."[42] We need to be challenged by Pope Francis's insights and initiatives and to follow in his footsteps.

We end with the prayer that those involved with the USM pray faithfully every morning:

> God our friend, mother and father, may you be praised

---

41. Küng, *Islam*, vi.
42. "Like My Predecessor," para. 4.

in your diversity of name and forms by the whole universe!
May we experience a world guided by your values of justice,
fraternity, equality, freedom, peace, hope, and love.
May your will be the motive force of all our dreams and actions!
Give us daily food for our body, mind, and soul.
Strengthen us to forget and forgive without counting the cost!
Forgive us our offenses as we forgive
Those who offended us in the past.
Bless all those who offend us now with your peace.
Strengthen us always to stand for truth without fear and to
walk in the path of light with hope, trust, optimism, and creativity!
Protect us from all evil forces and
liberate us from hatred, despair, and depression!
Om Shanti! Om Shanti! Om Shanti!

Bibliography

Apoorvanand. "On the Anniversary of Kandhamal Violence, the Least We Can Do Is Remember." *The Wire*, August 25, 2020. https://thewire.in/communalism/kandhamal-violence-anniversary-remembrance.

Atal, Yogesh. *Changing Indian Society*. Jaipur, India: Rawat, 2006.

Awasthi, Rajul. "India's 'Billionaire Raj Era': Time to Reform Personal Income Tax." *The Wire*, September 20, 2017. https://thewire.in/economy/indias-billionaire-raj-era-time-reform-personal-income-tax.

Banerjee, Brojendra Nath. *Struggle for Justice to Dalit Christians*. New Delhi: New Age International, 1997.

Basu, Indrajit. "Life after Demonetisation: How India's Poor Are Paying the Price." *Al Jazeera*, June 14, 2019. https://www.aljazeera.com/economy/2019/6/14/life-after-demonetisation-how-indias-poor-are-paying-the-price.

Bhargava, Rajeev, ed. *Secularism and Its Critics*. Delhi: Oxford University Press, 1998.

———. "What Is Democracy?" *Seminar* 389 (January 1992) 36–39.

Catholic Bishops' Conference of India. "Policy of Dalit Empowerment in the Catholic Church in India: An Ethical Imperative to Build Inclusive Communities." December 8, 2016. http://www.cbci.in/DownloadMat/dalit-policy.pdf.

Ceska, Andreas. "Art for Change 2017-IGNCA1." YouTube video, 3:27. December 25, 2017. https://www.youtube.com/watch?v=Dfnr-ukgAmw&ab_channel=andreasceska.

Chenoy, Kamal Mitra. *Violence in Gujarat: Test Case for a Larger Fundamentalist Agenda—Report of the Citizen's Commission on Persecution of Christians in Gujarat*. New Delhi: National Alliance of Women, 1999. https://cjp.org.in/wp-content/uploads/2020/07/Violence-in-Gujarat-Final_.pdf.

Constitution of India. May 2022. https://legislative.gov.in/sites/default/files/COI_English.pdf.

Dayal, John, and Shabnam Hashmi, eds. *365 Days: Democracy and Secularism Under the Modi Regime: A Report*. New Delhi: Anhad, 2015.

Desai, Akshay R. "National Integration and Religion." In *Sociology of Religion in India*, edited by Rowena Robinson, 54–67. New Delhi: Sage, 2004.
Dhage, Shivage K. "Poverty Alleviation Programmes in India: Issues and Challenges." In vol. 1 of *Poverty, Poverty Alleviation and Social Disadvantage: Analysis, Case Studies, and Policies*, edited by Clem Tisdell, 293–303. New Delhi: Serials, 2007.
Dolan, Kerry A., and Chase Peterson-Withorn, eds. "Forbes World's Billionaires List: The Richest in 2022." *Forbes*, 2022. https://www.forbes.com/billionaires-2022/.
Gelineau, Kristen, and Jon Gambrell. "New Zealand Mosque Shooter Is a White Nationalist Who Hates Immigrants, Documents and Video Reveal." *Chicago Tribune*, March 15, 2019. https://www.chicagotribune.com/nation-world/ct-mosque-killer-white-supremacy-20190315-story.html.
Golwalkar, Madhav S. *We, or Our Nationhood Defined*. Nagpur, India: Bharat Prakashan, 1947.
Gonsalves, Francis. "Populism and Religious Nationalism in India." *Concilium: International Journal of Theology* 2 (2019) 26–36.
Gonsalves, Manisha. "SCCs Inspiring NCCs." *The Examiner* 169:34 (August 25–31, 2018) 18.
Gonsalves, Peter. *Exercises in Peace Education*. Matunga, India: Tej-Prasarini, 2018. https://drive.google.com/file/d/1DHB1ojYUaL8UbQp7e_ulZUmmcAWzuUwl/view.
———. "Proposal: Peace Education Courses for School Teachers (Based on a Manual)." https://drive.google.com/file/d/1LW_zCqVb9yKwDdvQPB6DOaRFLTfgh6Eu/view.
Gorgan, Elena. "Antilia, the $2 Billion Private Residence, Has a Six-Level Garage for Over 160 Cars." *Auto Evolution*, January 4, 2022. https://www.autoevolution.com/news/antilia-the-2-billion-private-residence-has-a-6-level-garage-for-over-160-cars-178212.html.
Heredia, Rudolf C. "Justifying Reservation Quotas and Minority Rights: Recapturing the Constitutional Vision, I and II." *Vidyajyoti Journal of Theology* 76 (April–May 2012) 245–63, 357–70.
"India's Population at 1.21 Billion; Hindus 79.8 Percent, Muslims 14.2 Percent." *Business Standard*, August 26, 2015. https://www.business-standard.com/article/current-affairs/india-s-population-at-1-21-billion-hindus-79-78-muslims-14-12-115082600038_1.html.
John Paul II, Pope. "Letter of His Holiness John Paul II to Reverend George V. Coyne, SJ, Director of the Vatican Observatory, June 1, 1988." Vatican, Rome, 1988. https://www.vatican.va/content/john-paul-ii/en/letters/1988/documents/hf_jp-ii_let_19880601_padre-coyne.html.
Klyuev, Boris. *Religion in Indian Society: The Dimensions of "Unity in Diversity."* New Delhi: Sterling, 1989.
Kohli, Atul. *Democracy and Discontent: India's Growing Crisis of Governability*. Cambridge: Cambridge University Press, 1991.
Küng, Hans. *Islam: Past, Present, and Future*. London: Oneworld, 2008.
"Like My Predecessor John Paul II, Pope Tells Morocco: 'I Come as Pilgrim of Peace and Fraternity.'" *Zenit*, March 28, 2019. https://zenit.org/2019/03/28/like-my-predecessor-john-paul-ii-pope-tells-morocco-i-come-as-pilgrim-of-peace-and-fraternity/.
"Lipi Jesuits." Pax Lumina, n.d. https://paxlumina.com/lipi-jesuits/.

Mander, Harsh. "The Soul-Wounds of Massacre, or Why We Should Not Forget the 2002 Gujarat Pogrom." *The Wire*, February 27, 2022. https://thewire.in/communalism/2002-gujarat-anti-muslim-pogrom.

Mattam, Joseph, and Peter Arockiadoss. *Hindutva: An Indian Christian Response—The Twenty-Third Annual Meeting of the Indian Theological Association*. Bangalore, India: Dharmaram, 2002.

Quote Investigator: Tracing Quotations. "Be the Change You Wish to See in the World." October 23, 2017. https://quoteinvestigator.com/2017/10/23/be-change.

Radhakrishnan, Puthenveetil. "Globalization, Faith, and Development Politics." In *The Globalization Turbulence: Emerging Tensions in Indian Society*, edited by Prashant Kumar Trivedi, 180–205. New Delhi: Council for Social Development and Rawat, 2011.

Savarkar, Vinayak Damodar. *Hindutva*. Bombay: Veer Savarkar Prakashan, 1969.

United Nations. *The Millennium Development Goals Report 2015*. https://www.un.org/millenniumgoals/2015_MDG_Report/pdf/MDG%202015%20rev%20(July%201).pdf.

von Grebmer, Klaus, et al. *2022 Global Hunger Index: Food Systems Transformation and Local Governance*. Bonn, Germany: Welthungerhilfe and Concern Worldwide, 2022. https://www.globalhungerindex.org/pdf/en/2022.pdf.

"What's Unique?" Universal Solidarity Movement, n.d. http://universalsolidarity.in/what-is-unique/.

"Who Are We?" Nine Is Mine, n.d. https://www.nineismine.in/about-us/.

"With an Average Age of 29, India Will Be the World's Youngest Country by 2020." *Financial Express*, March 26, 2017. https://www.financialexpress.com/india-news/with-an-average-age-of-29-india-will-be-the-worlds-youngest-country-by-2020/603435/.

PART THREE

Theopolitical Debates: Just War and Responsibility to Protect

10

Confessions of a Just War Theorist: My Challenges Embracing a God of Absolute Nonviolence

M. T. Dávila

Introduction

A FEW YEARS AGO, a group of seminarians from various religious traditions came to my house as part of the annual day of service for our seminary. They were helping empty out our shed for demolition, a welcome aid to a home with a two-week-old baby and two very active toddlers. Once this task was done we sat around my kitchen table to share a simple lunch. The conversation turned to discussing the courses I typically taught. When we landed on a course on Christian approaches to the use of force, two Jewish students had a lot of questions. Specifically, they suggested that the possibility that just war theory could be a legitimate Christian approach to resolving conflicts did not seem congruent with the vision of Jesus they had learned in their studies. This echoed another moment a few years before that, when, as part of presenting a unit on Christian ethics, I introduced just war theory to a majority Jewish undergraduate classroom taking an introductory course on the Christian tradition.[1]

---

1. A note on my use of the term "Christian": While the Catholic Nonviolence Initiative (CNI), the 2016 conference in Rome, and the subsequent 2019 conference contained appeals encouraging official Catholic teaching on the ethics of the use of force to affirm gospel nonviolence as a central teaching of the faith, I consider this to be a question for the entire Christian family. I therefore use the term "Christian," not just "Catholic," when referring to gospel nonviolence and to the just war tradition.

For both of these groups, more familiar with the gospel story of Jesus than with the trajectory of the Christian tradition since, just war theory as a tool for navigating conflict in the world seemed absolutely incongruous with the "Christian message." For them the primary identity of Jesus is of him who blesses the peacemakers (Matt 5:9) and reminds his followers to love their enemies and pray for those who persecute them (Luke 6:27–28). I remember wanting to make my case that just war theory was not only a legitimate, ethical form of navigating conflict that helped reduce the tragic outcomes of war, if not prevent them altogether, but one that affirmed Christian values like love of neighbor. But they weren't having it. These students wanted to know where Jesus is in just war theory.

Among ethicists like me who work extensively on analyzing the usefulness of just war criteria for addressing conflict in today's world, the spring 2016 Gospel Nonviolence and Just Peace Conference in Rome and the document it generated landed with mixed reactions. Our main concern had to do with the possible repercussions of pushing aside just war theory as a tool for the ethical analysis of difficult cases relating to the protection of human life when the use of force is an option on the table for one or more of the parties involved.[2] The concern expressed had to do more with the possibility of doing away with a tool whose purpose is to limit violence and humanize potential targets and vulnerable populations, rather than any commitment to militarized responses to conflict. For many proponents of the just war tradition, myself included, the tradition has developed toward an increasingly strict presumption against justifying the intentional harming of human life and the environment and has come to serve as a crucial tool for supporting arguments for nonviolence. For many of us, just war theory does not normalize or even defend the existence of war. Having frameworks to deal with the tragedy of conflict as it has occurred in human history does not mean that we aim to normalize the morally tragic. On the contrary, these frameworks provide us with well-rehearsed and well-known tools for engaging different groups who are participating in conflict *for the defense of life*.

In the spring of 2017, I was asked to participate in the roundtable tasked to develop a fundamental theology of nonviolence for the Catholic Nonviolence Initiative (CNI). Our task was to develop the theological rationale for understanding the God revealed in the Bible as a God of radical or

---

2. See, "Theological Roundtable," 105–8, and these contributions by just war theorists that immediately follow this article in *Horizon* vol. 45: Christiansen, "Nonviolence," 108–14; Winright, "Just War," 114–19; Johnston, "Talking about War," 119–23; and Allman, "Practical Implications," 123–27. See also, generally, Shaddle, "Why We Still Need"; and Steinfels, "War Against Just War."

absolute nonviolence. As a just war theorist I wondered why I was working on this fascinating theological project aimed at developing a possible magisterial teaching on Christian nonviolence: the CNI roundtables, made up of international voices representing various viewpoints on the intersections of theology, conflict, anthropology, peacebuilding, ethics, public policy, ecclesiology, and other key themes, sought to build blueprints that would serve as foundations for a possible encyclical on Christian nonviolence. The process was dialogical, cooperative, and designed to take advantage of the expertise of the theological voices gathered. I count my participation in the roundtable on theological foundations as a profound honor.

This chapter is the product of our reflecting together during the DePaul University (Chicago) conference on Christian nonviolence. It is not a definitive declaration of my own positions on this project, but, rather, a description of my journey as a participant in the roundtable. Inevitably, this also includes reflections on my role as a public intellectual who has spent time arguing for and about the just war tradition.[3] This project has challenged me to consider methodological questions about how we do and source theology and ethics grounded on gospel nonviolence. But it has also encouraged me to recommit to the task of making available tools for ethical reflection and discernment that honestly consider conflict resolution "under the conditions of existence" and sin. Ultimately the biggest challenge to accomplishing this is the one described above that has been posed by my students. I am now painfully aware that I am hard-pressed to answer their question about whether Jesus or any gospel value can be found in the just war tradition.[4] My goal in engaging the just war tradition has never been to bring it closer to the gospel, but rather, to try to restrain, restrict, and judge the violence we have done to each other, both historically and in the present day.

---

3. See, for example, Dávila, "Breaking from the Dominance." See also Dávila and Winright, "Police Are Highly Militarized"; and Dávila, "Contribution."

4. Traditionally, just war theory resorts to Augustine and Aquinas to place just war criteria in the context of the love of neighbor and of the common good/natural law, respectively. See, for example, Cahill, "Theological Contexts"; and Watts, "Just War." The challenges of the last seventy-five years (including the Cold War and its end in 1989, Vietnam, the Rwandan genocide, various Gulf wars, and the War on Terror) have pushed many of us to reframe and reestablish the goals and limits of just war theory. For me, however, the theory continues to be grounded on the key Christian question of "What does love require of me?" at a personal, social, and national level.

Theological Nonviolence and the Ethics of Just War Theory

Throughout my participation in the Catholic Nonviolence Initiative project, I had to come to terms with being theologically nonviolent while from the point of view of ethics remaining a just war theorist. The specific roundtable I participated in was tasked with developing a foundational theology of nonviolence. I had the honor of working on this task with some of the most renowned theologians from around the world. The core question we examined was how to articulate a God of nonviolence:

> If nonviolence is viable it can only be because it is true, and it is only true if it corresponds to the way things really are, that is, the way God really is . . . and the way that God has chosen to create and sustain and redeem the world.[5]

As a cadre of theologians and ethicists from around the world having various life histories and experiences, our roundtable tackled this project with faithfulness, remaining honest to our particular contexts and histories. In the course of this project of developing a foundational theology that presented God as essentially nonviolent, I was most challenged by my historical consciousness, which cautioned me to carefully consider the implications of proclaiming "gospel nonviolence" and a God of radical nonviolence. Questions that kept complicating my thoughts about this task included: Who gets to define these terms? Who benefits? What realities do they include and imply? What kinds of practices do they normalize? Do they overlook people's histories of colonial, economic, and other forms of violence? In short, I was suspicious that the drive to promote a God of nonviolence would result in a tool that could effectively erase peoples' particular experiences of unjust violence. As a Puerto Rican and a Latin American, I recognized that members of the roundtable from the global South also had similar concerns. More specifically, we wanted to make sure that any proposal for a foundational theology of nonviolence would not gloss over the Catholic Church's complicity with colonial and religious violence throughout the ages. Proposals that describe a God of radical nonviolence need to serve the purpose of putting a mirror to the church's lamentable links to European colonialism, conquest, and expansion.

The roundtable understood this challenge, and explicitly included it in its construction of a foundational theology of nonviolence. While a God of nonviolence can be articulated throughout revelation in Scripture, faithfulness to that God has often not characterized the Christian life, historically

---

5. Catholic Nonviolence Initiative Roundtable #1, "Toward a Foundational Theology," 1.

and today. Our reflecting together included a journey through the Scriptures, where we identified a progressive understanding of God as nonviolent and the human person as created for relationships of kinship with one another grounded on this divine reality and image. We were meticulous in acknowledging what we meant by the term "nonviolence," and how this understanding of divine reality and of the purpose of human life has historically been clouded by the impact of sin and by the human condition in history. We concluded that a foundational theology of nonviolence is not an attempt to return to an idyllic garden of Eden where unjust suffering does not touch human lives. Rather, in our articulation of this theology, in acknowledging human history and the history of the Christian tradition, we affirmed a God of nonviolence who is carefully attentive and responsive to unjust suffering. We also affirmed that in this context the goal of human life is the establishment of relationships of kinship, as firmly revealed in the life, ministry, death, and resurrection of Jesus Christ. I believe that the roundtable reached these conclusions carefully, authentically, and humbly, submitting our articulation of a God of nonviolence to the greater scrutiny of those who have most suffered from the impact of the historical and present-day violence we do to each other. As a result of the care taken, I can attest to firmly upholding a theological vision of a God of nonviolence.

However, my own training and focus in the scholarly study of Christian ethics includes a robust engagement with just war theory. I have published several chapters and essays on the topic, examining both its usefulness for attending to particular forms of injustice globally as well its limits in taking into account minoritized voices among impacted populations (including women, religious and ethnic minorities, the indigenous, LGBTQ+ folk, and the extremely poor) and its limits in serving as an accurate determinant of how to legitimately use force in specific situations of extreme and unjust suffering. Throughout I have held that just war theory is a tool, not the only tool, but a well-rehearsed and generally recognized tool, for engaging others from various religious traditions and cultures in the task of limiting—if not delegitimizing altogether—the violence that we do to each other.

Just war theory makes a presumption against violence. This bears repeating again, as it is often an overstatement of advocates of an ethic of nonviolence that just war theory is a tool more frequently used to legitimize militarized responses to unjust suffering. But I have yet to meet a just war theorist whose central goal is not the absolute protection of life, and in more recent times, this has expanded to the protection of the environment as well. When it has been used as a checklist to approve military projects abroad for the benefit of a corporate or political interests, it has resulted in sinful campaigns of violence against vulnerable populations that do not bring the world any closer to peace.

When my students ask where Jesus is in just war theory, I point out this initial and strict presumption against the use of deadly force that is embedded in the criteria. A just cause and right intention do not legitimize the use of force, but rather demand the most absolute care in scrutinizing the bellicose drive of governments and individuals, a drive that Augustine was all too familiar with, and against which he warned in proposing that there might be an occasion that is sufficiently just to allow the use of deadly force against other human beings.[6]

In the criteria of last resort and reasonable hope for success, just war theory demands restraint from engaging in any use of force that bypasses the kinds of peacemaking processes we have been talking about throughout the entire CNI. This includes more limited or discreet agreements for cease-fires and temporary peace that establish safety for especially vulnerable populations while larger stakeholders negotiate a more secure and permanent agreement. Just war theory also demands that any use of force be limited in scope to what is absolutely necessary to achieve well-articulated ends, avoid mission creep (which is often a mask for the advancement of more sinister private and mainly economic interests), and avoid at all costs a protracted conflict. At the heart of just war theory is the restraint on the use of force, the protection of human life, and the minimizing of harm when force is deemed ultimately necessary.

As an ethicist, I found two other compelling reasons to hold onto the framework of the just war criteria. First, this tradition offers a common language—or perhaps I naively believe it to be so—through which to engage in conversations about accountability, restraint, the protection of life, and the minimizing of harm with broad sectors of the population. For decades this ethical language has been globally agreed upon, even if it has always been within the messy and violent context of the Cold War, expansionism, imperialism, terrorism, and violent capitalism. It continues to provide a common framework for concluding that most government-sanctioned killing, or any killing in conflict situations, is ethically unjust and categorically illegitimate. This common language is one that speaks at various levels of government decision-making, including in congressional hearings and presidential briefings (for what these are worth these days). Mark Allman reflects that

---

6. Augustine, *Contra Faustum*, #74: "What is the evil in war? . . . The real evils in war are love of violence, revengeful cruelty, fierce and implacable enmity, wild resistance, and the lust for power, and such like."

abandoning JWT [Just War Theory] reduces the church's influence in international affairs.... If the church were to no longer use the language, concepts, and ideas of JWT, it would no longer be speaking the language of international affairs. Its "place at the table" would no longer be needed, since a peace church has only one position on war: it is wrong always.... Should the church abandon JWT, it also surrenders its role as a moral authority in the interpretation and application of just-war principles in international affairs, which makes it easier for those who abuse the theory for national self-interest to wrap realpolitik in a veil of moral legitimacy.[7]

Second, while these criteria are not foolproof or absolute, and more often than not they are best used in hindsight, they *are* a tool, one to be used among many others that exercise our moral imagination with regard to how best to nourish and protect human dignity.[8] Tobias Winright describes how arguments for an ethic of nonviolence rely heavily on just war reasoning to assess the illegitimacy of *any* war.[9] The notion of a "just peace" or an ethic of nonviolence require reasoning that uses similar arguments to the criteria of just war theory in order to ground the judgment that the use of force is ultimately not a legitimately Christian alternative to conflict resolution.[10]

I admit that these reasons I've just discussed grow weaker the more I engage with and learn from nonviolent practices and thinkers. They are, decidedly, heavily dependent on a structure of power that limits who the actors making policy and military decisions may be. As most often articulated and used, just war theory does not take into consideration the clamor of masses of people who, themselves having applied just war principles to particular situations (for example, the global mass demonstrations against the preemptive war against Iraq), have judged the use of force against particular populations and governments to be completely illegitimate. It often fails to incorporate the wisdom and on-the-ground work of civil actors who offer

---

7. Allman, "Practical Implications," 124.

8. Winright, "Just War," 117–18: "Thought and imagination went into ongoing efforts to limit war.... None of these imaginative efforts aim to endorse war. Rather, they seek to limit war—narrowly clarifying when it is justified and how it is to be justly conducted—as well as to prevent it in the first place (*jus ante bellum*) and to prevent it from flaring up again (*jus post bellum*)."

9. Winright, "Why I Shall Continue," 147.

10. Winright, "Why I Shall Continue," 150: "As Lloyd Steffen has observed, 'just war thinking is itself an expression of a more basic approach to ethics,' one that includes elements of deontology, consequentialism, and virtue ethics. Put differently, there is an 'ethic that lies behind just war' that can be 'applicable to all kinds of ethical issues,' as well as for uses for force other than war" (quoting from Steffen, *Ethics and Experience*, 33).

nonviolent resolutions to some or all parts of what was previously thought to be an intractable conflict, detailed examples of which are presented in this edited volume. On this front Drew Christiansen points out that the evolution of the concept of the "responsibility to protect" (R2P) out of just war principles has "given rise to a complex of institutions, roles, and practices that could well endure beyond the current Western political distemper."[11]

It's painfully clear that for many, just war theory has been used to normalize war as a necessity in a sinful world, something that can be limited but not altogether eliminated. Laurie Johnston, herself an active member of the Community of Sant'Egidio, a key global actor in efforts aimed at nonviolent resolutions to armed conflicts, captures my sentiment most clearly:

> As much as war may be alien to Christian life and vocation, we cannot abandon the conversation, because that would be ceding the field to the warmongers. The virtue of JWT is that it refuses to regard warfare as a situation in which moral categories no longer apply. JWT is precisely the way that we can remain in the conversation about war without normalizing or glorifying it. . . . There is room for Christian ethics to speak about limiting war in a way that does not detract from our duty to be peacemakers.[12]

A Just War Ethicist Constructing a Fundamental Theology of Nonviolence? The Challenge of Integration

A key question for me throughout the CNI process has been that of the role of theology versus the role of ethics in the life of the faithful and of the church. Ideally, these are not distinct tasks. A Christian's journey of faith and discipleship ought to point toward a deeper integration of our essential belief in a God of mercy who is present in history and becomes incarnate in Jesus the Christ, with the tradition of ethical reflection and practices that witness this essential truth to the world. However, this crucial task of integration eluded me during the work of the roundtable. I fully affirmed the foundational theology of nonviolence that we were developing. I feel that it represents robust and realistic conversations about the broader human experience of violence and how God reveals Godself to be a God of mercy and nonviolence, creating out of wholeness and working in history toward restoration and reconciliation in wholeness and peace. But I've yet to fully adopt an ethic of nonviolence as proposed by the 2016 Rome document and

---

11. Christiansen, "Nonviolence," 114.
12. Johnston, "Talking About War," 122–23.

in the statement that came out of the subsequent meeting in the spring of 2019. What am I to glean, as an ethicist, from this inability to integrate the theological with the ethical on this particular issue? Could it be that I am simply too beholden to the taking up of arms as a tool for addressing unjust suffering in a sinful world, whether by governments or oppressed peoples?

Theology grasps at revelation from within the limited terms of human language and experience. The contribution to the topic of a foundational theology of nonviolence by Brazilian theologian Maria Clara Bingemer comes close to the kind of integration of the theological and the ethical that would address some of my key concerns. She asserts that in the Bible, God is portrayed as close to our violence, "debating and defying the violence that we do to each other. These stories include the human urge to have divine legitimation for the violence we inflict on others."[13] The biblical stories, in turn, reflect the violent language that was in usage at the time, proposing a God that might appear to be in line with our own bellicose urges, rather than reflecting what God is really doing at the time, resisting and judging violence as being contrary to the created order. It is perhaps the task of developing a new language to express a God of nonviolence who is working to transform human violence that would most readily address at least *this particular* Christian's challenge of integration.

The CNI roundtable working on a foundational theology of nonviolence struggled to articulate a God of nonviolence based on Scripture and tradition. Our goal was to locate nonviolence outside of human history, in the reality of who God is, but then, ultimately, within human history, in the broken and fallen histories of the creature that bears the image of a nonviolent God—you and me. This really was one of our deepest struggles as a roundtable: How is it possible to articulate a theology of nonviolence when human experience testifies to violence as a central experience of life in history and when the church has so often been silent or even complicit in so much of this violence? Ultimately theology ought to be grounded on who God is, a God who is nonviolent and, according to the gospel story, changes the world, transforms all of reality through an incarnational act of radical solidarity that is capable of turning hearts of stone into hearts of flesh.

The roundtable on a foundational theology of nonviolence attempted to articulate the full ideal of this God of nonviolence: the ideal of what creation is, who human beings are, how the community of the church and the sacraments are oriented toward the task of peacebuilding, and how this comes to be in and through the Holy Spirit working with us and within us,

---

13. Catholic Nonviolence Initiative Roundtable #1, "Toward a Foundational Theology," 7.

surprising us even in the face of our deepest impulses and instincts to be agents of violent retribution instead of peaceful reconciliation.

Given the construction of a foundational theology of nonviolence, what is the challenge for an ethic of nonviolence? Is the role of ethics, then, to approximate faithfully this theological idea? This task requires that we work toward shifting the hermeneutics that shape the construction of the knowledge of violence and how humans have come to regard violence as the *modus operandi* of societies or groups in conflict, toward one grounded on a God of nonviolence. Even in Scripture, humans come to know themselves first as a created good, but then, rather quickly, as creatures steeped in the blood of our brothers (Gen 4:1–16). Recent work in the hermeneutics of violence suggests that "it is very important that religions learn to come to grips with their particular traditions of violence and to find ways of living together in peace and mutual understanding."[14] The task of integrating a foundational theology of nonviolence with the ethical dictates of a life of Christian discipleship must necessarily pass through the very challenging task of understanding the ways that violence is deeply intertwined in humanity's self-understanding.

This hermeneutical shift requires further reflection. Some questions to consider would be: What kind of ethical analysis of present-day moments and situations of conflict and violence are needed? How do our analyses reflect history accurately without engaging in the erasure of the histories of colonialism or racism, for example? How should these analyses properly identify perpetrators and victims? How do we assign responsibilities and tasks aimed at restoration and reconciliation? How can these responsibilities and tasks help identify proper avenues and moments for nonviolent intervention?

As an ethicist, I have one crucial question still to consider as I engage with the challenge of integration: What are legitimate Christian responses to human suffering on a massive scale? Responses to this question must contend with the failures to intervene in the cases of Rwanda and Bosnia, the failure of a protracted war on terror that continues to claim lives without any measure of legitimacy, and the failure to have a proper set of tools in place to address the kinds of conflicts that arise from the massive displacement of peoples, such as that in Syria, which will become more frequent and more critical as the result of economic inequality and the ravages caused by climate change. What sort of defenses does human dignity call for? What kind of peace do we want to build and how is it best built? Does just war

---

14. Wiedenhofer, "Towards a Theological Hermeneutics," 111. See also Vahabzadeh, *Violence and Nonviolence*; and Ayyash, *Hermeneutics of Violence*.

theory contribute to the same kind of peace available through projects grounded in nonviolence? Or is it a different peace, tainted by violence and structured on power, networks of allies, and the definition of enemies, rather than our shared humanity?

Coming up with answers to these questions is a daunting task. I offered my participation in the roundtable and in the entire CNI project in the spirit of sharing a journey with people of faith who are deeply committed to the protection of life and furthering the Christian project of peace and wholeness in the world. I wish that my reflections here included a description of a clearer path on this journey, a resolution to the suspicions generated by historical and postcolonial consciousness, and a clear commitment to nonviolence as *the* Christian answer to ethical questions about the use of force. For now, however, I draw encouragement from the peace that comes from walking together in mutual respect, enlivened by the Spirit.

Conclusion: Committed to a Messy Journey

The Catholic Nonviolence Initiative insists that ethicists must come to terms with the fact that reliance on violence for the defense of human life stunts Christian imagination and our ability to approximate the ideal of a God whose identity is mercy and whose modality is encounter.[15] While the goal of Christian ethics might be the realistic building of practical tools for a discipleship that approximates that ideal, we are continually challenged by the weight of our own sinful tendencies, the weight of our histories, and the weight of countless Christian thinkers—including Augustine and Aquinas—who offered a tenuous yet decisive baptism of the natural right of the state to use armed forces as necessary for the defense of the common good, deeming them essential to the protection of human life and dignity. In other words, Christian ethicists like myself have a lot of theoretical, theological, and ethical baggage to get through. And it's not just us. Many Christians in the US and other nations with any sort of power continually bring up the right of a state to have military defenses whenever they are questioned about whether or not the use of violence to address conflicts and as a method of statecraft are faithful to the gospel.

Critical to any kind of ethical transformation will be building communities of faith that together walk the journey of exploring the role of violence in human history and in the story of the Christian tradition. The very process by which the roundtables negotiated and developed their particular topics, confronting the role of violence in our own reading of history in an

---

15. Dávila, "Hora de Reconsiderar," para. 9.

environment of solidarity, faithfulness to gospel nonviolence, and mutual respect, itself serves as a model for these kinds of reflections. The kinds of challenging and messy encounters I have described here seem to me to be the most effective at empowering people of faith to be agents of transformation in the world.

Developing Christian and interfaith communities called to live up to the ideal of a God of nonviolence, while at the same time building space for conversations open to a diversity of approaches to the ethics of using force will create the conditions for the hermeneutical shift required to squarely address conflict without the use of force.

In building ethical tools that approximate the ideal proposed by a foundational theology of nonviolence, I can propose that just war theory might have a role to play in its strong presumption against the taking of human life and its demand to minimize harm. While theology must challenge the ethical approximation of the ideal, the ethical cannot escape reality, numbers, data, history, and technologies. In other words, until there is full disarmament—for which I think all Christians must fervently struggle—I will not be able to yield on a legal framework to reign in and control the use of existing military capacities, and perhaps to even direct it toward the good in the most extreme of situations. After my comments at the DePaul University conference where I developed this reflection, two members of the audience approached me expressing deep gratitude for having articulated some of the ambivalence and suspicion toward an ethic of nonviolence that they had not been able to articulate thus far. They wanted to enter the conversation and were there as committed Christian disciples struggling with Jesus's call to radical nonviolence, but they had seen themselves as completely peripheral to the conversation until they heard about my own messy struggle and ambivalence. They felt validated, but most importantly, they felt invited into the conversation.

I come to the table of the conversation on gospel nonviolence as a person of faith who has relied heavily on just war theory as a tool to protect the common good and minimize harm to human life. The conversation thus far has been productive. It will also continue into the future as part of the messy journey of Christian discipleship. I can sincerely proclaim that the fact that the conversation has come thus far is truly the work of the Spirit. Therefore, even in my ambivalence, I shall remain in solidarity with the nonviolence movement as a co-sojourner and ally.

Bibliography

Allman, Mark. "Practical Implications of Abandoning Just War." *Horizons* 45:1 (June 2018) 123–27. https://www.cambridge.org/core/product/479380B250E94DD2D6BAB43C59BD89CF/core-reader.

Augustine, Saint. *Contra Faustum*. Translated by Richard Stothert. In vol. 4 of *Nicene and Post-Nicene Fathers*, First Series, edited by Philip Schaff. Revised and edited for New Advent by Kevin Knight. Buffalo, NY: Christian Literature, 1887. https://www.newadvent.org/fathers/140622.htm.

Ayyash, Mark. *A Hermeneutics of Violence: A Four-Dimensional Conception*. Toronto: University of Toronto Press, 2019.

Cahill, Lisa. "Theological Contexts of Just War Theory and Pacifism: A Response to J. Bryan Hehir." *Journal of Religious Ethics* 20:2 (Fall 1992) 259–65.

Catholic Nonviolence Initiative Roundtable #1. "Toward a Foundational Theology of Nonviolence." Fall 2018. https://nonviolencejustpeace.net/wp-content/uploads/2020/08/Toward-foundational-theology-of-nonviolence.pdf.

Christiansen, Drew. "The Nonviolence–Just War Nexus." *Horizons* 45:1 (June 2018) 108–14. https://www.cambridge.org/core/product/BD03357FA8F2DD3DE2A9C0D176618DAD/core-reader.

Dávila, María Teresa. "Breaking from the Dominance of Power and Order in Augustine's Ethic of War." In *Augustine and Social Ethics*, edited by Teresa Delgado et al., 145–62. Augustine in Conversation: Tradition and Innovation. Lanham, MD: Lexington, 2015.

———. "The Contribution of Reinhold Niebuhr's 'Moral Ambiguity' to Contemporary Discussions on the Morality of the Use of Force in a Post–Cold War World." *Political Theology* 5:2 (2004) 177–99.

———. "Hora de Reconsiderar la Cristianización de las Américas: La Modalidad de Dios es Encuentro." *Forum*, Catholic Theological Ethics in the World Church, November 1, 2019. https://catholicethics.com/forum/hora-de-reconsiderar-la-cristianizacion-de-las-americas-la-modalidad-de-dios-es-encuentro/.

Dávila, María Teresa, and Tobias Winright. "The Police Are Highly Militarized." *Sojourners*, February 2017. https://sojo.net/magazine/february-2017/police-are-highly-militarized.

Johnston, Laurie. "Talking about War." *Horizons* 45:1 (June 2018) 119–23. https://www.cambridge.org/core/product/EF04B05517F21E5B1896BB1AF51D7270/core-reader.

Shaddle, Matthew. "Why We Still Need Just War Theory." *Catholic Herald*, April 28, 2016. https://catholicherald.co.uk/why-we-still-need-just-war-theory/.

Steffen, Lloyd. *Ethics and Experience: Moral Theory from Just War to Abortion*. Lanham, MD: Rowman and Littlefield, 2012.

Steinfels, Peter. "The War Against Just War: Enough Already." *Commonweal*, June 5, 2017. https://www.commonwealmagazine.org/war-against-just-war.

"Theological Roundtable: Must Just Peace and Just War Be Mutually Exclusive?" *Horizons* 45:1 (June 2018) 119–23. https://www.cambridge.org/core/journals/horizons/article/must-just-peace-and-just-war-be-mutually-exclusive/1F6FF3717E9E36DE2908E1D6CE9CCE4C.

Vahabzadeh, Peyman. *Violence and Nonviolence: Conceptual Excursions into Phantom Opposites*. Toronto: University of Toronto Press, 2019.

Watts, Craig. "Just War, Pacifism, and the Ethics of Protection." *Encounter* 71:1 (Winter 2010) 35–62.

Wiedenhofer, Siegfried. "Towards a Theological Hermeneutics of Violence." In *Postcolonial Europe in the Crucible of Cultures: Reckoning with God in a World of Conflicts*, edited by Jacques Haers et al., 111–23. Currents of Encounter 34. Amsterdam: Rodopi, 2007.

Winright, Tobias. "Just War and Imagination Are Not Mutually Exclusive." *Horizons* 45:1 (June 2018) 114–19. https://www.cambridge.org/core/product/4820C6A058 3F84731E21C57E242DBCD6/core-reader.

———. "Why I Shall Continue to Use and Teach Just War Theory." *Expositions* 12:1 (2018) 142–61.

11

Just War: A Convenient Untruth

ROBERT EMMET MEAGHER

We shall know nothing until we know whether we have the right to kill our fellow men, or the right to let them be killed.

—ALBERT CAMUS, 1956[1]

WARS BEGIN NOT WITH the first shots fired but with the first lies told. Generic lies like "there have always been wars"; "war is part of human nature"; "wars have winners"; and "wars can be just, good, and even holy." Then there are the lies tailored to the moment: "we didn't ask for this"; "we can't just walk away"; "better dead than red"; "swift and surgical, over before we know it"; "we are the good guys here"; and "God is on our side." Let me give some examples of lies and promises drenched in blood.

Launching the twentieth century's first global conflict, the "Great War to End All Wars," Germany's Kaiser Wilhelm famously boasted in 1914 that Germany would rapidly defeat France in a matter of weeks and then Russia in several months, thus promising total victory in time to bring his troops home to celebrate Christmas with their loved ones. Six months later, swift victory and *fröhliche Weinachten* ("Merry Christmas") forgotten, Sigmund Freud added his own, even more lethal, lie to the Kaiser's:

1. Camus, *Rebel*, 4.

> When the fierce struggle of this war will have reached a decision, every victorious warrior will joyfully and without delay return home to his wife and children, undisturbed by thoughts of the enemy he has killed either at close quarters or with weapons operating at a distance.[2]

We might well ask what entitled Freud—neither prophet nor psychic—to offer such a blind and blinding assurance. Surely it was not his ignorance of war and of war's invisible wounds. Instead, as he explained, it was his professional confidence in the sophistication of "civilized" men who had shed what he called their "ethical delicacy of feeling." Unlike their superstitious, benighted forerunners—savage men who feared the vengeful spirits of the men they murdered—modern warriors know better than to allow their military service to haunt them. It remains hopeful for the future of humanity that he was so badly mistaken.

It was not only scientists and national leaders, however, who paved the road to World War I with lies. Poet and Military Cross recipient Siegfried Sassoon, or "Mad Jack" as he was known to his men in the Royal Welsh Fusiliers, reminds us otherwise in his poem entitled "They."

> The Bishop tells us: "When the boys come back
> They will not be the same; for they'll have fought
> In a just cause: they lead the last attack
> On Anti-Christ; their comrade's blood has bought
> New right to breed an honorable race.
> They have challenged Death and dared him face to face."
> "We're none of us the same!" the boys reply.
> "For George lost both his legs; and Bill's stone blind;
> Poor Jim's shot through the lungs and like to die;
> And Bert's gone syphilitic: you'll not find
> A chap who's served that hasn't found *some* change."
> And the Bishop said; "The ways of God are strange!"[3]

Strange indeed. Stranger still, however, was the bishop's blasphemous presumption that his or any war is God's doing, God's special cause. Surely it would be more honest to describe Europe's march to war in 1914 as a "descent into madness," in the words of former ambassador Joseph Mussomeli,

> when, without any sense of regret, remorse or equivocation, Europe grabbed itself by the throat and committed the greatest act of collective suicide in modern history. Not since the

---

2. Freud, *Reflections*, Essay II, 20.
3. Sassoon, "They," 27.

Peloponnesian Wars had a civilization so thoughtlessly and recklessly demanded its own destruction.[4]

We must be careful not to outdo them.

We who have lived through over thirty deadliest wars waged since the 11th of November 1918 can draw up our own lists of the lies told to ignite and sustain those conflagrations, but in doing so we should not overlook the "mother of all" war lies: that nuclear arms have made the world safe, that they are instruments of peace. Never mind that the human race and our beloved planet Earth have any number of times been a hair's breadth from nuclear annihilation and that we remain at this moment and always precariously balanced on that brink. Living, walking, working, loving, raising our children atop a catastrophe waiting to happen, we are assured only by our threats of assured mutual destruction, by the unthinkable. And yet we think it every day. What is wrong to do, however, is to threaten.[5] Our threats darken us. "Granted," writes Michael Walzer,

> killing millions of innocent people is worse than threatening to kill them. It is also true that no one wants to kill them, and it may well be true that no one expects to do so. Nevertheless, we intend the killings under certain circumstances. That is the stated policy of our government; and thousands of men, trained in the techniques of mass destruction and drilled in instant obedience, stand ready to carry it out. And from the perspective of morality, the readiness is all. . . . What we condemn in our own government, as in the police . . . is the commitment to murder.[6]

Albert Camus shared similar reflections on the lethality of thinking murderous thoughts in a historic address he gave at Columbia University in the spring of 1946, his first and only public address in the US, a talk that he entitled "The Human Crisis":

> At the end of this long night, we finally know what we must do in the face of this crisis-torn world. What must we do? Call things by their name and understand that we kill millions of people each time we agree to think certain thoughts. You don't think badly because you think you are a murderer, you are a murderer because you think badly. Hence, you can be a

---

4. Mussomeli, "100 Years On."
5. Ramsey, "Political Ethics," 134.
6. Waltzer, *Just and Unjust*, 272.

murderer without ever having killed, and this is why we are all more or less murderers.[7]

To the question, "what must we do?" Camus gave this answer: "The first thing to do is simply to reject in thought and action any acquiescent or fatalistic way of thinking."[8] Rather than rethink the policies of the Cold War, however, we in the US and our long-term opponent have resolved to double down and invest trillions of dollars in the decades ahead to updating and expanding our nuclear arsenals. "No policies in human history," writes Daniel Ellsberg, "have more deserved to be recognized as immoral. Or insane."[9]

"Why this madness?" is the first question that comes to my mind. We are told that it is all about our national security, the world's security; yet from the school duck-and-cover drills of my childhood in the 1940s to Donald Trump's delusory ongoing courtship of "Rocket Man," I don't believe a word of it; not when I follow the money. The Cold War and the arms race are and have always been, root and branch, an economic juggernaut, and the same is true of our hot wars. This realization came to Brigadier General Smedley Butler after a distinguished three-decade combat career in the Marine Corps, receiving two medals of honor and a chestful of other medals. When General Butler retired from the Corps he was the most decorated marine in its history. He later summed up his service in these words: "I spent thirty-three years in the Marines, most of my time being a high-class muscle man for big business, for Wall Street and the bankers. In short, I was a racketeer for Capitalism."[10]

Of war, in which his years had been steeped, he had this to say:

> War is a racket. It always has been. It is possibly the oldest, easily the most profitable, surely the most vicious. It is the only one international in scope. It is the only one in which the profits are reckoned in dollars and the losses in lives.[11]

Wars, of course, are not fought by businessmen, bankers, or brokers. Wars are fought by those who suffer its losses rather than by those who amass its profits.

It is ironic and angering that the most lethal and effective public lie told to enable empires, kingdoms, and nations to marshal armies and send them off to kill, destroy, and die is a lie invented by the church of the nonviolent

---

7. Albert Camus, as quoted in Columbia Maison Française, "Human Crisis," 42:31.
8. Columbia Maison Française, "Human Crisis."
9. Ellsberg, introduction to *Doomsday Machine*.
10. Butler, *War Is a Racket*, cover.
11. Butler, *War Is a Racket*, 23.

Christ, more specifically by bishops Augustine of Hippo and Ambrose of Milan in the fourth century. I have little doubt that it was a lie first fabricated in good faith, a "white lie" as we say, but one that like a cancer eagerly metastasized and spread, becoming more deadly with the passage of time. The lie I have in mind is what we know as "just war theory." While its original aim may have been to limit as well as to allow the use of deadly force, it has had far more success in unleashing violence than in controlling it. Like a Wikitext, just war theory and its precepts have been freely expanded and updated across sixteen centuries to address and accommodate the open-ended evolution of warfare and the deepening of humanity's addiction to it. When we consider the Crusades, the conquest of the Americas, the religious persecutions and wars of Europe, the Great War, the Good War, the Cold War, the Forever War, the invention of gunpowder, and the invention of nuclear fission, we may well wonder whether there is any war or weapon, any strategy or tactic, any exercise of force that just war theory won't eventually authorize or at least condone . . . provided we have the right intention (*recta intentio*).

I say this because in Christian ethics from the first century onwards the focus has fallen on the intentions behind our actions rather than on the consequences that result from our actions. Augustine summed this up in his notorious counsel to "love, and do what you will" (*dilige et quod vis fac*)[12] and thus maintained a sharp line between heart and hand, between inner disposition and outward act. The eminent philosopher and theologian Peter Abelard, seven centuries later, supported this view, arguing that God "pays attention not so much to the deeds that are done as to the mind with which they are done."[13] Add to this the doctrine of double effect and "the gloves are off." The late Oxford philosopher Elizabeth Anscombe made precisely this point, remarking honestly and harshly that this is "a marvelous way of making any action lawful." She went on to explain:

> This same doctrine is used to prevent any doubts about the obliteration bombing of a city. The devout Catholic bomber secures by a "direction of intention" that any shedding of innocent blood that occurs is "accidental." I know a Catholic boy who was puzzled at being told by his schoolmaster that it was an accident that the people of Hiroshima and Nagasaki were there to be killed; in fact, however absurd it seems, such thoughts are common among priests who know that they are forbidden by the divine law to justify the direct killing of the innocent. It is

---

12. Augustine of Hippo, *Homilies*, Tractatus VII.8.
13. Abelard, *Ethical Writings*, I.84

nonsense to pretend that you do not intend to do what is the means you take to your chosen end.[14]

Just war theory has indeed, over fifteen centuries, been increasingly weaponized to provide moral cover for the policies and practices of warring nations, while hoping to soothe the often tormented consciences of warriors. It still performs the first function quite effectively, as demonstrated by President Obama's explicit appeal to just war theory to defend his controversial policy of targeted assassinations. As for the soothing of war-fighters' consciences, Army infantry captain Michael Hoffman has this to say: "Let's be honest: most of the theory is there to make civilians feel better about sending someone's sons and daughters to war."[15]

So where did just war theory come from and why? A crucial question inviting a complex historical-theological response, while admitting of a much simpler one. I have developed the long version elsewhere and offer only the short version here. As I see it, the unexpected and radical redefinition of the Christian church in the fourth century was driven by the decriminalization and eventual privileging of the church by the Emperor Constantine. Prior to the Edict of Milan in 313 CE, the church was seen by Roman authorities as at worst subversive and at best marginal, a threat or a freeloader, in any event not a committed imperial stakeholder. And that was just as well from the church's perspective, for its kingdom was not of this world. That is, until Constantine embraced the church and offered her the keys, or at least a set of the keys, to his kingdom. Virtually overnight, the church that had eschewed military service in the Roman legions, as well as any imperial office involving the exercise of violence, now resolved to step up to its new responsibilities to defend Rome's borders as well as to maintain security and the rule of law within the empire. To pray for the emperor and the legions, as the ardent pacifist Tertullian had done, was one thing, but to partner with the emperor and march in the legions was quite another. To do this in good conscience required the recalibration of that conscience, and it was Augustine and his mentor Ambrose who took on that task. Essentially, this meant arguing that there are two kinds of killing, one that offends God and alienates the killer from God, and the other which does neither. With this simple distinction, Christian "just war" was born. War, after all, is all about killing. And so, with at least the theoretical possibility of sinless killing came the possibility of other forms of sinless physical violence, including torture, which Augustine explicitly defended, liberties that not only Christian nations but also the church freely exercised in the centuries to come.

14. Anscombe, "War and Murder," 51.
15. Hoffman, "On Soldiering," 9.

Today, most people are more comfortable speaking of moral injury than of sin, although they come down to the same thing. In contemporary terms, Augustine's contribution was to proffer war without moral injury, killing without moral injury. Throughout history, the goal of military strategists and the tentative promise of kings and politicians to their troops has been "killing without dying," killing the enemy while incurring minimal loss of life. Meanwhile, holding just war theory close, the church, in its care of souls, has shown the way to killing others without sin, without "mortal" or lethal sin, without "soul death." In all this, and in all these centuries of "just war" it is truly remarkable that the term "just war theory" has survived in our churches, our military academies, and our centers of power. What refreshing honesty! Just war has never been more than a theory, a failed theory, a theory daily disproven in war zones and execution chambers, a theory widely disavowed by veterans, who know what they are talking about, and by the silent, heartbreaking testimony of military and veteran suicides, roughly one every hour, a tragedy that the Pentagon and the Veterans Administration now recognize to be rooted principally in moral injury. Put simply, writes Captain Michael Hoffman, "the theory of moral injury is a direct challenge to just war theory. . . . Under just war theory, if I follow the rules, if I follow the field manuals, then I have done it right. My soul is safe."[16] But "doing it right" often doesn't make things right. It doesn't even come close. "In contrast to just war theory, which gives us ways to become comfortable with war," explains Hoffman, "moral injury reminds us that every death wounds. The last one kills."[17]

It is surely an understatement that, in the words of former Marine Captain Tyler Boudreau, "it is not possible to reduce one's regard for an enemy's life without reducing one's regard for all life. . . . You cannot achieve excellence in both war and humanity at the same time."[18] We simply can't have it both ways, as Augustine proposed and hoped. I would propose, instead, that there is simply no such thing as just war. Just war is an oxymoron. Just causes, yes, but not just wars. Legal wars, yes, because nations write laws that suit them and further their purposes. Arguments in defense of war without moral injury are as false and fabricated as denials that smoking causes cancer and emphysema. Killing wounds and too often kills the killer. It is years of listening to veterans, not years of reading books, that have convinced me of this.

16. Hoffman, "On Soldiering," 25.
17. Hoffman, "On Soldiering," 28.
18. Boudreau, "To Kill," final paragraph.

Having said this, I am not done here. Thus far I have concerned myself with untelling a lie: the promise of war without moral injury, the license to kill with a clear conscience. What remains is far more difficult: to acknowledge the resonant humanity of combatants and to consider the guilt of the bystander, the immorality of doing nothing. Here again I am indebted to the combat veterans I have come to know, respect, and care for, who are unquestionably men and women of extraordinary character and commitment. While nearly all those whom I know well have come to question quite radically the waging of war, they have retained a core commitment to service. In the military they learned to subordinate their own well-being, even their lives, to the safety and survival of their unit, their corps, and their country. They learned to dread letting down their fellow soldiers more than losing their own lives. In forming and living this life-and-death bond, they found a love that many or most of us may never experience apart from our own immediate families. Again, I turn here to Michael Hoffman. Speaking to civilians like myself, he tries to explain the bond of love between soldiers:

> I'm not sure I can help you understand this—I'm not sure I want to. To know this love, you need to know the pain at its center. And like most soldiers, I volunteered in order to spare you that pain. All I can offer you is this: it is a love that inspires and justifies sacrifice—the love of Achilles and Patroclus, of David and Jonathan. The love that passes all but a soldier's understanding.[19]

These words and the commitment they embody echo the familiar words of Jesus in the Gospel of John: "No one has greater love than this, to lay down one's life for one's friends."[20] Military training and service instills not only the willingness to take life, but also the readiness, without hesitation, to give one's own life for others. I am reminded here of what Army Major Sean Levine—an Orthodox priest and military chaplain—once wrote to me in describing his ministry: "I always approach veterans as those who have broken themselves upon the anvil of this nation's defense, often for causes way beneath the dignity of the sacrifice warriors are willing to make."[21] Even as we condemn war, should we not feel compelled to honor the sacrificial love that so many soldiers embody? It is this commitment to protect and defend others at the expense of their own lives that so many of the veterans I know are most loathe to abandon even though they have renounced war. I have in mind here one particular Marine combat veteran who told me that he had become a borderline pacifist. He was almost there.

19. Hoffman, "On Soldiering," 12–13.
20. John 15:13 (all citations to the Bible herein are from the NRSV).
21. Sean Levine, personal correspondence with author, used with permission.

To describe the remaining "border" between him and the total renunciation of lethal force, he pointed across the street to several children playing in his neighbor's front yard. Among those children was his own son. He then went on to say that if someone suddenly attacked those children, or any children for that matter, he would not stand by and let them be killed. That he could not live with. Instead, he would do whatever was needed to stop the attacker, even if it meant injuring or killing him.

Listening to his words, I was and remain conflicted, as even the nonviolent church has been and remains conflicted or, we might even say, confused. We can hear this confusion in the 2004 response of Pope Francis to a journalist's question regarding the church's position on US military intervention to halt the murderous advance of ISIS:

> In these cases, where there is an unjust aggression, I can only say this: it is licit to stop the unjust aggressor. I emphasize the verb: stop. I do not say bomb, make war, I say stop by some means. With what means can they be stopped? These have to be evaluated. To stop the unjust aggressor is licit.[22]

Like Pope Francis here, every recent pope from John XXIII on, while condemning war, has also affirmed the necessity and right to protect and defend the helpless. Pope John Paul II, in his homily to those gathered for Mass in Drogheda, Ireland, in 1979 asserted without equivocation that "violence is evil . . . a lie . . . a crime against humanity."[23] I agree with these words, as would so many veterans I know, including those who still could not live with themselves were they not to protect the helpless when it was in their power to do so, even if it meant sacrificing their own lives and putting their souls in peril. This is precisely the dilemma faced and the decision made, for example, by Dietrich Bonhoeffer and Ernesto Cardenal—two men who have been described as "militant pacifists." "Militant pacifist"—an oxymoron to be sure, a contradiction in terms, yes; but life is riddled with contradictions, not all of which we are able resolve in the moment, or perhaps ever. We know well how deeply Bonhoeffer struggled with his decision to join the plot to assassinate Adolf Hitler and his inner circle. That his cause was just and his plot necessary gave him little or no consolation. He knew what he was doing: planning a murder. He believed that in doing so he was committing a grave sin and that he would take that sin to his death and to his God and Savior, on whose mercy he would throw himself.

---

22. Boorstein, "Debate."
23. John Paul II, "Holy Mass in Drogheda," 9.

In his *Ethics*, Bonhoeffer reached for light in dark times, struggling to discern and accept his responsibility as a Christian confronting impenetrable, intransigent evil. He understood that the Christ to whom he prayed was "a breaker of the law" and that following him would demand the same of him. "The origin and the goal of my conscience," wrote Bonhoeffer,

> is not a law but it is the living God and the living man as he confronts me in Jesus Christ. For the sake of God and of men Jesus became a breaker of the law.... He came to be forsaken by God in His last hour. As the one who loved without sin, He became guilty: He wished to share in the fellowship of human guilt.[24]

Bonhoeffer came to understand that innocence, blamelessness, is not the highest or truest Christian calling. On the contrary, to follow Christ, to imitate Christ in a broken, sinful world, is to take on the sins of the world and to die for them, without excuse.

> When a man takes guilt upon himself in responsibility, and no responsible man can avoid this, he imputes his guilt to himself and to no one else; he accepts responsibility for it. Before other men the man of free responsibility is justified by necessity; before himself he is acquitted by his conscience; but before God he hopes only for mercy.[25]

What Dietrich Bonhoeffer came to understand and accept was that to be "sinless" in a sinful world can be irresponsible. Washing the world from our hands may produce clean hands, but is it what God calls us, called him, to do? This was the question that Bonhoeffer wrestled with and in the end decided in the negative, convinced that he was being called by God to repeat the sin of Cain and murder his brother, his fellow man, created, just as he was, in the image of God. Thomas Merton too, until his untimely death, struggled with total pacifism and the life he had embraced, the life of a monastic renunciant, concerned not to be a "guilty bystander."

Both Merton and Bonhoeffer rejected "just war." That was not a difficult call for them. But the total renunciation of violence was more troubling. When we turn for guidance to the Gospels, to the life and words of the nonviolent Jesus, we see that he went to his death without resistance, without threat. That was his choice, not to defend his life but to offer it freely, a choice that Christian martyrs have always embraced. Interestingly, the only use of lethal force that was never under any circumstance considered acceptable in early Christian just war theory was self-defense. But are self-defense and

---

24. Bonhoeffer, *Ethics*, 240.
25. Bonhoeffer, *Ethics*, 44.

the defense of others morally equivalent? Like Bonhoeffer, Ernesto Cardenal, who had been one of Merton's Trappist novices at Gethsemane and an equally committed pacifist, when confronted with the massacre of innocent children in Nicaragua, came to accept violent resistance as a necessary evil. He made a challenging case for his position in this controversial interpretation of the famous counsel of Jesus to not resist evil but rather to "turn the other cheek":[26]

> This doesn't mean not to fight. It means not to fight for yourself but for others. And Christ says to turn the other cheek, but it's your other cheek, not the other cheek of other people. Christians who don't fight for the revolution aren't turning either one of their cheeks. They're turning the cheeks of undernourished children, of the hopelessly ill, of abandoned widows, of workers robbed of their work.[27]

Another Catholic pacifist and mutual friend of Merton, however, objected to the militant words and actions of Cardenal and the liberation theology he espoused. In an open letter to Cardenal, Daniel Berrigan wrote these uncompromising words: "Thou shalt not kill. Love one another as I have loved you. If your enemy strikes you on the right cheek, turn to him the other. . . . We really are stuck. Christians are stuck with this Christ, the impossible, unteachable, irreformable loser."[28]

In agreeing with both of these statements, I am indeed "stuck" and fall silent. In this I suspect I am not entirely alone. Unable to conjure a satisfying conclusion to the issues I've raised, I will close instead with a familiar parable and a question.

First, the parable. Here I have in mind the lesson of the good Samaritan:

> A man was going down from Jerusalem to Jericho, and fell into the hands of robbers, who stripped him, beat him, and went away, leaving him half dead. Now by chance a priest was going down that road; and when he saw him, he passed by on the other side. So likewise a Levite, when he came to the place and saw him, passed by on the other side. But a Samaritan while traveling came near him; and when he saw him, he was moved with pity. He went to him and bandaged his wounds, having poured oil and wine on them. Then he put him on his own animal, brought him to an inn, and took care of him. The next day he took out two denarii, gave them to the innkeeper, and

---

26. See Matt 5:39; Luke 6:29.
27. Cardenal, *Gospel*, 113.
28. Berrigan, "Fortieth Anniversary," 32A.

said, "Take care of him; and when I come back, I will repay you whatever more you spend.... Go and do likewise."[29]

None of us can miss the lesson here. Passing by a "neighbor" or anyone in need and doing nothing is unacceptable.

Now the question: What if the good Samaritan had arrived on the scene earlier, when the neighbor was being stripped, beaten, and robbed? Can we simply stand by and do nothing? Do we wait and minister to the victim once the robbers have left and the neighbor lies half dead? Or do we do something else? Whose "other cheek" do we turn? What does "mercy" mean now? Clearly, these are violent men, unlikely to be stopped without violence. What instructive sequel to the parable of the good Samaritan can we, should we, write or even imagine?

I have raised this question not to undermine or soften my own and others' condemnation of war and commitment to peace. Precisely the opposite. By acknowledging the humane compulsion to protect and defend the vulnerable in extreme moments of immediate peril, a compulsion that has driven so many soldiers to risk and even sacrifice their lives, we may just remove a barrier to their joining the ranks of peacemakers. Why, you may ask, is this important? After all, those in military service and veterans represent less than 1 percent of the US population. True. But servicemen and women and especially combat veterans, like victims of war and refugees, speak with a fusion of passion and pain rarely found in others. They know war firsthand. They hate war and carry its wounds day and night. The nation listens to them; and if we in the peace movement listen to them, we will discover uniquely credible and committed allies, brothers and sisters willing, even aching, to put away the swords they have wielded and beat them into ploughshares.

Bibliography

Abelard, Peter. *Ethical Writings*. Indianapolis: Hackett, 2006.

Anscombe, G. E. M. "War and Murder." In *Nuclear Weapons: A Catholic Response*, edited by Walter Stein, 43–62. London: Merlin, 1961.

Augustine of Hippo. *Homilies on the Gospel According to St. John: And His First Epistle*. Translated by Henry Browne. A Library of Fathers of the Holy Catholic Church, vols. 26, 29. Oxford: J. H. Parker, 1848.

Berrigan, Daniel. "Fortieth Anniversary: Berrigan Debates." *National Catholic Reporter*, October 22, 2004.

Bonhoeffer, Dietrich. *Ethics*. Edited by Clifford J. Green. Dietrich Bonhoeffer Works 6. Minneapolis: Fortress, 2005.

---

29. Luke 10:29–37.

Boorstein, Michelle. "The Debate over What Pope Francis Meant When He Talked about U.S. Airstrikes in Iraq." *Washington Post*, August 22, 2014.

Boudreau, Tyler. "To Kill or Not to Kill." *The Progressive*, January 26, 2009. https://progressive.org/kill-kill/.

Butler, Smedley D. *War Is a Racket*. Port Townsend, WA: Feral House, 2003.

Camus, Albert. *The Rebel: An Essay on Man in Revolt*. Translated by Anthony Bower. New York: Vintage, 1956.

Cardenal, Ernesto. *The Gospel in Solentiname*. Maryknoll, NY: Orbis, 1978.

Columbia Maison Française. "'The Human Crisis,' Read by Viggo Mortensen, 70 Years Later." YouTube video, 1:32. April 28, 2016. https://www.youtube.com/watch?v=aaFZJ_ymueA.

Ellsberg, Daniel. *The Doomsday Machine: Confessions of a Nuclear War Planner*. New York: Bloomsbury, 2017.

Freud, Sigmund. *Reflections on War and Death*. Translated by A. A. Brill and Alfred B. Kuttner. New York: Moffat, Yard, 1918.

Hoffman, Michael. "On Soldiering." Unpublished manuscript. Used with permission of the author.

John Paul II, Pope. "Holy Mass in Drogheda. Homily of His Holiness John Paul II." September 29, 1979. http://www.vatican.va/content/john-paul-ii/en/homilies/1979/documents/hf_jp-ii_hom_19790929_irlanda-dublino-drogheda.html.

Mussomeli, Joseph. "100 Years On: World War I Ends, and Endless War Begins." *The Imaginative Conservative*, November 11, 2018. https://theimaginativeconservative.org/2018/11/100-years-world-war-i-joseph-mussomeli.html.

Ramsey, Paul. "A Political Ethics Context for Strategic Thinking." In *Strategic Thinking and Its Moral Implications*, edited by Morton A. Kaplan, 101–47. Chicago: University of Chicago Press, 1973.

Sassoon, Siegfried. "They." In *The War Poems of Siegfried Sassoon*, 37. London: William Heinemann, 1919.

Walzer, Michael. *Just and Unjust Wars: A Moral Argument with Historical Illustrations*. New York: Basic, 1977.

12

Responsibility to Protect and Nonviolence Discourse: Implications on Conflict Militarization in South Sudan

Elias Opongo, SJ

Introduction

SINCE THE LAST DECADE of the twentieth century, many countries across the world have experienced or are experiencing violent conflicts within their borders leading to loss of lives, destruction of property, psychological trauma, and ultimately destabilization of states. Confronted with this challenge, states and international bodies have explored the best options to address conflict in the twenty-first century. They continue to do that in the background of international law, guarding sovereignty of states and nonintervention in internal affairs of a nation-state, a doctrine that has been upheld since the 1648 Treaty of Westphalia. The Treaty of Westphalia underscored the sanctity of state sovereignty, and this has been upheld by subsequent international treaties regarding the modern state ever since. Though sovereignty has been praised for many years now for protecting the weaker states from the strong states, the concept has also received criticism in equal measure for protecting perpetrators of violence. The rule of nonintervention was widely abused by autocratic regimes to mete violence on dissenting citizens as was the case with Pol Pot in Cambodia and Idi Amin in Uganda, among others. The watershed moment came in the early 1990s with the explosion of intrastate wars around the world—notably, Rwanda's

1994 genocide. The resultant carnage and suffering, combined with the state's aversion to put an end to the killing and address the humanitarian needs of its people, shocked the conscious of the world. This prompted the United Nations (UN) to rethink the rule of nonintervention. Subsequently, the concept of responsibility to protect was born.

Conceptualization of Military Intervention and Responsibility to Protect

In many states, humanitarian military intervention has taken center stage in foreign policy decision-making,[1] multiple times sparking serious debates among policy makers. The controversy often revolves around this question: when is a state authorized to use its military against another? This question has greatly influenced the manner in which humanitarian agencies work today, mainly because unsolicited and unwanted external involvement equates to meddling in the internal affairs of another state against international law. However, as conflicts increase throughout the world, a number of humanitarian interventions have challenged sovereignty and the rule of nonintervention. There has been a shift to focus more on "the state's duty to protect the rights of citizens or situations that cause harm and loss of lives."[2] In situations of gross human rights violations, the UN Security Council has a duty to intervene within the framework of responsibility to protect (R2P), founded on humanitarian intervention principles.

During the Cold War, the term "humanitarian military intervention" adopted diverse meanings, often based on the political interests of intervening nations. In most cases, states would act unilaterally to execute a military intervention, usually ignoring the structures of the UN or regional bodies like the Organization of African Unity (or OAU, now known as the African Union, or AU). Such was the case of Vietnam's 1978 invasion of Cambodia, Tanzania's invasion of Uganda that same year, and India's invasion of East Pakistan in 1971. However, intervention by individual states was not encouraged during this period, and the international community examined such interventions through the lens of realpolitik. It was not until the fall of the Berlin Wall and subsequent end of the Cold War that there was a new enthusiasm within the United Nations for the advancement of more coordinated humanitarian military interventions, especially given that there were, in the 1990s, emergent intrastate conflicts in the Balkans and many parts of Africa.

---

1. Seybolt, *Humanitarian Military Intervention*, 1; Ramsbotham and Woodhouse, *Humanitarian Intervention*, 3–4.
2. Ramsbotham and Woodhouse, *Humanitarian Intervention*, 1.

The concept of humanitarian military intervention is elusively broad,[3] and the debates about it largely stem from the nominal vagueness of the term. First, it is "humanitarian," because it is meant to stop any threats to human lives. It is also "humanitarian," because "it refers to circumstances to which our moral sense and human sensibilities are being massively assaulted."[4] Humanitarian military intervention refers to "the threat or use of force across state borders by a state (or group of states) aimed at preventing or ending widespread grave violation of the fundamental human rights of individuals."[5] Secondly, it is "military," because it involves the use of armed force, while "intervention" entails the deployment of military forces into a country that has committed international aggression against another state[6] or prevented access to humanitarian assistance. As such, humanitarian military intervention has sometimes been interpreted as an "extreme case of interference in the internal affairs of another state."[7] It is also referred to as "humanitarian," because intervening states use force against another state that poses no immediate or strategic threats to their interests. Unfortunately, there have been instances in which states' interests—rather than humanitarian interests—have motivated them to intervene. The inconsistencies in the manner in which the UN has responded to humanitarian interventions has raised questions about its capacity for and levels of neutrality. For example, comparatively, while not diminishing the sacredness of life in any conflict, the UN did not evaluate the Kosovo conflict and Rwanda genocide in the same way, despite the level of gravity in the latter. To a great extent, "Kosovo arguably did not meet the test of genocide as defined in the international genocide convention as Rwanda certainly did."[8] Despite the obligation to intervene in cases of genocide, the international community failed to do so in Rwanda, and this exposed the biases involved in implementing some of these international laws.[9] In order to persuade the international community to respond obligatorily to situations of grave human rights violations, the UN adopted the responsibility to protect (R2P) principle. This principle

---

3. See generally Seybolt, *Humanitarian Military Intervention*; and Ramsbotham and Woodhouse, *Humanitarian Intervention*.
4. Frye, *Humanitarian Intervention*, 4.
5. Frye, *Humanitarian Intervention*, 5–6.
6. Frye, *Humanitarian Intervention*, 4.
7. Frye, *Humanitarian Intervention*, 4.
8. Frye, *Humanitarian Intervention*, 6.
9. Frye, *Humanitarian Intervention*, 7.

specifies that military interventions will be restrictive and selective so as to avoid unnecessary attacks against other states.[10]

Responsibility to Protect

Recognizing the need for change and importance of addressing the severe human rights violations, in 2000, UN Secretary-General Kofi Annan challenged world leaders to begin reflecting on the gross and systemic violence perpetrated against civilians. He called on leaders to offer ways to address systemic violence, as many claimed that humanitarian military intervention was a violation of state sovereignty. The Canadian government took the lead, forming the International Commission on Intervention and State Sovereignty (ICISS). The goal of ICISS was to find an appropriate international response to ensure that crimes committed against civilians would be addressed or prevented.[11] When the commission published its first report in 2001, the report was titled "Responsibility to Protect" and explained the conditions for humanitarian intervention; they included states' responsibility to prevent conflict and to rebuild after an intervention.[12] As such, intervention was no longer based solely on military action, given that diplomacy also played an integral role in preventing possible conflicts.

The 2004 doctrine of R2P put forward by the ICISS placed moral obligation on states to stop situations of gross violation of human rights.[13] Since then, there have been initiatives to articulate the moral imperative to hold state sovereignty accountable. For example, Kofi Annan produced a report entitled *In Larger Freedom: Towards Development, Security, and Human Rights for All*. Similarly, in 2004, the UN High-Level Panel on Threats, Challenges, and Change issued the report, *A More Secure World: Our Shared Responsibility*. Both of these publications call the world's attention to the changing nature of the conflicts, from interstate to intrastate. The former report proposes the formation of a "peacebuilding commission" to address the gap in the UN's response to interstate wars. This discourse has led to the reimagination of humanitarian intervention as a moral responsibility.

A laudable contribution of the ICISS was the deconstruction of the concept of sovereignty in its 2001 report, *Responsibility to Protect: Research, Bibliography, Background*. It argued that "sovereignty and intervention are

---

10. Rajan, *Conceit of Humanitarian Intervention*, 60–77.
11. Rajan, *Conceit of Humanitarian Intervention*, 11–20.
12. Rajan, *Conceit of Humanitarian Intervention*, 14.
13. Weiss, "To Intervene or Not," 141–57.

complementary rather than contradictory."[14] In other words, the sovereignty of a state is predicated on the state's ability to respect and protect the rights of the citizens within its borders. Hence, sovereignty does not give governments the autonomy to act arbitrarily within their own borders; rather, sovereignty goes hand in hand with the rights and responsibilities of states. The ICISS report underlined that "[s]tate sovereignty implies responsibility, and the primary responsibility of a state is the protection of its people. Where a population is suffering serious harm as a result of internal war, insurgency, repression, or state failure, and the state in question is unwilling or unable to halt or avert it, the principle of non-intervention yields to the responsibility to protect."[15]

The ICISS report also brought about a major shift in terminology. The controversial "intervention" was replaced with "protection."[16] In essence, the responsibility of the state and the international community was to prevent where necessary, react if prevention fails, and rebuild after the intervention. Effectively, a reaction was only to take place when there was evident need to protect human life. Subsequently, the aspect of respect for human rights was added to the traditional Westphalia aspects of territory, authority, and population. As a result, the emphasis was put on the state's responsibility to protect its citizens, and only after a state failed to do so was international intervention permitted. The R2P policy was adopted at the UN World Summit in 2005. Member states agreed that they have an obligation toward their citizens, which must be upheld and fulfilled at all times.

Militarization of Conflicts in South Sudan

Having gained independence from Sudan in 2011, South Sudan is the youngest nation in Africa. However, the joy of independence was short-lived when, in 2013, the country plunged into conflict due to a falling-out between President Salva Kiir and his deputy, Riek Machar.[17] The conflict was occasioned by Machar's public declaration in March 2013 of his intention to become the future president of South Sudan. At the time, political maneuvering was rife in the ruling party (Sudan People's Liberation Movement, or SPLM), in anticipation of the scheduled 2015 elections. Machar's

---

14. International Commission on Intervention and State Sovereignty, *Responsibility to Protect*, xi.

15. International Commission on Intervention and State Sovereignty, *Responsibility to Protect*, xi.

16. Tang Abomo, *R2P and the US Intervention*, 11–20.

17. "South Sudan Country Profile," paras. 1, 7.

announcement to vie for the top seat made President Kiir consider him a betrayer, and he replaced Machar with James Wani Igga, whom he regarded as a loyal supporter. Machar's supporters, mostly from his Nuer community, saw his removal as treachery. The result was mounting accusations and counter-accusations of corruption between the two leaders and their SPLM supporters. In the December 2013 SPLM party leadership meeting, these tensions exploded. Different leaders held different press conferences and publicly aired their anger at and mistrust of the rival group. Because the feud was between Kiir and Machar's ethnic groups of Dinka and Nuer respectively, on the evening of December 15, 2013, violence erupted in the capital of Juba between the Dinka and Nuer presidential guards. The fighting soon spread to the military's headquarters, and by December 16, there were gunshots reported all over Juba. The fighting in Juba targeted the Nuers, and within a few weeks, they were responding to the killings by attacking Dinka civilians and soldiers. Within months, South Sudan was divided into two, with some areas controlled by the government and others by Machar. The conflict has since sucked in other ethnic groups and spread to other areas.[18] Both Kiir's and Machar's support bases have suffered many casualties.[19]

As the conflict raged, hundreds of thousands of civilians were continuously displaced to neighboring countries. Periodically, regional bodies like the Intergovernmental Authority on Development (IGAD) tried to mediate in the conflict. However, hostilities persisted, because the agreements reached lacked an enforcement mechanism, and both parties often violated the terms. For example, both Kiir's and Machar's parties repeatedly violated the cessation of hostility agreement signed in 2014. Also, the transitional government, which both sides agreed to form, did not bear any fruit, because the two could not agree on the responsibilities of the government and its composition.[20] In August 2015, IGAD stepped in to craft a power-sharing deal following the blueprint of the 2014 peace deal brokered by John Kerry, former US Secretary of State.[21] Kiir expressed displeasure even as he signed the agreement; seemingly, he signed due to international pressure and threats of sanctions. Both Kiir and Machar agreed on implementing the agreement and, in April 2016, both sides formed the New Transitional Government of National Unity (TGNU).[22]

---

18. Ploch Blanchard, *Crisis in South Sudan*, 4.
19. Moggi, "Role of Religious Institutions," 118–28.
20. Moggi, "Role of Religious Institutions," 119.
21. International Crisis Group, "Salvaging," I, para. 1.
22. Ploch Blanchard, *Crisis in South Sudan*, 1.

The formation of TGNU did not end hostilities, however. Just before the power-sharing agreement was signed, its "provisions for a demilitarized Juba protected by a third-party force"[23] were withdrawn, an act engineered by Yoweri Museveni, president of Uganda. This left the control of the seat of power open to attack, and consequently, Machar returned to Juba in "April 2016 with over a thousand heavily armed bodyguards."[24] Later that July, the military loyal to Kiir clashed with Sudan People's Liberation Movement/Army-In Opposition (SPLM/A-IO), which was devoted to Machar and scuttling the implementation of the power-sharing agreement. The military pushed Machar fighters out of Juba, and Machar was exiled to South Africa. Keen to render a decisive blow on SPLM/A-IO, Kiir continued with military campaigns on the Machar fighters. Soon, the violence spread to previously peaceful states like Central Equitoria and South Equitoria. The military campaign also resulted in the rise of new rebel groups, such as the National Salvation Front led by Thomas Cirillo. Government forces and their allied militias have been accused of land grabbing, looting, premeditated attacks against civilians, and the killing of perceived opponents in the city of Wau. Kiir's decision to increase the number of states from the original ten at independence to twenty-eight and then to thirty-two only served to polarize the country and increase ethnic tensions. However, he later rescinded this decision in February 2020 to lure the opposition to the new peace agreement discussed below.[25]

After the 2015 power-sharing deal fell through, there was apparent unwillingness in IGAD and the international community to intervene in the South Sudan conflict. In 2016, President Obama suggested that both Kiir and Machar step aside. However, upon realizing that the regional heads were divided on the matter, Obama did not pursue this. He declared his support for IGAD's mediation work and, from then on, the US took a back seat.[26] The same apathy seemed to grip the European Union (EU)—none of its member states rose to take up the leading role formerly played by the US. With the pressure to negotiate having dissipated, Kiir armies and rebel groups continued to fight, kill, maim, rape women and girls, and displace millions from their homes.

Negotiations resumed in 2017, when the newly elected US President Donald Trump and the other TROIKA countries (UK and Norway) renewed pressure on the warring parties to come to the table. This led to the

23. International Crisis Group, "Salvaging," I, para. 2.
24. International Crisis Group, "Salvaging," I, para. 2.
25. See, generally, Mayai and Tiitmamer, "Return to Ten States."
26. International Crisis Group, "Salvaging," I, para. 3.

formation of the High-Level Revitalization Forum spearheaded by IGAD. Unfortunately, once more, negotiations did not succeed. The contentious issues were "power sharing, future security arrangements, and the question of whether Machar could return from exile to political life in South Sudan."[27] IGAD's faltering efforts were redeemed by Ethiopia's Prime Minister Abiy Ahmed and Sudanese President Omar al-Bashir who strived to bring Kiir and Machar to peace talks in Khartoum. Their efforts culminated in the Declaration of Agreement on a Permanent Ceasefire (known as the Khartoum Declaration), signed by both Kiir and Machar on June 27, 2018.[28]

President Kiir and former Vice President Machar committed themselves to a permanent cease-fire and pledged to settle the outstanding issues in the implementation of security arrangements as well as governance chapters of the 2015 Arusha Agreement, including effecting the cease-fire beginning on June 30, 2018. They further agreed to sign another agreement in two weeks' time on the composition of a new transitional government of unity, which would rule for thirty-six months until the 2022 general elections. Subsequently, on July 2, 2018, the South Sudanese parliament began debating a constitutional amendment bill that will extend President Salva Kiir's mandate for an additional three years. The extensions will enable President Kiir and the parliament to continue with their functions during the transitional period and avoid a constitutional vacuum in the country. However, there are four issues in the security arrangements where the parties failed to reach a compromise: (1) determination of demilitarized areas; (2) modalities and exemption from cantonment; (3) time frame for unification of forces; and (4) the number of parties' representatives in the Joint Transitional Security Committee.[29]

In February 2020, the government signed a new peace agreement with the opposition, which was referred to as the Revitalized Agreement on the Resolution of Conflict in South Sudan (R-ARCSS). As a result of this agreement, a Revitalized Transitional Government of National Unity (RTGONU) was formed, bringing together the president's coalition and that of his former deputy, Riek Machar. It is hoped that the government of national unity will finally bring peace to South Sudan. There are, however, concerns that another possible conflict could develop, given the lack of power-sharing agreements with a number of South Sudan's other rival factions, as well as

---

27. International Crisis Group, "Salvaging," I, para. 11.
28. International Crisis Group, "Salvaging," I, para. 12.
29. For a general chronology, see Woodard, "South Sudan's Peace Deals." Editor's note: The 2022 election was pushed back to 2024; see generally "South Sudan Extends Transitional."

armed insurgencies in the southern parts of the country, coupled with an imbalance in appointed government positions.

Militarized Interventions in South Sudan Conflict

In the aftermath of South Sudan's independence in 2011, and given its vulnerability to conflict, the UN Security Council adopted Resolution 1996 that same year, addressing postconflict reconstruction and security concerns in South Sudan. The resolution called for the formation of seven thousand military and nine hundred civilian police personnel under the UN Mission in South Sudan (UNMISS).[30] When the new country plunged into conflict in December 2013, the UN Security Council reinforced UNMISS, and the mission's priority shifted to the protection of civilians through Security Council Resolution 2155 of 2014. The new resolution now charged UNMISS with protecting civilians, ensuring that humanitarian aid reached the masses, monitoring the human rights situation in the country, and implementing the cease-fire agreement. As of November 2018, the UN had deployed 19,135 personnel in its mission in South Sudan with 14,011 continent troops and 1,823 police.[31]

From the time the conflict started in 2013, UN peacekeeping military interventions, regional protection provided by troops from IGAD countries, and efforts by the Ugandan national army have not succeeded in ending the hostilities against civilians. Millions of people have fled to neighboring countries, and hundreds of thousands have been killed or maimed. Thousands of children have been forcefully conscripted into joint militia groups, and many women and girls sexually assaulted. Journalists, activists, and aid workers have not been spared either. Between 2013 and November 2020, for example, about 124 aid workers were killed, most of them South Sudanese.[32] Dozens of activists and members of the press have been detained or reported missing. Government armies and rebel groups have severely overwhelmed UNMISS, often attacking its camps and sometimes resulting in the deaths of its soldiers. UNMISS is mandated to protect civilians and facilitate access for aid workers so they can deliver humanitarian help to the suffering population, but it records minimal success. Its main achievement, perhaps, is the protection of two hundred thousand civilians living in six UN camps across South Sudan, a very small number considering that millions have sought refuge in other countries. The Ugandan army, for its part,

---

30. UN Security Council, Resolution 1996, 3.
31. United Nations Peacekeeping, "UNMISS Fact Sheet."
32. "Second Aid Worker Shot," final para.

came to the rescue of President Salva Kiir in 2013 when Juba was threatened by a takeover from Riek Machar fighters. Some observers assert that the intervention of Ugandan forces "averted a bloodbath in the city, but [that] it also set the stage for prolonged conflict."[33] The prolonged conflict is largely due to the fact that Uganda has deliberately acted as an interested party in favor of Salva Kiir and, with its military presence, has aided Salva to take a strong political stand again Machar.

IGAD has equally contributed to the militarization of South Sudan. The IGAD summit of September 12, 2018, discussed deploying IGAD forces within the framework of the Regional Protection Force, or RPF (numbering four thousand troops), to support the thirteen thousand UNMISS forces. Accordingly, the IGAD chiefs of staff sent a team to Juba to assess the operational needs. The team gave its report in a meeting of military leaders held November 19–22, 2018, in Addis Ababa. Based on the report, which reviewed the composition and mandate of the regional protection forces, the leaders agreed to add 1,695 total troops from the five countries of Uganda, Kenya, Sudan, Djibouti, and Somalia. This number included 499 soldiers each from Kenya,[34] Uganda, and Sudan, while Somalia and Djibouti would contribute ninety-nine each. They arrived at the consensus to deploy IGAD forces in order to reassure the opposition groups that the guarantors would be physically present on the ground to prevent attacks on civilians like the ones that happened in July 2016 and December 2013. Besides protecting civilians, the IGAD troops were also tasked with protecting the opposition leaders during the remainder of the transitional period.[35]

The IGAD military leaders charged the Ethiopian foreign minister with engaging the African Union Peace and Security Council (AU-PSC) and the UN Security Council (UNSC) to allow the five countries to join the RPF deployed in South Sudan. It was up to the UN Department of Peacekeeping Operations, in coordination with the five states involved in the operation, to determine the nature and type of forces needed. In a briefing to the UN Security Council on November 16, 2018, the head of UN Peacekeeping, Jean-Pierre Lacroix, set three benchmarks for the integration of IGAD forces into UNMISS: "a continuing priority of protection of civilians in UNMISS' mandated tasks; the need to preserve a single peacekeeping force with one unified command and control structure; and [a requirement] that any addition to the force would have to be carried out consistent with

---

33. International Crisis Group, "Salvaging," I, para. 2.

34. Kenya rejoined UNMISS in 2017. For Kenya, see "Kenya Agrees to Rejoin," para. 1

35. "IGAD Military Leaders," final para.

the principles of peacekeeping and the standards to which we hold all troop and police-contributing countries."[36] The RPF has not done much as it is yet to be fully deployed (as of 2019).

Nonviolent Action as Responsibility to Protect

A militarized approach to conflict resolution has largely failed in many African conflicts. The protracted nature of the conflicts in South Sudan and DR Congo clearly demonstrated that there ought to be more concerted efforts toward dialogue, diplomacy, and integral development in order to address poverty, unemployment, and the provision of basic life necessities like food, housing, schools, hospitals, roads, and security. To a great extent, however, nonviolent approaches can be used to bridge differences between belligerents and fighting communities.

The nonviolent approach is founded on the acknowledgment of human dignity, safeguarding of the common good, and the defeat of such evils as hatred, marginalization, violence and the loss of life, injustice, corruption, ethnic discrimination, hunger, disease, and population displacement. It equally entails instituting governing structures that can ensure accountable leadership, which promotes values that respect life, justice, fairness, security of persons and property, and citizen participation in the society's democratic processes and organization. Such a nonviolent approach fosters trust, mutual respect, and common life goals.

The principles of nonviolence as practiced by Martin Luther King Jr. can act as guideposts in navigating the gray areas. These principles are:

- nonviolence as a courageous commitment to change;
- a way of life intended to build friendship and understanding founded on reconciliation and social cohesion;
- a strategy aimed at defeating evil rather than the person committing the evil acts;
- a willingness to accept suffering without any retaliation or revenge; and
- a commitment to avoiding both external physical violence and internal violence of spirit.[37]

For nonviolence to triumph, the principles must be applied simultaneously.

---

36. "UN Sets Benchmarks," para. 4.
37. King and Carson, *Stride toward Freedom*, 91–93.

Nonviolence *as a way of life* points to a perpetual denouncement of violence in order to bring about social change, and in the case of South Sudan, to end the conflict and foster a peacefulness throughout the country. This is why nonviolence is sometimes defined as winning over the hearts of enemies to one's position through self-sacrifice.[38] Martin Luther King Jr. emphasized that all nonviolent actions ought to be adopted as a way of life founded on love or *agape* (love in action), tolerance, and understanding, always seeking to create and build community where there is mutual understanding. Historically, on numerous occasions, the South Sudanese have resolved conflicts amicably in their communities without resorting to violence.[39] Dialoguing with the violator is a deeply African way of resolving conflicts. Traditionally, community councils of elders were critical for reaching amicable solutions to more weighty grievances that could not be solved at the family level.

Religious leaders have also made several attempts to bring peace to South Sudan through different nonviolent efforts. For example, during the civil war as well as the postindependence conflict, the New Sudan Council of Churches (NSCC), in collaboration with civil society and nongovernment organizations, has conducted numerous peace initiatives to end violence. One of the NSCC's most successful mediations was the 1999 Wunlit Peace Conference that brought together traditional and religious leaders from the Nuer and Dinka ethnic groups to dialogue about peace. The conference extensively addressed diverse issues affecting the country as well as strategies for solving the conflict between the Nuer and Dinka through dialogue, forgiveness, and reconciliation. Although the dialogue helped addressing seething issues between the two communities, the conflict was never entirely resolved, mainly due to continued armed violence against civilians and the political manipulations of armed groups against civilians. Despite these challenges, the fact that a nonviolent option could be brought to the table and temporarily accepted demonstrates that it is a fundamentally important way to seek an end to violent conflicts.[40]

Following the second of Martin Luther King Jr.'s nonviolence principles—creating friendship and fostering understanding—religious leaders worked closely with civil society groups and the international community to put pressure on the then-president of Sudan, Omar al-Bashir, and the leader of the South Sudan Liberation Army (SPLA), John Garang, to engage

---

38. King and Carson, *Stride toward Freedom*, 91.

39. Modi et al., "South Sudan's Costly Conflict," 40.

40. South Sudan Customary Authorities Project, *What Happened at Wunlit,* 8–12, especially 10.

in dialogue. The two eventually agreed to the Comprehensive Peace Agreement in 2005, which ended more than twenty years of violent conflict that led to the deaths of well over a million people.[41] Following the conflict that erupted in postindependence South Sudan, the government asked the religious leaders "to oversee the South Sudanese government in South Sudan's Committee for National Healing, Peace, and Reconciliation (CNHPR)."[42] The NSCC focused on people-to-people peace initiatives with the aim of ending violence in the country. The initiative generated a dynamic of peace conferences, bringing together different ethnic groups in conflict. The NSCC was influenced by the teachings of Jesus in the Gospel of Matthew (5:21-22, NIV): "You have heard that it was said to the people long ago, 'You shall not murder, and anyone who murders will be subject to judgment.' But I tell you that anyone who is angry with a brother or sister will be subject to judgment."

In another peace initiative, a Nuer traditional prophet, Gatdeang Dit, has been urging his community to ignore Nuer-Dinka ethnic feuds and intermarry with the Dinka as a way of creating friendship and fomenting understanding between the two groups. He only sanctions lethal force for the purpose of self-defense.[43] Government actions are often perceived as Dinka actions, because President Salva Kiir is Dinka. On the other hand, Machar, his rival, is a Nuer. The resulting cycle of interethnic retaliations and senseless attacks fueled by this rivalry has left many people dead without the ability to choose directly between Kiir and Machar. Jesus warned in the Gospel of Matthew (5:43-48, NIV):

> You have heard that it was said, "Love your neighbor and hate your enemy." But I tell you, love your enemies and pray for those who persecute you, that you may be children of your Father in heaven. He causes his sun to rise on the evil and the good, and sends rain on the righteous and the unrighteous. If you love those who love you, what reward will you get? Are not even the tax collectors doing that? And if you greet only your own people, what are you doing more than others? Do not even pagans do that? Be perfect, therefore, as your heavenly Father is perfect.

King's third principle of nonviolence calls for the defeat of the evil rather than the person(s) doing the evil. The goal of a nonviolent approach should not be to destroy the other but to end the structures of injustice or vice that exist in society. When conflict resolution mechanisms are directed

---

41. See US Committee for Refugees and Immigrants, "1.9 Million Dead," para. 1.
42. Modi et al., "South Sudan's Costly Conflict," 41.
43. Hutchinson and Pendle, "Violence, Legitimacy, and Prophecy," 422.

at people rather than violent structures, they lead to the destruction of people's psyches, physical lives, and property, ultimately failing to resolve the conflict and simply transferring it to a different realm.[44] Violent structures are those that propagate social, economic, and political inequalities in a society. In contrast, King's third nonviolence principle underscores the sacredness and dignity of human agency, closely related to the principles of love and nonretaliation. Love is superior to hate and, therefore, those who love their enemies are on a higher moral plane. Because human beings are to love one another, revenge is not justifiable. Advocates of nonviolence choose to forgive and reconcile with their enemies, rather than retaliate. When forgiveness and reconciliation are achieved, then a conflict can be transformed.

Unlike military interventions designed to contain the negative traits of human nature, nonviolent approaches tap into the good qualities—namely love, compassion, and forgiveness. In other words, nonviolence is a philosophy of love, sisterhood and brotherhood, and cultural emancipation that deeply respects the cultural values that promote and protect life; it strives to give the oppressed a sense of pride and dignity in their identity as human beings.[45] The *Encyclopedia of the United Nations and International Agreements* underscores that "nonviolence is a form of political protest, eschewing violence as a matter of principle."[46] Martin Luther King Jr. held that nonviolence aims not at overturning the state or government but at rectifying an evil or attaining a good within the existing political framework.[47]

Nonviolence is equally founded on *agape*—love in action—aimed at increasing understanding and tolerance within the community. The focus of *agape* is to strengthen bonds within the community through forgiveness and reconciliation, recognizing the dignity of every person.[48] Examples of *agape* at work are the various initiatives by religious and cultural leaders as well as civil society that led to the Wunlit Peace Conference; these efforts, in turn, influenced many other peace initiatives aimed at intercommunity reconciliation and dialogue. Among these was the Lilir Peace Conference held in 2000 in Bor, in South Sudan's Upper Nile region. It brought together the Dinka, Ayunak, Nuer, Jie, Murle, and Kachipo peoples to dialogue and end the violence between and among them. Similarly, in 2002, one hundred and seventy delegates—mainly from the Didinga, Toposa, Lotoko, and

44. See, generally, Nojeim, *Gandhi and King*.
45. Omoregbe, *Knowing Philosophy*, 34.
46. Osmańczyk, *Encyclopedia of the United Nations*, 634.
47. Colaiaco, *Martin Luther King, Jr.*, 185–87.
48. King and Carson, *Stride toward Freedom*, 94.

Dinka communities—gathered in Eastern Equitoria to dialogue for peace in what is known as the Nakwatom Peace Conference or, alternatively, the Chukudum Crisis Peace Conference.[49]

The above examples, though limited to some extent, demonstrate that nonviolent alternatives to a militarized approach to conflict can indeed work. Such processes are slow but have a fulfilling long-term impact, as far as effecting a change of attitudes and perceptions. As Ashworth and Ryan warn, "Quick fixes do not work. All this would be familiar to those who work for peace in Sudan. . . . The process must . . . be allowed to continue, for years if necessary."[50]

In collaboration with civil society, religious leaders have continued to lobby for peace and reconciliation in South Sudan, meeting privately with President Kiir and his rival, Machar, to persuade them to agree to peace. For example, the Catholic bishops have written pastoral letters calling for peace and dialogue and an end to the culture of impunity that has led to thousands of deaths. In their pastoral letter that immediately followed the bishops' conference of February 26–28, 2019, they stated:

> While the level of open conflict has reduced, the Cessation of Hostilities agreement is not holding, and all parties are involved either in active fighting or preparations for war. The value of human life and dignity is forgotten as human rights abuses continue with impunity, including murder, rape, widespread sexual violence, looting, and the occupation of civilian land and property. Organized crime is on the increase.[51]

The bishops also called for a genuine commitment to peace from political leaders through self-conversion and support for the peace process. The bishops reiterated that "[p]olitics alone will not resolve the conflicts in South Sudan. While many ordinary people long for peace, there is no will or commitment for peace amongst many of our leaders; hate speech and propaganda abound, and there is a thirst for revenge amongst many of our communities. What is needed is conversion, a change of heart, amongst individuals and communities."[52] Such a conversion is reflected in the life of Jesus, who always stepped away from revenge and embraced forgiveness. Further, the bishops called for the inclusion of cultural and traditional leaders in the search for solutions to interethnic conflicts. They equally encouraged the inclusion of a broad base of different members of civil society—professionals,

---

49. King and Carson, *Stride toward Freedom*, 95.
50. Ashworth and Ryan, "'One Nation,'" 47.
51. South Sudan Catholic Bishops' Secretariat, "Pastoral Message," 2.
52. South Sudan Catholic Bishops' Secretariat, "Pastoral Message," 1.

researchers, academics, church personnel, and peace practitioners. A broad consultation helps to identify the gaps in the implementation of the peace process, as well as identify peace mediators who can build trust between the parties. Such people must be impartial, have good knowledge of the situation in South Sudan, and be committed to sustainable peace for the country.

On the international level, there is also a need for a radical shift in the manner in which the UN and other states in the region have handled the conflict in South Sudan. The militarization approach has been insensitive to contextual imperatives and failed to broaden strategies for ending violence. In 2015, UN Secretary-General Ban Ki-moon acknowledged that, despite some progress made in implementing R2P principles, there were still major gaps that needed to be addressed, particularly in helping affected populations recover from conflicts. He stated, "While Member States today acknowledge their primary responsibility to protect, many have not prioritized policies designed to build national resilience to atrocity crimes. This may require new initiatives."[53] He generally acknowledged that the UN Security Council intervention in Libya under the R2P principle had raised questions regarding the challenge of making a "timely and decisive response" and avoiding the "misuse of the principle," as well as considering the kind of sustained and sustainable support "required after the use of force."[54]

The R2P military interventions have no framework for reconciliation and seem to assume that stability is only attained through peace enforcement, security, and democracy. This approach ignores the foundational value system of many African communities and, particularly, the communitarian approach to reconciliation. Peace agreements with top leadership alone are not sufficient. There has to be a broad-based consultation process that is inclusive and focused on short-, mid-, and long-term results. Ingrid Samset notes that, instead of focusing so much on humanitarian military intervention or militarization, it would be more productive to build strong communities and institutions to look into the reasons why violence is prevalent and what ought to be done to address it.[55] Focusing on the community and government institutions, along with mitigating the root cause of conflict, will increase the chances for sustainable peace, while drawing attention to soft approaches to peacebuilding.

Many peace agreements in South Sudan have collapsed because of their failure to address the root causes of conflicts or their failure to explore alternatives to violence such as dialogue and social reconciliation, which,

53. UN Secretary-General, "Vital and Enduring Commitment," 22.
54. UN Secretary-General, "Vital and Enduring Commitment," 9.
55. Samset, "UN Peacekeeping," 6.

in turn, enhance social cohesion. Social reconciliation processes presuppose an analysis of the root causes and historical patterns of conflicts, as well as intercommunal and interpolitical party dialogue aimed at creating a common future. Once there is an agreement on a common future, the parties can then agree on how best to change the structures that create conflict and harmful social-cultural attitudes and practices, such as attack-revenge cycles and attacks on the socioeconomic rights for the populations. Reconciliation, thus, becomes the culmination of a commitment to live together while building a common future. It goes beyond legal frameworks to a much deeper level of engagement between and among individuals and groups, leading to the transformation and healing of society. It is important to recognize that social reconciliation does not automatically emerge from public debates but rather from processes of conversion, repentance, and forgiveness. Otherwise, social reconciliation becomes merely a mirage.

Conclusion

Militarized humanitarian interventions in the South Sudan conflict have cost the United Nations millions of dollars, without hope of ending the conflict in the near future. The UNMISS may have also further fueled the conflict. Given the limited success of militarized conflict intervention carried out by the UN, government forces, and militia groups, it is crucial—in order to save lives—to reconsider R2P initiatives that incorporate nonviolent strategies. Dialogue, tolerance, and reconciliation are important elements for successful conflict resolution, but for such interventions to succeed, they must be founded on the framework of South Sudan's cultural value system. Like many African countries, South Sudan integrates the cultural mechanisms of dialogue and reconciliation into conflict resolution structures. Largely communitarian, this approach involves active mediation by elders who work with community members to find common solutions to conflicts. For example, the Wunlit Peace Conference discussed earlier included religious and political leaders as well as cultural leaders. Other approaches such as amnesty or pardon are built on the strong belief that, in certain situations, forgiving the offenders is more expedient for the public welfare than prosecution and punishment, which can lead to vicious cycles of revenge and hate.[56] Additionally, for conflict resolution strategies to be effective in Africa, there is a need to simultaneously link peacebuilding, democratization, governance, and economic development.

---

56. Baregu, *Understanding Obstacles to Peace*, 5–11.

Bibliography

Annan, Kofi. *In Larger Freedom: Towards Development, Security, and Human Rights for All.* New York: United Nations, 2005.
Ashworth, John, and Maura Ryan. "'One Nation from Every Tribe, Tongue, and People': The Church and Strategic Peacebuilding in South Sudan." *Journal of Catholic Social Thought* 10:1 (2013) 47–67.
Baregu, Mwesiga Laurent. *Understanding Obstacles to Peace: Actors, Interests, and Strategies in Africa's Great Lakes Region.* Kampala: Fountain, 2011.
Colaiaco, James A. *Martin Luther King, Jr.: Apostle of Militant Nonviolence.* London: Palgrave-Macmillan, 2016.
Frye, Alton. *Humanitarian Intervention: Crafting a Workable Doctrine.* New York: Council on Foreign Relations, 2000.
Hutchinson, Sharon E., and Naomi R. Pendle. "Violence, Legitimacy, and Prophecy: Nuer Struggles with Uncertainty in South Sudan." *American Ethnologist* 42 (2014) 415–30.
"IGAD Military Leaders Decide to Assess South Sudan's Security Situation." *Sudan Tribune*, October 22, 2018. https://sudantribune.com/article64620/.
International Commission on Intervention and State Sovereignty (ICISS). *The Responsibility to Protect: Research, Bibliography, Background.* Ottawa: The International Development Research Centre, 2001.
International Crisis Group. "Salvaging South Sudan's Fragile Peace Deal: Crisis Group Africa Report No. 270." March 13, 2019. https://www.crisisgroup.org/africa/horn-africa/south-sudan/270-salvaging-south-sudans-fragile-peace-deal.
"Kenya Agrees to Rejoin UN Protection Force in South Sudan." *Africa News*, February 2, 2017. https://www.africanews.com/2017/02/02/kenya-agrees-to-rejoin-un-protection-force-in-south-sudan/.
King, Martin Luther, and Clayborne Carson. *Stride toward Freedom: The Montgomery Story.* Boston: Beacon, 2014.
Mayai, Augustino T., and Nhial Tiitmamer. "The Return to Ten States in South Sudan: Does It Restore Peace?" *Weekly Review*, February 20, 2020. https://www.suddinstitute.org/publications/show/5e4fc6fae031b.
Modi, Lucy Poni, et al. "South Sudan's Costly Conflict and the Urgent Role of Religious Leaders." *Review of Faith and International Affairs* 17:2 (2019) 37–46.
Moggi, Paola. "The Role of Religious Institutions in Post-Conflict Reconstruction: The Contribution of the Catholic Radio Network to Peacebuilding in South Sudan." In *Transitional Justice in Post-Conflict Societies in Africa*, edited by James Stormes et al., 115–30. Nairobi: Paulines Africa, 2016.
Nojeim, Michael J. *Gandhi and King: The Power of Nonviolent Resistance.* Westport, CT: Praeger, 2004.
Omoregbe, Joseph. *Knowing Philosophy: A General Introduction.* Lagos: Joja Educational Research, 1990.
Osmańczyk, Edmund J. *The Encyclopedia of the United Nations and International Relations.* New York: Taylor and Francis, 1990.
Ploch Blanchard, Lauren. *The Crisis in South Sudan.* Washington, DC: Congressional Research Service, 2013. http://www.refworld.org/pdfid/52cff1494.pdf.
Rajan, Menon. *The Conceit of Humanitarian Intervention.* New York: Oxford University Press, 2016.

Ramsbotham, Oliver, and Tom Woodhouse. *Humanitarian Intervention in Contemporary Conflict*. Cambridge: Polity, 1996.

Samset, Ingrid. "UN Peacekeeping in the Congo: When Is the Job Done?" *Norwegian Peacebuilding Centre: Noref Policy Brief* 6 (June 2010) 1–7. https://www.cmi.no/publications/file/3717-un-peacekeeping-in-the-congo-when-is-the-job-done.pdf.

"Second Aid Worker Shot Dead in South Sudan in a Week." *The Defense Post*, November 3, 2020. https://www.thedefensepost.com/2020/11/03/aid-worker-shot-dead-south-sudan/.

Seybolt, Taylor. *Humanitarian Military Intervention: The Conditions for Success and Failure*. New York: Oxford University Press, 2007.

South Sudan Catholic Bishops' Secretariat. "Pastoral Message from the South Sudan Catholic Bishops' Meeting Juba, 26th–28th February 2019." Juba, South Sudan. https://cpn.nd.edu/assets/311222/sudan_bishops_pastoral_message_2019.pdf.

"South Sudan Country Profile." *BBC Africa*, August 6, 2018. https://www.bbc.com/news/world-africa-14069082.

South Sudan Customary Authorities Project. *What Happened at Wunlit? An Oral History of the 1999 Wunlit Peace Conference*. Nairobi: Rift Valley Institute, 2021. https://riftvalley.net/sites/default/files/publication-documents/RVI%202021.06.28%20What%20Happened%20at%20Wunlit__Pre-print.pdf.

"South Sudan Extends Transitional Government by Two Years." *Reuters*, August 4, 2022. https://www.reuters.com/world/africa/south-sudan-extends-transitional-government-by-two-years-2022-28-04/.

Tang Abomo, Paul. *R2P and the US Intervention in Libya*. Cham, Switzerland: Springer International, 2019.

UN High-Level Panel on Threats, Challenges, and Change. *A More Secure World: Our Shared Responsibility*. New York: UN Department of Publications, 2004. https://www.un.org/peacebuilding/sites/www.un.org.peacebuilding/files/documents/hlp_more_secure_world.pdf.

United Nations Peacekeeping. "UNMISS Fact Sheet: United Nations Mission in the Republic of South Sudan." https://peacekeeping.un.org/en/mission/unmiss.

UN Secretary-General. "A Vital and Enduring Commitment: Implementing the Responsibility to Protect: Report of the Secretary-General." UN General Assembly Security Council, July 13, 2015. https://undocs.org/A/69/981.

UN Security Council. Resolution 1996 (2011). S/RES/1996 (2011). July 8, 2011. https://digitallibrary.un.org/record/706698?ln=en.

"UN Sets Benchmarks for Deployment of IGAD Force in South Sudan." *Sudan Tribune*, November 18, 2018. https://sudantribune.com/article64770.

US Committee for Refugees and Immigrants. "1.9 Million Dead from Sudan's Civil War; More than 700,000 Deaths in 1998, Report Estimates." Relief Web, December 10, 1998. https://reliefweb.int/report/sudan/19-million-dead-sudans-civil-war-more-70000-deaths-1998-report-estimates.

Weiss, Thomas G. "To Intervene or Not to Intervene? A Contemporary Snap-shot." *Canadian Foreign Policy Journal* 9:2 (2002) 141–57.

Woodard, Alec. "South Sudan's Peace Deals: From the Khartoum Declaration to Power Sharing." *Africa Up Close: A Blog of the Africa Program at the Wilson Center*, October 18, 2018. https://africaupclose.wilsoncenter.org/south-sudans-peace-deals-from-the-khartoum-declaration-to-power-sharing.

13

Killing with Kindness: Can a Plague Cure a Plague?

MICHAEL L. BUDDE

A revolution is interesting to the extent that it avoids like the plague the plague it promised to heal.

—DANIEL BERRIGAN

Introduction

THE WORLD'S BEEN A mess for so long that it's understandable if you missed or have forgotten about one atrocity among others. On November 27, a report was made public—it spoke of the near-complete slaughter of a religious minority population yet again in the Middle East. These civilians had been attacked and plundered wholesale, and as one account summarized, "many had been brutally murdered; others had been taken prisoner and carried off into captivity."[1]

These atrocities were designed to horrify and frighten people worldwide. The report continues: "When they feel like inflicting a truly painful death on some, they pierce their navels, pull out the end of their intestines, tie them to a pole and whip them until, all their bowels pulled out, they fall lifeless to the ground. . . . [For other victims, the attackers] see if they

---

1. Frankopan, *First Crusades*, 2.

can manage to hack off their heads with one blow." The report continues by describing "the appalling treatment of women" with sexual assault practiced on a large scale.[2]

Massive human rights violations, ethnic cleansing underway, the systematic use of rape and torture against civilians—in the face of these crimes against humanity, the question of humanitarian intervention arises: whether to send soldiers into lands controlled nominally by another sovereign to put a stop to wholesale slaughter as quickly as possible. For many Christian ethicists, from a variety of traditions and regions, supporters of Christian pacifism and just war traditions alike—for nearly everyone, in other words—the general presumptions against war and violence can and should be set aside. In such extreme circumstances, the protection of the innocent trumps the sovereignty of states under international law, as well as the explicit prohibition on killing found in the gospel accounts of Jesus. Many of us here, I suspect, would share in the sense that given large-scale atrocities like this, using the military as a last resort to protect the innocent is an act of Christian love that we can endorse—such are the lessons of Rwanda, of ISIS, and countless other places. Many of us would support an armed intervention to protect civilians threatened by the atrocities just described.

The report in question became public on November 27, but you're excused if you missed it. It arrived on November 27, in the year 1095. In this case, support for humanitarian intervention endorsed the First Crusade, which sent a force of eighty thousand people to rescue persons being killed and endangered by Turkish soldiers as they engaged in conquest throughout what is now known as the Middle East. You may or may not find yourself echoing the affirmation of "*Deus Vult!*"—God wills it!—that issued from the crowd that heard Pope Urban II call for this rescue mission; you may not be encouraged by the pope's response back to them: "Let that be a war cry for you in battle because it came from God. When you mass together to attack the enemy, this cry sent by God will be the cry of all—'God wills it! God wills it!'"[3]

I start with the Crusades not to complicate matters beyond clarity, but to remind us all that we as Christians have been here before. Amid the contemporary debates about using force to protect the innocent—to set aside our sense that following Jesus is incompatible with being a killer—it is important to provide a larger context than one beholden to the urgency and immediacy of contemporary examples and imperatives. And I start with this example not to impugn the intentions of those among my brothers and

---

2. Frankopan, *First Crusades*, 2.
3. Frankopan, *First Crusades*, 2, 8, 28.

sisters whose Christian convictions lead them to support the constellation of practices and norms now known as the Responsibility to Protect (R2P). And it is not to agree with the killers in Al-Qaeda and Boko Haram that by definition any military move against them constitutes another "crusade" or war of Christian military aggression. I start here, as I said, to remind us that we have been here before.

R2P and the Need to Be Realistic

I will spare you the background on the development of R2P doctrine and advocacy, which seems to be a requisite part of most presentations in the field. I am aware, and you should be aware that R2P, as a set of norms and as codified in international bodies like the United Nations, are about much more than the use of military force. Indeed, the architects of R2P went to great lengths to add a host of preventative measures (and post-conflict policies) to responses to atrocities across borders in an attempt to distance the new norms from "humanitarian intervention," an earlier set of ideas and practices now suffering from public relations problems of various sorts. I take these distinctions seriously and appreciate the attempt to make the use of lethal force only one tool in the box, and hopefully not the first one seized; these pre- and post-conflict imperatives are not without their own problems, but such is best left for another time.[4]

Instead, I will focus on how Christians as members of the body of Christ—as Christians, in other words—ought to think and act in response to calls for the use of lethal force to protect persons being victimized or threatened with large-scale crimes against humanity. Many of the normative and descriptive assumptions attendant to R2P are reflected in, and have been taken up by, some significant emerging Christian theological frameworks. These include those schools of thought and practice that are known as just peacemaking, just policing, and others.[5] I take these approaches seriously, both because I know the people developing them are persons of good will and because they are serious attempts to think Christianly about the difficult issues involved in using lethal force to protect innocent communities around the world.

---

4. See, for example, Pandolfi, "From Paradox to Paradigm," 153–72.

5. Some leading spokespersons in these areas of Christian ethics attempt to distinguish R2P from their preferred frameworks, while others note the complementarity among frameworks. See, for example, Schlabach, "Just Policing," 73–88; and Winright, "Just Policing," 84–95.

Some of these efforts represent an attempt to apply a stringent version of just war theory to attempts to prevent or stop crimes against humanity where the in-place state is unable or unwilling to do so.[6] It is also the case that some scholars argue for the disconnect and incompatibility between just war theory and R2P.[7] I respect those who have developed just peacemaking or just policing (for present purposes, I use the terms interchangeably, although I am aware they are not identical), but I do not endorse their conclusions. Some of these approaches build upon a distinction between military action and the "police function," with the latter being more compatible with a thoroughgoing Christian commitment to nonviolence;[8] I find this distinction to be untenable on historical grounds, but I can only note rather than defend my position given the limits of this essay. As much as I might want to find a way to fit some measure of lethal means into the Christian love due to neighbors and to enemies, I do not believe such should be done.

Persons like me, who insist Jesus meant what he said in the Sermon on the Mount and elsewhere that Christians shouldn't kill people, even with a good cause, are generally regarded as unrealistic, detached from the realities of suffering and oppression in the world, and putting abstract purity of principle over the flesh-and-blood needs of the most vulnerable in society—leaving them to the wolves, in other words. One needs a bracing dose of realism, grounded in the experiences of at-risk others, lest abstract principle lead to the death of others.

I take such claims seriously. In that spirit, let me start with a few realistic assertions that, for reasons of time, I am only able to mention rather than defend in the time at hand.

Here is some realism to consider:

- State actors (those whom we hope will listen to our talk about ethical limits on military action—before, during, and after) mostly don't give a damn about our ethics when the chips are down. Christian or semi-Christian ethics may be a public relations card they can play when doing so is relatively low-cost in terms of losses, but our ethical niceties will go the way of innocent civilians in Dresden, Nagasaki, Tokyo, and the rice paddies of Vietnam. If you have doubts, read Nick Turse's book

---

6. See, for example, Himes, "Just War," 10–15, 28–31; Hoppe, "Just Peace," 68–76.; Schlabach, *Just Policing*; Winright and Johnston, *Can War Be Just*.

7. See Friberg-Fernros, "Allies in Tension," 160–73.

8. See Schlabach, "Practicing for Just Policing," 93–110; Schlabach, "Just the Police Function," 50–60.

Kill Anything That Moves for one set of cases.⁹ The distinctions and discriminations made by Christians do not and will not materially shift the decisions made by persons engaged in military invasions. Theologians may call for higher-risk approaches to war making that aim to minimize noncombatant deaths, for example, but these have been and will be overruled when the costs to intervenors threatens to exceed a fairly limited threshold, or one's comrades in arms are endangered.

- Military adventures, including those conducted under R2P auspices, will happen or not independent of what Christian leaders decide. Christianity hasn't been able to stop powerful countries from going to war in many centuries (some minor border disputes notwithstanding), and humanitarian invasions won't be launched or prevented to placate the demands of the churches. We have next to no influence in these arenas. To think otherwise is delusional. Whatever notions of justice, punishment, or compassion may be practiced by state actors in this area do not need Christian approval or grounding. In this area as in others, it's clear that the Christian tradition adds nothing much that secular states need in conducting their business.

- There have been some gains made in the area of gospel nonviolence in the past century—the delegitimation of war as an acceptable part of ordinary statecraft; opposition to some classes of tactics and weapons; and the acceptance of conscientious objection, the elevation of Christian pacifism as a defensible position in the church. But whatever these gains and whatever advances one hopes to see in the future may well be wiped out should Christians endorse the use of killing in the "limited" and "constrained" contexts described in R2P and its theological cousins. The world will certainly see more wars in the years ahead, as state actors worldwide are pressed upon by environmental collapse, mass expulsions of people, resource scarcities and the like; military experts worldwide are building such assumptions in their strategic plans. More and more of these wars will be labeled as R2P occasions, inasmuch as such may be easier to sell to domestic and international audiences than are wars for water, for oil, for land (although one can envision interventions justified by invoking a "responsibility to protect" certain ecologically significant areas when such is in the interest of one or more powerful states). What look like rare cases today are likely to become more common in the future; should it sign on to these ventures, the church will again be tarred with the brush of religiously sanctioned killing, and the gospel will be shown to be a sham yet again.

9. Turse, *Kill Anything That Moves*.

- R2P and its theological cousins presuppose the moral significance of scale: there is some magnitude of suffering and death sufficient to impel Christians to set aside his/her qualms about killing. The immediacy of threats to vulnerable populations, further, adds to the moral calculus—thousands, perhaps tens or hundreds of thousands, will suffer and die unless you bless the use of force. Afterward, however, the accounting may not be so simple. To whose account, for example, should one charge the two hundred and fifty thousand persons dead in Libya after the "successful" R2P intervention and overthrow of the Qadaffi regime?[10] Further, if protecting the vulnerable is the path by which the church takes up arms, it may also be the path that leads to a renewed militarization of Christianity and more weaponized religion in the world. How does the moral calculus shift if the casualty count includes not only those at risk unless Christians kill to save them, but also those killed in later wars that the church was powerless to resist, having already conceded the point to secular actors? Who will speak for those killed in later wars, who may have been spared had the church not lost its moral credibility by blessing the kinder, gentler forms of war promised by R2P defenders?

- There will always be actors and institutions that build some semblance of order using violence and coercion, but nowhere in the New Testament does it say that Christians have to help build or enhance the formal institutions of violent order-keeping—neither Rom 13 nor 1 Pet 2:13–17 nor anywhere else. Lethality-created order is like the weather: it's going to be here whether you like it or not, and sometimes—like a rainstorm that generates a flood, which can renew the soil—some good can come from it by the grace of God. It doesn't follow from that, however, that Christians are under an obligation to make the flooding more powerful, or to wash away one's enemies, just because these things happen sometimes on their own.

- Despite its obvious emotional appeal, upon inspection it is not obvious that the refusal of Christians to use lethal force to kill persons who are killing innocent persons is the same as being responsible for the death of those innocent persons. Such an assertion is more akin to gangster ethics—if you don't give me what I want, I'm going to kill this hostage and it will be your fault—than an unassailable chain of responsibility. By this logic, as Craig Watts notes, if the refusal of pacifists to take up arms in the name of rescuing certain innocent people is the ethical equivalent of killing them, then it must be conceded that everyone

---

10. See Davies, "Calculating the Millions-High Death Toll."

who has neglected to act in a way that could conceivably save someone's life anywhere is the ethical equivalent of a killer.[11]

Given the limits of space, here is what I will not do. For the most part, I will not develop some of the most important secular criticisms of R2P, even though I find them persuasive for the most part. These include:

1. the extent to which military interventions to "protect" at-risk populations has been the justification for colonial, neocolonial, and expansionist military attacks on weaker countries;
2. the degree to which R2P operates as an asymmetrical force in the modern world, a privilege held by the powerful and not the less powerful;
3. the impossibility of limiting the use of force in R2P adventures, or for managing the outcomes in ways that deliver on promises made. For example, despite protests to the contrary, it seems that one cannot protect internal populations from a despotic regime without engaging in "regime change"—the disavowal of "regime change" is an important part of current R2P advocacy, in order that the use of force is seen as limited in scope and ambitions; and
4. the degree to which R2P extends and masks the intrinsic violence of liberalism as a system of political economy, and the dubious nature of distinctions its theological defenders make between war making and (the presumably more benign) phenomenon of policing.

Additionally, I will presume for the moment that one is familiar with those parts of the scriptural tradition that point most directly toward the illegitimacy of lethal force employed by followers of Jesus. While such are important, by themselves they provide an incomplete sense of things. One needs to venture into the deeper waters of ecclesiology and eschatology to get a deeper sense of why lethality and Christian discipleship remain incompatible with one another. We lack time for this at present.[12] Instead, I want to examine only one feature of the theological case in favor of R2P—one shared by most theologians, even if not explored as deeply as some others.

The Importance of Right Intention

Christian advocates of R2P, just policing, and just peacemaking continue to make reference to St. Augustine as part of the project to defend military

---

11. Watts, "Just War," 39.

12. For one exploration, see the following chapter in this book on eschatology and ecclesiology.

force as part of peacemaking or police functions.[13] While many of his criteria have received considerable attention—legitimate authority, proportionality, and last resort, for example—I want to draw attention to one feature that receives relatively little attention in the theological reflections on just war as it relates to R2P—namely, the matter of right intention.

Lest anyone feel that focusing on one aspect only of just war theology is a poor test of the framework—getting four out of five or five out of six should be good enough, for instance—I am following the guidance of some of the best contemporary advocates of the tradition. Tobias Winright, for example, speaks for many who describe themselves as "strict constructionist" in their approach. Each criterion must be met, and one must be willing to reject a proposed course of warfare if all of the obligations of just war theory are not met. This is to take things beyond a "minimal or negative checklist" approach, serving instead "along the lines of a discipline that involves commitments, duties, and virtues as well as categories, criteria, and principles."[14]

Augustine's most famous passage on the matter, in which he claims that death and killing in warfare are not the worst things that can happen to a Christian, appears in *Contra Faustum Manichaeum*. It's often referred to as *Quid culpatur*:

> For what is culpable in warfare? Is it because some men, who will die anyway, are killed so that others may be tamed to live in peace? This censure is one of cowardly, not conscientious men. The desire to harm, the cruelty of vengeance, warlike and implacable intention, ferocity of rebellion, lust for domination, and similar motives, these are what are culpable in warfare.[15]

Not only does Augustine place intention and one's interior disposition at the center of whether war is just—or is simply murder—this move shapes what he does with the injunctions against violence in the Gospels (e.g., "do not resist evil," Matt 5:39; "turn the other cheek," Luke 6:29). These commands of Jesus are to be observed only in one's heart, only in one's intention and attitude toward one's adversaries. Killing can be an act of charity, and torture can be an expression of corrective love. As one commentator summarizes Augustine:

> Now the intention rather than the hostile act itself becomes the criterion of righteous warfare. Practically any hostile act was

---

13. I am aware that just war thinking admits of several formulations and articulations and that what is emphasized in one may be muted in another.

14. Winright and Johnston, *Can War Be Just*, xx.

15. Augustine, *Contra Faustum Manichaeum*, XXIII, 74.

justifiable provided it was motivated by love. The good Christian could suffer injury and yet retaliate, could love his [sic] enemy and yet kill him, both forgive and punish him. The evangelical precepts were transformed so that love was no longer an inhibition on warfare. In some cases, it even necessitated it.[16]

So central is intentionality to Augustine's understanding of just war that crusading warfare—war ordered by divine command, an aggressive warfare to avenge offenses against God—is valid because such is fought without the will to power, and with a properly ordered sense of love and internal disposition.[17] Those who build upon Augustine's just war thinking in crafting maxims of just policing and just peacemaking reaffirm the importance of intentionality in their theological projects.[18]

The matter of war making with love in one's heart strikes modern people as curious, if not downright nonsensical. And in fact, some contemporary defenders of just war theory radically circumscribe this notion of love in battle by elevating the notion of "callousness," a necessary "military virtue," needed alongside love toward one's target.[19] Yet Augustine's idea of intentionality is crucial if one is to maintain that just war making or peacemaking is to be something consistent with Christian convictions, and not merely an ideological window dressing provided for the dirty secular business of human slaughter. The need to create and sustain the virtue of love would seem to be even more important in the context of just policing or just peacemaking, in which deployed personnel are meant to operate with greater limits and restrictions than are operant in all-out warfare.

Lethal Means and the Means at Hand

This raises a critical and unevenly explored question: who will be the agents of lethal force employed in matters of Christianly inflected R2P and protection of the vulnerable? What institutions will provide these agents, and how have they been trained, socialized, and formed into the attitudes, dispositions, and convictions necessary to be efficient soldiers?

In some formulations, the agents of military intervention are to come from the United Nations, or from some other multistate institution like the African Union, or from regional security organizations. In reality, of course,

16. Russell, "Love and Hate," 111–12.
17. Russell, "Love and Hate," 113–14.
18. Schlabach, *Just Policing*, 75; Schlabach, "Practicing for Just Policing," 95; Pfeil, "Whose Justice?" 115, 127.
19. Biggar, *In Defence of War*, 148; see also O'Driscoll, "Heart of the Matter," 273–79.

national military institutions are the primary means of deploying military force, even for groups like the UN or African Union, who do not have their own military forces but instead rely on units loaned to them by member states (the latter is attempting to construct its own forces, the so-called African Standby Force). These are the institutions that will be charged with acting with right intention and love in the process of exerting lethal force on behalf of at-risk persons around the world.

And these institutions—national or multilateral—have their own ideas about intentionality, and about the formation and socialization necessary to create soldiers. These priorities predate the ideas of humanitarian interventionists and R2P advocates and take priority over whatever formation of persons one might want to see for just peace interventionary military forces. Foremost for modern military institutions is the formation of young people into efficient killers—people able and willing to kill upon the orders of others, to kill on their own initiative, and to do so under stressful conditions. On one level, this is a statement of staggering banality—of course soldiering requires teaching people how to kill—it's the job description. On another level, however, the matter is nowhere near as straightforward or obvious as it may appear.

In fact, conventional wisdom notwithstanding, it is very difficult to compel most people to kill other people. It's a problem that has occupied the best of military minds, of military psychologists, for decades, even centuries—contrary to the stereotypes, there seems to be a deeply ingrained aversion to killing another human being, even in conditions of combat and self-defense.

Some of you are familiar with the work of David Grossman, a retired Army colonel and psychologist whose book, *On Killing*, brought into public view how difficult it is for military forces to socialize young people into killers (Grossman now trains US police forces how to kill more quickly and with fewer hesitations).[20] Among other things, he reminded contemporary readers of the work of Brigadier General S. L. A. Marshall, the official combat historian of the European theater in the Second World War. Marshall's research discovered that only 15 to 20 percent of individual riflemen were able to fire their weapon at exposed enemy soldiers—the vast majority were unable to do so, even at risk to themselves. This extreme reluctance to kill—even in the "most just" of just wars—confirmed earlier research from the Civil War and World War I on high rates of refusal to fire and has been confirmed by subsequent research and experiences.

20. See, for example, McLaughlin, "One of America's."

None of this has been lost on those who create and deploy armies—the cross-cultural aversion to militarized killing is a problem to be solved, an obstacle to state action and ambition. Starting in 1946, the United States Army led the way in pioneering new approaches to military formation and socialization designed especially to overcome this aversion. These new approaches are constantly evaluated and refined, adjusted and abandoned as needed, all with the aim of solving the problems seen in World War II of soldiers' reluctance to kill. David Livingstone Smith, discussing the Marshall study, draws the following conclusion:

> Although it sounds very nasty, and Marshall never put it quite this way, his observations imply that military training should concentrate on overriding the recruit's moral integrity, so that he or she will have no scruples about killing on command. Moral reservations are—in Marshall's words—a "handicap" that prevents the soldier from doing his job.... The US armed forces overhauled their system of military training to try to solve the problems that Marshall identified.... Apparently as a result, US soldiers' ratio of fire increased during the Korean conflict, and by the time the Vietnam War rolled around, American troops had become much more efficient killers. But this situation created a whole new problem. The troops did better in battle, and the ratio of fire skyrocketed, but so did the incidence of combat-related psychological disorders.[21]

It's a fascinating topic, but one that can be summarized as involving more intensive psychological de- and reconstruction of recruits (taking apart their sense of self and replacing it with loyalty to the military and especially to their small unit); systematic indoctrination in what many participants describe as dehumanization of others; a hypermasculinity that generates sexual predation (among male and female recruits alike); and a profound disdain for civilian life and culture as weak, corrupted, and unworthy of the virtuous service of soldiers. These processes for formation begin in basic training, are sustained by military culture, and are deepened for those undergoing specialized training (e.g., elite forces of various types).

The literature is extensive, and the personal testimonies from those who have experienced it are extensive (even as a powerful code of silence discourages sharing with outsiders the nature and depth of the dehumanization necessary to make modern soldiers). From physical brutalization and sleep-deprived exertions to countless repetitive drills—complete with racist and sexist cadences, invectives and insider-outsider language, and combat

---

21. Smith, *Less Than Human,* 230.

conducted while using powerful stimulants and psychotropic drugs—the modern soldier is different from the romanticized citizen-soldiers of Hollywood war films and July 4 parades.

A sampler from Matt Young, a Marine Corps veteran who served in the recent imperial wars in Asia:

> I get it. The military fashions itself as the last bastion of true manliness, and in a world that feels unstable, it promises four years of a steady job, decent pay, health care and moral high ground over those who didn't serve.
>
> Then, they'll tell you, at the end of your active service you'll be left with a marketable set of skills so desirable employers will be lining up outside your door begging for you to take their jobs. You'll be wanted, a provider.
>
> The Marines have "How to Become a Man 101" down to a science. My fellow recruits and I suffered together. We were given a common language that sought to bond us, ensconce us in groupthink and separate us from the outside. We weren't allowed out in the civilian world without a partner to watch our backs, a "battle buddy." We were at war even when we were at home. We were never alone. I had more fathers than I knew what to do with.
>
> I shaved my head like one of my drill instructor's [sic] and copied from my senior Marines hard turns of phrase that relayed disgust of everything feminine, anything vulnerable. They called our girlfriends Susie Rottercrotch and told us fictional bull studs back home were having their way with them—women were not to be trusted.[22]

The result of all of this, according to Young:

> The infantry taught us to use language like "haji" and "raghead" and "target" and "towelhead" to dehumanize not just enemy combatants, but every Iraqi and Arab person we encountered. We screamed "kill" for every repetition of cadence during stretching exercises and calisthenics—"1!" "KILL!" "2!" "KILL!" "3!" "KILL!"—to make the thought of killing commonplace. Our senior Marines joked about raping Iraqi women, so we did too. They called Iraqi children terrorists in training and meant it. So did we.
>
> I developed ethnocentric thoughts that I shared without shame. I'd only been in the Marines for eight months before my

---

22. Young, "Hope the Military."

first deployment. But by then I was no longer a quiet, lost, empathetic kid.... I was bloodthirsty. I wanted to kill.[23]

With widespread reports of military personnel raping, abusing, mutilating, and killing civilians in conflict zones around the world—involving the armed forces of rich and poor countries alike—military leaders in general have attempted to blame so-called "bad apples" for such behavior. One study (from scholars supportive of the military enterprise) concludes, alas, that "most violations of the laws of war cannot be traced conveniently back to some preexisting psychological or physical pathology" among isolated soldiers. Important for the purposes of my argument, the authors of this study suggest that it is the dehumanization of military training, combined with "asymmetric conflicts involving insurgencies and unconventional warfare" that put troops at higher risk of committing atrocities.[24] Asymmetric conflicts, of course, are precisely the conditions in which R2P comes into play.[25]

These same experts on the psychological costs of dehumanization offer a telling admission relevant to precisely what one agrees to once one buys into just war theory.

> [O]ne response would be to suggest that all forms of dehumanization should be resisted, rather than being incorporated into military training. However, this view is also problematic for anyone who is not a pacifist. If we accept some version of Just War Theory, and therefore endorse the view that violent military force is sometimes required in defense of a just cause, then we are cornered by the reality that troops do need to be trained to kill. Indeed, for justified military actions, there is a strong moral argument that military training should, first and foremost, be directed at enabling our troops to kill in the most effective and efficient manner possible. We doubt this can be accomplished without allowing some form of dehumanization of the enemy....[26]
>
> On the modern battlefield, our troops are asked on the one hand to be ready to fight an enemy with clear-sighted and dispassionate efficiency, and, on the other hand, we expect them to be sensitive to the mores of a foreign culture, enabling them to win the hearts and minds of its citizenry while forming strong and mutually trusting working relationships with members of its military. In other words, we ask them to be both highly analytic

23. Young, "Hope the Military."
24. French and Jack, "Dehumanizing the Enemy," 169–70.
25. French and Jack, "Dehumanizing the Enemy," 170.
26. French and Jack, "Dehumanizing the Enemy," 177.

and highly empathetic. Hence, at first sight, it might appear that the demands of the modern battlefield are simply impossible to manage: they are bound to drive our troops insane.[27]

In the face of manifest problems generated by socializing people into overriding the aversion to killing, the military solution has become this: even more psychological manipulation and formation of soldiers by their own military. The goal is something that, for lack of a better term, might be called a humane dehumanization—which is about as logical as Augustine's killing as an act of love. First, dehumanize one's enemies and own soldiers, then rehumanize them at the end of their service.[28]

Finally, in an admission that sits awkwardly with Augustine's view and that of just war and just peace advocates after him, the authors of the study note:

> It strikes us that any attempt to square empathy or humanitarian concerns for an individual with committing acts of extreme intentional violence against that person represents a mindset that is too tortured and dysfunctional to condone. Troops should not be asked to love their enemies while inflicting suffering and death upon them. This is the mindset of an abuser, not a mindset we wish to encourage in troops who will return to civilian life.[29]

As if all of this were not enough, one ought also explore the literature on "combatant socialization," or the ways in which violent conflict builds company morale and efficiency. Much of this literature deals with the ways in which rape is used or tolerated by military forces as a way to bond soldiers to one another, as a form of compensation for soldiers' efforts, or as ways for soldiers to prove their masculinity.[30] A significant portion of this literature focuses on those areas where military forces have been deployed in peacekeeping operations, with troops from regional neighbors as well as from the industrial north. The prevalence of rape within a given military unit is another product of military socialization, both via training and combat exposure—lowering inhibitions, building appetites for violence and cruelty, and displacement of guilt onto victims.[31]

Then, there is the literature—from the United Nations, and from journalistic, NGO, and academic sources—about sexual violence and widespread

27. French and Jack, "Dehumanizing the Enemy," 180.
28. French and Jack, "Dehumanizing the Enemy," 191.
29. French and Jack, "Dehumanizing the Enemy," 192.
30. See Cohen, "Ties That Bind," 701, 704–5.
31. See Wood, "Rape as a Practice," 518–19.

civilian abuse perpetrated by UN peacekeeping forces.[32] Some of this occurs in places where sexual violence against civilians prompted calls for external intervention in the first place. At this point, it bears mentioning that I do not think that all soldiers are sociopaths, nor that all perpetrate heinous crimes in casual fashion as a result of military training and socialization. The wonder is that, given the power of these formative processes, there are not more incidents than there seem to be (although significant underreporting and secrecy remain powerful).

Still, even this cursory dip into the waters of military socialization should be enough to suggest that one cannot—cannot—hold on to even a shred of Augustine's regard for intentionality as constitutive of a just war and expect such to be operationalized by the modern military systems of the world. To the extent that just peacemaking, just policing, and R2P aspire to any sort of connection to Augustinian principles, to that extent they cannot but fall short.

In other words—these are your rescuers, these are your saviors, these are the instruments you are entrusting with the lives of civilians and innocents who are themselves at risk from other militaries and armed groups. Especially given the emphasis put on external invaders also providing humanitarian assistance after the end of armed conflict—and these soldiers will be crucial in the so-called *jus post bellum* stage of things—these dehumanized and dehumanizing human beings are your only means of conveying Christian-sanctioned violence and killing. There are no other options now available.

Is there anyone else able to fight the wars of just policing? What institutional forces will be deployed to rescue innocents at risk in other countries, in ways that meet the strict conditions Christian ethics hopes to maintain for R2P and related armed interventions? Powerful states have too much history to be reliable—too many bloody incursions made in the name of lofty values and selfless assistance. One would similarly feel uneasy about calling upon terrorists or mercenaries to conduct humanitarian violence (although the idea of using mercenaries has been raised several times in recent years). Multilateral institutions have no significant armed forces of their own. And all armies around the world, in countries great and small, take great pains to instill dehumanization, hatred, and prejudice into the character of their members so that they will kill on command. Who are the actors capable of implementing just policing/peacekeeping in ways that uphold the requirements of this school of thought?

---

32. For one example, see Moncrief, "Military Socialization." 715–30.

Theological defenders of armed intervention acknowledge the deficiencies of available means in the way they recommend the development of international police forces to implement their vision—and if one is to have international police, one also needs real international law and courts, regional enforcement agencies, and extensive cooperation with civil society organizations.[33] And yet, without the existence of such infrastructure—the problems with which I will overlook for now—one is left to advocate the pursuit of military interventions using the only tools at hand—the armed forces of states, as presently formed and socialized.

Even if one assumes for the sake of argument that things like international policing and courts with plenary jurisdiction are good things, the church can't make them or bring them into being. What options can the church implement in the here and now to construct the institutional capacities necessary to pursue the types of humanitarian intervention called for by Christian ethicists in these areas?

I have a proposal. If one is serious about conducting armed interventions in ways that respect the Christian convictions described herein, I suggest that you have no other choice than to bring back religious military orders—explicitly Christian armies. You heard me right—Christian military orders like the Knights Templar, the Knights Hospitallers, and more. The only way to make sure that one conducts war—excuse me, fulfill police functions—in ways consonant with just peacemaking, or with R2P compatible with Christian just war principles, is to have soldiers deeply formed by Christian convictions and practices; just the opposite of the formation steeped in bloodlust, misogyny, xenophobia, and enemy hatred typical of secular military institutions. While they may have done so imperfectly, Christian military orders attempted to engage in simultaneous deep formation and socialization of members—into martial dispositions and practices, and into Christian sensibilities and ways of inhabiting the world. Who else can kill with love? Who else will be adequately prepared to sacrifice persons under their command in the interest of Christian principles? Who else can be trusted to refuse orders given by self-seeking secular rulers who would exploit a humanitarian crisis for crass political or economic advantage?

I see no way around it. Unless one is willing to entertain the prospect of specialized military forces capable of acting in accord with the principles of Christian just peace/policing approaches, one is merely play-acting. It is absurd to believe that the powerful states of this age will conduct themselves in anything resembling the standards held by Christian ethicists looking to make room for violence of a highly constrained sort. They will ignore

---

33. See Winright, "Community Policing," 144–48.

those cases where intervention is needed but not in their self-interest; they will ditch limits on their warfighting options when the cost becomes too high, and especially if defeat becomes a real possibility; and they will use the ideological cover provided by well-meaning Christians to legitimize a range of objectives, some far beyond those countenanced by those well-meaning Christians.

So, we have returned full circle to the beginning—to a call for humanitarian intervention in the year 1095, to be answered best by reconstituted Christian armies. If either or both of these seem distasteful to you, if they violate some deep religious intuitions, I suggest one should be attentive to these reactions and take them seriously. They suggest that killing for Christian reasons remains a bridge too far, a contradiction at the level of visceral reaction that should be explored rather than buried under piles of exculpatory discourse. That, I suggest, is what *Deus Vult*—God wills—means in our time and place. . . .

Bibliography

Augustine. *Contra Faustum Manuchaeum XXIII*, 74. http://www.newadvent.org/fathers/140622.htm.

Biggar, Nigel. *In Defence of War*. Oxford: Oxford University Press, 2013.

Budde, Michael L. "An Interlude: Eschatology, the Church, and Nonviolence: Some Provisional Claims." In *Foolishness to Gentiles: Empire, Nationalism, and Discipleship*. Eugene, OR: Cascade, 2022.

Charlton, Linda. "Daniel Berrigan Linked to Plea to Weathermen for Nonviolence." *New York Times*, January 21, 1971. https://www.nytimes.com/1971/01/21/archives/daniel-berrigan-linked-to-plea-to-weathermen-for-nonviolence.html.

Cohen, Dara Kay. "The Ties That Bind: How Armed Groups Use Violence to Socialize Fighters." *Journal of Peace Studies* 54:5 (2017) 701–14.

Davies, Nicolas J.S. "Calculating the Millions-High Death Toll of America's Post-9/11 Wars." *MPN News*, April 26, 2018. https://www.mintpressnews.com/how-many-millions-have-been-killed-in-americas-post-9-11-wars/241144/.

Frankopan, Peter. *The First Crusades: The Call from the East*. Cambridge: Harvard University Press, 2012.

French, Shannon E., and Anthony I. Jack. "Dehumanizing the Enemy: The Intersection of Neuroethics and Military Ethics." In *Responsibilities to Protect: Perspectives in Theory and Practice*, edited by David Whetham and Bradley Jay Strawser, 169–95. Leiden, Netherlands: Brill, 2015.

Friberg-Fernos, Henrik. "Allies in Tension: Identifying and Bridging the Rift Between R2P and Just War." *Journal of Military Ethics* 10:3 (2011) 160–73.

Himes, Kenneth. "Just War, Pacifism and Humanitarian Intervention." *America* 169:4 (August 14, 1993).

Hoppe, Thomas. "Just Peace as a Leading Perspective: Towards the Concept and Task Profile of an Ethics of International Politics." *Studies in Christian Ethics* 20:1 (2007) 68–76.

McLaughlin, Kelly. "One of America's Most Popular Police Trainers Is Teaching Officers How to Kill." *Insider*, June 2, 2020. https://www.insider.com/bulletproof-dave-grossman-police-trainer-teaching-officers-how-to-kill-2020-6.

Moncrief, Stephen. "Military Socialization, Disciplinary Culture, and Sexual Violence in UN Peacekeeping Operations." *Journal of Peace Research* 54:5 (2017) 715–30.

O'Driscoll, Cian. "The Heart of the Matter? The Callousness of Just War." *Studies in Christian Ethics* 28:3 (2015) 273–79.

Pandolfi, Mariella. "From Paradox to Paradigm: The Permanent State of Emergency in the Balkans." In *Contemporary States of Emergency: The Politics of Military and Humanitarian Interventions*, edited by Didier Fassin and Mariella Pandolfi, 153–72. Cambridge: Zone, 2010.

Pfeil, Margaret. "Whose Justice? Which Relationality?" In *Just Policing, Not War: An Alternative Response to World Violence*, edited by Gerald Schlabach, 111–29. Collegeville, MN: Michael Glazer, 2007.

Russell, F. H. "Love and Hate in Medieval Warfare: The Contribution of St. Augustine." *Nottingham Medieval Studies* 31 (1987) 108–24.

Schlabach, Gerald. "Just the Police Function, Then." *Conrad Grebel Review* 26:2 (2008) 50–60.

———. *Just Policing, Not War: An Alternative Response to World Violence*. Collegeville, MN: Michael Glazier, 2007.

———. "Just Policing, Responsibility to Protect, and Anabaptist Two-Kingdom Theology." *Conrad Grebel Review* 28:3 (2010) 73–88.

———. "Practicing for Just Policing." In *Just Policing, Not War: An Alternative Response to World Violence*, edited by Gerald Schlabach, 93–110. Collegeville, MN: Michael Glazer, 2007.

———. "Warfare vs. Policing: In Search of Moral Clarity." In *Just Policing, Not War: An Alternative Response to World Violence*, edited by Gerald Schlabach, 69–92. Collegeville, MN: Michael Glazer, 2007.

Smith, David Livingstone. *Less Than Human: Why We Demean, Enslave, and Exterminate Others*. New York: St. Martin's, 2011.

Turse, Nick. *Kill Anything That Moves: The Real American War in Vietnam*. New York: Metropolitan, 2013.

Watts, Craig. "Just War, Pacifism, and the Ethics of Protection." *Encounter* 71:1 (2010) 35–62.

Winright, Tobias. "Community Policing as a Paradigm for International Relations." In *Just Policing, Not War: An Alternative Response to World Violence*, edited by Gerald Schlabach, 130–52. Collegeville, MN: Michael Glazer, 2007.

———. "Just Policing and the Responsibility to Protect." *Ecumenical Review* 63:1 (2011) 84–95.

Winright, Tobias, and Laurie Johnston, eds. *Can War Be Just in the Twenty-First Century? Ethicists Engage the Tradition*. Maryknoll, NY: Orbis, 2015.

Wood, Elizabeth Jean. "Rape as a Practice of War: Toward a Typology of Political Violence." *Politics and Society* 46:4 (2018) 513–73.

Young, Matt. "I Hope the Military Doesn't Change My Brother Like It Did Me." *Time*, March 13, 2018. https://time.com/5193840/military-afghanistan-service-marine-corps/.

Index

abandonment, 63, 96, 117, 121, 203–4, 218, 221, 253
Abba (Father), 56, 69–70
abduction, 164
abortion, 143, 183
Abrahamic, 177
academics, 36n4, 78–82, 84, 87, 98, 173, 189–90, 217, 239, 256
accompaniment, 42, 61, 65, 106, 128–29, 132, 134, 136, 156, 164, 166–67
accountability, 164, 185, 202, 227, 234, 248
Achilles, 218
activists, 107, 115, 164, 188, 232
addiction, 109, 215
Africa, 110, 120, 127–29, 137–38, 144, 150, 186, 228, 235, 240
    African Union (AU), 225, 233, 251–52
        African Standby Force, 252
        Peace and Security Council (AU-PSC), 233
    communities, 98, 145, 150, 153, 239
    conflicts, 102, 140, 225, 234
    countries, 101, 240
    culture, 149, 155
    Great Lakes region, 99
    Intergovernmental Authority on Development (IGAD), 214, 229–33, 252
    North, 36, 110
    Organization of Africa Unity (OAU), 225
    sub-Saharan, 129
agape, 235, 237
agents, 115, 139, 166, 176, 182, 184, 188, 237
    of change, 131, 133, 135, 154, 169, 208
    of violence, 206, 251
aggression, 52, 151, 162, 219, 226, 245, 251
Algeria, 75–76, 79, 81, 100
    Algiers, 76
    Fez, 76
    army, 79
    Bond of Peace, 76
    GIA (Groupe Islamique Armé), 75
    government, 79
    Lien de Paix, 76
    Ribat el Salam, 76, 84
    Tibhirine, 74–76, 79–80, 82, 84, 87–89
Allman, Mark, 202–3
altars, 105–6, 115
Amazon, 110
ambassadors, 133, 136, 139, 191, 212
Ambrose of Milan, Saint (Bishop), 215–16
    legions, 216
analysis, 47, 111, 156, 180n24, 198, 206, 240, 255
anamnesis, 65
animals, 85, 117–18, 151, 153, 221
    donkey, 46
    hare, 153
    lions, 112, 116, 118–19

animals (*cont.*)
   livestock, 130, 135–36, 135n16
      cattle, 46n47, 130–31, 135n16, 136, 142–43, 142n1, 151–52, 154, 156n37, 158, 254
         raids, 131, 135–36, 135n16, 142n1, 143, 151, 154, 156n37
      goats, 143, 152
      sheep, 46n47
         lambs (figurative), 64, 67
         wolves (figurative), 64, 246
   monkeys, 151
anonymity, 116–17, 120–21
Anscombe, Elizabeth, 215
anthropology, 86, 199
Antioch, 85, 118
Aquinas, Thomas, Saint, 37, 116–17, 187, 199n4, 207
   Summa Theologiae, 116
Arabs, 254
areopagus, 84, 84n26
Argentina, 164
   Buenos Aires
      Plaza de Mayo, 117, 164
arrest, 46, 67, 107, 118–19
arts, 183, 186, 190
   artisans, 38
      patient, 96, 99
   crafts, 186
   dance, 144, 153–55, 158
   drama, 183
   painting, 183
   writings, 82, 82n23, 176n1, 183
      literature, 36, 58, 110, 144, 152–53, 164, 253, 256
         poetry, 82, 144, 153, 212
Ashworth, John, 238
Asia, 110, 114, 120, 168, 186, 254
   South, 188–89
assassination, 36, 56, 115, 216, 219
assimilation, 80, 117
atonement, 35–36, 49–50
atrocities, 129–30, 136, 164, 173, 179, 239, 243–45, 255

Augustine of Hippo, Saint (Bishop), 199n4, 202, 207, 215–17, 249–51, 256–57
   Contra Faustum Manichaeum, 202n6, 250
   Quid culpatur, 250
Auschwitz, 111, 120
Austria, 110
   Hofer, Norbert, 110
authenticity, 36, 51, 78, 201
authorities, 105, 111, 119, 228–29, 250
   moral, 158, 170, 203
   police, 107
   political, 65–66
   Roman, 48, 119, 216
autonomy, 167, 170–71, 228

Baha'i, 177, 182
Balkans, 225
   Bosnia, 206
   Kosovo, 226
baptism, 61–62, 123, 207
Belgium, 99
   Brussels, 181
belonging, 37, 63, 76, 78, 83, 86–87, 151, 170, 186
Benedictines, 35
   Anselm of Canterbury, Saint, 35
Bible, 59, 63, 68, 88, 113, 133, 198, 205, 227. *See also under* Israel
   Cain, 220
   David, 218
   Deuteronomy, 48
   Eden, garden of, 201
   Exodus, 164
   Ezekiel, 43, 46
   Genesis, 137
   Gospels, 42, 47–48, 60, 62–64, 75, 83, 95–97, 165, 199, 207, 247
      apostles, 67, 95, 177
      Beatitudes, 41, 43, 59, 63
      Elizabeth, Saint, 61
      Jesus and, 37, 41, 46, 59, 61, 66–67, 69, 81–82, 198, 220, 244
      John the Baptist, 61–63, 117
      Judas, 95
      Last Supper, 49, 65, 95

Malchus, 67
  of John, 46n47, 61, 65, 67, 69, 123, 218
  of Luke, 49, 61–62, 115
  of Mark, 61–63
  of Matthew, 43–44, 61, 63–64, 95, 236
  nonviolence and, 59–60, 60n18, 93, 130, 138–39, 170, 197–200, 205, 208, 247, 250
  parables, 43, 221–22
    Good Samaritan, 87, 221–22
  Peter, Saint, 67, 95, 127, 130, 163
    letters of, 248
  Pilate, Pontius, 48, 66
  proclamation of, 79, 84, 88, 95
  Sanhedrin in, 48
  Sermon on the Mount, 43–44, 59, 63, 246
    transformative initiative, 44
  Simeon, 61
  synoptic, 46, 63
  Syro-Phoenician woman, 87
  teachings, 63, 137, 236
  Thomas, Saint, 177
  values, 139, 199
  Zacchaeus, 42
  Zechariah (father of John the Baptist), 61
Isaiah, 46–47, 58, 62, 121, 163
  Suffering Servant, 58, 121–22
Jeremiah, 43–44, 46
Jonathan, 218
Moses, 45, 164
New Testament, 37, 43, 248
Paul, Saint, 56, 68, 73, 128, 137
  Corinthians (first letter), 128
  Romans (letter), 56, 248
  Ephesians (letter), 56
Scripture, 37, 41, 56, 113, 137–38, 200–201, 205–6
Yahweh, 40–41, 121
Zechariah (prophet), 46
bishops, 58–59, 85, 105, 114, 136, 140, 177n4, 212, 215, 238
blame, 75, 146, 220, 225
blasphemy, 48, 112, 212

blessing, 44, 59, 63, 148, 152, 156, 191–92, 198, 248
body, 108, 156, 183, 192
  embodiment, 40, 61, 78, 218
  guards, 230
  of Christ, 68, 73, 86, 245
  organizational, 78, 110, 224–25, 229, 245
Bolivia, 164
bombs, 82, 110, 138, 169, 215, 219
bonding, 56, 76, 135, 145, 154–55, 218, 237, 254, 256
borders, 38, 110, 216, 218–19, 224, 226, 228, 245, 247
Bose Monastery, 89, 89n42
  Bianchi, Enzo, 89
Brazil, 110, 117, 164, 205
  Bolsonaro, Jair (President), 110
bridge, 60, 234, 259
building, 128, 145–46, 155, 172
brokers, 103, 147, 214, 229
brutality, 110, 243, 253
Bryant, Herschel Odell, 57n6
Buddhism, 166, 177, 183
bullying, 171–72, 189
Burkina Faso, 100
Burundi, 99

Caesars, 65–66
Cambodia, 224–25
  Pol Pot, 224
Cameroon, 100
campesinos, 115
Camus, Albert, 211, 213–14
  "The Human Crisis" (talk), 213–14
Canada, 227
  International Commission on Intervention and State Sovereignty (ICISS), 227–28
    Responsibility to Protect: Research, Bibliography, Background, 227–28
  Vancouver, 59
cancer, 215, 217
canonization, 35, 75, 113, 115, 122
  equipollent, 122

capitalism, 110, 202, 214
  businesses, 131, 135n16, 162, 214
  Wall Street, 214
Catechism of the Catholic Church, 133, 137–38
catechists, 133, 139–40
catechumens, 119, 133
cease-fires, 101, 202, 231–32
celebration, 46, 50, 64–65, 76, 79, 85, 115, 136, 163, 184, 187
  of Christmas, 211
  of life, 87, 155
cenobites, 89n43
Central African Republic (CAR), 100–101, 127
  anti-balaka, 100
  Bozizé, François (President), 100
  coup d'états, 100
  president, 100
  Seleka, 100
Central America, 74, 80–81
centuries
  first, 37, 45, 119, 215
  fourth, 89n43, 205, 207, 215–16
  nineteenth, 164
  second, 36, 85, 119
  third, 36, 119
  twentieth, 57n6, 73–74, 82n23, 211, 224
  twenty-first, 224
Chad, 100
character, 37, 40, 48, 123, 218, 257
charism, 57, 80–81, 84
charity, 119, 122–23, 250
  propter caritatem, 123
chastity, 75
Chevigny, Paul, 109
Chile, 164
China, 114
Christian writing, early
  Letter of the Churches of Lyons and Vienne, 36
  Martyrdom of Montanus and Lucius, 36
  Syriac, 36
Christiansen, Drew, 204
Christmas, 97, 211
  fröhliche Weinachten, 211

chronology, 83, 231
Cicero, 58n12
Cilicia, 119
citizens, 112, 143, 172, 179, 185, 224–25, 228, 234, 254–55
civil
  rights, 164
  society, 132, 134, 137, 235, 237–38, 258
  unrest, 16, 46
  war, 127
    Africa, 101, 127
    Angola, 127
    Mozambique, 98
    South Sudan (*see under* South Sudan)
    Uganda, 127
    US, 252
civilians, 165, 216, 218, 227–35, 238, 243–44, 246, 253–57
civilization, 182, 213
clans, 130, 145–46, 149, 152, 167
cleansing, 40, 115, 152–53, 244
clergy, 88, 113, 138
climate change, 121, 206
coercion, 109, 120, 248
Coffey, David, 57n8
collaboration, 77–78, 80n22, 128, 133–36, 139–40, 158–59, 188–89, 235, 238
collusion, 113, 115
Colombia
  Medellin, 77
colonialism, 98, 114, 200, 206–7, 249
communion, 42, 52, 56n5, 57, 60, 64, 76–77, 79–80, 87, 89, 150
communism, 107, 165, 169, 211
communitarianism, 80, 239–40
compassion, 44, 52, 86, 183, 237, 247
  acts of, 106, 116, 119–20, 183
  of Jesus, 41–42, 51, 115–16
  peace and, 153, 157–58
complementarity, 103, 190, 228, 245n5
Concilium, 114
conflict resolution, 96, 99, 133, 162, 166, 172, 189–90, 199, 203, 234–36, 240

INDEX 265

Congo, Democratic Republic of (DRC), 100, 111, 127, 237
Congo, Republic of, 100
congregation, 83, 189
conquest, 46, 200, 215, 244
conscience, 79, 112–13, 131, 138, 144n7, 185, 216, 218, 220, 247, 250
consecration, 66, 75, 80, 86
consequentialism, 203n10
conservatism, 115
constructionist, 250
consumerism, 183
contemplatives, 75, 79, 87
contradiction, 45, 219, 228, 259
controversy, 115, 216, 221, 225, 228
convents, 96, 98
conversion, 41–43, 114, 163, 176, 238, 240
corruption, 47, 50, 229, 234, 253
cosmos, 73, 177, 183, 191
counsel, 66, 146, 155, 162, 215, 221
courage, 134, 168–69, 183, 234
covenant, 43, 56n5, 62–63, 65
cowardice, 51, 153, 250
creatures, 60, 205–6
credibility, 100, 222, 248
crime, 46, 48, 98, 107–9, 111–12, 131, 221–22, 227, 239, 257
   against humanity, 219, 244–46
   age of criminality, 167, 170
   and cattle (*see under* animals)
   decriminalization, 216
   organized, 238, 248
cross (Christianity), 35–38, 44, 47–51, 64–67, 70, 83, 86, 121–22
   crucifixion, 35, 47–50, 57–58, 67, 70, 86, 111, 115–16, 120–22
cruelty, 50, 111, 118, 202n6, 250, 256
culture of peace, 128, 133, 137, 140, 154, 158, 173
culture of violence, 128–29, 131, 142–43, 162, 189
Cunningham, Lawrence, 112
curse, 148–50, 149n17, 150n22, 152, 181

cycles (of hostility), 129–30, 136, 236, 240
Czechia, 113
   Bohemia, 113

danger, 35, 81, 100, 107, 110, 112, 117–18, 130, 151, 164
Daniel-Rops, Henri, 113
Day, Dorothy, 62
defense of life, 138, 173, 198, 207, 220
democracy, 100, 178–79, 178n13, 234, 239–40
demons, 41, 63
denominations, Christian, 76, 89n42, 115, 134
deontology, 203n10
depression, 143, 192
desert, 61–62
destruction, 83, 108, 114, 129, 138, 151, 173, 213–14, 224, 236–37
   mass, 169, 213
   of creation, 69
   of death, 69
   of Mother Earth, 189
   of temple, 46–47
Deus Vult, 244, 259
devil, the, 131
   Sheitani, 131
dialectic, 60, 121
dictators, 37, 55, 88, 109, 114–15, 167, 224, 249. *See also* regimes
diplomacy, 98–100, 227, 234
disability, 97, 144n7
discernment, 43, 81–82, 109, 199, 220
disciples, 43, 59, 61–62, 64–65, 67–70, 82, 95, 97, 128, 138, 208
   discipleship, 35, 51, 60, 68, 204, 206–8, 249
discipline, 171, 182–83, 187, 250
discrimination, 50, 121, 132, 134, 139, 144n7, 164, 179, 189, 234
   religious, 55, 247
disinterest, 103

displacement, 135, 143, 161, 165, 167, 171, 206, 229–30, 234, 256
disrespect, 130, 152–53, 156n37
dissent, 109–10, 224
diversity, 75, 81, 131, 162, 166, 189, 208, 225, 235
　religious, 84, 87, 89, 177, 178n7, 191–92
Djibouti, 233
dogma, 37, 88, 113
domination, 38, 162, 166, 169, 250
donations, 49, 179, 182–83
dreams, 81, 97, 192
drugs, 105–9, 108n9, 120, 167, 170, 184, 254
dysfunction, 256
earth, 43, 55–56, 61, 63, 68, 73, 83, 182, 191, 213
　Charter, 55
　Mother, 182, 186–87, 189
　peace on, 45, 60, 64

East Pakistan, 225
Easter, 83
ecclesiology, 77n12, 88, 115, 199, 249, 249n12
ecoclubs, 183
ecology, 59, 121, 182–83, 189, 247
ecumenism, 78, 80, 80n22, 89, 89n42–43, 132, 136, 184, 189, 191
egalitarianism, 178
El Salvador, 74, 76–78, 81–82, 84, 86–87, 105, 115
　army, 74
　batallón ATLACATL, 74
　San Salvador, 74
elderly, 97, 100, 114, 135, 146–47, 147n13, 150n21–22, 151, 154–55, 158
elders, 134–36, 153–54, 173, 235, 240
elections, 76, 96, 101, 142, 172
　Central African Republic (CAR), 100–101
　India, 178
　Kenya, 136, 142
　Philippines, 109, 167

Senegal, 102–3
South Sudan, 228, 231, 231n29
United States, 230
electricity, 187
Ellsberg, Daniel, 214
emotion, 156, 248
empathy, 189, 255–56
emphysema, 217
empire, 38, 58, 61, 65–66, 85, 111–12, 117–19, 214, 216
　emperors, 58, 68, 85, 114, 216
　imperialism, 202, 254
　Holy Roman, 58
　Roman (*see* Rome)
encyclicals, 59, 199
Encyclopedia of the United Nations and International Agreements, 237
endangerment, 244, 247
English language, 76, 146
enmity, 45, 49, 64, 129, 139, 202n6
entrepreneurs, 98
environment, 62, 87, 154, 189, 208
　of earth, 55, 154, 182, 198, 201, 247
　of nonviolence or peace, 129, 134, 140, 188
　of violence, 128, 131, 137
epiclesis, 86
epiphany, 86
equality, 144, 157, 166, 168, 185n30, 192
　in-, 56, 128, 130, 180, 206, 237
equity, 144, 157
equivocation, 212, 219
Erasmus of Rotterdam (priest), 58
eremites, 89n43
eschatology, 41, 47, 65, 78, 249, 249n12
ethicists, 198, 200, 202, 204–7, 244, 258
ethics, 59, 61, 163, 166, 198–208, 203n10, 212, 246, 248–49
　Christian, 197n1, 199, 204, 207, 215, 220, 244, 245n5, 246, 257–58
　ethicists, 207, 244, 258
　integration with theology, 204, 206
　study of, 197, 201
　virtue, 152, 203n10

INDEX 267

Ethiopia, 231, 233
  Addis Ababa, 233
  Ahmed, Abiy (Prime Minister), 231
Eucharist, 64–65, 85
Europe, 110, 186, 200, 212, 215, 252
  European Union (EU), 110, 230
Eusebius of Caesarea, 35n1, 119
evangelísastai, 62
evangelization, 58, 79, 81–82, 133, 138, 190, 251
evil, 40, 49, 202, 202n6, 234, 236–37
  confronting, 49, 51, 117, 220
  forces, 192, 250
  nonviolence and, 236
  overcoming, 62, 138
  resisting, 64, 95, 184, 221
  responding with
    evil, 82
    good, 82, 163
  violence and, 51, 219, 221, 250
exclusion, 41, 44–45, 52, 57n10, 79, 88, 111, 122, 143–44, 156–57, 185
execution (killing), 74, 85, 113, 118, 217
exorcism, 41, 63
expansion, 61, 77–78, 89, 98, 149, 182, 200–202, 214–15, 249
expertise, 99, 159, 199, 247, 255
extrajudicial killing, 106–9, 170–71

factions, 102, 231
farming, 39, 103, 107, 113, 116, 120, 135, 142n1, 151, 155, 183
fasting, 62, 182
fear, 48, 68, 81, 108–9, 139, 148, 149n17, 212
  without, 70, 76, 87, 192
fellowship, 41, 64–65, 76, 182–83, 220
  table, 41, 64–65, 144, 157
female, 143–44, 156, 156n37, 253
  circumcision, 143, 155–56
  genital cutting (FGC), 143
  genital mutilation (FGM), 143, 143n5, 155–57, 156n36–37
    termination of (TFGM), 143n5, 156n36, 160

femininity, 254
fidelity, 62, 66–67, 82, 103, 116–17, 122
films, 107, 254
flesh, 60, 68–70, 205, 246
followers, 36, 44, 50, 64, 68, 80n22, 88, 138, 198, 249
foreign
  affairs, 168, 225, 233
  people, 39, 43, 60, 87, 110, 114, 150, 190, 255
foundational theology, 200–201, 204–6, 208
France, 75, 100, 110, 113, 181, 211
  Le Pen, Marine, 110
  Rouen, 113
Francis of Assisi, Saint, 58, 98, 191
fraternity, 63, 191–92
French language, 62n20, 76
Freud, Sigmund, 211–12
funerals, 107–9, 115

Gandhi, Mahatma, 62, 176–77, 176n1, 177n6
garbage, 105, 107, 187
gender, 143, 155, 156n37, 157, 158n39–40, 162, 166, 168–69, 172, 185n30
generations (human), 129, 131, 133, 140, 144, 146, 149–50, 153, 191
genocide, 127, 178, 199n4, 225–26
geography, 81
Germany, 38, 135, 150n22, 211
  Berlin Wall, 225
  Dresden, 246
  Hitler, Adolf, 219
  Wilhelm (Kaiser), 211
gestures, 65, 78, 81, 150
Gichohi, Angela Wangui, 151
Global Hunger Index, 180
global South, 200
globalization, 111, 121, 180
Godself, 204
goodwill, 98, 188
Gospel Nonviolence and Just Peace Conference, 198, 204
grace, 44, 62, 77, 248

268 INDEX

grassroots, 128–34, 136, 139–40, 154n31, 158–59, 158n40, 172
gratuitousness, 40, 42–43, 52, 97
Greek, 62, 85
groupthink, 254
Guatemala, 100, 103, 117, 120
   Recovery of Historical Memory (REHMI), 120
      Guatemala, Nunca Más, 120
guerillas, 98
guidance, 137, 220, 250
guilt, 73, 218, 220, 256
Guinea, 100
gypsies, 97

happiness, 86, 108–9, 154–55
harmony, 45, 55, 99, 150, 153–54, 157–58, 182, 184, 190
hate speech, 238
hatred, 39, 129, 138–39, 192, 234, 237, 240, 257
   of conscience, 113
   of enemies, 44, 236, 258
   of justice, 114
   of love, 115–17
   of mercy, 115
   of war, 222
   religious, 36, 50, 105, 111–12, 115
healing, 41, 44, 104, 121, 128, 166, 184, 236, 240, 243
health, 87, 132, 143–44, 155–56, 177, 183–87, 254
   care, 132, 184, 186, 254
   lack of, 107
hegemony, 113–14
Hengel, Martin, 38
herbs, 143, 150, 184
hermeneutics, 56, 59, 64, 69, 121, 206, 208
heroism, 73, 106, 116, 122–23
Hinduism, 166, 177–78, 182, 187
   Ganpati, 187
      Lord Ganesh, 187
   Hindutva (*see under* India)
HIV/AIDS, 97, 103, 143
Hollywood, 254
homelessness, 97, 183

Horsley, Richard, 39
Hospitallers, 258
hostility, 80n22, 112, 128–29, 132, 134, 229–30, 232, 238, 250
human rights, 106–7, 109–10, 132, 163, 166–67, 172, 183, 227–28, 232
   violations, 55, 166, 170, 225–27, 238, 244
humanity, 129, 153, 157, 206–7, 212, 215, 217–18
   crimes against, 219, 244–46
   God and, 36, 40, 43, 45, 49, 57
   humanization, 50, 198
   dehumanization, 45, 140, 253–57
   humanitarianism, 99, 101, 132, 172, 225–27, 232, 239–40, 244–45, 247, 252, 256–59
Hungary, 110
   Orban, Viktor (Prime Minister), 110
hunger, 62–63, 83, 110, 119, 121, 180, 234

ideology, 45, 47, 251, 259
idolatry, 62, 87, 190
image of God, 133, 137–38, 220
imitation of Christ, 35–36, 74, 123
incarnation, 56–57, 60–61, 60n18, 68–70, 79, 88, 204–5
inclusion, 40–41, 88, 156–57, 182, 189, 238–39
inclusivity, 157
independence, 100, 102, 137, 165, 228, 230, 232, 235–36, 247
India, 110, 176–91, 225
   adharma, 180
   Adijati, 179
   ahimsa, 176
   billionaires, 180
      Ambani, Mukesh, 180n21
         Antilia (home), 180
      Forbes list of, 180n21
      Mittal, Lakshmi, 180n21
   BJP (Bhartiya Janata Party), 178, 178n11
   Brahmins, 178

INDEX   269

caste system, 178–80, 190
   Adivasis, 177n4, 179
   BCs (backward classes), 179
   Dalits, 177n4, 179
   Jati, 179
   OBCs (other backward classes), 179
   tribals, 179
      STs (scheduled tribes), 179
   Vanyajati, 179
   Varna, 179
Catholic Church, 177, 177n3–4
   Bishops' Conference, 177n4
   Bombay, Archdiocese of, 186
   Kottar, Diocese of, 186
   Latin church, 177n3
   Policy of Dalit Empowerment, 177n4
   Syro-Malabar church, 177n3
   Syro-Malankara church, 177n3
   Trivandrum, Diocese of, 186
Constitution, 178–79, 179n16
   affirmative action, 178–79, 179n16
dharma, 177–78, 177n6, 180
"Freedom of Religion" bill, 178
GDP, 185
Golwalkar, Madhav S., 179n17
Gujarat, 178
   Dangs District, 178
   genocide against Muslims, 178
gurus, godmen, 180n24
Hindi, 178n11, 185
Hindutva (Hindu nationalism), 178–79, 178n11, 179n17, 181
   pseudonationalism, 179
International Day for the Eradication of Poverty, 185
Jainism, 177, 183
karma, 180
Kerala, 186, 189
   Kochi, 189
Madhya Pradesh, 181
   Indore, 181, 184
Maharashtra, 187
Modi, Narendra (Prime Minister), 110, 178, 180
Mumbai (Bombay), 181, 186
   Malad West, 186

Nehru, Jawaharlal (Prime Minister), 177, 177n6
New Delhi, 185
   Christian Brothers, 185
   "Nine Is Mine" Campaign, 185, 185n31
   Rocha, Steve (brother), 185, 185n31
Orissa, 178
   Kandhamal District, 178
polarities, 177, 180–81
PRATYeK, 185
public distribution system (PDS), 180n22
religions, Cosmic/Mystic/Indic, 177
RSS (Rashtriya Swayamsevak Sangh), 178n11
Salesians of Don Bosco (SDB), 188
   Gonsalves, Peter (priest), 188
   Exercises in Peace Education, 188–89
   Peace Education courses, 188–89
satyagraha, 176
Savarkar, Vinayak Damodar, 179n17
secularism, 177–78, 177n6, 181
SEZs (special economic zones), 180
Sikhism, 177, 183
southern, 186
Tamil Nadu, 186
Theological Association (ITA), 179n17
tribal religions, 183
Universal Solidarity Movement of Value Education for Peace (USM), 181–84, 191
   action plan for social transformation, 183
   Alengaden, Varghese (priest), 181, 184
   Five Conditions, 182–83
   Five Paths, 182–83
   good deeds, 182
   youth, 181, 184–89
Zoroastrianism, 177, 183
   Parsees, 183
indigenes, 110, 117, 142, 145, 157, 159, 165–66, 170, 177n4, 201

individualism, 40, 75
infographics, 171
infrastructure, 109, 131, 183, 258
innocent, 36, 106, 111, 121, 127, 140, 213, 215, 220–21, 248
  protection of the, 244–46, 248, 257
inspiration, 77, 79, 84, 98, 164, 172, 176, 181–82, 190–91, 218
  divine, 81–82, 82n23, 89
insurgency, 228, 232, 255
integral human development, 133, 139, 181, 234
intellectuals, 78, 81, 87, 119, 199
intentionality, 109, 117, 123, 165, 202, 215, 228, 244, 249
  recta intentio, 215
  violence and, 58, 161, 198, 215, 250–52, 256–57
intercommunity, 237, 240
interethnic, 127, 145, 236, 238
interfaith, 103, 136, 176, 181–82, 191, 208
international
  community, 100–102, 110, 225–26, 228, 230, 235
  courts, 258
  law, 224–26, 244, 258
interreligious, 184, 188–89, 191
  dialogue, 78, 80, 89, 89n43
  groups, 132, 136
intervention, 100, 134, 206, 224, 228, 230, 239–40, 247, 257, 259
  humanitarian, 225–27, 239–40, 244–45, 252, 258–59
  military, 219, 225–27, 232–33, 237, 239–40, 244, 249, 251–52, 258
  non-, 248, 257
  R2P (responsibility to protect), 225, 248, 257
Iraq, 203, 254
  ISIS, 181, 219, 244
Ireland, 219
  Drogheda, 219
Islam, 75, 79, 80n22, 89n43, 165–66, 170, 177, 181–82
  Al-Qaeda, 181, 245

Boko Haram, 245
Islamists, 181
Muslims, 75–76, 79, 87, 100, 167, 170–72, 178, 181
  Christians and, 76, 80, 84–85, 100, 102, 134, 166, 172, 191
  Rohingya, 110
Israel, 164
  biblical, 38, 39n16, 40, 43, 47–49, 61, 66
    Ashkelon, 119
    Caesarea, 35n1, 119
    Egypt and, 46
    Essenes, 39n16, 61
    Galilee, 38–39
    Gaza, 119
    Gentiles in, 39–40, 45
    Hasmonean period, 45
    Herod Antipas, 38–39, 66
    Herod the Great, 38
    Herodians, 66
    priests (*see under* priests)
    Jericho, 221
    Jerusalem, 46–47, 49, 66, 221
    Jordan River, 61
    Judea, 38
    Law, 38, 40, 44–45, 48, 67
    Levite, 221
    Nazareth, 37, 57, 60, 82, 87–88
    Passover, 46, 122
    Pharisees, 39n16, 45, 61, 66
    Sadducees, 39n16, 46
    Samaria, 38
    taxation (*see under* taxation)
    temple, 38–40, 46–48, 46n47, 61, 66
    Zion, 40
  Women in Black, 164
Italy, 89, 97n3, 98–99
  Assisi, 191
  Milan, 215–16
  Rome, 95–96, 103, 197n1, 198, 204
  Trastevere, 96, 100

Japan, 114
  Hiroshima, 111, 120, 215
  Nagasaki, 215, 246
  Tokyo, 246

INDEX 271

Jesuits, 74–82, 84, 86–89, 189–90
  Berrigan, Daniel, 221, 243
  Catholic University of El Salvador, 74
  Dall'Oglio, Paolo, 89, 89n43
  Ellacuría, Ignacio (*see under*
    theologians)
  GC 36 (36th General Congregation of
    the Jesuits), 189
  González Faus, José Ignacio (*see
    under* theologians)
  Jacob, Binoy, 190
  Kerala, 189
  Loyola Institute of Peace and
    International Relations
    (LIPI), 189–91
    Centre for Art and Peace (CAP),
      190
    Centre for Science and Religion for
      Peace (CSR), 190
    Ezhuthu magazine, 190
  Lopez, Amando, 74
  Lopez, Ignacio Lopez y, 74
  Martin-Baró, Ignacio, 74
  Mathew, Roy, 190
  Montes, Segundo, 74
  Moreno, Juan Ramon, 74
  of UCA of El Salvador (*see under* El
    Salvador)
  Rosato, Philip J. (*see under*
    theologians)
  South Asian, 189–91
Jesus martyrs, 111, 114–15, 122
Judaism, 38–40, 45–48, 61–63, 66–67,
  177, 183, 197
  Second Temple, 40
judgment, 44, 47–48, 113, 203, 205, 236
jus ante bellum, 203n8
jus post bellum, 203n8, 257

Kalashnikovs, 101
Kaushat, Irmtraude, 135
Kenya, 136, 142–45, 150, 150n22,
  152, 156, 156n36, 158,
  158n40, 233, 233n34
  Agĩkũyũ people, 144, 149n17,
    150n22, 160
  cũcũs, 150n22

AIC Church, 132
Borana people, 130–31, 130n14,
  133–36, 135n16
Catholic Women's Association, 158
Constitution of, 144, 144n7
  Bill of Rights, 158
counties, 142–44, 142n1, 154n31
cowrie shells, 147
diviners, 150
eastern, 140
Elgeyo Marakwet county, 142, 149,
  149n19, 150n21, 152,
  152n28, 153n29, 155n34
footprints, 150–51
Gabbra people, 136
Human Rights Commission, 132
Kajiado county, 156
  Isinya, 156
Kalenjin people, 146, 146n11,
  147n14, 150, 155
Kanu (Kenya African National
  Union), 150n22
Kiswahili language, 145–46, 145n9
legetiet (*leketio*, *leketyo*, birth belt),
  147–49
Institute of the Blessed Virgin Mary
  (Loreto Sisters), 155n35,
  156
  Gachiri, Ephigenia (nun), 155n35,
    156n36–37
  Christian Initiation for Girls,
    156n35
  *Rite of Passage for Christian
    Boys*, 156n37
  Loreto Abundant Life Centre, 155,
    156n36
Machakos, Catholic Diocese of, 140
Marakwet people, 142n1
milk, 149–51, 161
Moi, Daniel arap, 150
Murang'a Catholic Diocese, 156n36
murenju, 148
Nairobi, 150n22, 154n31
  matatus, 150n22
North Rift Region, 142–45, 142n1,
  147, 152, 155, 157
nakedness, 145, 149–50, 150n22

Kenya (*cont.*)
  northern, 127, 130, 130n14, 132–34
    Marsabit, 132, 136
      Catholic Diocese of, 136
        Kihara, Peter (Msgr. Bishop), 136
      Joao (priest), 134
      Leyai, 134–35
      Leyai IDP (Internally Displaced Persons camp), 135
      Turbi massacre, 136
    Parliament, 158n40
    Pokot people, 145–46, 149
    Rendille people, 130, 130n14, 133–36
      dowry, 135n16
      Maasai, 135n16
      Morans, 135–36, 135n16, 143, 152
    Samburu county, 142, 146n10–11, 151–52, 151n24, 152n27, 154, 154n31
    Samburu people, 135n16, 143, 145, 147
      beading, 143, 143n6
    seemweett, 147
    strikes (labor), 150
    Turkana county, 142, 145n9, 155
    Turkana people, 143, 145–46, 147n13, 154–55, 154n31, 155n32
      language, 146
    West Pokot county, 142, 146n12, 148n15, 151, 151n25, 154n31, 155
  Women's Guild, 158
kidnapping, 74–75, 89n43
  hostages, 102, 248
kindness, 118, 153, 243, 248
King, Martin Luther, Jr., 62, 114–15, 234–37
kingdom, 46, 63, 114, 214, 216–17
  of God, the, 37, 40–44, 48–51, 56, 58–59, 63–65, 67, 74, 78–79, 85, 87
    proclamation of, 41, 44, 46, 70, 83
kinship, 201
Korea, 114
  conflict, 253
  North, 100
    Rocket Man (Kim Jong Un), 214

lactation, 150, 161
laity, 58, 89n42, 186
land, 39–40, 102, 114, 150–51, 238, 244, 247
  grabbing, 165, 230
language, 101, 140, 144n7, 146, 153, 158n38, 168–69, 202–3, 205, 253–54
last resort, 51, 202, 244, 250
Latin America, 36–37, 50, 77, 109, 117, 200
  church, 81, 88, 115, 186
  desaparecidos, 117
  disappeareds, 117
  theology, 41, 79, 111
law, international, 224–26, 244, 255, 258
Lederach, John Paul, 128, 130, 159
legends, 144, 153
legitimacy, 51, 147, 180, 197–98, 201–3, 205–6, 247, 249–50, 259
lepers, 45, 97
lethality, 211, 213–14, 217, 219–20, 236, 245–46, 248–49, 251–52
Levinas, Emmanuel, 86
Lewis, Thomas A., 77n12
LGBTQ+, 166, 201
liberalism, 77, 249
  neo-, 180
liberation, 56, 61, 64, 75, 84, 88
  ecclesiology, 115
  theology, 77–79, 111, 115, 221
Liberia, 127, 145
liberty, 62
Libya, 101, 103, 239, 248
  Fezzan region, 101
  Haftar, Khalifa, 102
  Qadaffi regime, 248
  Sabha, 101
  Serraj, Fayez, 102
lies (falsehoods), 211, 214–15, 217–18
limits, 130, 198, 199n4, 201, 203, 205, 238, 246
  lack of, 49
  on war, 202, 203n8, 204, 215, 240, 246–47, 249, 251, 259
literacy, 113, 183
liturgy, 36, 80, 85–86, 85n39, 113, 169
looting, 152, 230, 238

Lord's Prayer, 64
loyalty, 112, 170, 229–30, 253
Luther, Martin (priest), 113

magisterium, 199
majority, 39n16, 46, 80, 88, 102, 106, 129, 132, 135n16, 136, 140, 197, 252
   majoritarianism, 178
Mali, 127
Mandela, Nelson, 185
manipulation, 45, 129, 139, 235, 256
marginalization, 41–42, 45, 50, 65, 165, 167, 182, 234
   areas, 129–32, 139
   of minorities, 179
   of women, 144
margins, 105–6, 112, 116, 120, 123, 128
marriage, 135n16, 145–46, 153–54, 236
   husbands, 107, 143, 145–49, 151, 154
   in-laws, 145
   inter-, 135, 236
   wedding, 65
   wives, 107–8, 146, 153, 164, 212
martyrdom, 35–38, 35n1, 36n4, 44, 49–52, 74–77, 79–80, 82–86, 105–6, 111–26, 220
   Acta, 112, 116
   Agapius, 119
   Agnes, Saint, 119
   Ares, 119
   Beckett, Thomas, 113
   Bonhoeffer, Dietrich (*see under* theologians)
   Dionysius, Saint, 119
   Elijah, 119
   Emerentiana, Saint, 119
   Huss, John, 113–14
   Ignatius of Antioch, 85, 118
   Joan of Arc, 113
   King, Martin Luther, Jr. (*see* King)
   Kolbe, Maximilian, Saint, 114
   liturgy and, 36, 85, 85n29
   memory of, 36, 74, 88
   More, Thomas, 113
   Probus, Saint, 119
   Romero, Óscar (*see* Romero)
   Savonarola, Girolamo, 113
   Theodosia, 119
   Zaragoza, 117
   martyrs at the margins, 105, 116–23
Marxism, 77–78, 98
   Afro-Marxism, 98
Mary, Blessed Virgin, 60–61, 156, 187
masculinity, 162, 166, 169, 172, 253–54, 256
massacres, 111, 120–21, 136, 221
materiality, 65
mediation, 58, 96, 101–3, 166, 172, 230, 235, 240
mediators, 79, 98–99, 102–3, 162, 239
medical care, 76, 84, 150, 184
medieval period, 35, 112
meekness, 43–44
mentorship, 147n13, 154, 157, 216
messiah, 46, 48, 61–62, 65
method, 96, 103, 133, 136, 164, 169, 169n24, 188, 199, 207
Mexico, 110
   Mexico City, 103
Middle East, 81, 89, 110, 114, 243–44
migrants, 63, 97, 99, 110, 121, 191
militance, 178n11, 219, 221
military, 170, 203, 212, 217, 226, 244–45, 249, 251, 253–54, 256–57
   action, 113, 201, 225, 227, 230, 245–47, 249, 255
   armies, 214, 253, 257
      Algeria, 79
      Christian, 258–59
      El Salvador, 74
      France, 113
      Philippines, 165, 169
      South Sudan, 230, 232, 235
      Uganda, 232
      United States, 216, 218, 252–53
   campaigns, 230
   Christian, 258
      Knights Hospitallers, 258
      Knights Templar, 258
   culture, 253, 256, 257
   forces, 169, 226, 245, 252–53, 255, 258
   institutions, 252, 257–58

military (cont.)
   intervention, 219, 225–27, 232, 237, 239, 249, 251–52, 258
   leaders, 46, 233, 255
   militarization, 46, 224, 228, 230–34, 238–40, 248, 253
   morale, 256
   orders, 258
   paramilitary, 166
   personnel, 217–18, 247, 252, 255
   police and, 162, 166, 172
   presence, 105, 163–64, 207–8, 229, 232–33, 256
   responses, 198, 201
   service, 212, 216, 218, 222
   soldiers, 37, 61, 82, 103, 129, 218, 222, 229, 232–33, 244, 251–58
      Second World War, 98, 253
   training, 167, 217–18, 253, 255–57
   troops, 170, 211, 217, 232–34, 253, 255–56
   veterans, 217–19, 222, 254
mining, 111, 180
ministry, 38–41, 49–51, 66, 176, 181, 184, 186–87, 201, 218, 222
minority, 110–12, 158, 178–79, 179n16, 201, 243
   minoritarianism, 178
Miserere, 114
misinformation, 157
misogyny, 258
missiological, 189
modernity, 45, 57, 84n26, 159, 212, 224, 249, 251–57
monks, 35, 75–76, 79–81, 84–85, 87–89
   monasteries, 75–76, 79–80, 84, 87–89, 96, 220
   novices, 21, 75
moral, 80n22, 164, 198, 203, 213, 216, 253
   authority, 158, 170, 203
   comparison, 181, 204, 221, 237, 248, 254
   framework, 170
   immorality, 214, 218
   injury, 217–18
   responsibility, 114, 226–27, 248, 253, 255

Morocco, 191
Mott, Lucretia, 164
Mount Everest, 185
Mozambique, 98–101
   barbudos armados, 98
   FRELIMO, 98
multilateral 252, 257
music, 183
   songs, 116, 118, 120, 144, 149, 153–55, 158
mutilation, 255. *See also under* female
Myanmar, 110
mysticism, 79, 84, 177
myths, 144, 153, 157

narratives, 108–9, 108n10, 120, 122, 142, 145, 151
   Christian, 37–38, 61–62, 111–12, 116, 119, 122
neocolonial, 249
neoscholastic, 57
Netherlands, the, 110
   Wilders, Geert, 110
neutrality, 39, 177n6, 226
New Zealand, 181
news, 74, 108, 108n9
   good, 42, 62, 65, 83, 88, 128, 137
   journalists, 99–100, 106–7, 131, 162, 171, 186, 219, 232, 256
   letters, 172
   papers, 171
NGOs (nongovernment organizations), 103, 185, 235, 256
Nicaragua, 221
Nicene-Constantinopolitan Creed, 60
Nicholas of Cusa, Cardinal, 58
Niger, 100
nonbeliever, 87, 89n42
nonviolence, 135, 138, 166, 173, 176, 183, 198, 201, 208
   active, 55, 62, 68, 163, 166
   Catholic Nonviolence Initiative (CNI) (*see under* Pax Christi International)
   Christian, 73–74, 138, 166, 199, 207–8, 246
   ethic of, 201, 203–4, 206, 208

gospel, 93, 138–39, 197n1, 198–200, 208, 247. *See also under* Bible
   King, Martin Luther, Jr. and, 234–37
   peace and, 55–56, 58–60, 62, 66, 68, 70, 164–66, 171, 207
   responsibility to protect and, 224
   spaces of, 161, 164–65
   theology of, 33, 55, 58–60, 198, 200–201, 204–6, 208
      Christology of, 55–56, 60, 70
      incarnation of, 60, 60n18
      God of, 197, 199–201, 204–6, 208
   victory of, 68
North America, 186
Norway, 230
nuclear
   groups, 76
   weapons (*see under* weapons)
nucleus, 48
nuns, 101, 139
   Carmelites, 96

oaths, 156–57
obedience, 40, 67, 75, 112–13, 130, 149, 156, 164, 213
obligation, 163, 168, 226–28, 248, 250
odium
   amoris, 115
   conscientiae, 112–13
   fidei, 50, 105, 112, 114–15, 117
   justitiae, 114–15
   misericordiae, 115
operandi, 183, 206
operant, 251
oppression, 39, 41, 84, 120, 165, 237
   defenders of, 114–15
   forces of, 45, 49
   historical, 66, 120
   Jesus and, 42, 45, 50, 62–63, 67, 79, 246
   power and, 44, 66
   religion and, 39, 42, 45, 102
   sin and, 50–51, 205
optimism, 184, 192
orders
   military, 258
   religious, 76, 83, 138

   social, 80, 111
orphans, 46, 62–63, 100, 108, 185
Orthodox Church, 89n43, 218
orthodoxy, 69
oxymoron, 217, 219

pacifism, 59, 216, 218–21, 244, 247–48, 255
pagans, 47, 119, 236
Paglia, Vincenzo (Bishop), 105
Palestine, 37–39, 45–46
paradox, 83, 121, 129, 177, 180
Paraguay, 164
parents, 131, 143, 150, 158, 166, 182, 184–85, 187–89
parishes, 186
partnership, 166, 172, 216, 254
pastors, 36, 59, 88, 134, 142, 148, 160, 189, 238
patriarchy, 134, 143
Patroclus, 218
Pax Christi International, 139, 166n16
   Catholic Nonviolence Initiative (CNI), 139, 166, 166n16, 170, 197n1, 198–200, 202, 204–5, 207
peace
   as an open workshop, 95–98, 97n3, 104
   building, 85, 99, 128, 132–34, 136, 152, 172, 199, 227, 239
      activities, 58, 145, 147, 153, 190
      as mission, 137, 166
      Christian, 137–38, 205
      demystifying, 133–34
      process, 145–46, 151, 159, 163, 240
      violence and, 158, 171–72, 176
      women and, 142, 145, 148, 153, 157, 158n40, 159, 168, 172
   keeping, 166–67, 172, 232–34, 256–57
   making, 41, 44, 62–64, 99, 132, 154, 167, 204, 222, 250
      as blessed, 59, 63, 198
      Jesus and, 43, 56, 60–62
      just, 245–46, 249, 251, 257–58
      process, 44, 202

peace (cont.)
   process, 98, 132, 139, 162–63, 168–69, 172–73, 238–39
   theology, 56, 58–59
periphery, 84, 145, 180, 208
persecution, 215
   of Christians, 43–44, 50, 63, 67, 70, 105, 111, 198, 236
      by Rome, 66–67, 112, 118–19
   of Jesus, 48, 67
   of Latin American Christians, 36
Peru, 77
Philippines, 105–10, 120, 124–26, 165, 167–69, 174
   Abra, 167
   Bangsamoro, 170
      Comprehensive Agreement on the (CAB), 165, 168–70
      Government, 168
      Organic Law, 168–69, 173
   Communist Party of the, 165, 169
      New Peoples' Army (CPP-NPA), 165, 169–70
   Constitution, 170
   Councils of Elders, 173
   death penalty, 167, 170
   Duterte, Rodrigo (President), 106–7, 109–10, 117
   Foreign Affairs, Department of, 168
   Government of the Republic of the (GRP), 165
   Juan, Constantino de, 107–8, 108n9, 118, 120
      Remy, 109
   Manila, 120
   Marcos, Ferdinand (President), 167, 170
   Mindanao, 103, 167, 169, 171–72
   Miriam College, 165–66, 171–72
      Center for Peace Education, 165–66, 165n14
      Zone of Peace, 171–72
   Moros, 165, 167
      Islamic Liberation Front (MILF), 165
   National Acton Plan on Women, Peace, and Security, 173
   National Democratic Front, 170
   National Police, 106
   Payatas, 107–8
   presidents, 103, 109–10
   QCPD, 108n9
   Santos, Kian de los, 106
   Solidarity with Orphans and Widows (SOW), 108, 108n11
   Supreme Court, 107
philosophy, 78, 86, 166, 171, 215, 237
piety, 36, 113, 116
plague, 177, 243
ploughshares, 222
Plowshares Eight, 164
   Rush, Molly, 164
pluralism, 78, 84, 182, 188
pneumatology, 56–58, 57n10
policing, 106–7, 109, 120, 131, 150, 213, 249
   function, 246, 250, 258
   international, 258
   just, 245–46, 249, 251, 257–58
   killing by, 106, 108–9, 252
   military and, 162, 166, 172, 232, 234, 246
   personnel, 106–7, 150, 232
   Philippine National Police, 106
policy, 177n4, 185, 199, 203, 213, 216, 225, 228
political parties, 45, 66, 101, 150, 165–66, 178n11, 228–29, 240
pollution, 40, 45, 183, 187
polyvalent, 35
populism, 105–6, 109–11, 110n15, 110n17 117, 122, 170, 178
Portugal, 98
postconflict, 232
postindependence, 235–36
potential, 127, 131, 133–34, 136–40, 143, 156n36, 198
praxis, 49, 51, 58, 65–66, 68, 77–78, 114
pregnancy, 107, 143, 144n7, 153, 161
prejudice, 139, 257
priest, 77–78, 87, 95, 101–2, 134, 139–40, 168, 215, 218, 221
   India, 178, 181
   Israel, biblical, 38–39, 45, 61
      chief, 38

high, 46, 67, 95, 163
prison, 62–63, 75, 83, 97, 106–8, 114, 118–19, 243
professionals, 98, 100, 106, 134, 212, 238
profit, 101, 214
progressive, 200
propaganda, 109, 238
prophets, 43, 46–47, 79, 81, 84, 88, 99, 176–77, 212, 236
   Old Testament, 47
     Ezekiel, 46
     Isaiah, 46–47
     Jeremiah, 43–44
     Zechariah, 46
   prophetic mission of Jesus, 50, 62, 65, 83
Protestantism
   Anabaptists, 58
   Anglicans, 102
     Williams, Rowan, Bishop, 123
   charismatics, 57
   Mennonites, 58
   Pentecostals, 57, 57n6
   Presbyterians, 102
   Reformation, 113
protests, 47, 96, 101, 150, 150n22, 164, 167, 170, 237, 249
pseudonationalism, 179
psychology, 161, 224, 252–53, 255–56
   pathology, 255
psychosocial, 156
publicans, 65, 87
purity, 41, 45, 48, 85, 87, 118, 181, 246

race (characteristic), 144n7, 212–13
race, arms, 164, 214
racism, 55, 206, 253
radicalism, 52, 83–84, 87, 198, 216, 218, 239, 251
   conversion, 42
   Islam, 75, 181
   nonviolence, 200, 208
   solidarity, 65, 205
   terrorism, 79
realism, 204, 207, 245–46
realpolitik, 203, 225
rebellion, 66, 98, 101–2, 131, 230, 232, 250

redemption, 35–36, 47, 51, 84, 136, 200, 231. *See also* salvation
refugees, 63, 99, 110, 121, 129, 158, 222
   camps, 110, 129, 232
regimes, 112–13, 117–18, 120, 150n22, 164, 248–49
   autocratic, 88, 114–15, 224, 249
   populist, 105–6, 109, 111, 117, 122
rehabilitation, 109, 113, 162
reinocentrismo, 78
repentance, 41–42, 61–63, 240
repression, 111, 115, 121, 228
rescue, 233, 244, 248, 257
resistance 39, 51–52, 64, 95, 112, 202n6, 220–21, 248, 255
   violence and 44, 47, 63, 66, 165, 176, 205, 221, 250
responsibility to protect (R2P), 195, 204, 224–28, 234, 239–40, 245–52, 245n5, 255, 257–58
   Christianity and, 245, 249–51, 257–58
restoration, 41, 68, 97, 128, 147, 171, 204, 206
restraint, 199, 202
resurrection, 57, 62, 65, 67–68, 70, 83, 201
retaliation, 48, 64, 150n22, 163, 234, 236–37, 251
revenge, 129–30, 139, 202n6, 234, 237–38, 240
revolution, 38–40, 46, 48, 78, 80, 87, 221, 243
riots, 96, 101, 150n22
rites, 156–57, 177n3
   of passage, 143, 152, 155–57, 155n35, 156n37
ritual, 41, 45, 48, 112, 152–53, 177, 181
Rome (empire), 24, 38–40, 45–48, 58, 61, 65–68, 85, 112, 118–19, 177, 216
   arenas, 85, 118–19
   Constantine (Emperor), 68, 216
     Edict of Milan, 216
   Decius (Emperor), 112
   denarii, 221
   Diocletian (Emperor), 112

Rome (empire) (*cont.*)
  gods, 112
  legions, 216
  Nero (Emperor), 112
  Pax Romana, 65–68
  pietas, 112
  pontifex maximus, 66
  Trajan (Emperor), 112
Romero, Óscar, Saint (Bishop), 50, 84, 105, 111, 115–16, 122, 124–25
roundtable discussion, 198–201, 204–5, 207
Russia, 99–100, 110, 211
  Gulags, 111, 120
  Moscow, 100
  Putin, Vladimir (President), 110
Rwanda, 127, 199n4, 206, 224–26, 244
Ryan, Maura, 238

Sabbath, 80n22
sacraments, 157, 205
sacredness, 80n22, 149–50, 157, 171, 226, 237
sacrifice, 36, 49, 66, 66n31, 112, 131, 133, 140, 218–19, 222, 258
  self-, 183, 235
Sadducees, 39, 46
salvation, 35–36, 56, 68, 113, 122. See also redemption
Samset, Ingrid, 239
Sant'Egidio, Community of, 96–101, 103, 204
  Johnston, Laurie, 204
  March for Peace, 99
  People of Peace, 99
  Riccardi, Andrea, 99
  School of Peace, 99, 103
Sassoon, Siegfried, 212
  "They" (poem), 212
scapegoating, 73
Schoonenberg, Piet, 57n8
  Der Geist, 57n8
science, 189–91, 212, 254
secrecy, 112, 156n37, 257
secular, 73, 84, 177, 179, 181, 189–90, 247–49, 251, 258

self-interest, 203, 259
Senegal, 102
  Casamance, 102–3
  Sall, Macky, 102–3
servant of God, 58, 63–64, 67, 68, 70, 121–22
sex, 89n42, 143, 144n7, 148, 156–57, 238, 253
  abuse, 115, 158n39
    rape, 120, 158n39, 161, 230, 238, 244, 254–56
  assault, 232, 244
  violence, 238, 256–57
sexism, 55, 253
shalom 62–63
Shanti, 192
Sharp, Gene, 169, 169n24
Sierra Leone, 127, 145
sin, 42, 50–51, 59, 122, 199, 201, 217, 219–20
  forgiveness of, 41, 59, 64, 68, 70
  Jesus and, 35, 41–42, 48–50, 65, 220
  of the world, 45, 51, 122, 220
  sinners, 41–44, 46, 64–65, 121
Singapore, 110
slaughter, 110, 117, 243–44, 251
Small Christian Communities (SCCs), 186–87, 235–36
  Neighborhood Children's Council (NCC), 186–87
  Care for Mother Earth Ministry, 187
  Food and Diet Ministry, 187
  Spiritual Connections Ministry, 187
  Sports Ministry, 187
  Talent Search Ministry, 187
  RSCJ (Religieuses du Sacré-Cœur de Jésus), 186
    Furtado, Daphne (nun), 186
    Gonsalves, Manisha (nun), 186, 188
Smith, David Livingstone, 253
smoking, 217
social
  justice, 36, 80n22, 97, 138
  media, 109, 171
    Facebook, 171

Twitter, 171
teaching of the Catholic Church, 133, 137–38
socialization, 130, 169, 251–53, 256–58
socioeconomic matters, 84, 119–20, 122, 144, 155, 186, 240
sociopaths, 257
sociopolitical matters, 84, 111–12, 121, 186
Socrates, 82, 119
solidarity, 42, 52, 88, 122, 150n22, 176, 208
   of Jesus, 48–50, 65–66
   radical, 65, 205
   Solidarity with Orphans and Widows (SOW) (*see under* Philippines)
   universal, 181–82
   Universal Solidarity Movement of Value Education for Peace! (*see under* India)
solidary, 191
Somalia, 127, 233
sonship, 56
soteriology, 35–36
souls, 104, 192, 217, 219
South Africa, 230
South Sudan, 100, 102–3, 127, 130, 133, 136–37, 224, 228–36, 238–40
   Arusha Agreement, 231
   Ayunak people, 237
   Bor, 237
   Catholic Bishops' Secretariat, 238
   Chukudum Crisis Peace Conference, 238
   civil war, 136–37, 235
   Committee for National Healing, Peace, and Reconciliation (CNHPR), 236
   Comprehensive Peace Agreement, 236
   Declaration of Agreement on a Permanent Ceasefire (Khartoum Declaration), 231
   Didinga people, 237
   Dinka people, 229, 235–38
   Equitoria
      Central, 230
      Eastern, 238
      South, 230
   High-Level Revitalization Forum, 231
   Igga, James Wani, 229
   Jie people, 237
   Joint Transitional Security Committee, 231
   Juba, 229–30, 233
   Kachipo people, 237
   Kiir, Salva (President), 102, 228–31, 233, 236, 238
   Kuron peace village, 136
   Liberation Army (SPLA), 235–36
      Garang, John, 235–36
   Lilir Peace Conference, 237
   Lotoko people, 237
   Machar, Riek (Vice President), 102, 228–31, 233, 236, 238
   militarization, 224, 228
   militia groups, 230, 232, 240
   Murle people, 237
   Nakwatom Peace Conference, 238
   National Salvation Front, 230
      Cirillo, Thomas, 230
   New Sudan Council of Churches (NSCC), 235–36
   New Transitional Government of National Unity (TGNU), 229–30
   Nuer people, 229, 235–37
      Gatdeang Dit (prophet), 236
   parliament, 231
   Revitalized Agreement on the Resolution of Conflict in South Sudan (R-ARCSS), 231
   Revitalized Transitional Government of National Unity (RTGONU), 231
   Taban, Paride (Bishop), 136
   Toposa people, 237
   Torit, 136
   UN Mission in South Sudan (UNMISS) (*see under* United Nations)

South Sudan (cont.)
  Upper Nile region, 237
  Wau, 230
  Wunlit Peace Conference, 235, 237, 240
sovereignty, 58, 110, 224–25, 227–28, 244
sowing, 83, 88, 109
  seeds of peace, 133, 136, 138, 188
Spain, 116
  Madrid, 181
  Zaragoza, 117
spirituality, 41, 57, 80–82, 182, 186–87, 190
sports, 135, 162, 186–87
  football, 187
    World Cup, 187
stability, 38–39, 66, 75–76, 88, 146, 224, 239, 254
stakeholders, 168, 185, 202, 216
Stang, Dorothy, 62
Ste. Croix, G. E. M. de, 118, 126
Steffen, Lloyd, 203n10
stereotypes, 139, 144, 156n37, 189, 252
strangers, 62–63, 134–35
strategy, 77, 81, 98, 147–48, 151, 153, 188, 190, 226, 234–35, 240
  military, 215, 217, 247
  nonviolent or peaceful, 168–69, 189, 235, 239–40
studies, 36–38, 45, 133, 146, 162, 183, 197, 201, 253, 255–56
  research, 84, 149, 151
  scholars, 37, 40–41, 43–44, 46–47, 63, 171, 201, 246, 255
  students, 96–98, 106, 166–67, 169–72, 183–84, 186, 188–90, 197–99, 202
subservience, 109, 113
substitutionary, 35
Sudan, 100, 127, 145, 228, 231, 233, 235, 237
  al-Bashir, Omar (President), 231, 235
  Darfur, 127
  Khartoum, 101, 231
    Declaration, 231

People's Liberation Movement (SPLM), 228–29
  Army-In Opposition (SPLM/A-IO), 230
  Upper Nile region, 237
suicide, 119, 180, 212, 217
  bomber, 82
  kamikaze, 82
Sunday school, 133, 139
superstition, 190, 212
surrender, 85–86, 108, 203
sustainable
  development, 155, 157, 159
  peace, 55, 127, 131, 139, 155, 157, 159, 239
symbolism, 36, 40, 46–47, 65, 146–49, 153, 155
synod, 80n22
Syria, 89, 89n43, 110, 206
  Assad, Bashar (President), 110
Syriac Christianity, 36, 89n43
  Mar Musa (Monastery of San Mosè L'Abissino), 89n43S

tactics, 73, 215, 247
Taizé Monastery, 89
  Taizé, Roger de (brother), 89
Tanzania, 225
Taoism, 166
taxation, 103, 180
  Israel, biblical, in, 38–39, 42, 44, 46, 61, 66, 236
technologies, 108
temptation, 61–62
Teresa of Calcutta, Saint (nun), 122, 138
  Nobel Peace Prize of, 138
terrorism, 55, 79, 121, 127, 170, 181, 202, 243, 254, 257
  post-9/11, 181
  war on (see under war)
Tertullian, 118, 216
testimony, 47, 81, 83–86, 151, 159, 217, 253
Thailand, 74
theocracy, 45–46, 84
theologians, 36–37, 41, 49, 58, 95–96, 200, 247, 249
  Abelard, Peter, 215

Balthasar, Hans Urs von, 57
Barth, Karl, 60, 69
Bingemer, Maria Clara, 205
   Mística e Testemunho em Koinonia, 74n5
Boff, Leonardo, 40, 79
Bonhoeffer, Dietrich, 114–16, 219–21
Brock, Rita Nakashima, 36
Buck, P. Lorraine, 119
Cardenal, Ernesto, 219, 221
Comblin, Joseph, 59, 62
   Théologie de la Paix, 59
Congar, Yves, 57
Coste, René, 56n5, 58–60, 67n32
   Il est notre paix, 59, 67n32
Dear, John, 67
Dulles, Avery, Cardinal, 77n12
Dupuis, James, 57
Durrwell, François-Xavier (priest), 66n31
Ellacuría, Ignacio, 50–51, 67, 74, 78, 81, 86, 116, 120, 122
González Faus, José Ignacio, 116–17
Gushee, David, 44
Gutiérrez, Gustavo (priest), 40–41, 48, 77–78, 77n12
Hellholm, David, 64n22
   Eucharist, 64n22
Herzog, William, 47
Hofheinz, Marco, 69
Jegen, Carol Frances (nun), 59
Kasper, Walter, 49, 57
Küng, Hans, 191
Latin American, 41, 79, 111
Luz, Ulrich, 43
Merz, Annette, 39
Moltmann, Jürgen, 67
Moss, Candida, 36, 36n4
Myers, Ched, 47
Rahner, Karl, 114
Rosato, Philip J., 57
Sanders, E. P., 39, 46–47
Sänger, Dieter, 64n22
   Eucharist, 64n22
Schillebeeckx, Edward, 36, 49
Schockenhoff, Eberhard, 63
Schwager, Raymund, 45

Sobrino, Jon, 37, 42, 45, 64, 67, 74, 111, 114–15, 120–22
Stassen, Glen, 44
Thiessen, Gerd, 39
Third Quest, 37
Weaver, J. Denny 36
Will, James E., 59–69, 65, 67n32
   A Christology of Peace, 59–60, 67n32
Williams, Delores, 36
Winright, Tobias, 203, 203n8, 245, 250
   Just War, 203n8
   Why I Shall Continue, 203n10, 250
Wright, N. T., 40, 43, 47–49
theopolitical, 195
Third World, 114–15, 121
tokenism, 157
torment, 121, 216
torture, 55, 118, 120, 164, 216, 244, 250, 256
trade, 131, 135, 155, 168, 173
training, 62, 135, 156n37, 167, 172, 184, 188, 201, 213, 218, 251–57
transcendence, 60, 70, 138, 145
transportation, 134–35
transreligious, 88–89
Trappists, 74–76, 221
   community of Notre Dame de l'Atlas, Tibhirine, 74–76, 80–81, 87
   Amedée (priest), 75
   Chergé, Christian de (prior), 75–76, 79, 81–82, 84–86
   Dochier, Luc (brother), 75–76, 84
   Favre-Miville, Paul (brother), 75
   Fleury, Michel (brother), 75
   Jean Pierre (priest), 75
   Lebreton, Christophe (priest), 75, 82, 82n23, 85
      Born from the Gaze of God, 82n23
   Lemarchand, Bruno (priest), 75
   Ringeard, Célestin (priest), 75
Gethsemane, 221
Merton, Thomas, 62, 220–21
trauma, 131, 139, 224

treaties, 101, 163, 168, 173, 224
  Arms Trade (*see under* United Nations)
  Nuclear Ban (*see under* United Nations)
  Westphalia, 224, 228
triadic, 44
tribes, 101, 177n4, 179, 183
Trinity, 56–58, 57n8, 57n10, 60–61, 66n31, 70
  Christology, 55–60, 64, 68–70, 86
    Christomonism, 57
    of peace, 55, 58–60, 68–69
    Spirit, 56–57, 56n5, 57n6, 57n8, 57n10, 60, 69–70
  Father, 48, 56–58, 61, 63–64, 66–70, 66n31, 236
  Holy Spirit, 56–63, 57n8, 65–70, 66n31, 67n32, 73, 79, 82, 86, 205–8
    Veni Creator Spiritus, 56
  homousios, 68
  ousia, 68
tripersonal, 57
triune, 57, 70
TROIKA countries, 230
Turkey, 110, 244
  Erdogan, Recep (President), 110
Turse, Nick, 246
  Kill Anything That Moves, 246

Uganda, 127, 136, 224–25, 230, 232–33
  Amin, Idi (President), 224
  Museveni, Yoweri (President), 230
  Odama, Baptist (Archbishop), 136
Ukraine, 99
United Kingdom (UK), 230
  England, 113, 164
    Berkshire, 164
    Greenham Common, 164
    London, 181
  military, 113, 164
    Military Cross, 212
    Royal Welsh Fusiliers, 212
United Nations (UN), 100–101, 103, 107, 121, 168, 225–26, 232, 237, 239, 256

Annan, Kofi (Secretary-General), 227
  In Larger Freedom: Towards Development, Security, and Human Rights for All, 227
Arms Trade Treaty (ATT), 168, 173
as international body, 110, 185, 225, 245
Bachelet, Michele (High Commissioner for Human Rights), 106
Ban, Ki-moon (Secretary-General), 239
conferences, 59, 168
delegates, 168
High-Level Panel on Threats, Challenges, and Change, 227
  A More Secure World: Our Shared Responsibility, 227
Human Rights Council, 106
MDGs (Millennium Development Goals), 185, 185n30
Mission in South Sudan (UNMISS), 232–33, 233n34, 240
Nuclear Ban Treaty, 173
Office of the High Commissioner for Human Rights (OHCHR), 106–7
peacekeeping, 158n39, 226–27, 232–33, 240, 251–52 257
  Peacekeeping Operations, 232–33, 257
    Lacroix, Jean-Pierre, 233
Security Council (UNSC), 158n39, 162–63, 225, 232–33, 239
  Resolution 1325, 158, 158n39, 162–63
  Resolution 1996, 232
  Resolution 2155, 232
  Women, 162
World Health Organization, 143n5
World Summit, 228
United States, 38, 98, 110, 115, 150n22, 207, 213–14, 222, 229–30, 252
  Berkeley, 190

Chicago, 95, 169, 199
Civil War, 252
Congress, 202
July 4 parades, 254
Kerry, John, (Secretary of State), 229
military, 219, 253
  Army, 253
    Grossman, David (colonel), 252
      On Killing, 252
    Hoffman, Michael (captain), 216–18
    Levine, Sean (major), 218
    Marshall, S. L. A. (brigadier general), 252–53
  chaplains, 218
  Marines, 214, 217–18, 254–55
    Boudreau, Tyler (captain), 217
    Butler, Smedley (brigadier general), 214
    groupthink, 254
    Young, Matt, 254
  Pentagon, 217
  Veterans Administration, 217
Mussomeli, Joseph (Ambassador), 212
New York, 181
Obama, Barack, 216, 230
presidents, 202
Puerto Rico, 200
Regional Protection Force (RPF), 233–34
Trump, Donald (President), 110, 214, 230
Wear Orange Day, 169
  Pendleton, Hayida, 169
  Global 16 Days Campaign, 169
  Global Week of Action against Gun Violence, 169
United States Conference of Catholic Bishops, 59
The Challenge of Peace, 59
universality, 61, 64, 81, 84, 89, 105, 110, 122, 181–83, 185
universe, 192
universities, 74, 78, 81, 84, 84n26, 86, 96, 190, 199, 208, 213
  Catholic University of El Salvador, 74
  Columbia, 213

DePaul University, 199, 208
Oxford, University of, 215
Santa Clara University, 190
Universidad Centroamericana José Simeón Cañas (UCA), 74, 77, 79–80, 87–88
  Ramos, Celina, 74
  Ramos, Julia Elba, 74
univocal, 36, 181
Uruguay, 164
utopian, 78

Vatican, 97n3, 98, 105, 115, 135, 139
  canon law, 37
  Councils
    Chalcedon, 68–69
    Constance, 114
    Nicaea, 68–69
    Second Vatican, 37, 57, 59, 69, 77n12, 80, 80n22, 82, 88, 105, 117
    documents (*see under* Vatican)
    signs of the times, 82
  Dicastery for Promoting Integral Human Development, 139
  documents
    apostolic letters
      Maiorem Hac Dilectionem, motu proprio, 122
    encyclicals
      Mater et Magistra (John XXIII), 59
      Pacem in Terris (John XXIII), 59
      Populorum Progressio (Paul VI), 59
      Redemptoris Missio (John Paul II), 84n26
    Second Vatican Council, 59, 79, 80n22
      Gaudium et Spes, 59, 77n12, 80n22, 169
      Lumen Gentium, 77n12, 88
      Nostra Aetate, 80n22
  Inquisition, 113
  popes, 58, 75, 89, 102, 113, 177n3, 219
    Benedict XV, 58

Vatican, popes (*cont.*)
    Francis, 89, 101–2, 120, 122, 138–40, 169–70, 189–91
        other popes and, 219
        Sant'Egidio, Community and, 96–97, 99
        World Day of Peace and, 128, 148, 163
    John XXIII, Saint, 59, 96, 219
    John Paul II, Saint, 78, 97–98, 97n3, 104, 165n15, 173, 190–91, 219
    Paul VI, Saint, 59, 165, 165n15
    Pius XII, 59
    Urban II, 244
    World Day of Peace, 59, 99, 128, 138, 163, 165n15
veneration, 86, 122
vengeance, 130, 212, 250–51
victimization, 41, 111, 245
victory, 40, 58, 68, 81, 100, 113, 153, 211–12
Vietnam, 199n4, 225, 246, 253
    war (*see under* war)
virtue, 122–23, 153, 156–58, 204, 250–51, 253
    ethics (*see under* ethics)
vocation, 51, 77, 79, 85, 96, 99, 166n16, 204
    calling, 44, 51, 97, 112, 220
voice, 113, 128, 130–31, 199, 201
    women, 134, 144, 157, 158n40, 159
vulnerability, 157, 232, 254
    vulnerable population, 45, 129, 146, 162, 198, 202, 222, 246, 248, 251

Walzer, Michael, 213
war
    as racket, 214
    asymmetric, 249, 255
    banks and, 169, 214
    battle, 109, 113, 161, 244, 251, 253–56
    Cold, 59, 199n4, 202, 214–15, 225
    combat, 214, 218, 222, 247, 252–54, 256

conscientious objection, 247
Crusades, 215, 244
crusading, 245, 251
culpability, 250
delegitimizing, 201, 247
Forever, 215
Good, 215
Great, 211, 215
Gulf, 199n4
interstate, 227
intrastate, 224–25, 227
just, 199n4, 203n8, 203n10, 204, 211, 216–17, 220, 250–52, 256–58
    criteria, 198, 199n4, 202
    principles, 203–4, 258
    reasoning, 203
    theory (JWT), 58–59, 197–98, 199n4, 200–204, 208, 215–17, 220, 246, 250–51, 255
    thinking, 203n10, 250n13, 251
    tradition, 197n1, 198–99, 244
Korean, 253
mercenaries, 257
on Terror, 199n4, 206
Peloponnesian, 213
US Civil War, 252
Vietnam, 199n4, 246, 253
warriors, 135, 135n16, 143, 147–49, 152–53, 158, 212, 216, 218
World
    First, 58, 211–13, 215, 252
    Second, 58–59, 98, 252–53
    third, 101
water, 129, 143, 150–51, 187, 247
waters (figurative), 249, 257
Watts, Craig, 248
weakness, 41–42, 59, 63, 70, 73, 203, 224, 249, 253
wealth, 39, 45, 102, 111, 149, 166, 180, 255
    money, 100, 113, 117, 132, 134, 140, 182–83, 214
    property, 130, 132, 154, 182, 224, 234, 237–38

weapons, 143, 161–63, 168–69, 212, 215–26, 247–48, 252
  arms, 37, 61, 130–32, 143, 158, 161, 169, 173, 205, 247–48
    control, 168, 171, 173
    race, 164, 214
  chemical, 110
  cruise missiles, 165
  disarmament, 101, 163, 208
  guns, 101, 108, 138, 158, 167–69, 171, 211, 229, 252
    bullets, 83
    gunpowder, 215
  knives, 83
  mines, 102–3
  nuclear, 164, 169, 171, 173, 213–15
    General Electric, 164
  swords, 45, 64, 67, 95, 118–19, 127–28, 130–31, 163, 222
Weber, Jörg, 57n10
  Geist-Christologie, 57n10
West, the, 114, 181, 204

widows, 46, 62–63, 108, 154, 221
wisdom, 63, 82, 139, 146–47, 152, 154, 203, 252
witness, 35, 73, 85, 103, 114, 127, 131, 138, 148, 204
  Christ, to, 36, 51, 80n22, 116–17
  love, to, 116–18
  of martyrs, 35n1, 36, 51, 74–75, 85, 88
womb, 83, 147, 152
World Council of Churches, 59
  Process of Justice, Peace, and Creation, 59
worship, 41, 61, 133, 136
wounds, 98, 104, 121, 143, 212, 217, 221–22
Wycliffe, John, 114

xenophobia, 258

zeal, 35n1, 45

www.ingramcontent.com/pod-product-compliance
Lightning Source LLC
Chambersburg PA
CBHW032058220426
43664CB00008B/1050